International Relations Then and

The new edition of this classic history of International Relations has been completely revised and updated throughout and remains a major guide to the intellectual lineage and development of the field.

In *International Relations Then and Now* the authors examine the historical antecedents and the emergence of theories of the state system during the 18th and 19th centuries culminating in the short-lived League of Nations. They look at the foundation of International Relations as an academic discipline and the competing theories that emerged within it. In an entirely new part to this volume, they also consider contemporary developments within the theories and methodologies of International Relations, including feminism and postcolonialism.

International Relations Then and Now is an indispensable text for students and scholars interested in the history of the development of International Relations.

A. J. R. Groom is Emeritus Professor of the University of Kent and holds an honorary doctorate from the University of Tampere in Finland. He has also taught at University College London and has been Guest Professor at the Graduate Institute Geneva – where he was awarded a PhD – Renmin University and Xi'an International Studies University of China, Sciences-Po Paris, the IEP de Lille, the Diplomatische Akademie Wien, the Universities of Colorado Boulder, University of Southern California, Dalhousie, Cape Town, and the University of Turin. Professor Groom has been particularly active in professional associations, having been the Founder and for ten years Chairman of the European Standing Group for International Relations, Chairman of BISA and Vice-President of ISA, a member of the Executive Committee of the European Consortium for Political Research and a Board Member of the Academic Council for the United Nations System. He has been Editor of the academic journals *Global Society* and *ERIS*. His academic interests include conflict resolution, track II diplomacy, international organisations, functionalism and European politics. Among his other interests are opera and music, food and wine and travel. He is a fervent supporter of Lincoln City, from where he hails.

André Barrinha is a Lecturer in International Security at the University of Bath and a Researcher at the Centre for Social Studies, University of Coimbra, Portugal. Dr Barrinha joined the University of Bath in September 2017, having previously worked at the University of Coimbra and Canterbury Christ Church University. He holds a PhD in International Relations from the University of Kent. From 2004 to 2006 he was a researcher at the Institute of Strategic and International Studies, Lisbon. His main research interests are within the fields of Critical Security Studies, European Security and International Relations Theory. Dr Barrinha is one of the coordinators of the UACES RN INTERSECT: Technology-Security-Society interplays in Europe. Between 2016 and 2018 he was one of the founders and conveners of the British International Studies Association European Security Working Group.

The late **William C. Olson** was a retired Dean and Professor Emeritus of American University's School of International Service and founder of the international collegiate honor society Sigma Iota Rho. From 1970 to 1979, he directed the Rockefeller Foundation's Bellagio study and conference centre on Lake Como in Italy. Earlier in his career, he directed the Foreign Affairs Division of what is now the Congressional Research Service at the Library of Congress and was an Associate Dean of Columbia University's School of International and Public Affairs. He was a trustee of the Social Science Foundation at the University of Denver and what is now known as World Learning, an organisation that promotes international understanding by placing students with host families. His memberships included the Cosmos Club and the Council on Foreign Relations. Dr Olson published and co-wrote scholarly works, including *The Theory and Practice of International Relations* (1966).

"This book stands out because of its exceptional historical depth which perfectly shows how International Relations are first a human adventure in which political actors, thinkers and societies participate while fluctuating between war, peace, power and social crisis. It is also an impressive and very pedagogic perspective on the literature, and particularly the English language IR theory. It is a tremendous narrative of our international past and present."

Bertrand Badie, *Sciences Po, France*

"Combining an overview of the history of the international system with evolving theoretical discourses in the discipline, Groom and Olson, with their new co-author, Barrinha, have produced what will likely be an invaluable teaching source for scholars in International Relations."

Vivienne Jabri, *King's College London, UK*

"Anybody looking to find an introductory text to either learn about or teach the discipline of International Relations could start with this text. The authors have done an admirable job of surveying and synthesising a vast number of texts on the subject from the seventeenth century on, with some going back to even earlier epochs. They show that the international concerns of governments and thinkers alike have always had common roots and intertwining expression. Such a book could only have been written by longstanding and experienced teachers of the subject, in this case A.J.R. Groom and William Olson, here ably aided by a young scholar, André Barrinha. It is particularly recommended for early years undergraduates but could also be read by any interested members of the general public. It is written with clarity and style, both traits often lacking in academic IR texts."

Andrew Williams, *University of St. Andrews, UK*

International Relations Then and Now

Origins and Trends in Interpretation

Second Edition

A. J. R. Groom, André Barrinha and William C. Olson

Routledge
Taylor & Francis Group

LONDON AND NEW YORK

Second edition published 2019
by Routledge
2 Park Square, Milton Park, Abingdon, Oxon, OX14 4RN

and by Routledge
52 Vanderbilt Avenue, New York, NY 10017

Routledge is an imprint of the Taylor & Francis Group, an informa business

First edition published by HarperCollins Academic 1991

British Library Cataloguing-in-Publication Data
A catalogue record for this book is available from the British Library

Library of Congress Cataloging-in-Publication Data
A catalog record has been requested for this book

ISBN: 978-0-415-18020-7 (hbk)
ISBN: 978-0-415-18021-4 (pbk)
ISBN: 978-0-429-06106-6 (ebk)

Typeset in Times New Roman
by Swales & Willis Ltd, Exeter, Devon, UK

MIX
Paper from
responsible sources
FSC   FSC™ C013985
www.fsc.org

Printed in the United Kingdom
by Henry Ling Limited

For
Isobel, Rafael and Sara

Contents

Figures

Preface to the second edition

If it were a house, *IR Then and Now* would be a property in need of renovation. The foundations were solid and the building was in a good state but in need of maintenance and some decoration. Most importantly, it needed an extension (which, as is often the case, took longer to build than expected). As with any renovation, this was very much a process of deciding what to keep and what to take out. The preface to the first edition is the front door plaque which was largely left as found. Much of the rest suffered changes of some nature, but some of its key features were kept. For instance, as in the first edition, there is no introduction and the conclusion is more a moment for a pause than a full stop. And we are already well aware that there was much left to tell, but a choice had to be made between engaging in a potentially endless update of the second edition or to draw a line at some point and leave open the possibility of a third edition; one that may include chapters on international political sociology, the Anthropocene or cyberspace.

This second edition of *IR Then and Now* is a dialogue between three generations. Each of the three authors first learned the discipline in different historical and cultural contexts: Bill in the US in the late 1930s, John in the UK during the 1950s and André in Portugal in the 2000s. The outcome is a journey through the evolution of the discipline in which history and present are often too entangled to be distinguished from each other. The ambition very much present in the first edition to look at the evolution of the discipline even before it existed, to weave it in the developments in the real world, and to make often difficult and elaborate ideas and theories accessible and adequately framed in the the context in which they were created, hopefully remains in this second edition. Fundamental innovations in IR, such as social constructivism, feminism or post-colonialism were brought in and all the chapters were carefully revised. The more attentive reader will notice the bibliographic appendixes were removed and the theories about 'now' suffered significant changes so that the label could remain, or so that they could adequately fit in the 'then' section. Finally, there is no Epilogue to this edition. Instead it has an open-ended conclusion. A time perhaps for a pause between this and a future edition.

Preface to the first edition (1991)

At the turn of our century the philosopher Santayana noted that "those who cannot remember the past are condemned to repeat it."[1] This is true for academe as well as statecraft, for disciplines as well as books. As we see it, the function of this little book is to open up a panorama of past and present ideas about international relations, both as politics and as conceptions, to those who are fascinated by the unfolding of world events and have already taken the trouble to inform themselves about what is going on and why.

This 'advanced beginner' may be a university student, a young foreign service officer, a new don, perhaps a researcher or a serious journalist. Young or old, he or she may be a member of what Gabriel Almond terms[2] 'the attentive public,' the intelligent layman who wants to be better informed not only about the present but also the past, especially the ideas that have shaped the way philosophers and practitioners look at international affairs. Our book is a sort of intellectual map to guide one from ancient insights to contemporary debates.

Emphasis in the book is on two dimensions: one of space, the other of time. Most of the recent work in International Relations (hereinafter referred to as IR) has been in English, including translation of much of consequence from Ibn Khaldun to Raymond Aron, just as the distinguished Danish scholar, Niels Amstrup, chose to present his superb recent monograph, 'The study of international relations: old or new?' (Institute of Political Science, University of Aarhus, March 1989, 58 pp.) in that language. Yet, as there are signs that this particular manifestation of ethnocentrism is beginning to give way to a truly international basis of theory, we are already planning a second edition reflective of this transformation.

As for time, we have struggled in the early part of the book to produce an abbreviated pre-history up to the end of the Age of Enlightenment, and have then taken five chapters to cover most of the last two centuries. The second half of the book interprets the state of the study of IR today (by which we mean from 1960). This segment has been divided topically rather than sequentially, simply because it is too early to tell which of several current approaches will prevail. Throughout we have proceeded on the assumption that facts do not speak for themselves. Lord Keynes was right when he pointed out that facts tell us what our theories suggest they should reveal. It behoves us therefore to know our theories and the version of reality that is implied by them. As reality changes, theory tends to change with it.

One other point, on style. We have tried to take to heart the advice given to writers fifty years ago by William Strunk and E.B. White: to use language to clarify and to promote understanding, not to obscure. We have tried to avoid the pitfalls of 'jargon.' But where a new scholarly term reflects something more clearly than ten old ones do, we use it. So onwards into the past, the better to understand the present and – just possibly – to prepare for future worlds.

Acknowledgements

For the second edition, we inherited a rich past in comments from our colleagues and our students and have endeavoured to put that to good use. We are in their debt. We would particularly like to thank Antoinette Groom for her support and endurance. Without her, this book would have never seen the light of day. At the same time, we thank the Olsen family for permission to make use of Olsen's work, especially in the first part of our 'little book.' We like to think that he would approve of our endeavours.

This book would not have been possible without the contribution of Bronwen Edwards, Jack Young and Ned Watkins, whose research assistance was crucial in different phases of the process. We also need to thank Canterbury Christ Church University, in particular Professor David Bates' Politics and the International Relations Programme for their financial support, as well as Mattia Cacciotari for having accepted the challenge of reading the whole manuscript in a very short period of time. His feedback was crucial to improving this final version.

Finally, a word of gratitude to Routledge. The second edition of this book was long due. Their patience and support throughout has been much appreciated.

Sometimes the best words have been said the first time around, avoiding the need for new words to be uttered. That is the case here:

"Although the writing of any book entails a modicum of pain as any author, successful or otherwise, will attest, we have enjoyed writing this book for the opportunity it has given us to read where we had not read before and re-read what we had often first read long ago; for the collegiality and friendship of working together; for the professional support, criticism, comment and encouragement of our friends; and above all, to learn a little more of what our subject has to offer. Our hope is this 'little book' is to convey to the reader our sense of intellectual adventure and to share the stimulus and insight that we have derived from writing it."

Notes

1 George Santayana, from *The Life of Reason* (1905–1906), Vol. 1, *Reason and Common Sense*, cited in John McCormack, *George Santayana: a Biography* (New York: Alfred A. Knopf, 1987), p. 173.
2 Gabriel Almond, *The American People and Foreign Policy* (New York: Harcourt, Brace, 1950), *passim*.

Part I

'Then'

The formative years

1 The antecedents

When a new academic endeavour, approach or a field emerges it is likely that there will not be a specific moment at which it came into existence. Instead there is a process which contains some benchmarks such as particular events. In the chapters that follow we shall identify such benchmarks as part of a process that goes back to the Ancient worlds not just of Europe but the antecedents in Asia, the Manchu world and elsewhere. Gradually the focus comes to Europe as far as International Relations (IR) is concerned, which reveals well-known milestones such as the symbolic but largely mythological Peace of Westphalia of 1648.[1] Thus, the disparate factors and experiences come together to form what we hope is a coherent chronology as IR emerges, takes shape and makes its mark. So let us, briefly, turn first to the antecedents from ancient worlds.

Masterpieces of the past cannot be ignored by the serious student seeking insights into the understanding of contemporary international relations. Even in Pharaonic literature, we can find references to the Kadish treaty during the era of Ramses II that reflects some of the modern concerns in international society.[2]

Ancient diplomacy and philosophy

Any orthodox reading of the ancestors of IR scholars usually starts with a reference to the *History of the Peloponnesian War*, the work of the famous Athenian historian and general, Thucydides. His account of what was one of the defining periods in the history of Ancient Greece could well have been entitled the 'diplomacy' of the Peloponnesian war. Inasmuch as Thucydides developed no systematic theory of interstate relations, its principal value for our purposes lies in his description of the negotiations, the policy alternatives, the strategic concepts, the diplomatic skills (or lack of them) exhibited by plenipotentiaries as Athens tried first to avoid the war and then to win it. Important and lasting elements of IR are to be found in Thucydides' writing, notably lessons which derive from the confrontation of land power and sea power in geographical terms.[3]

A number of other classical Greek authors delved into topics and approaches that are central to today's discipline. For instance, the view that 'man is the measure of all things' is attributed to the sophist Protagoras, an antecedent of contemporary behaviouralist thought, especially in relation to perception and images. When Socrates proclaimed himself to be 'a citizen of the world,' he shared the cosmopolitanism of the Stoics. Although he showed little interest in inter-state relations except by implication, Aristotle demonstrated the connection between ethics and politics which preoccupies many writers today, and Plato anticipated Machiavelli, Hobbes and Hans Morgenthau in his realism, "firmly representative of the collective Greek mind in apparently recognizing that war remained a central, if tragic, feature of international life."[4] Despite their philosophical differences, both Plato and Aristotle recognised that a consequence of unequal size among city-states was that "the strong would normally strive to become stronger and the weak seek to avoid becoming weaker."[5] Their contradictory views of justice between states led to schools of philosophy that prevailed for centuries. As Fred Parkinson has put it in his *Philosophy of International Relations*, this "cleavage between the normative and the empirical runs right through the history of thought in international relations."[6]

The Asian legacy should also be taken into consideration. As early as 771 BC the important principle that treaties should be regarded as being between equals was recognised in China. During the 'Age of Philosophers,' Confucius (551–479 BC) and later his principal follower, Mencius, tried to promote government by moral value. In the fourth century BC there appeared the first more or less systematic treatise on interstate politics ever written, *The Book of the Lord of Shang*, or Kung-sun Yang, the exact date of which is uncertain because many Chinese scholars and statesmen over a period of time apparently contributed to its final form.[7] In paving the way for the Ch'in dynasty, which ended in 221 BC, this great work, while promoting the rule of law to govern the relations of princes, precluded any role for an informed public in government. In the discipline of military science, the views of another Chinese thinker, Sun Tzu,[8] are cited even today, both in terms of strategy and tactics.

Meanwhile, far to the South and West in India, Prime Minister Kautilya (321–296 BC), known as 'The Crooked' because of his explicit rejection of any place for morality in politics, produced an influential treatise entitled *Arthashastra*. Adam Watson in his helpful and succinct analysis of Kautilya's thought[9] points to the fusion of Indian practice and Persian scope and concept. Kautilya's manual anticipated that of Machiavelli some fifteen centuries later. Behera used Kautilya's work to speak critically of IR as a discipline, stating:

> The impoverishment of traditional IR's political thought becomes further evident on its chosen ground – political realism – that it does not recognise our own Indian political philosopher, Kautilya, as "the father of realpolitik." Kautilya is not taught in any "principal IR theory courses."[10]

Watson writes "he described . . . the relations between one ruler and another, and explained how a prince, whom he called the conqueror, might exploit the pattern to bring all India into a Persian type of empire."[11] This was an imperial system not a system of competing states. Watson identifies Kautilya's precepts including that in which:

> [a]ny state that touches yours must be considered an enemy, because that is where you want to expand and because he may want to expand against you. Any state beyond the enemy, who touches him but not you, can be considered your friend.[12]

In short, the enemy of my enemy is my friend. Kautilya was a master at pointing to the chain effect of alliances as one set of protagonists having an impact upon another.

While Kautilya had a tool box full of dirty tricks, Watson points out that Kautilya, nevertheless:

> [s]tresses that peace should be preferred to war, and peace should even be preferred to armed and watchful neutrality in wars between other kings . . . If by the use of bribery or in any other way a king can attain his goal while avoiding the actual use of force, then that king is reaching his goal on the cheap.[13]

Kautilya advocated a lenient policy of occupation apart from the defeated king for whom there was no place. Otherwise it was a "very substantial local autonomy, leaving the local legitimacies as far as practical intact."[14]

In contrast to this somewhat cynical guide came the dramatic renunciation of armed conquest by the Emperor Asoka (265–238 BC) after leading his forces to one of the bloodiest victories in early Indian history. Converted to Buddhism, Asoka then advocated conquest by persuasion and reason. Although regarded as a wise emperor, his exemplary reign unfortunately was followed by centuries of violence and conflict.[15] In the longer run, that compilation of Hindu wisdom over the centuries, the *Bhagavadgita*, justifies the reconciliation of actual participation in war with spiritual peace.

Antecedents of religious thought

In the Biblical tradition, the Old Testament represents a literature rich in political insights. The international relations of the children of Israel rested upon deep philosophical and religious foundations. Christ's critique of Rome, as set forth in the majestic yet simple form of the Sermon on the Mount, provided a guide to political behaviour, however seldom it may have been followed by those in power throughout history. The devotion to peace of early Christians, who believed in cooperation, underwent transformation by the third century AD when St Augustine considered the possibility of 'just war.'

Much later, after the seventh century AD, the Koran provided many political guidelines for followers of Mohammed, such as for making peace, the observation of treaties, and militancy in the spread of Islam. Knutsen, in his *History of International Relations Theory*, acknowledges that "the Islamic perspective of world politics was mitigated by pragmatism" inherent in their understanding of the world with "peaceful relations and cultural and commercial ties . . . Muslim scholars embraced the ancient Graeco-Roman heritage . . . By keeping alive arguments that were lost in the West, they maintained a tradition . . . [they] went beyond the texts." They fitted older ideas to new contexts by fusing ideas from the Greco-Roman world with the Koran.[16] For instance, in tenth-century Persia, the Muslim philosopher Al-Farabi saw politics essentially as a struggle of each against all.[17] Another Islamic philosopher and thinker, a North African born in Tunis who lived in 'Moslim Spain,' Ibn Khaldun (1332–1406), argued that "while human civilization requires political leadership for its organization,"[18] it seems also true that "savage nations are better able to achieve superiority than others."[19]

From the point of view of what might be termed the 'linear' development of ideas about international relations, however, it is Europe that really matters in terms of how *world* politics as we conceptualise it today emerged. The legacy of the European nation-state system, despite many variations, has essentially been adopted as the world system in our time. The 'Christian' period of world politics was not particularly peaceful. Europeans lived in the Holy Roman Empire, which belied all three terms that made up its title. Yet in the thirteenth century, St Thomas Aquinas saw the world as reflecting God's plan, which mortals must endeavour to comprehend and to which their temporal affairs must conform.[20] Aquinas embraced Augustine's notion of a just war in which there is the authority of a sovereign in whose command the war is being waged (not a private dispute), a just cause and a right intention.[21] It was in that same century that Europe saw what was perhaps the first of its many peace plans, that of Pierre Dubois (1250–1320) seeking to pacify Europe by enhancing the power of France at the expense of other states in order to recover the Holy Land.

The early fourteenth century saw Dante Alighieri produce his remarkable *De Monarchia* (c. 1313), designed to secure unity through a world state under an emperor.[22] Shortly thereafter, Marsilius of Padua followed with what arguably was the first treatment of the problem of sovereignty, though he only went far enough to indicate that, as an interstate problem, it certainly deserved "rational enquiry."[23] Like Dubois, its overriding objective was a revitalisation of the Crusades, but his means to that end would require the princes of Christendom to strive towards a common goal. It would be some time before the ideal of a peace system as an end in itself would occur to the philosophers of Europe, although the farsighted Dutch philosopher, Desiderius Erasmus, did issue a *Plea of Reason, Religion and Humanity against War* in 1518.

Building a barricade: Europe, sovereignty and the 'Other'

Our starting point in the process of the emergence of a field later called International Relations was that at which there was the Caliphate, the Byzantine Empire and the Far West in Europe. The three met in the Iberian peninsula, but this ended on January 2, 1492 when Granada fell to the Christians, thus ending 700 years of Muslim governance, culture, science and philosophy in Western Europe. At the same time, the conquest of the Americas by the Portuguese and the Spanish and others got underway. The Muslims and the American civilisations were quickly characterised and treated as the 'Other' by the conquerors.

Europeans asserted their supremacy, the superiority of their civilisation, their right to exercise their manifest destiny, to bear the white man's burden, to engage in a *mission civilisatrice* and to pillage the world. Even relations between European states were hierarchical, and because of their differing capacities, this stratification was nothing when compared with that between the European-centric world and the 'Other' beyond the barricade.

Renaissance Italy: the anarchical precedent

Although it is no accident that Niccolò Machiavelli was called "the champion of realism,"[24] he was not as 'Machiavellian' as is often thought. Having boldly advised 'the Prince' in 1513 how to manage his affairs with other princes, based upon his own considerable diplomatic experience, he also put forth more cautious views in *The Discourses on Livy*,[25] praising the Roman republic, which belied the sinister reputation earned for him by his earlier, more cynical book of advice. The political environment within which he wrote – a kaleidoscope of warring Italian city-states – parallels the current world system, at least in certain particulars. In the first place, neighbours who were outside the system were not necessarily considered barbarians. They were people with whom a prince might have to deal, hopefully at arm's length, but perhaps at peril of losing some degree of independence (as the Milanese found out when, to enhance their security, they went outside the limited peninsular configuration to invite in French troops in the fifteenth century). Like the earlier systems, it was one of independent city states, but with each participant more insecure than those making up the ancient configuration. The Peace of Lodi in 1454 nevertheless reflected a sort of collective security system reminiscent of the time of the Delian League[26] or the Ch'in dynasty. Within the Italian peninsula, the 'international' system was characterised by diplomatic intrigue, conspiracy, betrayal and amorality, all conveniently lumped together under the name of 'Machiavellism.'[27] If there was an ethic at all, it was to serve the state, or rather the interest of the prince whose province it was. In a sense, *The Prince* was its book of rules. It was a book of rules placed in the Index in 1559, and Machiavellian became a synonym for immoral politicians in France in 1581 and in England in 1589. 'Raison d'état' (Reason of State) was to become a widespread notion in the next century,[28] bringing many of the ideas envisaged by Machiavelli to the centre of European politics in the seventeenth century.

The origins of international law

In parallel, with Italy's 'anarchical society,' to borrow Hedley Bull's title, the fifteenth and sixteenth centuries witnessed early manifestations of international law as a discipline. This could not have occurred in Rome, whose empire had neither the need nor the use for it, nor in medieval times, when law was rudimentary and local. Although hardly the father of the subject as some of his contemporaries claimed, Francisco de Vitoria (1480–1546), followed by another Spaniard, Francisco Suarez, did much to delineate the *jus gentium* (now somewhat broadened from its original meaning). In Italy, the study of international law on a religious foundation was advanced by the diplomat Ottaviano Maggi in 1566. Shortly thereafter, his Protestant country-man, Alberico Gentili, developed an entirely new approach, which saw war more as a political than a religious matter, arguing in his study of war in 1588 that "if men in another state live in a manner different from that which we follow in our own state, they surely do us no wrong."[29]

At about the same time, the French philosopher Jean Bodin considered sovereignty to be a central concept in this field, which was characterised by unlimited power over citizens and subjects, unrestrained by law. Bodin's contribution was a milestone. As Anderson points out:

> Bodin was the first thinker systematically and resolutely to break with the mediaeval conception of authority as the exercise of traditional justice, and to formulate the modern idea of political power as the sovereign capacity to create new laws, and impose unques-tioning obedience to them.[30]

According to Bodin, sovereignty belonged to the state (commonwealth) not to men; it was perpetual and absolute, "the source of all power and authority inside the commonwealth [only limited by] . . . divine or natural law, regime type and covenants."[31] Bodin also reiterated the principle of *pacta sunt servanda* by highlighting that it was "essential that princes keep their promises."[32] Part of the modern edifice for the study and practice of IR was now in place.

However, the principal credit for advancing the discipline of international law as a practical concern for the policy-makers of his day must go to Hugo Grotius (1583–1645). Like Plato, Aristotle, St Augustine and St Thomas of Aquinas before him, Grotius, whose career included a stint as an ambassador, was progenitor of a whole school of thought, which has adherents down to the present day – the so-called 'English School.'[33] Writing during the Thirty Years' War, his work on the law of war (in which he counselled moderation and, to a lesser degree, peace) derived its principles of reason from the actual nature of world society in his day. The definitive work for law between states for many years, *De Jure Belli ac Pacis*, published in 1625, must take its place in the early development of the discipline simply because interna-tional law was the context within which IR subject matter was considered by scholars of that era. To Grotius, clear rules must govern even wars: "violence is characteristic of wild beasts, and effort should be put forth . . . be tempered with humanity, lest in imitating wild beasts too much we forget to be human."[34] If Bodin provided the cornerstone of the edifice of IR, namely sovereignty, Grotius built on the idea of the interaction of sovereign princes to postulate an international society of sovereign states ruled by reason, custom and binding agreements. This was in many respects a new world and a conceptual framework for studying it.

Even though international law may be considered the 'root discipline' of IR, none of these savants of the law gave much time to concocting peace plans. That was left to others. Among the most significant of them (in terms of seminal ideas, not in terms of actually producing any striking alteration in the power structure) was Emeric Crucé. Crucé put his faith in trade in which individuals behaved in a rational manner, respectful of others. While sovereign states existed, he saw the desirability of a general assembly, which could adjudicate on differences after each had said his piece. He was an early, perhaps original, protagonist of the idea that trade creates a stake in peace. In this sense he was a forerunner of Mitrany and his *Working Peace System*.[35] War was already seen as *depassé* in this conception.

Even though a book Crucé wrote in 1623 was considered by Quincy Wright[36] as the first truly systematic study of International Organisation, it received far less attention than the 'Grand Design of Henry IV,' drawn upon and revised by numerous authors over a considerable period of time. Each author made changes according to his own political predisposition and objectives. The best known of these was the Duc de Sully, who in 1638 was trying to lay the groundwork for a Christian republic. The design, regarded by Sir Harry Hinsley as a source of endless confusion, had been seen by some earlier writers as the forerunner of contemporary proposals for maintaining lasting peace among states. In point of fact, this and most other peace plans of the period were more hegemonic than universal in purpose.

With Bodin, Grotius, Crucé and Machiavelli we are beginning to get a feel for notions that are recognisable as antecedents of what we now conceive to be IR. The picture will be a little clearer if we also include Thomas Hobbes. Hobbes described life without a Leviathan as "solitary, poore, nasty, brutish and short,"[37] in which danger was ever present. The security dilemma is all-consuming for political relations since if a prince did not provide an adequate and prudential capacity to defend his domain, he was likely to lose it to an adversary. And since there was no outside force or coercion on which he could rely, he was reduced to self-help, which created a system of relations fraught with danger where power politics reigned supreme. As Hobbes himself put it:

> Hereby it is manifest, that during the time men live without a common Power to keep them all in awe, they are in that condition which is called Warre; such a warre, as is of every man, against every man. For WARRE, consisteth not in Battell only, or the act of fighting; but in a tract of time, wherein the Will to contend by Battell is sufficiently known; and therefore the action of *Time*, is to be considered in the nature of Warre; as it is in the nature of Weather. For as the nature of Foule weather lyeth not in a showre or two of rain; but in an inclination thereto of many days together; so the nature of Warre, consisteth not in the actual fighting; but in the known disposition thereto, during all the time there is no assurances to the contrary. All other time is PEACE.[38]

Already we can see a glimpse of great traditions of political thought which have coursed through thinking across the centuries and which are already relevant to an academic subject that knows not yet its name. State-centric power politics can be found in Bodin, Machiavelli and Hobbes and liberal institutional theories about an international society in which individuals and organisations based on cooperation are to be identified in the thoughts and writings of Grotius and Crucé. We lack a third tradition, as yet, of structural analyses.

The significance of Westphalia

The quest for alternative systems, however fanciful, must have been irresistible. In a sense, the inchoate Italian system extended itself to the rest of Europe, culminating in the bloody, militarily inconclusive Thirty Years' War (1618–1648). More conclusive was the Peace of

Westphalia which ended it, recognising as it did a new international system based not upon the city but increasingly upon a wider territorial base, though not yet in every case the nation. To many students of the subject, IR began at Westphalia essentially in the form which continues today, more than three centuries later.

Complex as their negotiations turned out to be, what the princes at Westphalia did was very simple, not unlike what had occurred in different circumstances and for very different reasons 400 years earlier at Runnymede where the Magna Carta was signed. To oversimplify, they defied the highest authority. Consisting of several bilateral understandings, the Westphalian agreements brought an end to the religious wars of the Reformation. They *legitimised* the new order, which now rested upon sovereign, independent states. At least in theory. No longer did princes have to seek the Pope's or the Emperor's permission to deal with one another as equals. Theirs were competing interests with common norms. This demonstrated, if nothing else, that European diplomacy had matured after a century which was "one of the most formative periods of thought in international relations."[39]

Yet it is easy to read too much into what emerged from Westphalia.[40] People from earliest times have tended to believe that history repeats itself, but as Frederick Schuman observed in one of the first widely used IR textbooks, "of course, it does not."[41] Similar circumstances do produce similar reactions, as Arnold Toynbee tried to demonstrate in his ambitious 'challenge and response' theory. What Westphalia created was less a model than a profoundly significant and novel development in the relations of sovereign states and the analysis of those relations.

Within a few years, Baruch Spinoza was able to give unreserved acknowledgement to the existence of a system of sovereign entities and to concentrate on the relations between them. He regarded wars as legitimate, writing in 1677 that the sovereign "may live entirely as he pleases and is not bound by the will of another."[42] Although the study of IR may be said to have its origins at Westphalia because of the diplomatic and political phenomena that took place there, it should not be thought of in terms of a sudden revelation to those who thought they were establishing a revolutionary order. Nevertheless, the views of leading commentators on the state in its relations with others now take on more importance in the development of thought about the nature of what can at last technically be termed 'international relations' than before Westphalia. *Raison d'état* now was seen to be more compelling in determining the actual behaviour of princes than the reason of nature of Grotius or the reason of humanity and religion of Erasmus.

The central authority of the Papacy and the Holy Roman Emperor having been weakened, the more informal mechanisms of the balance of power now were strengthened. At the same time, men of vision, who could rise above the system and thus be less constrained than politicians, continued to think and to write opinions not bound entirely by the dictates of national interest. One was Baron Samuel von Pufendorf who, in contrast to Grotius, differentiated between ethics and law in an influential book published in 1672. Several decades later, a professor of the 'law of nature and nations,' Christian von Wolff, would appear, in his *Jus Gentium Methodo Scientifica Petractatum* (1749), to have been one of the first to adopt a kind of 'scientific method' to which some modern thinkers give so much weight. More important than either Pufendorf or Wolff was Emmerich de Vattel (1714–1767). In *Le Droit de Gens* in 1758 ("the first direct onslaught on the traditional international law")[43] Europe was urged to "form a political system in which nations inhabiting this part of the world are bound together by their relations and various interests into a single body," as it was no longer "a confused heap of detached parts."[44] He did not mention the still detached *other* parts of the world, which would gradually become enmeshed in the European colonial system. In rejecting accepted ideas about the law of nations, Vattel turned instead to "the well-known principle of the balance of power, by which is meant an arrangement of affairs so that no state shall be in a position to have absolute mastery and dominate over the others,"[45] in a shift in emphasis that was to prove prophetic in the development of classical theory in IR.

Hinsley has drawn our attention to the interaction between the notions of Christendom and Europe or, after Westphalia, the European state-system which had escaped from the political notion of a united Christendom with its inherent favouring of the power of the Pope and working concepts of a Holy Roman Empire. Gradually, Christendom became limited to Europe with a decline in its pretentions beyond Europe in part because of the blocking power of the Ottoman Turks.[46] The state-system post Westphalia was the dominant organising force.

The state in international relations

But what of the state itself? What was its nature? What *should* it be? Some intellectual giants grappled with the external dimensions of the state as well as with its internal nature. Thomas Hobbes, John Locke and Jean-Jacques Rousseau concentrated upon governance, but they all also concerned themselves explicitly with the state in relations with other states. Already a noted translator of Thucydides (whom he called "the most Politik Historiographer that ever writ")[47] Hobbes published his famous *Leviathan* three years after Westphalia. As mentioned earlier, to him, states lived in a state of nature, a hostile world lacking both cooperation and balance between states. In addition to *Leviathan*, Hobbes commented on the state of nature in *De Cive*, stating:

> [n]either if they cease from fighting, it is therefore to be called Peace, but rather a breathing time, in which one enemy observing the motion and the countenance of the other, values his security not according to the Pacts, but the forces and counsels of his adversary.[48]

His term, 'the body politic' lends itself well to IR, avoiding both the utopian overtones of 'world society' and the cynical undercurrents of nationalism. Some decades later Locke gained attention with his two treatises on government (1690), which concentrated upon the philosophy and organisation of government and in which he made the distinction between the state of war and that of nature. He did not, however, develop the implications of this distinction for world politics.[49] Although, of the three, only Locke had diplomatic experience, Rousseau had more to say about international affairs. Early in the eighteenth century, he endeavoured to apply his renowned Social Contract theory to states as they related to one another, which led him to be confusing and contradictory. In one place he urged that "all the European powers form among themselves a sort of system which unites by the same religion, the same international law, by customs, literature, commerce, and by a kind of balance of power," but in another "that the pretended brotherhood of the nations . . . seems nothing but a term of derision" and "if the present system is founded on a rock, it is all the more on that account exposed to storms" which keep them in a "constant state of unrest."[50] Needless to say, it would not be all that difficult to argue that he was right on both counts, given the capriciousness of world politics that has already been noted.

Knutsen[51] further points out that:

> Rousseau portrays man as peaceful and kind . . . War is a *social* undertaking; it is a product of human civilization . . . all other contract thinkers argue that the social contract ends conflict among men, but for Rousseau it creates the preconditions for war.

Nurture triumphs over nature since "Man is born free; and everywhere he is in chains," as the first line of the *Social Contract* puts it.[52]

Diplomacy and the balance of power

Known at the time for his conservative philosophy, David Hume's contribution to international thought is seen principally in his perceptive historical essay, 'Of the balance of power' (1742), in which, as Stanley Hoffmann has pointed out, he demonstrated "an acute awareness of the advantages of such a system, of the delicacy of its operation, and of Britain's special position."[53] Like Voltaire (*nom de plume* of François-Marie Arouet), who wrote of a 'Christian Europe' in 1751, Hume saw in the multiplicity of states of differing natures an element of common sense, which had in fact been practised in the balancing process, a process whose principal instrument was diplomacy.

Hitherto hardly more than a form of 'aristocratic cosmopolitanism,' diplomacy itself matured. Cardinal Richelieu was the first to establish the art as a permanent activity and "not merely a hurried endeavour."[54] Later descriptions tended to concentrate upon procedure, style and technique, or the symbols of diplomacy, but among these thinkers concerned in an innovative manner with the philosophy of interstate contact, three are noteworthy. Not surprisingly, their commentaries on the art followed the publication of the landmark philosophical treatises on the nature of government itself, of which foreign relations had become more and more a formalised feature. Nearly 150 years after Gentili had described the nature and function of the legation, Abraham de Wicquefort reviewed the lessons of a lifetime in describing *The Ambassador and His Functions*. Although full of practical insights, he unfortunately exhibited neither the charm nor the depth of understanding of François de Callières. This grand master of diplomatic method observed in *On the Manner of Negotiating with Princes* (1716) that:

> [i]t is a fundamental error, and one widely held, that a clever negotiator must be a master of deceit . . . apart from the fact that a lie is unworthy of a great Ambassador, it actually does more harm than good.[55]

Drawing to some degree upon his experience as Secretary of War, James (later Lord) Bolingbroke extended the concept of diplomacy to encompass policy in several fascinating letters on the study of history, written between 1735 and 1742. His *Idea of a Patriot King* (1746) is significant for the contemporary student of IR in that he endeavoured to bring state and nation together in a single context. The force of nationalism would become the chief determinant of the politics of the latter part of the eighteenth century. It culminated in wars where the *levée en masse* produced massive contingents of troops so fiercely loyal to the French nation and its Emperor, Napoleon, that a mighty coalition of other European states would have to be drawn together to defeat them.

The vision of peace

The writings of these pragmatic men of affairs (although only Bolingbroke might be regarded as a specialist in foreign policy) must not obscure the value of the admittedly more visionary work of William Penn, John Bellers and the oft-cited Abbé St Pierre, however little their prescriptions actually affected the relations between states in their time. A Quaker often in trouble with the law in England for applying deep religious conviction, Penn left his homeland to found a colony based upon pacifist principles in the United States and there to consolidate his ideas about improving the old world. In his *Essay towards the Present and Future Peace of Europe* (1693), he was realistic enough to write that men "will hardly be brought to think of peace unless their appetites be some way gratified."[56] In a similar vein Bellers advanced reasons for a 'Christian Commonwealth' in 1710, laying down certain broad principles for a peaceful international order. By very different means Charles François Irénée Caste, the Abbé St Pierre, drew upon the labours of many others (including Sully), even changing his own ideas in successive drafts of a renowned project for achieving perpetual peace in Europe.

What is really at issue here is neither literary purity nor philosophical originality, but rather the persistence of 'the pursuit of peace' as an approach to the study of IR. The more men practised, and through the discipline of military science, perfected the art of war, the more they longed for the possibility of peace. The trouble then was, as it is today, that peace is rarely, if ever, the ultimate value in the determination of foreign policies of states. That value usually is self-preservation, and sometimes self-extension, based upon some notion of the 'national interest.' Most of the plans for general peace were designed as a means for serving better the interests of a particular prince or state. What is different about Penn is that he thought of peace for its own sake and not for the self-interest of any particular State.

Difficult as it may be to say just when the Age of Enlightenment came to an end, it was certainly still in flower when Thomas Paine published *Common Sense*[57] in 1776. The openness that had encouraged scientific enquiry by such men of that age as René Descartes, Frances Bacon and Isaac Newton, also set the stage for innovation in many fields of thought. The 'pre-history' of the discipline of IR was about to be replaced by the internationalisation of the political process, in the form of a military coalition brought into being to restore the balance of power, to be followed by what came to be called the Concert of Europe.

Notes

1 See Benjamin de Carvalho, Halvard Leira and John M. Hobson, 'The Big Bangs of IR,' *Millennium*, Vol. 39, No. 3, 2011.

2 The Kadish Treaty of the thirteenth century BC between the Hittites and Egyptians was possibly the oldest peace treaty known today. For an analysis of early practice in the diplomacy of ancient times, see Raymond Cohen and Raymond Westbrook (eds), *Amarna Diplomacy: The Beginnings of International Relations* (Baltimore: John Hopkins University Press, second edition, 2000).

3 See Richard Ned Lebow, *The Tragic Vision of Politics: Ethics, Interests and Orders* (Cambridge: Cambridge University Press, 2003).

4 Robert Purnell, 'Theoretical Approaches to International Relations: The Contribution of the Greco-Roman World,' in Trevor Taylor (ed.), *Approaches and Theory in International Relations* (London: Longman, 1987), p. 27.

5 *Ibid.*, p. 25.

6 Fred Parkinson, *The Philosophy of International Relations* (London: Sage, 1977), p. 11.

7 On the Book of Lord Shang, Handelman (1995, p. 264) stated that "The origins of the Book are apocryphal, its text likely compiled from various writings, c. 250–150 B.C. The text purports to recount discussions, policies, and theories of the state of Ch'in, c. 350 B.C. The Book was a manifesto for the totalistic, bureaucratic remaking of social order under the control of human agency, relatively autonomous of the operations of the natural cosmos." Quoted from Don Handelman, 'Cultural taxonomy and bureaucracy in ancient China: The book of Lord Shang,' *International Journal of Politics, Culture, and Society*, Vol. 9, No. 2, 1995, pp. 263–293.

8 Sun Tzu, *The Essential Art of War*, transl. Ralph D. Sawyer (New York: Basic Books, 2005).

9 Adam Watson, *The Evolution of International Society* (Oxford: Routledge, 1992), pp. 78–83.

10 Quoted from Michael Liebig, 'Kautilya's Relevance for India Today,' *India Quarterly*, Vol. 69, No. 2, 2013, p. 110.

11 Watson, *op. cit.*, p. 78.
12 *Ibid.*, pp. 80–81.
13 *Ibid.*, p. 82.
14 *Ibid.*, p. 83.
15 Fredrick L. Schumann, *International Politics* (New York: McGraw-Hill, 1933), p. 32.
16 Torbjørn L. Knutsen, *A History of International Relations Theory* (Manchester: Manchester University Press, 1997), second edition, p. 2.
17 Richard Walzer, 'Aspects of Islamic Political Thought: Al-Farabi and Ibn Xaldun,' *Oriens*, Vol. 15, 1963.
18 *The Mughaddimah* (*An Introduction to History*), transl. Franz Rosenthal (Oxford: Routledge and Kegan Paul, 1967), p. 256.
19 *Ibid.*, p. 107.
20 See *Aquinas Selected Political Writings*, edited by A.P. D'Entrèves (Oxford: Blackwell, 1954).
21 For Aquinas' words, see Torbjørn L. Knutsen *A History of International Relations Theory* (Manchester: Manchester University Press, 1992), first edition, p. 22.
22 Dante, *Monarchy* (London: Weidenfeld and Nicholson, 1954).
23 Cited by F.H. Hinsley, *Power and the Pursuit of Peace: Theory and Practice in the History of Relations between States* (Cambridge: Cambridge University Press, 1967, first published in 1963), p. 15.
24 Mary G. Dietz, 'Trapping the Prince: Machiavelli and the Politics of Deception,' *The American Political Science Review*, Vol. 80, No. 3, 1986.
25 Niccolo Machiavelli, *Discourses on Livy* (Oxford: Oxford University Press, 2008).
26 The Delian League was formed in 478 BC by Greek city states under the leadership of Athens against the Persian Empire.
27 Friedrich Meinecke, *Machiavellism* (1957), cited in Hinsley, *op. cit.*, p. 368.
28 Steven Forde, 'Classical Realism,' in Terry Nardin and David Mapel (eds), *Traditions in International Ethics* (Cambridge: Cambridge University Press, 1992), p. 63.
29 Cited by P. Savigear, 'European Political Philosophy and International Relations,' in T. Taylor, *op. cit.*, p. 38.
30 Perry Anderson, *Lineages of the Absolute State* (London: Verso, 1979), p. 50.
31 Knutsen, *op. cit.*, p. 74.
32 *Ibid.*, p. 4.
33 See Chapter 7 this volume.
34 Cited by P. Savigear in T. Taylor, *op. cit.*, p. 40.
35 David Mitrany, *A Working Peace System* (Chicago, IL: Quadrangle Press, 1966 [1943]).
36 Quincy Wright, *The Study of International Relations* (New York: Appleton-Century-Crofts, 1955) is a masterful study of the discipline at that time.
37 Thomas Hobbes, *Leviathan* (London: Dent, 1914, Part I, chapter 13), p. 65.
38 *Ibid.*, p. 64.
39 Parkinson, *op. cit.*, p. 33.
40 A recent article makes this point and debunks 1648 and 1919 as "the Myths that your teachers still tell you." See Benjamin de Carvalho, Halvard Leira and John M. Hobson, 'The Big Bangs of IR,' *Millennium*, Vol. 39, No. 3, 2011.
41 Parkinson, *op. cit.*, p. 15.
42 Quoted in *Ibid.*, p. 38.
43 Hinsley, *op. cit.*, p. 166.
44 E. De Vattel [1758], *The Law of Nations* (New York: AMS Press, 1987).
45 *Ibid.*
46 Hinsley, *op. cit.*, p. 156.
47 Hinsley had a similar view. He writes, "Thucydides is still the author of the best book on that subject," that subject being "international aggression, continuous, calculated, pathologically inspired." Hinsley, *op. cit.*, p. 275.
48 Cited in Theodore Christov, *Before Anarchy: Hobbes and His Critics in Modern International Thought* (Cambridge: Cambridge University Press, 2016), p. 112.
49 Savigear, *op. cit.*, p. 39.
50 Cited by Hinsley, *op. cit.*, p. 61.
51 Knutsen, *op. cit.*, pp. 114–115.
52 Jean-Jacques Rousseau, *The Social Contract* (London: Dent, 1913), p. 3.

53 "The balance of power," in David I. Sills (ed.), *International Encyclopaedia of the Social Sciences* (New York: Macmillan and the Free Press, 1968), p. 508.
54 Cited by Sir Harold Nicolson, *The Evolution of Diplomatic Method* (London: Constable, 1953), pp. 50–51.
55 Cited by Nicolson, *Ibid.*, p. 63.
56 Cited by Hinsley, *op. cit.*, p. 41.
57 Thomas Paine, *Common Sense and the Crisis* (Garden City, NY: Anchor Books Edition, 1973).

2   The 'international' idea and the reordering of Europe

Had the French writer Albert Grosser been right in dubbing IR a US speciality, it would have been appropriate to begin our study at about the time of the birth of 'the first new nation.'[1] But that is really only coincidence. To be sure, the war of independence began in 1776, but that was also the year of the publication of Adam Smith's *Wealth of Nations*, and shortly after that came the first use of the term 'international' by Jeremy Bentham.[2] As William T.R. Fox has put it, "the word is symbolically important because it registers the norm-expectation that the interstate system is becoming and ought to be an inter-nation-state system."[3]

To Bentham, the force of public opinion would make states keep their pledges, so that "international integration was not so much attainable and undesirable as utterly unnecessary."[4] Besides his contribution to nomenclature, Bentham's recognition of the importance of international law was influential, especially the need for codification and a tribunal. He was an advocate of open diplomacy and embraced the notion of the harmony of interests. He viewed colonies as a burden to be dispensed with and that Europe would be better off without them, and more peaceful. His 'plan for a universal and perpetual peace' (1797) stressed the importance of free trade. His thought has echoes in that of advocates of a League of Nations decades later. To Adam Smith, the state could not be trusted anyway, so he advocated a system of political economy based on *laissez-faire*. Both Bentham and Smith understood the interaction of economics and politics. Although dimly understood at the time, a third discipline, demography, which would have profound implications for international relations, especially in racist attitudes and fears, began to emerge at this time with the publication of Thomas Malthus' essay on the principle of population in 1798. In the realm of public international policy, Edmund Burke championed the traditional rights of "the natives of Hindustan and those of Virginia"[5] against the Crown. On the other side of the Atlantic, the concepts of the Declaration of Independence reflected the work of Edmund Burke[6] and included ideas from Jean-Jacques Rousseau and other European thinkers, supplemented by those in *The Federalist Papers*, notably the ideas of Hamilton on national commerce and its implications for international politics.

By the end of the eighteenth century, both through the philosophical insights of James Madison and Thomas Jefferson and the effective diplomacy of John Jay and Benjamin Franklin, a US contribution had begun in world affairs. These men shared a belief with many in Britain that lasting international peace was a possibility, though this was tempered by the view of those like George Washington who felt that the United States should steer clear of entanglements with Europe. The tensions between a liberal universalist ideology and an isolationist one that were to clash in post First World War US foreign policy, were already in evidence in the early years of the Republic. A commonly held view was that, since no real conflict existed between the basic national interests of all states, there need be no delay in creating a workable international order. Optimism, based upon the ideas of Bentham, Penn and others, continued to dominate thought in the two countries well into the nineteenth century. Britain was preoccupied with its emerging position of world leadership. The United States was preoccupied with its internal development. Both possessed the elemental security of the seas as a gift of nature that enabled them to share a broader vision.

In continental Europe, the intellectual climate was very different. Neither Rousseau, who thought that international conflict rendered impossible any real progress, nor Immanuel Kant, who took the opposite view that progress might well be achieved as a result of conflict, had shared this optimism. The Age of Enlightenment had come to a close with an eruption of violence which began with the French revolution and ended with the double defeat of Napoleon. Once *l'Empereur* was twice defeated and banished, peace was to be organised upon a traditional basis at the Congress of Vienna in 1815. Like the Peace of Westphalia a century and a half earlier, the Congress of Vienna followed a series of continental wars, but there was one great difference. The Thirty Years' War had left the continent exhausted, with vast tracts laid waste and economies ruined in a Europe which had already been disintegrating for a long time. Napoleon's war did not. His own country had just gone through a revolution as had the United States, their respective constitutions having been adopted within a few months of one another. Regimes which had fought long battles remained in power. In the emergent configuration, what would now be called the state system, came to dominate world politics. One reason this endured (at least for a time) was that the defeated Power was to be made part of the system. Unhappily, that principle was neither perceived nor applied at the peace negotiations following the next general war a century later, though as Henry Kissinger[7] demonstrated, the lesson was not entirely to be lost as the defeated Powers in 1945 – Italy, Japan and Germany – were incorporated freely into the West in the context of the Cold War.

Another kind of theory, largely ignored by the policy-makers if not the intellectuals of the time, took the form of a renowned essay[8] put forth in 1795 by Kant. Never travelling more than forty miles from his home in Königsberg, Kant nevertheless endeavoured to create a practical plan for the abolition of war the world over. He argued that what was needed was less a treaty *of* peace to end the French revolutionary wars than a treaty *for* peace. As he himself put it in the final paragraph of *Perpetual Peace*, "it may well be said that this Treaty for universal and eternal peace constitutes not only a part, but the final objective in its entirety of law within the confines of common sense."[9] This represented a fairly widespread image of international relations in which good states (i.e. for Kant, republics) make peace by following good policies.

The statesmen-thinkers

The influential thinkers of the Westphalian era – Spinoza, Vattel, Pufendorf – had written as individuals with no professional accountability, as outsiders commenting upon the system and advocating its reform. The new pre-eminent minds – Castlereagh, Metternich, Talleyrand and Tsar Alexander I – were themselves statesmen occupying positions of high responsibility in the states that made up the system, promoting its restoration once the disturber had been put down.

Such fundamentally contrasting types of statesmen as the idealistic Alexander I of Russia and the practical Pitt the Younger of England argued – separately – for some sort of a league of governments, which would undertake to help one another prevent war and encourage political stability. As early as 1804, Pitt actually recommended in a state paper that the Powers "should bind themselves mutually to protect and support each other against any attempt to infringe upon" their respective positions.[10] Whether because of these sometimes contradictory ideas or in spite of them, the statesmen of Vienna were to succeed in creating a relatively stable post-war order. But it was the balance of power rather than the peace plans of the centuries upon which practitioners were now to seize as the keystone of European security.

No overview of nineteenth-century thought concerning international politics can ignore the essentials of the power configuration emerging from the Congress of Vienna. Ideas for planning the peace as promulgated by Kant provided no more than a kind of backdrop for the events now taking place on the stage of conference diplomacy. It was the doers, the statesmen of the victorious Powers, who were to make the peace. The actors were the treaty makers, not the peace planners.

As the eighteenth century gave way to the nineteenth, the dominant state system comprised five major Powers in Europe (Prussia, Russia, Austria, Britain and France), a multiplicity of minor Powers, such as Spain and Sweden, and a new state, as yet untried as a Power, geographically outside Europe (the United States). That system had been challenged by a brilliant disturber, but France now renounced its claims to what Napoleon had conquered. A German confederation of some thirty-eight states was established, with Prussia strengthened and Austria enabled to maintain its basic status with some gains here, some losses there, but now turned more towards Central Europe, the Balkans and North Italy than the German states. Britain enhanced its power, especially overseas, but also by virtue of being able to manipulate the balance of power on the continent, apparently as it chose, a condition which produced the epithet 'perfidious Albion.' Russia gained both territory and prestige, its ruler regarded as the saviour of Europe until his indecisive behaviour cast doubt upon his right to any such role. In each instance it was to be the quality of thought as well as the political astuteness of the top negotiators which, given the power of their respective states, granted them the right to be there in the first place and determined the outcome of their deliberations.

Tsar Alexander had the merit of thinking in systemic terms in that it was not always men or revolution that determined outcomes, but they could also be derived from the processes of a system, and such processes therefore also had to be addressed. Holsti identifies the Tsar's three essential ideas as "domestic constitutionalism; the independence of Europe's nations, based on the principle of nationality; and a federation of Europe."[11] Constitutions could seem to offer evolution especially when allied to self-determination. Constitutional national states could then form a European body based on international law. However, this was not to last even though the Tsar proposed creating a European army with a permanent Allied General Staff "primarily to protect small states and to deter aggression. By 1818, however, the Tsar had converted to reaction, and so he came to see this project as a means for a coordinated crusade against liberal-national revolutions."[12] In Holsti's words, the Tsar:

> [s]aw that the best formula for creating an international order was to combine domestic harmony *within* the members of the European family by the devices of constitutionalism and self-determination, with guarantees, consultations, and international principles to regulate relations *between* states. He was concerned with a generic problem of the international system and not just with the particulars of the French Revolution and the Napoleonic eras. His colleagues were less interested in that question and sought to deal primarily with the source of the last war, namely the French Revolution. The Tsar sought to create a general system of peace; his colleagues focused on the principle of equilibrium, with little else. The Tsar anticipated the ideas and problems of the nineteenth century; his colleagues wanted to avoid them or, should they manifest themselves through revolution, to crush them.[13]

Among the workaday statesmen perhaps the most influential was Viscount Castlereagh, the British Foreign Secretary (1812–1822). It was his conception of the European balance of power that was to prevail. His intellectual stamp, which was on most of the Treaties, rested upon a few simple but well-conceived principles: first, lasting peace depended upon a real balance of power being established in Europe; second, France being reintegrated into the system but being at the same time confined to limits going back to ancient times; third, the continuation of the alliance after the peace settlement; fourth, a clear recognition that British interests should take into account the emerging plans for reconstructing the continent of Europe. In order to achieve all this (and he did achieve most of it) he knew he would have to act as mediator between the other allied Powers.

Castlereagh's systematic thinking came to dominate the conference, but it was Prince Metternich's more pragmatic approach to international politics which, day by day, set the actual pace. As a noted interpreter of international conferences, Sir Harold Nicolson, has put it, "in his attitude to internal and external affairs the whole of Metternich's political theory can be summarized in the one word 'equilibrium.'"[14] His guiding light was to snuff out revolution wherever and whenever it manifested itself and, better still, to prevent it from occurring. The balance of power was the prime means to achieve this, whether it was relevant to internal disputes or not. After the Congress System had broken down and the Quadruple Alliance (Prussia, Austria, Russia, Britain) had been abandoned by a Britain under George Canning increasingly antagonistic towards the so-called Holy Alliance, Metternich was forced to resign in the face of the revolutionary winds of 1848. Now after nearly forty years as Austrian Foreign Minister, the venerable statesman bitterly observed, "I ruled Europe sometimes but I never governed Austria."[15] Given the intricacies of Austrian politics in the end it was his thought and his conception rather than Castlereagh's that left its mark upon the conduct of international affairs.

Talleyrand, the third principal actor, brought his influence to bear only later in the conference, because it was his lot to try to bring his country back into the centre of European policy. As a tactician, Prince Charles de Talleyrand succeeded brilliantly but, as these words reveal, his views of the balance of power were more pragmatic than theoretical, more adaptive than consistent:

> If Europe were composed of states being so related to one another that the minimum of resisting power of the smallest were equal to [the] maximum of aggressive power of the greatest, then there would be real equilibrium. But the situation in Europe is not, and will never be such.[16]

The French Minister's talents, writes Nicolson, "transcended opportunism, they amounted to genius."[17]

Even though the period separating two great conferences – Vienna and Versailles – has often been referred to as *Pax Britannica*, was this really a century of peace? If by 'peace' is meant the absence of any fundamental, intended threat to the balance of power, the answer is 'yes.' If it means the absence of wars, even those involving the great Powers in adjusting the balance by border changes, then the answer must be 'no.' The first answer is both more persuasive and more useful to the student of IR, although it would never satisfy the peace seekers who became more activist as the century wore on. What needs to be understood is what was meant by the catch phrase, *Pax Britannica*. Britain, which had acquired strategic pieces of the French and Dutch colonial territories as a result of the Congress, had persuaded the ambassadors of Austria, Prussia and Russia to agree not even to discuss the question of British maritime rights during the negotiations. The British government would now be free to remain aloof or to intervene in continental affairs, whenever and wherever it wished, without necessarily committing to any other Power in advance.

In light of the importance that was to be attached to public opinion after the next great peace conference, it is instructive to note its relative unimportance at the Congress of Vienna.

Nevertheless, in a *Handbook*[18] released just after the First World War by the Foreign Office as being of probable use to those in the attentive public concerned with international affairs, Webster noted the efforts by diplomats to influence public opinion and, through public opinion, the negotiators at Vienna. There had been a real journalistic struggle in Prussia. Talleyrand was himself believed on more than one occasion to have stirred up dissent for his own purposes. The Tsar's ambassador in London was instructed that an effort was to be made to influence public opinion in a direction favourable to Russian interests. Webster concluded that the total impact of these episodes was insignificant. Only the ideas of the plenipotentiaries mattered. An effective role in international affairs for potential challengers outside governments was to be postponed. Those in power neither wanted nor needed it; they merely ignored the public.

What took the place of the Congress system was the 'Concert of Europe,' an informal international-state association which worked fairly well until the Crimean War (1853–1856). This did not mean that the governments always continued to support one another, as Castlereagh had hoped. Once a coincidence of perceived interests gave way to contention, an order based on the consensus of values inevitably broke down. "History teaches us, and invariably we disregard her lesson," one authority has observed in what is almost a theorem: "that coalitions begin to disintegrate the moment that the common danger is removed."[19] Within less than a decade, the tidy Congress system had broken down, as had been predicted by one leading political thinker of the time, Friedrich von Gentz, called the Secretary-General of Europe for his organisational and political skills at the Congress of Vienna.[20] Earlier he had attacked Kant's ideas, writing that "it is impossible to establish an eternal system of public law by means of a general treaty." The "question of the probable duration of this European League, which has temporarily overcome the gulf of competing political pretensions but cannot overcome it for ever, or even for very long, is thus the most important question facing the statesmen."[21]

The Congress of Berlin in 1878 that followed the Prusso-Turkish War of 1877–1878 was characterised by *The Times* as the "first instance of a real Parliament of the Great Powers,"[22] but only a few years later, the desirability of such a parliament was apparently shared by the British Prime Minister. William Gladstone endeavoured to revive the Concert of Europe in 1893 through a 'Council of the Great Powers' (all of which at that time were still, but not for long, wholly or partly European). General belief in the feasibility of international cooperation through the formal organisation of Powers with common values, however, was to wane after Bismarck was forced to resign. As for formal international organisation, that potentially rich harvest was to remain in seed for later generations. But that seed had been planted, at least in theory, during a century in which for the first time the idea of international institutions was seen as a feasible forum for managing the relations among states.

The philosophers

If the diplomatic interplay of the nineteenth century may be said to have been ushered in by statesmen-thinkers, it also had its share of political philosophers who never held power, but who, in the long run, were probably more influential for not doing so. Several widely divergent authorities, David Ricardo[23] and Friedrich List[24] to name but two, were convinced that economics and politics could and should not be separated. Their views contributed to the history of ideas in International Political Economy that was to constitute one of the growing points of the discipline in the late twentieth century. Challenging the entire system by word and deed were numerous groups making up the peace movement, which in the second half of the nineteenth century had to be taken more seriously than it had been by the diplomats at Vienna, when as a 'movement,' it hardly existed. All of this was nourished in its many contradictions by a European society which allowed them all to exist and indeed, to a greater or lesser degree, to thrive.

Most of these seminal writers about the state and politics writ large, while never holding responsible positions in government, accepted prevailing societal assumptions and values. Georg Hegel's (1770–1831) philosophy of history, particularly his dialectical method of thinking (thesis, antithesis, synthesis),[25] was different. He succeeded in doing what neither Kant nor Rousseau had attempted, which was to produce a comprehensive theory based on impersonal forces propelling humanity in a sort of preordained route of progress. Hegel reversed the order in what Parkinson regards as the first theory of IR to be conceived entirely in terms of social dynamics.[26] War between states was simply a fact, neither to be praised nor condemned, so there was no point in moralising about what should govern relationships between governments. This amoral approach to international politics reflected a break with the immediate past. Like Burke, Hegel was sceptical about formal agreements, such as treaties. They both had "a great deal of faith in the regulatory capacity of custom in international relations"[27]. Hegel rejected the whole idea of international integration. Universal diplomatic custom was a better basis for bringing about order among states. For this reason, he concentrated upon the state and international relations, as would Marx, but for different reasons.

Knutsen notes that "Hegel was enormously influential, partly because he included all the major early nineteenth-century themes in his vast synthesis; partly because his arguments were so abstract that adherents of all ideologies found some support in his work."[28] In the end Hegel provided the basis for an organic version of nationalism giving succour to conservatives. Knutsen comments that "Conservatives found in Hegel a conception of the nation-state as an 'imagined community,' a consensual community and a nation." In that regard, "Hegel's arguments constituted a Teutonic counterpart to Burke's conservative view of the British state as an organic, historically created whole and a necessary precondition for social order and individual freedom."[29] Chris Brown highlights elements of Hegel's thoughts which find expression in German thinking about the individual, the state and nationalism, which sees the state as the repository of the loyalty of the individual as the doctrine of nationalist calls for the organic nation to become a political entity.[30]

Meanwhile several other theories or approaches to international politics were being advanced in the field of international law. For example, James Mill wrote an influential series of *Essays* for the *Encyclopaedia Britannica*, which placed considerable emphasis upon public opinion, or as he put it, "the approbation or disapprobation of mankind."[31] He even went so far as to advocate that steps be taken to educate public opinion, postulating that:

> [t]he book of the law of nations, and selections from the book of trials before the international tribunal, should form a subject of study in every school and a knowledge of them a necessary part of every man's education . . . a moral sentiment would grow up, which would, in time, act as a powerful restraining force upon the injustice of nations.[32]

Yet, while he favoured an international court with real power to treat offences against the law of nations, Mill rejected any intention of backing up such a court by armed force. Another believer in the rule of law in the tradition of statesmen-scholars, though never a decision-maker like Castlereagh or John Quincy Adams, was a US international lawyer, Henry Wheaton (1785–1848), an experienced career diplomat widely known for the precision of his writing. In 1836, the year he became Minister in Berlin, he published the first of many editions of a widely read standard work, which was translated into several languages. One basic principle was put this way:

> [t]he peculiar subjects of international law are Nations, and those political societies of Men called States . . . a State is also distinguishable from a Nation, since the former may be composed of different races of Men, all subject to the same supreme authority.[33]

Highly influential over a period of many years, Sir James Lorimer, in his *Institutes of Nations* (1883) also revealed himself to be a master of the middle ground in the field of international law between national independence and cosmopolitan values. He advocated both the loosest possible bonds in its organisation and a court whose awards should if necessary be enforced by an international army.

Political economists, sociologists and strategists

From an entirely different perspective, the political economists continued to stand out, some for their writing (such as List), some for their parliamentary skill (such as John Bright) and some for both (such as Richard Cobden).[34] They believed in as little government intervention as possible, either in domestic or foreign affairs. A Member of Parliament who founded a major opposition newspaper, Cobden argued in his *Free Trade as the Best Human Means for Securing Universal and Permanent Peace* (1842) that unfettered commerce would create such a powerful incentive for peace that men would prevent their governments from using war as the chosen instrument for serving their interests. Another Progressive Radical of the so-called Manchester School was John Bright, a brilliant orator who wrote little but was much written about, particularly by Cobden. An early manifestation of functionalism (though it was not then called that), Bright's philosophy was based on three essential elements: first, existence of a 'harmony of interests' among states; second, an intimate connection between peace and free trade; and third, abolition of the monopoly of trade, which Bright saw as being fundamental to what he termed 'the colonial system.' His parliamentary colleague Cobden even went so far as to contend that free trade constituted "the international law of the Almighty." The theory of peace, while still perhaps rudimentary, was advancing on several fronts, though there was as yet still no theory of IR as such. Or at least it was not called that, though two kinds of theory had begun to emerge. One grew out of a need to *explain* the nature of power relations; the other reflected a deep desire to *change* it.

As for the theory of war, the nineteenth century also produced significant advances. One important thinker achieved notoriety for his maxim: "war is a mere continuation of politics by other means."[35] When Karl von Clausewitz wrote this in *Vom Kriege* (*On War*) in 1823, he spelled out a theory of war as an instrument of national policy.[36] To Clausewitz, peace seemed hardly more than a temporary respite from the normal, yet he warned against "the most soulless analysis, and as if in a horrid dream" trying to "connect this base of abstractions with facts belonging to the real world. Heaven preserve every theorist from such an undertaking."[37] Some years later, a Swiss who served in the French and Russian armies, Baron Antoine Henri Jomini, further systematised military science, concentrating not upon politics and diplomacy, but war itself. In his 1838 *Précis de l'Art de la Guerre* (*Summary of the Art of War*), Jomini made a theoretical attempt to demonstrate that there is a fundamental principle in all operations of war, a principle which should preside over measures adopted so that they may be successful. Jomini was at one time a paramount figure in his field in Europe, although unlike Clausewitz he may later have been neglected because he was referring to a type of war that was no longer relevant.[38] Although neither a war theorist nor a military special-ist, another nineteenth-century thinker deserves attention, if only because he came close to anticipating 'conflict resolution.' C. de Mougins de Rocquefort implied in 1889 that govern-ments must reconcile themselves to the possibility of legitimate sanctions and compromises on national sovereignty if wars were ever to be prevented or contained.[39]

Closely related to thinking about war and strategy were questions of resources, land mass and location. Alexis de Tocqueville had produced in 1832 a disturbingly prophetic study entitled *Democracy in America*.[40] In some ways, he can be regarded as one of the first modern exponents of what came to be known as geopolitics, predicting that because of their respec-tive size, position and resources, as well as their political institutions and capabilities, Russia and the United States would, in time, become the major power centres of the world (he also expressed grave reservations about the ability of democracies either logically to define a for-eign policy or to adhere to it persistently once defined). In the context of defining goals for the peace movement in 1866, Michael Chevalier was to be perhaps the first to promote European unification expressly for the purpose of providing an essential counter-weight to what he called the "political colossus"[41] on the far side of the ocean, the United States of America.

Long-range prediction in international politics also fascinated two influential writers of the time, Auguste Comte and Herbert Spencer. The founder of Western sociology, Comte was the first modern thinker to recommend the empirical investigation of the facts of soci-ety and politics along scientific lines. His critique of the widely known and by some highly regarded *Project* of the Abbé St Pierre revealed both a theory of international relations and of foreign policy:

> The idea of the worthy Abbé was in itself good, but it erred by the false combination by means of which he wished to carry it out, for he proposed a coalition of kings . . . He might as well have proposed that wolves should guard sheep . . . soon, by the power of public opinion, enlightened by the press . . . the people will actually govern.[42]

What Comte wanted was a League of Peoples, not of states. Like Comte, Spencer (who coined the term 'survival of the fittest' in 1864) believed that the conflict between individu-als and the world in which they live could only be resolved by applying ethical principles to contemporary society. But this had to be based upon knowledge acquired by free individuals, not the initiative of organised society. At about the same time, another sociologist, Lester Ward, was drawing distinctions between territorial groups called races, nations or states. He was convinced that war would disappear as international understanding was developed through education (a concept later institutionalised in Archibald Macleish's preamble to the constitution of UNESCO, which begins with the words "as wars begin in the minds of men, it is in the minds of men that the defences of peace must be constructed").

The conventional consensus

Certain notions can be said to have been accepted by most, though certainly not all, of the nineteenth-century thinkers about the nature and improvement of international relations. Despite sharp differences of opinion and even of action, consensus seemed to prevail on the presumably obvious, though increasingly challenged, legitimacy of the state. What were the elements of this consensus? In the first place, the state and its continued existence in any one of its existing forms was taken for granted, as it had been certainly since Westphalia. Second, even though strategists like Clausewitz and statesmen like Metternich expected war to occur from time to time among such states, there was a general acceptance of an essential interest among them in maintaining the existing order. Third, undergirded by a shared belief in international law, peace was regarded as the normal characteristic of relationships. Even Bismarck's use of force fused with 'blood and iron' was designed more for internal German unification than expansion, except in the case of Alsace-Lorraine. Fourth, although the prime value remained the national interest, acceptance of the idea of the existence of some kind of international interest had also been prevalent. Even the expression 'harmony of interest' was often used to describe one of the underlying realities – or even principles – of the world political economy of the period, despite the all-too-evident competition between the Powers for advantage. Finally, the sometimes almost mystical belief in the balance of power as the way of accommodating these contradictory values was widespread.

All this represented the conventional nineteenth-century world view, and many of these consensual precepts were to continue to affect international thought right up to the totally unexpected outbreak of a general war early in the twentieth century. But all was not, in fact, well. The liberal revolts that had broken out all over the Continent of Europe in 1848 were evidence of an underlying discontent and reluctance to accept the prevailing value systems of elites in the respective countries which together made up European society. There were alternative paradigms or conceptual frameworks. One was a gradually changing peace movement. Another was Marxism, which seemed to burst suddenly upon the consciousness of society. And a third was nationalism.

Notes

1 Cited by William T.R. Fox and Annette Baker Fox, 'The Teaching of International Relations in the United States,' *World Politics*, Vol. XIII, No. 3, April 1961, p. 339.
2 See Jeremy Bentham, *An Introduction to the Principles and Morals of Legislation* (London: The Athlone Press, 1970), edited by J.H. Burns and H.L.A. Hart. Wright, Quincy. *The Study of International Relations* (New York: Appleton-Century Crofts, Inc., 1955), p. 3.
3 Correspondence with Olson, July 1988.
4 Quoted in F.H. Hinsley, *Power and the Pursuit of Peace: Theory and Practice in the History of Relations between States* (Cambridge: Cambridge University Press, 1967, first published in 1963), p. 81.
5 R.J. Vincent, 'Edmund Burke and the Theory of International Relations,' *Review of International Studies*, Vol. 10, 3 July 1984, p. 216.
6 For more on Burke and IR, see R.J. Vincent, 'Edmund Burke and the Theory of International Relations,' *Review of International Studies*, Vol. 10, No. 3, 1995, pp. 205–218.
7 Henry Kissinger, *A World Restored* (New York: Grosset and Dunlap, 1964), p. 167.
8 Immanuel Kant, *Perpetual Peace*, Boston World Peace Foundation, 1950, transl. Lewis L. Beck.
9 Cited by Fred Parkinson, *The Philosophy of International Relations* (London: SAGE, 1977), p. 68.
10 Sir Harold Nicolson, *The Congress of Vienna: A Study in Allied Unity 1812–1822* (New York: Harcourt, Brace, 1946), pp. 241–242. Perhaps his earliest claim to fame as a writer came from his *Peacemaking 1919* (London: Constable, 1933) in which he describes the Versailles conference "as I experienced it myself," p. 6.
11 Kalevi J. Holsti, *Peace and War* (Cambridge: Cambridge University Press, 1991), p. 119.
12 *Ibid.*, p. 122.
13 *Ibid.*, p. 122.
14 Nicolson, *op. cit.*, p. 39.
15 *Ibid.*, p. 274.
16 *Ibid.*, p. 155.
17 *Ibid.*, p. 154.
18 Webster, Sir Charles Kingsley, *The Congress of Vienna 1814–15*, Great Britain, Foreign Office, Historical Section. *Peace Handbooks*, Vol. 24, No. 153 (London: HMSO, 1920), pp. 93–97.
19 Nicolson, *op. cit.*, p. 260.

20 See Friedrich von Gentz, *Fragments in the Balance of Power* (London: Peltier, 1806).

21 Hinsley, *op. cit.*, p. 198.

22 Hinsley, *op. cit.*, p. 137.

23 See David Ricardo, *On the Principles of Political Economy and Taxation* (London: John Murray, 1817.

24 See 'Edward Mead Earle, Adam Smith, Alexander Hamilton, Friedrich List: The Economic Foundations of Military Power,' in Edward Mead Earle (ed.), *Makers of Modern Strategy* (Princeton, NJ: Princeton University Press, 1941); also, Friedrich List, *The Natural System of Political Economy* (London: Longman, 1904), transl. Sampson S. Lloyd.

25 Knutsen summarises Hegel's dialectics thus: "In the Hegelian approach, history must be understood in terms of *ideas* rather than events. History is the evolutionary process through which the Absolute Idea attains full consciousness of itself as spirit (*Geist*) and realizes itself in the form of a new world spirit (or *Weltgeist*) of reason, freedom and equality. For Hegel, this process is not linear, but dialectical; a given thought will always contain inherent contradictory aspects and will produce its own negation. Thus, a given state of affairs (the 'thesis') will inevitably produce a conception of an opposite state of affairs (the 'antithesis'). The contest between the two will, in turn, be resolved in an *Aufhebung*: a reconciliation and fusion (a 'synthesis'), which includes the key elements of the original thesis as well as the antithesis, but which is more than and different from both," in Torbjørn L. Knutsen, *A History of International Relations Theory* (Manchester: Manchester University Press, 1992).

26 Cited by Parkinson, *op. cit.*, p. 75.

27 Tony Burns and Ian Fraser, *The Hegel-Marx Connection* (New York: Springer, 2000).

28 Torbjørn L. Knutsen, *op. cit.*, p. 148.

29 *Ibid.*, p. 149.

30 Chris Brown, *op. cit.*, p. 66.

31 See Hinsley, *op. cit.*, p. 88.

32 *Ibid.*, pp. 90–91.

33 Henry Wheaton, *Elements of International Law* (Boston, MA: Little, Brown, 1966), eighth edition, p. 29.

34 The views of both Bright and Cobden are perceptively reviewed in Part I of Hinsley, *op. cit.*, in 'A History of International Theories,' especially pp. 96–124.

35 Karl von Clausewitz, *On War*, taken from the Penguin edition (Harmondsworth: Penguin, 1968), p. 119.

36 Karl von Clausewitz, *On War*, ed. and trans. by Michael Howard and P. Paret (Princeton, NJ: Princeton University Press, 1976).

37 Clausewitz, Penguin edition, *op. cit.*, p. 250.

38 See Crane Brinton, Gordon A. Craig and Felix Gilbert, 'Jomini,' in Edward Mead Earle, *op. cit.*

39 *De la Solution des Conflicts Internationaux* (*On the Solution of International Conflicts*). Cited by Hinsley, *op. cit.*, p. 138.

40 Alexis de Tocqueville, *Democracy in America* (London: Colonial, 1900).

41 Cited by Hinsley, *Ibid.*, p. 122.

42 Cited by Hinsley, *Ibid.*, p. 106.

3   Transforming the world
Marx, the peace movement and war

The internationalist paradigm that would dominate thinking about world affairs in the early part of the twentieth century had its origins, within the context of British liberalism, in the peace movement of the nineteenth century. More revolutionary was another alternative to convention, represented by Karl Marx, who opposed the entire system. Both declined to accept the state's judgement about the legitimacy of the military option and particularly the people's role in war. Many dissenters joined the Internationals as an expression of their concern and desire for change.

The Marxist alternative

Karl Marx, one of those who rejected the right of the bourgeois state to speak and to act for the people, expanded his ideas in England, but did not live to see them implemented where he least expected it: in Russia. He and his principal collaborator, Friedrich Engels, have been characterised as the last of a number of thinkers on international affairs in the nineteenth century who placed great emphasis upon the meaning of historical progress.[1] When they wrote the first sentence of *The Communist Manifesto* in 1848[2] – "A spectre is haunting Europe: the spectre of communism" – many countries were either in revolt against the existing order or were about to be. The revolts turned out to be more liberal than communist, and for the most part they failed. The old order was given a new lease of life. In a sense, so was Marx, the most influential political thinker of the nineteenth century, and his ideas are still the source of debate, sometimes violent. In his commentary on political economy in 1859 (which incidentally was his only theoretical work relating the non-European world to his general philosophy of history),[3] Marx observed that "mankind always takes up only problems it can solve."[4] Engels agreed and acted upon that premise.

Two of their political ideas are of particular concern to students of the development of international thought. One was the conception of the state itself. The other was their interpretation of the relations between states. To Engels, who was a social Darwinist, the state was "the executive committee of the ruling class" which exploited the working class for its own advantage. Were there no classes, there would be no need for the state: it would "wither away." Before that could happen, however, there would have to be the overthrow of a class-ridden society. Applied on a world plane, the class struggle would produce a stateless world without class antagonisms. Hence war was the only road to peace.

The state, far from providing the basis for international law, organisation and peace, was itself necessarily and by its very nature the enemy of peace. The system could not be improved neither could the balance of power be tinkered with; they had to be replaced. Yet Marx was, according to Hinsley, "firmly attached to a belief in perpetual peace. If he said little about it, it was because he believed that it would follow automatically upon the withering away of the state."[5] A rebel outside the system in the nineteenth century, Marx's ideas were to have a tremendous impact on the twentieth.

A related work of considerable significance was *Gemeinschaft und Gesellschaft* (*Community and Society*), published in 1887 by Ferdinand Tönnies when he was only thirty-two. Little noticed at first, it was to become a major work in both the theory and application of sociology to the state and the emerging capitalist economy. In discussing its tendency "to be cosmopolitan and unlimited in size," Tönnies postulated that the capitalist society "through a long process spreads itself over the totality of its people, indeed over the whole of mankind."[6] Though greatly influenced by Marx, Tönnies disagreed with him on what brings about social change.

Imperialism and nationalism were never principal preoccupations of Marx (who, incorrectly, saw nationalism in decline), but Marxist writers were later to deal extensively with both these phenomena, notably Nikolay Bukharin on imperialism and the world economy; Vladimir Ilyich Lenin in his famous work on imperialism as the highest state of capitalism; and Karl Kautsky who established the twin criteria of territory and language. This gave rise to a challenging 'debate' to which we shall return later. But the Marxists were not the only philosophical activists of this period.

The peace movement as an alternative

Certain segments of the peace movement, which flourished in England, France, the United States, the Netherlands and other Western countries after the Crimean War, and particularly after the Franco-Prussian War, also opposed the existing state system. They felt that inherently it sanctioned war. The aggressive unifier of Italy, Giuseppe Garibaldi, was a leading figure in the International League of Peace and Liberty, set up in 1867 by Charles Lemonnier, an outspoken federalist advocate of a United States of Europe. In discussing this movement, Hinsley refers to "the strong undercurrent of distrust of government which marked even English and American liberal views," including such writers as Henry Thoreau and William Lloyd Garrison. In England, Bright, who was no Marxist, had argued in the 1850s that "wars were financed by the working class, which stood to lose most by them," while Cobden was convinced that "the intercourse between communities is nothing more than the intercourse of individuals in the aggregate"[7] to which the intervention of governments was but an obstacle. The Benthamites agreed, yet another group outside the conventional consensus went even further: the anarchists. William Goodwin (1756–1836) had seen the state as an institution whereby such privileged groups as the military and the diplomats – "all the train of artifices that has been invented to hold other nations at bay, to penetrate their secrets, to traverse their machinations, to form alliances and counter-alliances"[8] – sought to impose their will on the people. An international organisation of governments would be only one more obvious manifestation of the state's effort to preserve its status.

Not all peace activists rejected international organisation as an unnecessary evil. Some saw it as the only way to guarantee peace. In the United States, one of the most articulate, William Ladd, published a *Dissertation on a Congress of Nations* in 1832 and followed up with another essay on such a congress some eight years later. In 1843 the first Universal Peace Conference (a non-governmental enterprise despite its official-sounding title) took place in London, based upon a manifesto of the American Peace Society. Complementing Cobden, whose book relating to free trade and peace has already been noted, were William Ellery Channing, the founder of the Massachusetts Peace Society (later to become national) and Charles Sumner, who regarded the Constitution of the United States as proof that war as an institution in society could actually be outlawed. Both were writing, speaking and organising with enthusiastic vigour.

The first of many journals produced by the peace movement appeared in 1819 under the auspices of a group calling itself the British Society for the Promotion of Permanent and Universal Peace, the name itself, *The Herald of Peace*, implying a certain expectation of a world to come. On the Continent, La Societé des Amis de la Morale Chrétienne (the French Peace Society), founded in 1821, had many branch societies by the 1890s, stimulated no doubt by Henri de Saint Simon in his *De La Réorganisation de la Societé Européenne* (*On the Reorganisation of European Society*) a few years earlier.

From opposition to participation

By mid-century the ideas of the peace movement apparently began to have an effect upon governmental behaviour, with the *Manchester Examiner* in 1853 stating that:

> The principles of the Peace Society, fanatical as they are, have unquestionably gained ground among us; statesmen shrink from war now, not only on account of its risks, its costs, its possible unpopularity, but from a new-born sense of the tremendous moral responsibility.[9]

This sense was not confined to England. Western society had become more integrated and more representative, all of which "reconciled the mass of public opinion to the state . . . A new kind of publicist, not at loggerheads with the government, found an interest in the field of international relations."[10] This was the reverse side of the coin of the peace movement. Its main adherents were coming to believe that the road to peace ran through influencing public opinion in order to change public policy, not through challenging the state itself.

No such shift was taking place in Marxist thought, but only the more radical members of the peace movement were drawn to the Marxists' fundamental transformation approach. The movement as a whole came to occupy the middle ground between the opposition to Rousseau, Kant, Bentham and their followers to a formalised international organisation and the equally radical advocacy by such writers as Penn, Bellers and Saint-Simon of some form of federal union. The peace movement gradually had become part of the conventional nineteenth century, not an alternative to it. Its adherents, looking at the world around them, concluded that the *grounds* for war had almost disappeared in the international politics of civilised states. That war existed at all was due simply to the "stupidity and criminality" of governments, and hence international organisations made up of those governments were undesirable because politicians could not be trusted. To these activists, the opinion of the public would exercise its benevolent influence which, with international law, would ensure peace. Given these happy premises, inter-state organisation seemed hardly necessary.[11]

This conviction had produced a change of tactics in the peace movement: parliamentary representation. Cobden and Bright had already led the way in this, followed by such men as Senator Marcoartu of Spain and Professor Mancini, a member of the Chamber of Deputies in Rome, one of several thinkers instrumental in fostering the peace movement in Italy as a result of the Franco-Prussian War. That experience led to the formation of societies in the Netherlands and Belgium as well. In the years before the Hague conferences at the turn of the century, their efforts concentrated upon the promotion of arbitration at various assemblies, notably a congress of all the peace organisations in Paris in 1878 and the formation of the Inter-parliamentary Union in 1892. Speaking before the 1893 Congress, W. Evans Darby, the secretary of the British Peace Society, warned that what was necessary was to provide the state, not with policies but with principles upon the basis of which governments should then have the responsibility of making policy. Otherwise, the peace movement would be charged with "arrogant meddlesomeness."[12] The effort to influence those in power took the form from 1900 onwards of inviting minsters to attend. Some did so and received reports annually on the peace resolutions passed by successive congresses.

A recurring debate: idealism versus realism

These developments may now be seen as harbingers of what was to become the study of international relations, characterised by two drives. One was the desire to understand and to promote peace. The other was to accomplish this by influencing government policy, by making public opinion a factor in international politics. A striking example of two approaches of this and the related subject of morality in foreign policy is seen in dramatic speeches in the House of Commons following the Ottoman suppression of Balkan peoples in 1875. William Gladstone, an opposition MP at the time, stated in 1876 what might be called the internationalist view:

> My hope, therefore, is twofold. First, that, through the energetic attitude of the people of England, their Government may be led to declare distinctly, that it is for the purposes of humanity alone that we have a fleet in Turkish waters. Secondly, that fleet will be so distributed as to enable its force to be more promptly and efficiently applied, in case of need, on Turkish soil, in concert with the other Powers, for the defence of innocent lives, and to prevent the repetition of those recent scenes, at which hell itself might almost blush.[13]

By contrast, Prime Minister Benjamin Disraeli put the national interest first in a classical 'realist' statement:

> We must remember that our connection with the East is not merely an affair of sentiment and tradition, but that we have urgent and substantial and enormous interests which we must guard and keep . . . We have, therefore, entered into an alliance – a defensive alliance – with Turkey, to guard her against any further attack from Russia. We believe that the results of this Convention will be order and tranquillity.[14]

One reason for citing this particular colloquy is that the so-called realist-idealist debate would continue well into next century as the discipline of IR came to maturity. The more difficult epistemological question is how one assesses the statesman who is idealist in rhetoric and realist in action. This is particularly difficult when 'the national interest' is elevated to a high ethical plane.

Many such 'debates' are no such thing in the sense that there was an active debate such as between Gladstone and Disraeli. The idea of a debate between 'realist' and 'idealist' became a pedagogical device to organise a plethora of ideas and concepts into a suitably digestible form for both scholars and students to partake. It was a device that was treated with derision by practitioners. The 'debates' then became an organising myth to be used with care and taken with more than a pinch of salt for the most part. Opposite ideas do not necessarily imply a debate but a difference which may be fundamental, the respective adherents of which hold rigid and stereotypical images of the world and each other. Such differing images may be beyond debate and unbridgeable.[15]

Throughout the second half of the nineteenth century a number of intellectuals in several countries advanced theories of IR, though few, if any, called them that. Among the most advanced was Gustave de Molinar who, in comparing the peace plans of St Pierre and Kant in a notable study published in Paris in 1857, linked the idea of a universal organisation to a tribunal and an international police force which would have no domestic jurisdiction at all. In Britain, John Noble soon proposed a Supreme Court of Nations, Leone Levi published a *Draft Project of a High Court of Arbitration* and Lorimer challenged the assumption that any given status quo could ever be regarded as permanent, ridiculing the old Grand Design of Henry IV as being "meaningless in the mouths of princes as of other people."[16] In Germany, J.K. Bluntschli anticipated in 1878 what was later to emerge as one of the basic principles of both the League of Nations and the United Nations. He argued that the independence of member states be protected, that voting be weighted in favour of great Powers, that disputes be decided by majority vote and that, if such decisions had to be carried out by force, this should be the responsibility of the most powerful states.[17]

A fascinating French figure was Joseph-Pierre Proudhon (1809–1865), whose thought passed through distinctive phases, from favouring global utopian associations to international functional federalism and eventually confederalism in world politics. Having started out in the 1840s as an anarchist, Proudhon had within twenty years begun to re-examine the world order systematically in a study of war and peace in 1858, followed by his *Du Principe Fédératif* (*On the Federal Principle*) in 1863, designed to forge instruments for the prevention of war through federalism. Thus, federalism was seen as the handmaiden of functionalism, which in the rise and proliferation of public international unions (outlined in Paul Reinsch's book on the subject published in 1911) indicates the nature of European perspectives on IR in the nineteenth century.

By the turn of the century, however, the committee on a United States of Europe of the 1900 Paris Congress of Political Sciences had taken pains to reject a federal approach. Now the continental peace movement was, in the face of growing tension between European nations, turning away from federation just as British activists were moving towards it. It was in this atmosphere of increasing anxiety about the possibility of war and the cost of armaments that the Tsar persuaded other monarchs to meet in a major conference at The Hague in 1899, to be followed by another in 1907. Contradictory expectations and explanations accompanied both, and everyone tried to capitalise on them to press his own views. Some saw them as the culmination of decades, even centuries, of gradual development of the rule of law in international politics. Others saw in the Hague meetings the assumption that since wars were bound to occur, their conduct needed to be better regulated.

At all events, there was an intensified interest in law and new theories about it. In 1899, T.E. Holland came out with a series of thoughtful studies in international law, as well as his *Letters on War and Neutrality*, which appeared over four decades starting in 1881. Sir Henry Sumner Maine, whose *Ancient Law in Relation to Modern Ideas* advanced the sociology of law, produced the second edition of his definitive work on international law in 1906. All of these represented the urgency as well as the anticipation of increased reliance upon law in the world of sovereign states. This was pioneered by Latin American states, which developed systems of arbitration through the growing panoply of inter-American agreements and institutions, including the Pan-American Union founded in 1890. The reason for the sense of urgency lay in the opposite view of reliance: the state, in the form of the redefined and revivified nation, had to rely upon itself.

From agents to structures

The suggestion has already been made that 'debates' in IR were no such thing for the most part since there was little interaction, no thrusting debate. What there was were analyses within the various traditions of political thought which go back centuries to ancient times in Europe and even beyond Europe to India and China. We have already examined in a cursory fashion the realist tradition and the Grotian and Kantian traditions, but these emphasise the importance of actors or agents. What of structures? How far can the strutting princes get on a world stage that is shaky and having its foundations undermined? It is time therefore to move from actors to structures, and two conceptions of structure were evident over the turn of the century – geopolitics and the nexus between capitalism and imperialism.

The possibility of war and the threat to the world order towards the end of the century revived interest in several countries in what was to become known as geopolitics.[18] Anthropologists and geographers such as Friedrich Ratzel had shown certain connections between culture, national divisions and migration, on the one hand, and topography, resources, positions and climate, on the other, without drawing from them any particular strategic implications. Then, three broad-gauged thinkers combined politics and strategy in a way not witnessed since the simpler days of Machiavelli. One was American, one British and one Swedish, each assembling geographical information and interpreting it for foreign policy purposes. The first, Admiral Alfred T. Mahan, made explicit one of the principal assumptions that had guided US strategy since the promulgation of the Monroe Doctrine, namely that a state with predominant sea power could, if it chose to, blockade its rivals and dominate world politics. This paradigm of strategic thinking, set forth in Mahan's *The Influence of Sea Power upon History* (1890), was highly influential in Britain since it vaunted the *Pax Britannica* that came from Britain's domination of the seas. It was also popularised in Germany by Admiral Turpitz who used the thesis to justify German naval expansion as a requirement for great Power status. The British reacted and the Anglo-German naval arms race ensued, darkening the European horizons. Mahan's thesis depended on the notion that movement by sea was faster, more economical and safer than movement over land in terms of the time/space ratio. This had facilitated the projection of economic, political, military and cultural power of a succession of global leaders beginning with Portugal, the Netherlands and finally Britain. They were protected by, exploited and dependent on sea power to a greater extent than others who either did not have easy access to the sea and a maritime culture, or who were vulnerable to hostile land power. France, for example, no matter how powerful, was a hexagon vulnerable to land attack from all sides of the hexagon and therefore had to attend to this as well as develop sea power, which gave Britain a structural advantage in its rivalry with France. As Mahan pointed out:

> [i]f a nation be so situated that it is neither forced to defend itself by land nor induced to seek extension of its territory by way of the land, it has, by the very unity of its aim directed upon the sea, an advantage as compared with a people one of whose boundaries is continental.[19]

The time/space ratio was a function of technology, and the balance was changing with the advent of transcontinental railways. They, too, became corridors for the projection of all sorts of power in North America and Trans-Siberia. They were an iron way for state building. It was not for nothing that Cecil Rhodes wanted a line from the Cape to Cairo to consolidate British Africa, or the Germans built a line from Berlin to Baghdad to penetrate the Ottoman Empire. The thesis of dominance of sea power was soon matched by a land school strategy enunciated by Sir Halford Mackinder and others. Addressing the Royal Geographical Society in 1904 on "The geopolitical pivot of history," Mackinder spelled out his well-known "classic warning":[20]

> Who controls East Europe
> commands the Heartland;
> Who rules the Heartland
> commands the World Island;
> Who rules the World Island
> commands the World.

The term 'geopolitics' had actually been coined by a Swede, the political scientist and geographer Rudolph Kjellen (1864–1922), who in describing a novel theoretical, organic system of government, influenced German thinking, particularly the man who was to turn geopolitics into a pseudo-science for Hitler – Karl Haushofer. It was Haushofer's influence which made geopolitics a factor in policy; other, more responsible students of the geographical impact upon politics were only brought into IR analyses later.

Changes in the time/space ratio also evoked a global structural clash between the Rimland (sea power) and the Heartland (land power), sometimes called the Great Game, which was played out in Central Asia as the Tsarist Empire pushed South and East and the British Empire blocked it in the Ottoman Empire, Persia, Afghanistan and, in 1902, in an alliance with Japan. After the Second World War the United States occupied Britain's position in a series of alliances and treaty arrangements.

Imperialism and its critics

A hundred years ago sitting in a study or library in Central Europe, not to mention the Café Landolt in Geneva where Lenin is supposed to have carved his name on a table, were a number of scholars-intellectuals-activists who were struck by the predominant political, economic and cultural structure of their times – imperialism. Around them was the clash between the old dominant Empires of Britain, France, Portugal and Spain and the thrusting newcomers Germany and Italy seeking their slice of the colonial cake. They had vicious polemical arguments among themselves about the relationships between capitalism and imperialism.

Was imperialism the highest stage of capitalism as Lenin argued forcefully in 1916?[21] Or would capitalism put an end to capitalism as Schumpeter later suggested?[22] Or was there no necessary connection, as Hobson maintained in his magisterial study on imperialism?[23] Lenin's position had an oft-repeated five-point definition of "essential fractures":

> (1) The concentration of production and capital, developed to such a high stage that it has created monopolies which play a decisive role in economic life; (2) the merging of bank capital with industrial capital and the creation, on the basis of this "finance capital," of a financial oligarchy; (3) the export of capital, as distinguished from the export of commodities, becomes of particularly great importance; (4) international monopoly combines of capitalists are formed which divide the world; and (5) the territorial division of the world by the greatest capitalist princes is completed.[24]

Imperialism was the penultimate state of capitalism. The final stage of global monopoly through imperialism was being played around Lenin as he wrote in 1916 at the height of the Great War.[25] Lenin was responding in part to Hobson[26] – a radical journalist who like much of the civilised world had been horrified by British practices in South Africa such as the brutalities of the concentration camps. Hobson made some cutting remarks that colonial territories served, first of all, the governing classes rather than the indigenous governed, but he could also be seen as a Keynesian *avant la letter* in that he advocated the multiplier effect: "there is no necessity to open up foreign markets; the home markets are capable of indefinite expansion. Whatever is produced in England can be consumed in England, provided that the 'Income,' and power to demand commodities, is properly distributed."[27]

Hobson's position was that imperialism was not necessary for the well-being of capitalism whereas that of Schumpeter was that capitalism would put an end to imperialism. In a masterly essay Schumpeter[28] explained what is alleged to be imperialism – it was an outgrowth of nationalism and state-building. To build a new nation-state, not only was a nation necessary in the hearts, minds and the behaviour of its future citizens but so was a military machine to build such an entity. In Germany, the Prussian military machine was an example. Once the state is established, however, the machine is not dismantled but acts as the spearhead of overseas expansion.

What then would put an end to this atavistic military machine? Schumpeter's answer was capitalism, because to function most efficiently, that is to maximise profit, capitalism requires free trade and the opening of colonial markets. In his view, free trade also guaranteed access without the costs of war or colonial rule.

The debate about the relationship between capitalism and imperialism was not the only consideration of the global phenomenon of Empire. Schumpeter had hinted at imperialism as being a form of social Darwinism. The idea was that victorious colonial wars demonstrated the survival of the fittest and that they would raise the level of civilisation precisely because they had demonstrated their fitness to rule. Might was right and it was right that it should be so. As Treitschke put it, "every virile people has established colonial power" while for the Italian dictator, Benito Mussolini, "Fascism sees in the imperialistic spirit a manifestation of its vitality."[29]

Others had a gentler view, whether hypocritical or not, as they shouldered the 'white man's burden,' as their 'manifest destiny' to fulfil a 'mission civilisatrice' (civilising mission). Theirs was the task of bringing to the 'other' the benefits of European civilisation – its religion, its governance, its economy and its culture in a package of exploitation, law and order whether the 'other' wanted it or not. It was an aristocratic view of imperialism. As Stokes put it:

> At its heart was the belief that political power tended constantly to deposit itself in the hands of a natural aristocracy, that power so deposited was morally valid, that it was not to be tamely surrendered before the claims of abstract democratic ideals, but was to be asserted and exercised with justice and mercy.[30]

Lord Milner exemplified this claiming that "British influence is not exercised to impose an uncongenial foreign system upon a reluctant people. It is a force making for the triumph of the simplest ideas of honesty, humanity, and justice."[31]

But strategic notions there were too. The Romans had found that they needed to incorporate new areas to protect the ones previously integrated, and the colonial Powers did likewise. To protect the Indian sub-Continent – the jewel in the crown – Britain necessitated possession of Gibraltar, Malta, the Suez Canal (Palestine and Egypt), Aden, South Africa, Singapore, Malaya and the Falklands Islands to cover all the global maritime choke points. But an empire could also be a financial and political burden which made universal free trade seem attractive, and so, in the distant future, free trade was a factor which put an end to formal empire.

Towards a more systematic study of IR

What about diplomacy within and reacting to these structural constraints? Was this an aspect of an alternative to power politics? It was generally not so regarded in the nineteenth century. Though not on a par with the great Callières, another renowned diplomat, Count Vincent Benedetti, drew upon his experience, particularly in unsuccessful negotiations, only to pass on useful lessons in technique in his *Studies in Diplomacy* in 1896. However, in another study ten years later, *The Practice of Diplomacy*, an American, John W. Foster, not only brought up to date the entire procedural dimension of the field but made some plausible new suggestions on the formulations and execution of foreign policy. In discussing the development of diplomatic theory, Nicolson asserts that:

> In spite of dramatic periods when violence momentarily became more authoritative than reason, it is possible to recognize a distinct upward curve of progress . . . from the narrow conception of exclusive tribal rights to the wider conception of inclusive common interests.[32]

The first glimmerings of IR as a discipline had appeared with the publication of Reinsch's *World Politics at the End of the Nineteenth Century* (1900). More a critique of imperialism (including American) than an all-encompassing systematic treatment of the whole fabric of international affairs, the Wisconsin political scientist nevertheless did deal with such topics as The Hague Conference, popular opinion towards international questions, parties, international administration and demands for policing the world. While the political scientists assembled in Paris that year (as was to be the case in the third decade of the twentieth century) were focusing upon organisation, Reinsch concentrated upon power. His work suggests that a discipline of IR had its real beginnings in studies of imperialism, not in world order, as has so often been suggested. A different framework was set forth by Norman Angell between 1908 and 1914 in several editions of the best seller *The Great Illusion*, which he contended was the assumption "that a nation's financial and industrial stability, its security in commercial activity – in short, its prosperity and well-being, depended upon its being able to defend itself against the aggression of other nations."[33] He concluded that all this carries with it "the paradox that the more a nation's wealth is protected the less secure does it become."[34]

Tracing the intellectual development of theory in IR must never be confined only to intellectuals, if by that often-misapplied term is meant people who are not in the intergovernmental sense 'responsible' or accountable. For example, the famous memorandum of His Majesty's representative in Berlin, Sir Eyre Crowe, constituted as thoughtful a piece of foreign policy analysis as one will find in the literature of the field.[35] In warning Whitehall in 1907 about the intentions and plans of the German decision-makers no longer restrained by Bismarckian statesmanship, he may have turned British foreign policy around. The balance of power, while certainly not abandoned, was given a new interpretation; instead of acting outside as the balancer, Britain now felt it more advisable to join with France and later Russia as a weight in the continental balance itself. Once committed, she could neither manipulate the system nor tip the scales at its convenience. But the purpose was still the same: to avoid a general war. It failed.

Even though the delegates to the renowned conferences (1899 and 1907) in the Netherlands had devoted a high proportion of their time to the law of war and of neutrality in time of war, their meetings are generally known as The Hague Peace conferences. Together with the Algeciras Conference in 1906 they galvanised the peace movement to even more intense activity. However menacing world politics had become, including the coming of the war itself, peace activists continued to propose remedies, not out of naïveté in all instances but out of a well-intentioned conviction that if the proper kind of machinery for international cooperation could be created, a war might be prevented. In 1908 the Universal Peace Congress adopted:

> [a] scheme for a complete Society of Nations, with a single executive as well as a legislative Council to supervise an international code and a court to apply it, and for the reduction of national armies to the minimum required for police purposes.[36]

In another domain, in 1910, the then recently created Carnegie Endowment for International Peace started publishing *International Conciliation*, arguably the first professional journal in the field of IR. The Endowment's founder, the industrialist-philanthropist Andrew Carnegie, had addressed a letter to the Universal Peace Congress in 1904, urging somewhat optimistically that a union of all the leading states renounce war and announce their intention of enforcing this declaration. Nothing happened. In setting up a US$10 million endowment for peace, Carnegie ensured that the income would be utilised for other socially useful purposes once the problem of peace was solved, as he was confident it would be within a relatively short time, if only enough money were applied to its solution. Naïve as this seems, it was a reasonable expectation for an industrial pragmatist of the pre-First World War era.

In the nineteenth century, the industrial revolution had represented a quickening of pace in the application of the reasoning of scientific method to the development of an empirical theory about the physical world, so that its findings could be used for its manipulation. The method that revealed the 'secrets' of nature, which were then applied in the form of the industrial revolution, could also be used in the context of the social environment as well as the physical environment. Bismarck had been one of the first to use such notions in a comprehensive way when he initiated social reforms. Others followed, including those who applied these principles to relations among states. As the nineteenth century progressed, three of the four great traditional afflictions of humanity had become (at least so far as parts of Western Europe and North America were concerned) amenable to societal control. Famine could be banished by the application of science and capital to agriculture. Pestilence could be defeated by public health programmes, public education and investment in the engineering of the infrastructure of the new industrial cities. Poverty would be banished. The last great curse remained – war. By a logical progression, the application of scientific research and empirical findings to the physical environment first, and then to the domestic social environment, suggested that the *international* environment might also be subject to social engineering.

This sense of progress, of betterment, of pride was brutally interrupted by a calamity – the justly named Great War. Those very states, which had justified their world hegemony by their white man's burden, their duty to teach others how to live, their *mission civilisatrice*, their manifest destiny, used the tools of the industrial revolution to arm and supply great armies. They now found themselves mobilising whole societies for years on end in a war that destroyed the Eurocentric world order. The industrial revolution produced the gun; the French Revolution and the ensuing flowering of nationalism motivated people to pull the trigger. This contrast with the confident and widespread belief in progress was devastating for some. For others it was a spur. If war was now too terrible to be allowed to happen again, it had to be understood and measures taken to control it. Peace was regarded then, as it is by many today, as the supreme task of those engaged in the analysis of international politics. To others, that task was to analyse the nature of power in the relations of states. These twin objectives were about to merge.

Although no effort had yet been made to create a separate discipline of International Relations, four different threads which would be woven into its fabric began to form in the nineteenth century. One was the traditional pattern of diplomacy and of international law. A second was the internationalist tradition that combined progressive thought with public activism in the peace movement. This would dominate the period of the first consensus in the new discipline in the early years following the First World War. In stark contrast stood the third, *Realpolitik*, which would come to dominate the period of second consensus following the Second World War. The fourth was Marxism which, except for the true believers, was for some time to play only a secondary role in the development of the discipline, even if it was, and remains, always present even if its form changes.

Ironically, the whole process was accelerated by the coming of the First World War. Within a year of the outbreak of hostilities, novel post-war proposals were being advanced. Hobson, for example, shifted from criticism of imperialism to a provocative pamphlet, *Toward International Government*, in which he advocated the eventual creation of a legislature entitled to utilise force against violators of international agreements. G. Lowes Dickinson went even further, proposing that an international army be empowered to maintain *internal* order, although he was later to conclude that a world state (or even the loosest federation that might be called a state) was not yet a serious political consideration. Because of his bellicose reputation, many are unaware of the early advocacy by Theodore Roosevelt of a 'League of Peace,' based upon the commitment to use force by the great Powers in a form of collective security. Another American, Walter Lippman, wrote in *The Stakes of Diplomacy* in 1915 that any post-war organisation could command what he called "a world patriotism" only if it were able to demonstrate its utility to its member-states, and nothing resembling a "Federation of Mankind" was in the offing. Nevertheless, the "supreme task of world politics" was "a satisfactory organization of mankind,"[37] which would develop gradually from a Western league.

In order to implement these ideas, new organisations sprang up in various Western countries looking towards a lasting peace. Even before the war, the British League of Nations Society had been set up in 1913. The American League to Enforce Peace (1915) followed, with the Organisation Centrale pour une Paix Durable (Central Organisation for a Sustainable Peace) in the Netherlands (1916) and the French Association de la Paix par le Droit (Association for Peace through Law). In non-belligerent Sweden, August Schevan went so far in promoting world law as to assert that existing states would be "stripped of sovereignty and independence, and transformed into subdivisions of humanity."[38] Few others agreed, though the Union of Democratic Control, established in London in 1914, actively supported the abolition of secret diplomacy, the renunciation of alliances and the establishment of universal disarmament. Most agreed that an actual union of states was not required, but an organisation of the Powers was. The main question was how far sovereign states should go in restricting their own freedom of action. Increasingly, this was to turn on how far they could take their publics with them.

A further proposal took the form, in terms of voting rights as well as a name, of *A League of Nations* (1917) by H.L. Brailsford. He proposed restricting membership in a Council to the great Powers, who also would possess a larger vote than the smaller states in a legislative assembly and a court.[39] Another idea not generally expressed in the growing pro-league consensus came from North Americans (perhaps not surprisingly in light of what was to happen later), whose League to Enforce Peace advocated provision for members' withdrawal. So many proposals had been advanced that by 1916 Randolph Bourne compiled his *Towards an Enduring Peace: A Symposium of Peace Proposals and Programs*, convinced that they represented the framework for a new world order.

An interdisciplinary experiment

The first of what might be termed 'mainstream' IR appeared during the war. Books or chapters were written by such economists as Arthur Greenwood in Leeds, political scientists as Raymond Buell in Harvard, international lawyers as Geoffrey Lawrence in Bristol, geographers as Isaiah Bowman in Johns Hopkins and historians as David Heatley at Edinburgh, whose *An Introduction to the Study of International Relations* (1916) was years ahead of its time. Featuring chapters on war and peace since 1815 and on the causes of modern wars by two historians, one on international economic relations by an economist and one on international law by an international lawyer, this pioneering effort corresponded favourably with the consensus of principal topics that would emerge after the war. Even more striking from the perspective of an emergent discipline is the fact that this first real textbook was written at the suggestion of the Council for the Study of International Relations, a British group that was constituted during the First World War with the aim of promoting the debate on international affairs to the general public.[40]

Across the Atlantic, the growing importance of the public was reflected in writings of such leaders of the American establishment as the President of Columbia University, Nicholas Murray Butler, who argued in 1913 that "the rise in the world of a real public opinion . . . makes war increasingly difficult and increasingly repulsive,"[41] and former Secretary of State Elihu Root in his "Need of popular understanding of international law" in 1916. Before the United States entered the war, a few Britons were already trying to influence the course of public opinion about the world after the war. Graham Wallas even anticipated later thinkers by taking a psychological view of the world in his controversial *The Great Society* in 1917. In 1918, G. Lowes Dickinson developed his ideas in *The Choice before Us*, another clear indicator of the impact public opinion was expected to have upon the peace process once it took place. All of this set the stage for the US President's approach to the conduct of foreign policy based upon public understanding and acceptance of a world "safe for democracy." Leonard Woolf wrote a major British study of *International Government*[42] in which he advocated that various categories of dispute could be dealt with in legal form. International public unions formed an emerging network that required international administration which could give rise to law-making to achieve standardisation. Writers like Reinsch and Woolf were creating a new international conceptual framework which was to become *matériel* for decision-makers at Versailles.

Long and Schmidt,[43] in their innovative and insightful collection of essays, made a distinction between internationalism and imperialism (as opposed to realists and idealists). It is a distinction which now we would like to reiterate and emphasise. It is the most salient, if now somewhat forgotten, starting point for a discipline that came into its own after the First World War. Engels was to see with remarkable prescience how that was to be when he wrote:

> No war is any longer possible for Prussia-Germany except a world war and a world war indeed of an extension and violence hitherto undreamt of. Eight to ten millions of soldiers will mutually massacre one another and in doing so devour the whole of Europe until they have stripped it barer than any swarm of locusts has ever done. The devastation of the Thirty Years' War will be compressed into three or four years, and spread over the whole Continent. We will see famine, pestilence, general demoralisation both of the armies and of the mass of the people; hopeless confusion of our artificial machinery in trade, industry and credit, ending in general bankruptcy; collapse of the old states and their traditional state wisdom to such an extent that crowns will roll by dozens on the

pavement and there will be nobody to pick them up; absolute impossibility of foresee-ing how it will all end and who will come out of the struggle as victor; only one result is absolutely certain: general exhaustion and the establishment of the conditions for the ultimate victory of the working class. This is the prospect before us when the system of outbidding in armaments is driven to extremities, and at last bears its inevitable fruit.[44]

It is to the aftermath of that catastrophe that we must now turn as IR emerged as a more recognised discipline.

Notes

1 Parkinson, *Philosophy of International Relations*, p. 87.
2 Karl Marx and Friedrich Engels, *The Communist Manifesto* (New York: Russell and Russell, 1963 [1848]).
3 Shlomo Avineri, *Karl Marx on Colonialism and Modernization* (Garden City: Doubleday, 1968), p. 4.
4 Cited by Avineri, *Ibid.*, p. 33.
5 Hinsley, *Power and Pursuit of Peace*, p. 112.
6 Ferdinand Tönnies, *Community and Society*, trans. and ed. by Charles P. Loomis (London: Harper and Row, 1957), pp. 258–259. First published in 1887.
7 Hinsley, *Power and the Pursuit of Peace*, p. 106.
8 Parkinson, *Philosophy of IR*, p. 146.
9 *Ibid.*, p. 114.
10 *Ibid.*, p. 115.
11 The relationship in Europe, and to some extent in the United States, between public opinion, government and the peace movement, is thoroughly discussed by Hinsley in chapter 7, especially pp. 114–126.
12 Hinsley, *Power and the Pursuit of Peace*, p. 132.
13 Quoted in Hans J. Morgenthau and Kenneth W. Thompson (eds), *Principles and Problems of International Politics* (New York: Alfred A. Knopf, 1950), p. 53.
14 *Ibid.*, p. 56
15 There has been quite a lot written on the division of the history in IR in debates. For more, see Joel Quirk and Darshan Vigneswaran, 'The Construction of an Edifice: The Story of a First Great Debate,' *Review of International Studies*, Vol. 31, No. 1, 2005, pp. 89–107 and Wæver O. 'Still a Discipline After All These Debates?' in Dunne T, Kurki M, Smith S (eds), *International Relations Theories: Discipline and Diversity,*. (Oxford: Oxford University Press, 2016), fourth edition, pp. 300–321.
16 Cited by Hinsley, in *Power and the Pursuit of Peace*, p. 134.
17 *Ibid.*, p. 135.
18 See Lucian Ashworth, 'Realism and the Spirit of 1919: Halford Mackinder, Geopolitics and the Reality of the League of Nations,' *European Journal of International Relations*, Vol. 17, No. 2, 2011; and Oyvind Osterud, 'The Uses and Abuses of Geopolitics,' *Journal of Peace Research*, June 1988.
19 Alfred T. Mahan, *The Influence of Sea Power upon History, 1660–1783* (Boston: Little, Brown, 1849), twelfth edition, p. 29.
20 F.L. Schuman, *International Politics*. (New York: McGraw-Hill, 1948), fourth edition, p. 408. For perhaps the best summary of the long-term significance of Mackinder's ideas for students of IR, see Wight, Martin, *Power Politics*, edited by Hedley Bull and Carsten Holbraad (New York: Penguin, 1978), pp. 72–77.
21 V.I. Lenin, *Imperialism: The Highest Stage of Capitalism* (Moscow: Foreign Language Publishing House, no date).
22 Joseph Schumpeter, *Imperialism and Social Classes* (New York: Meridian Books, 1955).
23 J.A. Hobson, *Imperialism* (London: Allen and Unwin, 1965 [1902]).
24 Quoted in Tom Kemp, *Theories of Imperialism* (London: Dobson, 1967), p. 75.
25 See David Long and Brian Schmidt (eds), *Imperialism and Internationalism in the Discipline of International Relations* (Albany: SUNY Press, 2005).
26 J.A. Hobson, *Imperialism: A Study* (London: Unwin Hyman, 1988 [1902]).

27 Quoted in Tom Kemp, *Theories of Imperialism* (London: Dobson, 1967), p. 33.

28 Joseph Schumpeter, *Imperialism and Social Classes* (New York: Meridian, 1955).

29 Quoted in A.P. Thornton, *Doctrines of Imperialism* (New York: John Wiley, 1965), p. 74.

30 Quoted in *Ibid.*, p. 36.

31 Quoted in *Ibid.*, p. 205.

32 Harold Nicolson, *Diplomacy* (New York: Oxford University Press, 1964), third edition, p. 17.

33 Norman Angell, *The Great Illusion: A Study of the Relation of Military Power in Nations to Their Economic and Social Advantage* (London: Heinemann, 1910), p. 24.

34 *Ibid.*, p. 31. We shall return to Angell below.

35 'Memorandum by Sir Eyre Crowe on the Present State of British Relations with France and Germany, January 1, 1907,' *British Documents on the Origins of the War*, edited by G.P. Gooch and H. Temperley (London: HMSO, 1928). The main sections are quoted in Fred Sondermann, David McLellan and William C. Olson, *The Theory and Practice of International Relations* (Englewood Cliffs: Prentice-Hall, 1979), fifth edition, pp. 119–122.

36 Hinsley, *Power and the Pursuit of Peace*, p. 143.

37 Cited by John Morton Blum (ed.) in *Public Philosopher. Selected Letters of Walter Lippmann* (New York: Ticknor and Fields, 1985), p. xxii.

38 Hinsley, *Power and the Pursuit of Peace*, p. 144.

39 *Ibid.*, p. 145.

40 Helen McCarthy, *The British People and the League of Nations* (Manchester: Manchester University Press, 2011), p. 119.

41 Nicholas Murray Butler, *The International Mind: An Argument for the Judicial Settlement of International Disputes* (New York: Charles Scribner's Sons, 1912), p. viii.

42 See Peter Wilson, in Douglas Long and Peter Wilson (eds), *Thinkers of the Twenty Years' Crisis* (Oxford: Clarendon Press, 1995).

43 David Long and Brian C. Schmidt (eds), *Imperialism and Internationalism in the Discipline of International Relations* (Albany: SUNY Press, 2005), p. 10.

44 Quoted in W.B. Gallie, *Philosophers of Peace and War* (Cambridge: Cambridge University Press, 1978), pp. 92–93.

4   The period of the first consensus

A quest for peace

In assessing efforts to analyse, to understand, or even to change the relations between countries after the First World War, we must look – if only briefly – at the preparations for the Paris Peace Conference that followed it. By the time the Conference at Versailles got underway a wealth of material awaited possible (though by no means certain) use by the respective plenipotentiaries. In the end, the peace treaty contained, in addition to traditional terms of settlement which usually follow a war, provision for a formal post-war organisation, which certainly could not have been created at short notice. In contrast to the irrelevance of Kant's ideas at Vienna, there can be little doubt that the ideas of the peace movement, particularly societies promoting a post-war organisation of states, at least indirectly affected the outcome at Paris. It was this novel feature of the peace settlement that had most to do with the development of the study of IR, namely, the League of Nations. And the individual who had most to do with adoption of the idea in the first place was a former President of the American Political Science Association, Woodrow Wilson. Again, in contrast to Vienna, he was the only world leader who could be called an intellectual with a formula for reordering the political universe. Ironically, he overlooked the lessons of his own specialty, *Congressional Government*,[1] and lost the battle in Congress to bring his own country into the League.

Wilson may have been the great driving force for the League, but the ideas were mediated through the plans of the Big Four – Britain, France, Italy as well as the United States. But their leaders Lloyd George, Clemenceau, Orlando and Wilson himself did not have the freedom that the Tsar, Metternich, Castlereagh and Talleyrand had enjoyed in making a 'new world order' in Vienna as they approached the analogous task at Versailles. They were constrained by a new factor – public opinion.

This public opinion – formed by elements of an attentive civil society – embraced a 'Wilsonian' logic of sorts. Since it was the people that suffered in the trenches and the privations at home, they knew the cost of war and rationally this would cool their ardour for war. It was necessary, therefore, to have democratic control of government by and for the people as a whole, and not dynastic disputes and rivalries pursued at so much human cost. Democracy was therefore the first plank for peace. The second was not only the creation of democratic states but democratic nation-states. States should be nations and nations should be states thus giving full play to the people's sense of identity. But there was also a harmony of interest between peoples who manifestly would benefit more from functional cooperation rather than competitive warfare. The third plank was thus to create an institution – the League of Nations – to promote peace and well-being by peaceful association. This institution was to be founded on collective security, such as pertained within states, based on shared values whereby these values were reflected in a set of rules freely agreed upon, together with a means to change the rules as the situation changed, and sanctions to bring back any deviant into the fold. Wilson was quite fierce about this, envisaging coercive sanctions. However, as in domestic society where the number of persons denied their liberty is small, so it would be at the international level if the League reflected shared values, had mechanisms for peaceful change and procedures for arbitration, mediation and the like. The aspiration was for the League to reflect successful democratic practices and the welfare state within society 'writ large' to the international level.

All these developments implied a movement in conceptions of sovereignty. No longer was it a case of 'L'État, c'est moi' or of a family dynastic holding, be it for Habsburgs or Bourbons among others, but sovereignty had moved to a democratic nation-state. The movement was to continue towards internal and external sovereignty as well as positive and negative sovereignty as the process of globalisation strengthened and embraced a myriad of fields.[2]

For a while, the League of Nations promised for the first time to organise all of international society through what might be called 'global social engineering.' Britain initially saw in the League an instrument for maintaining world peace but gradually came to utilise it mainly to promote British foreign policy goals. Although far more sceptical, France was just as ready to make use of this unprecedented agency to serve its own national interests. The third European member, Italy, was so disillusioned and diplomatically, economically and militarily weak that its constitutional monarchy, soon supplanted by the world's first fascist dictatorship, scarcely mattered. Japan, courteous and cooperative to the letter, became disaffected as it observed other Powers' behaviour. In striking contrast to Vienna, there was no Talleyrand for the defeated Power at Paris – Germany was kept down by the victors for as long as they saw it in their interest to do so. Excluded because of its communist system of government with its international revolutionary pronouncements and activity, the USSR only joined in the new organisation's activities in the mid-1930s. Proceeding with their strategy and diplomacy outside the League, the United States did play a crucial role in the debt and reparations settlement and hosted two naval conferences mainly concerned with the balance of naval power in the Pacific Ocean (which was codified in the Washington Naval Treaty of 1922 but remained, by choice, outside the principal arena). US citizens were members of the League Secretariat. However, Wilson was gone, struck down by illness and political ineptitude.

The 'succession' states in East and Central Europe saw distinct advantages in the system designed to protect them from larger potential predators. The Scandinavians, who after centuries of bitter rivalry were becoming a model of international organisational innovation, also slipped readily into the League pattern. The Latin American states gradually acquired a sense of regionalisation and solidarity, recognising, as did the Scandinavians, that these values protect weaker states unable to assert their rights through military power, and some of their delegates became well-known champions of international law and order. Two large countries played a minor role: India because of its status of relative dependency upon London, and China because it continued to be rent by internal strife and international interference. What all of this meant in terms of the political environment for scholarship was that, while there was a certain fascination with the dream and to some degree the realisation of world organisation, the overriding reality was that Europe was still the epicentre of world politics. Its two strongest member states, Britain and France, reverted to traditional diplomacy. The League gradually came to be merely a function of the European balance of power.

Such a 'realist' view was largely muted both in Britain and the United States, however obvious it became on the continent, and in the years to come. Liberal internationalism – and in Britain even pacifism – profoundly affected public opinion in both countries, influencing the manner in which many political leaders addressed world affairs. At the same time, close observers recognised that, whatever its form, the system had to deal with real problems, the solutions to which often had to be sought outside the League machinery. During what G.M. Gathorne-Hardy terms "the period of settlement," these included: the reparation and debt problems left over from the war; security; the settlement in Eastern Europe; disarmament; the place of the USSR in world affairs; the political isolation of the United States; economic crisis; and regional issues.[3] While governments obviously held responsibility for dealing with these questions, those that had been democratically elected could do so only to the extent to which they enjoyed the support of their respective electorates. No longer could the public be isolated. Instead, if solutions were to be found, it had to be educated, not necessarily to one point of view but to the point of understanding what was at stake. Recalling the experience of John Maynard Keynes in trying to teach the elements of economics to statesmen at Versailles (an effort which failed), Webster reflected upon both the source and object of much that went into the early promotion of international studies in a democracy. He commented, "We have, in fact, reached the age in politics when expert knowledge must be brought within the reach of the mass of the people if it is to have its full influence upon affairs."[4]

Educating the public

'Reaching the masses' was the populist approach. A second approach was to the elitist Establishment. A better-informed public was the objective in both instances. As a result of informal talks during the Conference, the French, the British and the Americans agreed to create new private institutions for the purpose of raising the level of international understanding of opinion leaders in their respective countries. In London, what was to become the Royal Institute of International Affairs (RIIA) was established in order to "advance the sciences of international politics, economics and jurisprudence, and the study, classification and development of the literature in these subjects, to encourage and facilitate the scientific study of international questions."[5] In the United States, the Council on Foreign Relations was set up, not in the then relatively provincial national capital, but in New York City, the bastion of corporate and banking power. In retrospect, leaders of the Council recalled its origins and development in this way:

> Under the pressure of a public opinion which was impatient to be done with war-making, decisions had to be made in haste; and the minds of diplomats, generals, admirals, financiers, lawyers and technical experts were not sufficiently well furnished to enable them to function satisfactorily on critical issues at top speed. Realizing their own shortcomings, some of these men began to talk about a way of providing against such a state of things in the future.[6]

In a description of its 'Program of Studies' in 1929, the Council's aim was stated as being "to develop, by scientific and impartial study, a better understanding of international problems, and an intelligent American foreign policy."[7] In both centres, there was a tacit expectation that *scientific* studies in IR would prevent the next war.

In Paris similar efforts proved abortive. A somewhat comparable institution, the École Libre des Sciences Politiques, had been founded in 1871 but was mainly concerned with diplomatic history. There was no regional equivalent of the RIIA although there were some quasi-academic bodies such as the European office of the Carnegie Endowment for International Peace. French participants were also active in the professional meetings of the International Studies Conferences in the 1930s, some of which took place in Paris.

The most important continental centre was in Geneva, the Institut Universitaire de Hautes Etudes Internationales (HEI) (Graduate Institute of International Studies), the difference being that HEI was primarily an academic institution awarding degrees in international studies, not the public opinion forming base. Its location in the city of the League of Nations afforded it a special opportunity in the development of international studies by facilitating contacts between academics and practitioners from all over the world. The purpose was to train the international leaders of the future.

In Germany the Deutsche Hochschule für Politik und Wissenschaft group opened its doors in October 1920 modelled on the French École Libre. As in Paris, the Carnegie Endowment organised lectures, but all this came to an end with Hitler, and henceforth Haushofer and geopolitics ruled the roost giving Hitler's expansionism 'scientific' cover.[8] Germans, however, still had a major contribution to make, but abroad as *émigrés*, especially in the United States.

The populist approach was practised in quite different ways, taking one form in Britain, another in the United States. The Union of Democratic Control was less interested in the objective presentation of broad international affairs information to the British public then it was in getting Parliament to assert more control over the actual conduct of foreign policy.[9] The aim of the Foreign Policy Association, on the other hand, was "to carry on research and educational activities to aid in the understanding and constructive development of American foreign policy."[10] Everything from dinner meetings to highly readable topical brochures were utilised to provide background for anyone in the United States who wanted to take part in its activities or subscribe to FPA services. No claim to being scientific was made.

All of these organisations, populist or elitist, played a crucial role in the development of IR in so far as they were performing independent research and 'teaching' functions. In some ways, they were ahead of most universities, where any new discipline required time to take root if it was to be taken seriously. For that to happen, a literature of a distinct order would have to be produced.

Meanwhile the peace societies, having appeared to gain so many of their nineteenth-century objectives through the establishment of the League, were for a time at least relatively quiescent, as were 'cause' or special interest groups of various kinds. Newspapers continued to perform their traditional although, for them, secondary role of chief educator in international affairs. It would be difficult to locate anything systematic or disciplinary in their reams of copy, though a few pundits like Walter Lippmann and the more academic David Mitrany, who wrote the foreign affairs leaders in the *Manchester Guardian* during the 1920s (and would later become known as the father of the functionalist theory), for many years set a high standard of journalistic analysis as, later, did E.H. Carr in *The Times*. The views and perhaps even more importantly the moods of people in democratic societies had become a real factor in shaping government decisions. In the words of Sir Harry Hinsley, looking back from the 1960s:

> Before 1914 it is almost impossible to find evidence that French or British or American public opinion ever acted as a deterrent to decisions in foreign policy, as opposed to being an incitement to the men who took them. It is almost equally impossible to show that French and British and American foreign policy has ever been free from the hampering effect of public opinion – if only from the hampering effect – since that date.[11]

This necessity to be sensitive to the will of the people, greatly encouraged by Wilson's popular war aim of "open covenants, openly arrived at," created what ambassadors and other foreign affairs professionals derisively, and liberal internationalists proudly, called 'The New Diplomacy.' Much as members of the diplomatic community deplored it, they could no longer ignore public opinion. And, it must be added, much as the internationalists longed for it, they were unable fully to achieve it. Even Wilson is said to have come around to "open covenants, secretly arrived at" during the protracted negotiations at Versailles. The implications for the way IR were now to be studied were enormous. One of the leading chroniclers of IR describes how the problem of war would be handled:

> Various simplistic determinisms . . . among which economic determinism and the devil theory of war were probably the most fashionable, flourished. In a way the belief in the possibility of discovering *the* cause of war reflected the prevailing optimism; for if the cause could be isolated, the cure could be prescribed . . . the historian in this respect frequently had little more to offer than the political scientist. The tremendous research effort on war guilt seemed only to document the badness of the diplomats and their system and to contribute little to understanding the causes of war and the conditions of peace.[12]

Yet the educational dimension was slow in being perceived; "past experience seemed to have little to teach," and the old system "was thought of as absolutely bad."[13] Precious little attention had been given to the analysis of the political functions, which, even in a reorganised system of states, would still have to be performed.

Teaching IR

To fill the vacuum, political scientists had two immediate options: to concentrate, as they had sometimes done, upon form rather than function, or to devise innovative ways of analysing the political process as it then operated. In the United States, the profession tended to opt for the former, which allowed international organisation to become the first focus of a new study or branch of an older discipline. IR likewise found a home in major university centres, where its leaders were influenced not so much by international history as in Britain but by international law and the fledgling political science. Harvard established a Bureau of International Research in 1924, whereas in Chicago Quincy Wright began his magnificent project on the Causes of War in 1926. At Yale a Department of International Relations was set up in 1934 as the first department in the United States under Nicholas Spykman together with the Swiss, Arnold Wolfers, and Frederick S. Dunn. The previous year the Fletcher School of Law and Diplomacy had been founded.[14]

In the United Kingdom, the field's beginning can probably best be dated from the creation in 1919 at the University College of Wales at Aberystwyth of the first academic Chair in International Politics, named after Woodrow Wilson, with Sir Alfred Zimmern the first of several distinguished occupants. Neither he, a classicist, nor his immediate successor, the diplomatic historian Sir Charles Webster, were trained as political scientists, but they were deeply aware of the charge implied in the Trust Deeds defining their task as studying "International Relations with special reference to the best means of promoting peace between nations."[15]

Zimmern was, organisationally, a particularly influential figure, since not only was he the first holder of the first ever academic Chair of International Politics, he was also the first holder of the Montague Burton Chair at Oxford in 1930. Zimmern was, as Jeanne Moorfield argues, a muddled liberal.[16] He had gained practical experience in the Foreign Office, and he was muddled because he tried to reconcile nationalism and internationalism into a common liberal framework. There was a Germanic Hegelian tinge to his thought in which he likened nations to families in search of an international commonwealth. Like Charles Manning, a holder of the Chair at LSE, he was difficult to fathom and a believer in a liberal, harmonious, but differentiated world.

When IR emerged in the UK, it was on its own, so to speak, not as a branch of political science as was often the case in the United States. Indeed except for the London School of Economics and Political Science, which antedated the war by many years, and possibly the noted PPE (Philosophy, Politics, Economics) degree at Oxford, the discipline of political science or government, but not usually called as such, tended to occupy a distinct place in British higher education *after* IR did, not before. Across the Atlantic it was the other way round, which understandably created a certain tension between the two disciplines in the United States, which for some continues to rankle to this day. In light of all this, what can one say about the then respective capabilities of other recognised academic fields for studying IR?

Contributing disciplines

The most logical place to begin is with Law, as in many countries in Latin America and, to a lesser degree, continental Europe, Law faculties were the locus of whatever international studies there was in Latin America and, to a lesser degree, continental Europe. As a discipline, Law reflected little attempt either to block or to nourish the new discipline, although of the thirteen books which may be regarded as the early mainstream IR texts, three were written by international lawyers, more than from any other discipline except history. Indeed the first comprehensive *Cumulative Book Index* (1922–1928) grouped together that literature in both fields under the heading 'International Law and Relations,' a combination which was kept in practice until the *Index* of 1943–1948 appeared a generation and a war later. Both the American, Elizabeth Read in her *International Law and International Relations*,[17] and the Briton, Pearce Higgins, Professor of International Law at Cambridge, in his *Studies in International Law and Relations*,[18] discussed the substance of IR.

But legal methodology could not easily accommodate such earnest purposes as peace planning, internationalism, and certainly the growing force of pacifism. Indeed the legal profession tended to take pride in continuing to analyse international legal questions in its conventional manner, based upon cases, precedents and procedures. In a striking exception, Higgins lectured in Illinois in 1927 on 'Some difficulties in international relations' in which he observed that:

> [i]t will be appreciated that international relations are involved in difficulties of the greatest complexity and it follows that the conduct of international business demands that those who are engaged in it should possess abilities of the highest order. For their success, statesmen and diplomatists should be able to rely on the intelligent understanding of those for whom they are acting, and this can only be acquired if their citizens will take the necessary trouble to make themselves acquainted with the problems with which they were endeavouring to solve.[19]

In all fairness, it must be noted that by 1925 the periodic Conferences of Teachers of International Law (CTIL), created in 1911 as one of the earliest undertakings of the Carnegie Endowment, embraced 'related subjects,' which really meant IR. The restriction of the agenda to Law at CTIL's initial conference, which fell between the second Hague Conference and Sarajevo, itself reveals the elementary fact that before the war the only place where the word 'international' was likely to be found in curricula was in Law schools. Their professors no more dealt with the balance of power, sabre rattling, dollar diplomacy, or military strategy in their classes than did the agendas of the peace societies for reordering the relationship of states.

All the same, the new discipline of IR may be said to have sprung from Law, especially in the United States. Had the element of international legal considerations been missing, its foundation would have lacked one of its sturdiest building blocks. Law was central to IR (though not vice versa). In 1928, N. Politis produced his innovative *New Aspects of International Law*, shortly to be followed by a comprehensive survey of research on international law[20] since the First World War by a scholar who was to become a key thinker of a new discipline, Quincy Wright of Chicago. This is only a sampling of new literature; no fewer than 150 titles appear in the first Cumulative Index under 'International Law and Relations,' half of them explicitly on Law (fewer than fifty are listed under 'World Politics,' most of them cross listings with the other category). In the United States, the legal approach dominated early writing in IR; in Britain, it was History.

Like Law, History has almost always been divided along different *schools* of historians for different political purposes and even practise different approaches to evidence. Nevertheless, there were well-established principles for the guidance of 'objective historians.' In contrast, an historian, Sir Charles Webster, Zimmern's successor at Aberystwyth, felt obliged to observe in his inaugural address in 1923 for the new Chair in International Politics that:

> There is no general acceptance of the principles of the study. Indeed, even if such principles had existed before the Great War, that event has so sapped the foundations of international order, and changed so remorselessly our conception of International Relations, that a recasting of our ideas would be necessary . . . no ordered and scientific body of knowledge did exist in 1914.[21]

Noting his freedom from restraint in setting new guidelines from among "the various lines of developments suggested," Webster understandably – perhaps inevitably – chose modern History as his point of departure. As a discipline, History was bound by its own methodological canons. Historians generally have been reluctant to render judgements about government policies and actions until the record is in. Others, more determined to develop studies that would prevent the outbreak of another, even more terrible war, could not wait that long. In the fullness of time, historians could be counted upon generally to interpret what happened, if not always to agree exactly upon which events had occurred or why. They could hardly be expected to help to *make* them happen – the very thought was unprofessional. Neither lawyers nor historians were future-oriented. The expertise of both had been relied upon heavily at Versailles; neither was programmed to institute a new order. As Fox has pointed out, historians (at least in the United States) were so preoccupied with reassessing the question of whether Germany was in fact guilty of starting the war that they had little or no interest in this new subject.[22] In Britain, however, a number of historians, notably Webster, Mowat and later Carr, made crucial contributions.

What then of the economists? Had not the most influential book to come out of the Peace Conference been John Maynard Keynes' *The Economic Consequences of the Peace*?[23] While his 1931 book was to carry the title *Unemployment as a World Problem*,[24] his mind did not turn to the larger disciplinary question of how to analyse and present IR as an integrated field, probably because he did not think it could be done and possibly because he thought it would not have been worth the effort if it could. Other immediate post-war publications by economists reveal only a few works of general international scope, such as Michael Pavlovitch's *The Foundations of Imperialist Policy*.[25] Although in a sense interdisciplinary (economics, history, sociology and military science), these gave little evidence of interest in a new social science discipline to deal with IR as a whole, only parts of it.

While the more traditional disciplines fell short of dealing comprehensively and systematically with IR, others fell even shorter. Sociology was caught up in developing its own scientific methodology, which for many years apparently found in IR a subject with too many variables to be capable of scientific analysis, to say nothing of prediction. To be sure, 1926 saw the third edition of Tonnies' *Community and Society*,[26] with a new introduction in which Pitirim Sorokin discussed not only Aquinas and Hegel but Ibn Khaldun and Confucius as well.[27] Neither demography nor ethnology had yet demonstrated their relevance for understanding and analysing IR, despite the ethnic basis for most of the nationalist movements, which finally found expression at Versailles in the creation of the successor states and despite the contention which could be made that there had occurred the crowning triumph of the nation as the basis for the state system. To be sure, a few tentative steps had been taken by A.M. Carr-Saunders in *The Population Problem*,[28] but he was not at the time concerned with a discipline of IR.

Geography was destined to occupy a prominent place in IR, although in a quite different way from that in which the work of Mahan and Mackinder had been conducted. Sir Halford's own *Democratic Ideals and Reality: A Study of the Politics of Reconstruction*[29] in 1919 revealed an interdisciplinary comprehension of the relation of the field to world politics, as did the work of Isaiah Bowman in *The New World: Problems in Political Geography*.[30] In all fairness, it must be observed that two developments were to occur which blunted geography's long-term involvement in any new discipline of IR. One was the 'bad name' later given to the field by 'geopolitics' as it was developed and used by the Nazis. The other was a possibly related shift from a human, cultural and political approach to a more scientific and thus more reputable physical geography, leaving political interpretation to others.

Understandably, the contribution of military science was a mixed one in the immediate post-Versailles years. On the one hand, pacifism was growing to the point where anything considered to be tainted with militarism was hardly given a hearing, certainly by those who felt that more careful analysis and understanding of interstate politics within the evolving League system would produce the solution to the whole problem of war itself. Contrary to this constraint was the undeniable fact that a great many ideas about strategy, tactics, logistics had been learned from the war, the doubtful utility of gas warfare and the probable utility of air power, to name but two. The need to educate the public was not lost on military planners any more than it had been on peace planners, as was demonstrated by Major-General Sir George Aston's *The Study of War for Statesmen and Citizens*,[31] and by books of two other influential and widely read British analysts of military problems, B.H. (later Sir Basil) Liddell-Hart[32] and Major-General J.F.C. Fuller,[33] both of whom put their arguments in a broadly political context. To these must be added the views of Giulio Douhet, an early and influential theorist of air power in the interwar period.[34]

The psychological dimension was suggested by Harold Lasswell's *Propaganda Technique in the World War*,[35] although his *World Politics and Insecurity* eight years later would prove more enduring. The sleeping giant of propaganda, discredited by the war, was yet to reawaken, but it would only be a matter of time before it foreshadowed a new sub-discipline – international communication theory. Except for the work of C.E. Playne and Gustave LeBon, the psychological literature explicitly related to IR was relatively meagre in the decade following the war.

The emergence of a consensus

What of IR itself? Was there any similarity in the sense that authors made use of this concept? Was there any consistency in the manner in which they subdivided the subject matter?

Did they come from several disciplines? If so, this suggests the dimension of a new discipline, or at least of what might be called an 'interdiscipline.' As early as 1916, as we have seen, the Council for the Study of International Relations published a series of studies representing history, economics, law and journalism, becoming the first book to make use of the term which was eventually to label the new discipline. The second was D.P. Heatley's *Diplomacy and International Relations*.[36] This was followed at once by the first to use it exclusively as a title, *International Relations*[37] by S.H. Allen, a former Kansas Supreme Court Judge; it proved actually to be a well-organised treatise on international law. Possibly the first academic text as such was *International Politics*, published the same year by the British social thinker, C. Delisle Burns.[38]

Of the many works on every conceivable aspect of international affairs between the war and the demise of the League system in the 1930s, less than fifteen can be seen to represent overall treatments resembling textbooks of a discipline. Four were entitled *International Relations*, five others having that term as part of the title; of the remaining three, two used 'society' and three preferred 'politics.' The authors were equally divided between Britain and the United States. From these efforts, certain generalisations can be advanced about how the subject first came to be defined in a mainstream literature dealing comprehensively with the world system.

Although there was a surprisingly high degree of consensus, there were differences of opinion on what should be included and, even more so, excluded. For example, that old stand-by of the eighteenth and nineteenth centuries, the balance of power, was rarely mentioned in this new literature of the first third of the twentieth. History, law and organisation were given primary attention, with little space usually allotted to psychological, sociological, demographic and especially military factors. Economic considerations were usually brought in, though not in any consistent manner. Little attention was as yet being paid to the nature of the study and especially to the methodology of the field.

To what extent was this literature 'idealist or liberal internationalist?' The short answer is, 'not much.' All the authors possessed an international, as contrasted to a narrowly nationalistic, outlook. None of them thought for a moment that war as a human institution was over for good. To be sure, public opinion was now more important than ever before, but it served only to extend the political process, not to replace it. But it is not an exaggeration to say that the new IR literature was designed to overcome some of the dubious assumptions and hopeful expectations of the liberal internationalist, widespread as their influence may seem to have been especially among the attentive public. The mainstream literature of the 1920s did not particularly reflect this paradigm, however much some of those outside the IR professional literature may have done so.

The organisational base

Several non-academic organisations came into being at this time as a result of the impulse for the systematic analysis of international politics or the promotion of peace in a responsible manner. In the United States, these efforts apparently sprang, partly at least, from a desire to compensate for what was regarded as the profound moral and political blunder of its having declined, because of the nature of its constitutional structure and a doctrine of isolationism, to become part of the League of Nations. In Britain, the principal effort was being made at Chatham House under the scholarly direction of Arnold J. Toynbee, who masterminded a colossal annual called *Survey of International Affairs*. The sister house to the Royal Institute, the US Council on Foreign Relations, also featured study groups and an annual survey, *The United States in Foreign Affairs*, all of which tended to concentrate upon US foreign policy in contrast to Toynbee's more universal approach. In 1931 the Council produced the survey (which unfortunately did not become a periodical one), *American Agencies Interested in International Relations*. Like Chatham House and its *International Affairs*, the Council published a learned quarterly journal, *Foreign Affairs*. The difference in the title 'International' for the British and 'Foreign' for the Americans may be a subconscious perceptual difference – the one internationalist, the other a national perspective. In any case *Foreign Affairs* featured articles by the world leaders and included exceptionally competent brief reviews by such recognised scholars as Robert Gale Woolbert, of the rapidly growing literature in world politics and economics. However, these provided less a picture of an incipient academic discipline with an emerging body of theory than a reflection of the State Department's traditional regional–functional compartmentalisation of the world. Little attention was given to whatever scant theoretical work may have appeared, nor to what might be termed disciplinary development. The object was to educate the business, financial and legal elites, not academics, although some professorial members (often rapporteurs of study groups, such as, in later years Henry Kissinger and Zbigniew Brzezinski) could help to educate an influential public.

In Boston, in 1931, the World Peace Foundation made a signal contribution to the development of the study in the form of a sweeping survey[39] of what was being taught in this field all over the country, to be matched two years later by a similar effort by Chatham House, *International Studies in Great Britain* by S.H. Bailey, a leading figure in promoting systematic studies. The Institute of International Education (IIE) published some scholarly works, such as Parker T. Moon's *Syllabus on International Relations*,[40] but tended to concentrate upon student exchanges. Founded in 1924 by Edward R. Murrow, who early in the Second World War was to become a renowned radio journalist, the IIE nevertheless did share the then prevalent assumption that greater knowledge could only create a deeper and broader understanding, which in turn could not but contribute to a more peaceful world. Eventually, the Chatham House–CFR model would be adapted to informing various elites throughout the world, but at first the English-speaking countries were virtually alone in this kind of endeavour.

The first international conferences on IR

Two more institutions provided a place for the nurturing of ideas that contributed to developing the discipline. One has already been mentioned, the Conference of the Teachers of International Law and Related Subjects, which published the works of some towering figures in the field such as Manley O. Hudson (law), Pitman B. Potter (organisation), Quincy Wright (foreign relations) and Nicholas J. Spykman (sociology), a number of whom wrote specifically on methods of teaching. The second was the International Institute of Intellectual Cooperation, set up in Paris under the League's auspices. Both of these represented attempts to analyse world affairs objectively as well as assessing how the subject was being taught. Among the more significant of the Institute's efforts were the International Studies Conferences.

The first such gathering of experts on coordinating the work of institutions dedicated to 'higher international studies' took place at the *Deutsche Hochschule für Politik* in Berlin in 1928. Among the delegations from Austria, France, Germany, Britain, Italy, The Netherlands, Switzerland and the United States, four institutional bases for analysis were represented:

1   Centres of study and discussion, such as those conducted at Chatham House.
2   Special courses, such as those taught at the Geneva Graduate Institute of International Studies or the Academy of International Law in The Hague.

3   Teaching Institutes outside the University proper, such as the École libre des Sciences Politiques in Paris or the Diplomatic Academy in Vienna.
4   University faculties, such as the London School of Economics and Political Science or the faculties of political science at some Italian universities.

In an analysis based upon the work of the Sub-Committee of Experts and of the Annual Conference of Institutes for the Scientific Study of International Relations, Professor (later Sir) Alfred Zimmern of Oxford noted after the Paris conference four years later that:

> Anyone drawing up a university syllabus for the study of international relations will find himself on the horns of a dilemma. Either he will limit himself to the subject in its narrower, technical sense, or he will include studies which provide an indispensable foundation for the understanding of the nature, purpose and working of the machinery.[41]

If one chose the former, the results might be "profoundly dehumanising," but if he chose the latter he might be overwhelmed in trying to decide "where does the subject begin and end?"[42]

These important conferences continued to be held periodically until the outbreak of war in 1939, although as more countries succumbed to authoritarianism open debate on IR became more difficult since such governments tended to restrict academic freedom in what they saw as a sensitive area. However, such meetings resumed in 1946, earnestly going over essentially the same ground. Previously each succeeding year saw more emphasis upon specific issues such as population, land utilisation and the perfecting of the League machinery for peaceful settlement of disputes, and less upon the 'scientific' organisation of International Studies as such. There was a parallel literature on imperialism and colonisation which fed into international studies, broadly conceived. A definition of sorts did begin to take shape during consideration of an agreement upon an IR bibliography, but it was not conclusive. The 1929 conference in London passed no less than ten resolutions, covering everything from the designation of national centres, to an interlending library and to the 'equivalence of degrees.' For our purposes, Resolution IX would prove more practical, calling for a "meeting of teachers concerned with international studies for the purpose of discussing among other matters methods of teaching, relations and arrangements of subjects, relations of academic teaching and practical experience." In subsequent years several such meetings were held until the 1960s, known in Britain as 'the Bailey meetings,' which in turn would eventually become the British International Studies Association. According to David Long the final demise of the International Studies Conference was due to some skulduggery by political scientists in the framework of UNESCO.[43]

The place of liberal 'internationalism'

Although, as we have seen, the mainstream literature did not necessarily represent the liberal internationalist approach, that perspective or bias was highly visible in other endeavours in the immediate post-First World War era. It clearly occupied the high ground of advocacy, although any distinction made or contradiction noted between scholarship and polemics would have been met with heated objections. Hopeful assumptions about the future of world affairs were prevalent in the writing of some educators of the period, notably in Zimmern's *The Development of the International Mind* (1925) and *Education for World Citizenship* (1931), and Ben Cherrington's *Methods of Teaching International Attitudes*. Each of these highly motivated writers was perhaps trying to 'make a point' more than primarily to make progress towards more scientific study. In one of his more lyrical expressions, for example, Zimmern said in 1924:

> For the world of our vision is no single field of waving grain, every ear like its fellow and blown the same way by the same breeze, but an infinitely diversified landscape, seen, as an airman would see it, from above, land and sea, city and country, cornland and pasture, orchard and forest, all placed at the service of man, of a humanity united in one great community of mutual understanding.[44]

Attitude outweighed analysis. Not only that. In approaching politics in the Greek sense of the term, Zimmern broadened hopelessly the range of what IR should encompass rather than endeavouring to narrow the definable and manageable dimensions of a discipline. Arguably, this actually set it back. Nevertheless, these efforts did represent a sincere impulse of a significant body of those engaged in its early development and may well have led the way to the scholarly emergence of normative theory. Although the idealists did not see themselves as such (especially if by 'idealists' one meant 'unrealistic'), it was this feature, along with the popularity which IR teachers enjoyed in interpreting headlines or 'current events,' which drew criticism and academic rivalry from many in the conventional disciplines. Another unrelated factor inhibiting legitimacy were 'cause groups,' which in their zeal for international change allowed ends to colour means. A remarkable exception was the Foundation for the Advancement of the Social Sciences, located at the University of Denver and doubling as one of the first formal Departments of International Relations in the United States.[45]

The early role of government and foundations

States were slow to recognise the value of a comprehensive and objective approach to foreign affairs, which would in effect place its own sometimes narrow policies within a broader context. In Britain, the government appears at first to have resented the creation of a second source of information and analysis in detail at Chatham House, which incidentally served to provide the Opposition with ammunition with which to attack Whitehall's cherished aims. This sometimes awkward relationship between democracy and public affairs was as important in defining the nature of the new discipline as was the yearning for a peaceful world order. It helps to explain why in authoritarian states the study of international politics or foreign policy could only exist as an explanation and justification of state policy. It also sheds light on why IR, at least at first, only developed in a few democratic countries, where it could enjoy indirect government support without being subject to official control.

While governments, foundations and institutes for quite different reasons could stimulate the systematic study of IR, the field had to find its home in the university. As mentioned earlier, the academic dimension in Britain initially took the form of Chairs in three Universities: the University College of Wales at Aberystwyth (1919), the London School of Economics and Political Science (1923) and Oxford (1930), each held initially by scholars of high intellect and genuine commitment to the scientific study of world politics. In the United States, university activity took two forms: the first was obviously the gradual increment of courses, usually based in departments of political science, covering world politics or some similar designation. The other was the establishment and growth in numbers at the rate of about two a decade of a dozen non-governmental professional schools or centres for the training of diplomats and other hopefuls for international careers.

Even though their primary function was seen to be training for the diplomatic service rather than contributing to the emerging field of international studies, their programmes did represent a beginning of professionalism.

Another critical institutional base affecting the way in which IR developed was provided by philanthropic institutions, especially the Carnegie Endowment, the Rockefeller and later the Ford foundations. They were active in the United States and also in Europe. Apart from the funding of chairs at Aberystwyth, LSE and Oxford, there was little philanthropy in Britain. In the United States their contribution should not always be regarded as an advance, especially in cases were scholars were tempted to trim their proposals to the whims of foundation officers. Another dimension of philanthropic endeavour took the form of gifts from the Carnegie Endowment of seminal current books on IR to libraries all over the country, which later encouraged intercollegiate conferences of what were usually called 'International Relations Clubs' (IRCs) featuring debates on crucial foreign policy issues of the day. Many a future diplomat, author, or professor of IR got his or her start through active participation in IRCs. On balance, the field could hardly have progressed as it did in this formative era without the assistance and, in many cases, wisdom of philanthropy.

Shifts in the balance of power in the wake of Japan's destructive challenge to the League system marked the beginning of worldwide disillusionment with that system. Other shocks were soon to follow. Inevitably they led to new approaches for thinking about world politics. They also led to a quickening of interest in the latest news from all over the world. The press, bored by dull League Assembly debates of plenipotentiaries from states for the most part miniscule in their weight in the balance of power, thrilled to the highly newsworthy shelling of Chinese cities by Tokyo's military forces on the offensive.

The effect of such striking events upon the orderly fostering of a scientific discipline was both destructive and salutary – destructive because they concentrated attention upon the short run and the spectacular, and salutary because they forced specialists to give more weight to power realities and their systematic analysis. As we shall now see, with the discipline beginning to mature, the consensual base of its innocent phase also began to erode. It would take a second world war for consensus to return. Then it would rest upon quite different intellectual foundations in a quite different world of politics.

Looking again

We owe an intellectual debt to the group of scholars in Britain and Canada who have trawled extensively through the literature of the inter-war period.[46] In particular they have looked at the writings of Angell, Brailsford, Woolf, Noel-Baker, Mitrany, Zimmern and others and revealed a treasure trove of ideas. They have castigated the sloppy identification of idealists or utopians revealing that they were so few and far between as to constitute an endangered species. The writers cited here were practical, experienced men of the world who were familiar with the full range of its ways. They were active in politics and not at all inhibited in challenging each other's ideas. If anything really united them it was their intellectual approach and their liberalism. They realised that politics and especially international politics could be both coercive and cooperative. They looked for an explanation of movement between these two poles – in both directions. Above all, they were pluralists. There was no great debate with others, be they the rising tide of realists, imperialists or advocates of a Marxist-Leninist interpretation of the globalisation of capitalism.

The literature was by now primarily Anglo-American and increasingly in a German-American mode as the realist tradition came to the fore. Apart from fitfully in France, continental IR was crushed by the conformity required by authoritarian regimes, and it was not to play its rightful role for decades. Brian Schmidt sums up the 'debate about a debate' thus:

> By unreflectively accepting the dubious notion, largely invented and perpetuated by realists, that the earliest generation of IR scholars were idealist utopians who failed to engage the underlying realities of international politics, scholars have failed to give careful consideration to the various ideas that were put forth between the two World Wars.[47]

Not only realists but others must plead 'guilty,' and it is important to represent early texts in the field of IR in their real context to understand not only the origins of the discipline but also its development after the Second World War.

Notes

1 Woodrow Wilson, *Congressional Government* (Boston, MA: Houghton Mifflin, 1885).
2 For a succinct analysis of these concepts see Andrew J. Williams, Amelia Hadfield and J. Simon Rofe, *International History and International Relations* (Oxford: Routledge, 2012, chapter 4).
3 G.M. Gathorne-Hardy, *A Short History of International Affairs 1920–1939* (Oxford: Oxford University Press, 1950), fourth edition, pp. 1–141. The "political isolation of United States" was dropped somewhere between the first and fourth editions, probably because of the war debts question, and the "Islamic world" was substituted for "regional issues."
4 C.K. Webster, *The Study of International Politics* (Cardiff: University of Wales Press, 1923), p. 27.
5 *Handbook of Institutions for the Scientific Study of International Relations* (Paris: Institute of Intellectual Cooperation, 1929), pp. 68–69.
6 *The Council on Foreign Relations* (New York: CFR, 1 January 1947), p. 5. See also the *IIC Handbook*, p. 95 (see note above).
7 *IIC Handbook*, p. 95.
8 Niels Amstrup, *The Study of International Organisation. Old or New? A Historical Outline (1500–1939)* (Aarhus: Institute of Political Science, University of Aarhus, March 1989), pp. 21–38.
9 H.M. Stanwick, *Builders of Peace, Being Ten Years' History of the Union of Democratic Control* (London: The Swarthmore Press, 1924), p. 23.
10 *IIC Handbook*, p. 96. This book's brief recapitulation of reports from all over the world is especially instructive in showing how the membership, dues and activities' structure varied between the RIIA, the CFR and the FPA. Both the 'sister houses' had programmes of studies, but the FPA did not; the Council and Chatham House (RIIA) had a limited membership by invitation after formal nomination, whereas the Association was open to anyone who paid $3 per year dues (more than 10,000 joined). Dues for the Council were $100 in the same year, 1929.
11 Hinsley, *Power and the Pursuit of Peace*, p. 285.
12 W.T.R. Fox, *The American Study of International Relations* (Columbia: Institute of International Studies, University of South Carolina, 1966), p. 5 n.
13 *Ibid.*, p. 11.
14 Niels Amstrup, *op. cit.*, pp. 28–29.
15 Webster, *The Study of International Politics, op. cit.*, p. 5.
16 See her chapter in David Long and Brian C. Schmidt (eds), *Imperialism and Internationalism in the Discipline of International Relations* (Albany, NY: SUNY Press, 2005), pp. 93 *et seq.*
17 Elizabeth Read, *International Law and International Relations* (New York: The American Foundation, 1925).
18 Pearce Higgins, *Studies in International Law and Relations* (Cambridge: Cambridge University Press, 1928).
19 Higgins, *Studies in International Law and Relations*, p. 36.
20 Wright, Quincy, *Research in International Law Since the World War* (Washington DC: Carnegie Endowment, Division of International Law, 1930).
21 Webster, *The Study of International Politics*, p. 4.

22 Fox, *The American Study of IR*, pp. 4–5.

23 J.M. Keynes, *The Economic Consequences of the Peace* (New York: Harcourt, 1919).

24 J.M. Keynes, *Unemployment as a World Problem*, edited by Avery Wright (Chicago: Chicago University Press, 1931).

25 Michael Pavlovitch, *The Foundations of Imperialist Policy* (London: Helm Publishing, 1922).

26 Ferdinand Tonnies, *Community and Society* (New York: 1965 [1887]).

27 Tonnies, F. *Community and Society*, third edition, 1926, p. vii.

28 A.M. Carr-Saunders, *The Population Problem* (Oxford: Cloveden Press, 1922).

29 Halford J Mackinder, *Democratic Ideals and Reality* (New York: Kenny Holt, 1919).

30 Isiah Bowman, *The New World: Problems in Political Geography* (New York: World Book Co, 1928 [1922]).

31 George Aston, *The Study of War for Statesmen and Citizens* (London: Longmans Green, 1927).

32 Basil H. Liddell-Hart, *Great Captains Unveiled* (Edinburgh: Blackhood, 1927).

33 J.F.C. Fuller, *War and Western Civilization* (London: Duckworth, 1932).

34 Giulio Douhet, *The Command of the Air* (New York: Coward McCann, 1942), transl. Dino Ferrari.

35 Harold Lasswell, *Propaganda Technique in the World War* (London: K. Paul, Trench, Trubner, 1927).

36 David Heartley, *Diplomacy and the Study of International Relations* (Oxford: Clarendon, 1919).

37 Steven Allen, *International Relations* (Princeton, NJ: Princeton University Press, 1920).

38 C. Delisle Burns, *International Politics* (London: Methuen, 1920).

39 Farrell Symons, *Courses in International Relations in American Colleges, 1930–31* (Boston, MA: World Peace Foundation, 1931).

40 Parker T. Moon, *Syllabus on International Relations* (New York: Macmillan, 1925).

41 A.E. Zimmern, 'Education in International Relations: A Critical Survey,' *Education Survey*, Geneva, League of Nations, III, 1, March 1932, p. 35.

42 *Ibid.*, p. 36.

43 David Long, 'Who Killed the International Studies Conference?' *Review of International Studies*, October 2006.

44 A.E. Zimmern, 'Education in International Goodwill,' *The Sixth Earl Grey Memorial Lecture* (Oxford: Oxford University Press, 1924), p. 14.

45 Ben M. Cherrington, *The Social Science Foundation of the University of Denver, 1926–1951: A Personal Reminiscence* (Denver: Social Science Foundation, 1973).

46 Brian C. Schmidt, 'Anarchy, World Politics and the Birth of a Discipline,' *International Relations*, April 2002; Lucian M. Ashworth, 'Did the Realist-Idealist Debate Ever Happen?' *International Relations*, April 2002; David Long and Peter Wilson (eds), *Thinkers of the Twenty Years Crisis* (Oxford: Clarendon, 1995); Lucian M. Ashworth, 'Where Are the Idealists in Interwar International Relations?' *Review of International Studies*, April 2006; David Long and Brian C. Schmidt (eds), *op. cit.*

47 Brian C. Schmidt, *op. cit.*, p. 23.

5 The impact of the collapse of the League system

A time of change in international politics produced a change in ideas about the world. The initial post-First World War decade had reflected an essential concurrence in the mainstream literature because there was a certain degree of consensus in politics. The second decade produced no such consensus. Hence, although a composite model from basic texts of the first decade of the discipline's formal growth could reasonably (if not very scientifically) be constructed, we were now confronted with a pattern of distinctions. Between the collapse of the League and the extension of the European war to most of the world by 1941, there were almost as many conceptual frameworks as there were authors to explain the meaning of rapidly shifting events.

Conventional wisdom contended that internationalist assumptions, having dominated early post-war thinking about world politics, were gradually being replaced by realism as the League of Nations inexorably demonstrated its inability to cope with aggression. Neither paradigm was very often expressed in unadulterated form. Internationalists had seen the League as an alternative to power politics while their challengers merely regarded the Assembly as another arena for its pursuit. Internationalists struggled for acceptance even after it was apparent that the League experiment was failing. But we must not throw out the baby with the bathwater. The League was a success in functional cooperation as the Bruce Report attested in 1939.[1] Moreover, the idea of a general, permanent, international secretariat of a universal international organisation dealing with all manner of world affairs took root. A world without such an organisation is unthinkable now and to this extent the League left a successful mark.

The beginning of the end of consensus

The Japanese attack at Mukden, which contributed significantly to discredit the League of Nations, took place in 1931, two years after the Wall Street crash and two years before Hitler became Chancellor. It is a convenient year of division in the development of ideas in IR. Obviously this is no accident, merely serving to illustrate a rather obvious feature of this new discipline: the direct impact of events in world politics upon not only the relative emphasis respective authors gave to the same topics but upon their assumptions as well. The same could be said of such disparate writers as Thucydides and Grotius, even more so of Machiavelli and Kant. Not surprisingly, the international law, international organisation and the peace literature tended to remain at least implicitly hopeful, but writers in the subfield of foreign policy as in diplomatic and international history, were rarely anything but 'realistic,' never being taken up by those whose wishful thinking expected too much or even something fundamentally different of League politics. To such authorities the inadequacy of the League, far from causing a 'sea change' in interpretation, was to some degree anticipated in their treatments. Of the dozen or so 'mainstream' writers only Raymon Leslie Buell in 1929 went into a second or revised edition of *International Relations*, and he told the public a tale of woe rather than of hope.

As the literature developed, further breaks with tradition emerged, as fears and expectations of a new war were reflected in new titles. Yet mainstream texts continued to cover international institutions designed to prevent war, although less was claimed for them. Credit for 'correcting' the naïveté of the literature of the League period was first to be bestowed upon a British diplomat-journalist-academic, Edward Hallett Carr, after a 'softening up' in the United States, by Reinhold Niebuhr, and later upon Georg Schwarzenberger and Hans Morgenthau, two of many driven out of Central Europe by Nazism who profoundly enriched US, and to a lesser extent British, intellectual life. Actually, the realist phase had begun to surface years earlier. For example, the caution of most early post-Versailles IR specialists was only confirmed by Charles Hodges, who introduced a background text on world politics with these words:

> This endeavour has been cast along realistic lines . . . To those who seek short cuts to the outlawry of war and to world peace in ready-made idealism, we commend the whole pageant of human progress as a struggle against human nature, successful only where leadership had proceeded slowly and painfully over the solid ground of prevailing world realities.[2]

This Hobbesian perspective appeared in print just *before* the multiple crises that accompanied the shift from the optimistic 1920s to the forlorn 1930s. Hodges saw IR as the 'apex' of the social sciences. In one sense, his treatment was consistent with the literature of the first decade, devoting even more space to international law and organisation than most, but it was in an essentially realist context.

Putting aside specific country or regional studies and dozens of titles that concentrated upon the closely related fields of international law, history, foreign policy, international organisation and especially peace, we can identify about forty titles in what we have termed 'mainstream' IR from 1916 to the entrance of the United States into the Second World War. Even if by 'idealist' we mean no more than stressing the efficacy of law and organisation, only about half of these can be said to be even primarily idealistic in tone. The long-range effects of political events are rarely understood at the time they occur, particularly in the still relatively unfamiliar domain of international developments that challenge the very foundations of the existing order. So that while diplomats, reporters and some pundits realised that something crucial was happening in Asia, academics tended to continue their painstaking efforts to develop, enhance and especially to organise scientifically the teaching of the new discipline. Most of them concentrated not on current events but on continuing the efforts initiated more than a decade earlier, to all appearances undeterred and hardly discouraged by what was occurring on the new battlefields of actual interstate contact.

Defining the subject-matter

A landmark in these patient efforts, at least in Britain, was an extensive survey undertaken in 1933, under the chairmanship of Sir William (later Lord) Beveridge, by the British Co-ordinating Committee of Institutions for the Scientific Study of International Relations. The survey not only covered the entire range of student and adult education in the country at that time, but the study of international law and relations as such in universities as well, including a few 'separate' Departments of International Relations. Objectivity in methodology and presentation seemed to be one of the keystones in the scientific approach, just as education was the key to creating an informed citizenry.[3]

The editor, S.H. Bailey, made it clear that, in this subject especially, there should be no trace of propaganda from the state. But just what was meant by 'this subject?' Was this eminent committee now prepared to give a definition of the new discipline? According to Bailey, this question could be considered from two viewpoints – the theoretical or ideal, and the practical or possible. On the theoretical side, it encompassed these subdivisions:

(a) International History – particularly diplomatic relations.
(b) Economics and the Theory of International Trade.
(c) The Structure of International Relations, or of the Great Society – a composite study of geographical, economic, social, psychological, ethical, political and other factors influencing international conduct.
(d) Principles, history, philosophy and International Law, mainly public.
(e) Study of what has been called 'the technique of peace,' that is, growth, structure and practice of both national and international institutions for the conduct of international relations.

Practical problems produced in the committee a consensus on several factors, notably the absence of uniformity and facilities for teaching history, economics and international law, the time-factor for IR students required to cope with an already overloaded undergraduate schedule, and the problem of whether the subject should be postgraduate, undergraduate or both. The generalisation can probably be made that, whereas in the United States considerable intellectual effort was going into the preparation of textbooks analysing the comprehensive field, the main effort in the UK was upon teaching, conferring about the nature of the subject and deciding how universities could better accommodate it. The US writers taught, to be sure, just as the British teachers wrote, but the latter tended to make their mark through specialisation, not an overall treatment of problems on the global scale.

Within a few years after the Bailey survey, two US studies (1934, 1937) were completed under the competent eye of Edith Ware on all aspects of US IR studies and, indeed, activities. They were sponsored by a duly impressive 'American National Committee on International Intellectual Cooperation,' a veritable Who's Who of world-minded intellectuals headed by Professor James T. Shotwell of Columbia and The Carnegie Endowment. In her 1937 preface, Edith Ware cited Secretary of State Cordell Hull's charge to the Third World Power Conference in Washington in 1936:

> You meet in a spirit of friendly cooperation with no thought of chauvinism or political jealousy . . . you also advance the cause of peace. And the cause of peace is the cause of civilization; religion, science, culture and social betterment only go forward in a world without war.[4]

Hull asked, "Shall the brains of the world be used to lighten the burdens of man, or shall they be used for the purposes of war?" Ware's book did not answer the question, but in 1937 there was ample reason to wonder. Hundreds of pages were devoted to organisational activities on an international plane, from temperance societies to The American Tariff League, but with no more than twenty pages to the study of IR in academic institutions, seven of which concentrated upon the several professional schools then in being or planned.

How were the political scientists and others, who were writing the textbooks for actual IR courses, now looking at the subject? The frequency of general texts remained about the same as in the earlier period. However, consensus on what the student of IR should learn was much more difficult to find among authors, most of whom were now Americans. Narrower, more specific treatments of world economics and politics became more commonplace. At least in the literature, the discipline of IR did not advance in ways that had been anticipated. Hitherto plausible certainties accompanying an incipient *science* of IR gave way to doubt, just as optimism gave way to pessimism in world politics. Indeed, the literature of this middle period, particularly outside the mainstream on both sides of the Atlantic, may even be regarded as retrogressive. Consensus on what topics needed to be given major treatment gave way to novelty, challenge and experimentation. Hence, while Ramsey Muir was still looking back to *The Political Consequences of the Great War*,[5] titles by responsible writers such as David Davies,[6] James T. Shotwell[7] and even Buell[8] reflected current concerns about the international situation. The cover of one book, an update of *The Great Illusion* of 1910, featured "Angell warns again!" This 'apocalyptic' literature looked ahead to what seemed to be a growing probability of another major conflict. Concentration was no longer upon the system but upon its collapse.

Contrasts in the new mainstream literature

Although only six comprehensive texts appeared between the Mukden Incident of 1931 and the Munich Crisis of 1938, eight more were published by the time the Japanese struck at Pearl Harbor three years later. Dominant among them was Frederick L. Schuman's *International Politics*, whose three editions in this second decade (1933, 1937, 1941) had many competitors. Yet while the term 'mainstream' remains useful to describe those authors whose perspective was universal rather than regionally or functionally restricted, the tidy formulations of the previous, more optimistic decade gave way to a variety of interpretations that have little in common but their non-consensual realism and scope. Indeed, there was little agreement on the components of a distinct discipline as the fragile new world order fell apart. In contrast to the participants in the Bailey conferences, most US textbook writers showed little interest in 'the discipline' during what they increasingly implied would turn out to be a pre-war decade. Why?

To find the answer to this, there is no better place to begin than with the decade's most successful author in the field, if the widespread adoption of Schuman's *International Politics* text in the United States is any guide (British students were reading international history, principally as set forth by the anti-Wilsonian, Gathorne-Hardy). In a "Preface for social scientists," Schuman argued that hitherto international lawyers and historians had monopolised the study of IR. Jurists had looked at the subject from the perspective of the international public law. Historians treated world politics in a general way "by the usual word jugglery and the intellectual acrobatics habitually indulged in by those who conceive of social science as a vehicle for dispensing moral judgements."[9] In apparently ignoring any real interdisciplinary collaboration in approaching the subject, Schuman failed even to mention economists, geographers or others who presumably had something to contribute to an understanding of international politics. His approach was based upon what he termed "the new political science," not the old variety "circumscribed by barren legal and historical concepts" but one which showed that:

> Political science, as one of the social sciences, is concerned with the description and analysis of power in society – i.e. with those patterns of social contacts which are suggested by such words as rulers and ruled, command and obedience, domination and subordination, authority and allegiance.[10]

A new vocabulary would even be necessary along with novel ideas in order that political scientists might "escape from these frustrations," namely "the blind alley of legalism" and "elaborate fact gathering on a variety of topics which they are unable to put together into a unified scheme of interpretation."[11]

The methodological revolution, which thirty years later would provide both methods and the language of an even newer political science, did indeed overcome these particular frustrations, but at the expense of producing frustrations of their own based upon excessive claims and a certain inability to communicate. In describing The Western State System (which he seemed to identify with "the whole state of modern world society"), Schuman devoted as many chapters to "world anarchy" as to the rise of modern world society and world order combined, leaving a lonely final chapter for "toward tomorrow." Disorder hence replaced international law and organisation in the scheme of things, a distinct departure from the previous decade.

Schuman's power-based analysis is countered by an economic base of power in *The Great Powers in World Politics*[12] by journalist Frank Simonds and Brooks Emeny, a Yale professor (who soon left academe to pursue the other educational target of the early theoretical practitioners, public opinion, as president of the Foreign Policy Association). Their study of international politics and economic nationalism frankly eliminated everything that was not a part of what was termed 'the world that matters,' fundamentally economic in nature and encompassing Western Europe, the United States and Japan. Here was indeed one of the first modern examples of international political economy, although it would be nearly fifty years before international political economy would signify a growing point in the discipline.[13] Full of maps and charts, this interpretation set forth the factors of national power and their relative standing among the contending states in Europe and East Asia, with the United States as 'the third centre of industrial power.' By the time the student reached the relatively brief last section, 'Can peace be preserved?' he had every reason to doubt it.

A new word now appeared in the literature, one which in time would become very familiar – 'theory.' The first presentation occurred in a long tome by a political scientist whose roots in history were as strong as Schuman's. Frank Russell's *Theories of International Relations*,[14] unsophisticated by later quantitative and behavioural standards, must be regarded as a landmark contribution to the discipline. As Russell put it:

> There is no book in any language, as far as I know, that attempts to present from the earliest times, and in the light of environmental influences, more significant ideas, whatever their character or implications may be, that men have entertained concerning international relations.[15]

A possible exception might be F.S. Marvin's *The Evolution of World Peace*.[16] Despite contributions by such distinguished scholars as Toynbee on Hellenism and G.P. Gooch on the impact of the French Revolution, the book must be regarded as a polemic for what today might be called the peace paradigm.

A second theory book was less historical and more philosophical: Salvador de Madariaga's *Theory and Practice in International Relations* (1937). Recalling his years in the League Secretariat in Geneva, de Madariaga was struck by the contrast between what people were thinking or saying about international relations and what they, and particular others in chancelleries throughout the world, were actually doing. What did he have to say about theory? Although perhaps not much in light of advanced analyses to be seen later, he was nevertheless original and full of insight. As one "temporarily taken away from his real vocation, that of a man of thought, into the field of action," de Madariaga set forth a series of theoretical propositions linking these two worlds (italics his):[17]

1   International relations is a form of politics.
2   Politics may be defined as "*all manifestations of life endowed with power to influence collective events.*"
3   "The State is based entirely on moral forces . . . much gnashing of teeth, and much disappointment, might have been avoided if people had realized that it is impossible to expect of a world community which is groping towards its State (with a capital S), that it should go further and rise higher and become more efficient than the state (with a small s) of the moral forces which compose it allows."
4   The world community, like every other community, may be defined by "the solidarity which binds together all its members; *Solidarity may be defined as the interdependence between parts of a whole, without which the whole does not exist.*"
5   Sovereignty (from a moral, not a legal perspective) "*is a tendency, both primary and reactive, to consider or to assert the national will as the sole, or at least as the final determinant of action.*"

To pursue the ideas of these quite diverse writers – Schuman, de Madariaga, Marvin, and Russell – more fully would be rewarding even today, but before returning to the literature of the time, let us see what was going on in another arena – the International conference.

International conferences

Several shelves, both at Chatham House and at the headquarters of the Council on Foreign Relations, are filled with papers and verbatim reports (mostly in French) from the ISC (International Studies Conferences). The proceedings of one of the most fruitful of these, which took place in Prague about a year before the outbreak of the Second World War, were published in Paris under the title *University Teaching of International Relations*. Noting that other discussions of teaching IR had recently taken place (London, 1935; Madrid, 1936), the rapporteur cited a "substantial consensus of agreement" and three propositions:[18]

1   Within the general mass of the social phenomena of the present-day world there is a distinguishable body of material which lends itself to separate study under the name of International Relations.
2   It is desirable that this material should form the subject of teaching in Universities and institutions of University rank.
3   It is desirable also that such adjustments as may be necessary should be made in the academic framework to enable this teaching to take place under the best conditions.

As for sub-topics, Zimmern also ecumenically suggested that "the indispensable nucleus of the subject" was contained in political science, political economy, international law, geography, history, sociology, and political and moral philosophy.[19] He even asked whether other subjects should be included, namely psychology and, in their more general aspects, law, biology, geology and demography, adding many questions about methodology and academic organisation and winding up with a concern about ultimate values: "What is the good implicit in the notion of a peaceful solution? Is Peace an ultimate good? Or are there other values superior to it? If so, can they be defined and applied to the problem under review?"[20] These were considered the real questions, rather than the urgent practical issues that were soon to lead to the Munich conference of European statesmen, which split off German-speaking Sudetenland from the rest of Czechoslovakia and gave it to Hitler (neither Czechs nor teachers of IR were invited). Nevertheless, for four days, the professors discussed philosophy and pedagogy, including reports on the status of teaching IR in several of the countries represented: Australia, Austria, Canada, Denmark, The Netherlands, Norway, Romania, Switzerland and Yugoslavia, with "bulky volumes" circulated to the Conferences by the American Coordinating Committee.

What is most striking in these reports is the consistent theme that, even though general formal acceptance of IR as a discipline or a separate department was yet to come, except, perhaps, in Britain, universities were at last becoming responsive, somewhat reluctantly within their existing faculties, to the insistently growing interest in world affairs and the need for its systematic study. Exchanges were exceptionally rich in both conceptualisation and innovation, the first with respect to the nature, scope and methodology of IR, and the second with how to organise instruction more effectively within a compartmentalised academic environment. In closing, the rapporteur marked the relative progress of US effort and experience:

> The broad fact that emerged was that the study of international relations is very much more systematically developed in the Universities of the United States than in any other part of the world and that this development has taken place almost entirely since 1918. Even allowing for the great preponderance of the United States in the number and size of its University institutions, no other country could show a volume of work in the academic field comparable.[21]

Mainstream books in dark times

Shortly after the Prague conference ended two mainstream books appeared that portended a new consensus. One was a complex volume containing essays by no less than thirty-four authors. Frances J. Brown, Charles Hodges and Joseph S. Roucek, editors of *Contemporary World Politics*, designed their book as one of the first truly interdisciplinary (as contrasted to multidisciplinary) texts and not a mere collection of individual papers by experts in different fields.[22] While not designed as a text, the other was to have as much to do with bringing about a shift in attitude as any other analysis in the history of the discipline. Like others in this second decade, Carr's *The Twenty-Years' Crisis 1919–1939: An Introduction to the Study of International Relations* (1939) bore little resemblance to previous mainstream books.

As a leader writer for *The Times*, Carr had been impressed by the contradiction between how Hitler's successes were bringing another war ever closer and how public opinion was expressing itself in his country. Carr had spent years in the Foreign Office before turning to journalism and was later to find himself, as occupant of the IR chair at Aberystwyth, a man with a triple vantage point. Consistent with the purposes of Chatham House (with which he had for years been closely associated) Carr defined what he meant by "the science of international politics." Discussing the "beginnings of a science," he observed that utopianism had occupied the place in the development of this new science not unlike that which had occurred earlier in the physical sciences, including medicine, that is, "the desire to cure the sickness of the body politic has given its impulse and its inspiration to political science mixing,"[23] of which international politics is a part. Responding to a popular demand:

It has been created to serve a purpose and has in this respect followed the pattern of other sciences . . . The course of events after 1931 clearly revealed the inadequacy of pure aspiration as the basis for a science of international politics, and made it possible for the first time to embark on serious critical and analytical thought about international problems. Utopia and reality are two facets of science.[24]

There were other politico-intellectual phenomena, Carr argued, that had to be understood before any attempt could be made to examine the crisis in actual international relations such as the dichotomy between ethics and politics. The last of these, along with utopianism versus realism, made up a philosophical dimension of political outlook; collectively they go far towards delineating what later would be called a paradigm. With reference to the nature of a post-crisis international order, Carr asked whether the nation itself would continue to exist as the unit of power in such an order, concluding that one prediction could be made with some confidence, "the concept of sovereignty is likely to become in the future even more blurred and indistinct than it is at present."[25] Carr's significance lay in what Fox characterised as "four great virtues":

He relentlessly exposed the hollowness of the edifice of then prevailing Anglo-American "utopian" international thinking. He had a sense of the sweep of modern European history and was well-equipped to identify the salient changes which marked the passing of the European age in world politics. He was a pioneer in bringing the insights of Karl Mannheim and the sociology of knowledge to bear on the relation between thought and action in world politics. Finally, whether or not he always got the right answers, he asked very good questions.[26]

Where he might have got it wrong was in a realist theoretician's defence of appeasement as late as 1939, which was revised in subsequent editions.

After Carr and the relative dearth of mainstream literature in the depression decade, three conventional texts were published before the United States at last entered the Second World War following the attack on Pearl Harbor. Two of them were harbingers of the new realism. One, *Elements of International Relations*[27] by Frederich Middlebush and Chesney Hill, warned against preoccupation with current events and the 'blood and thunder' aspects of international affairs, resulting in the danger of superficiality, loss of a sense of perspective and failure to grasp the 'fundamentals.' The other represented the then best example of the 'state of the art,' Walter Sharp and Grayson Kirk's *Contemporary International Politics* (1940), which was "not designed to provide any simple or complete answers to these complicated and perplexing aspects of a new world that through infinite travail is struggling into being," but rather "to explore and examine those fundamental forces which . . . are most responsible for the motivation of foreign policies."[28]

All of these authors were interdisciplinary realists. Where Zimmern was the consummate internationalist, they represented the new mainstream pragmatism.

The third text was in the internationalist tradition. *Foundations of Modern World Society*[29] appeared before analyses grounded upon the war took over. In presenting what might be called a 'welfare' approach to the subject, Linden Mander dealt with problems of health, crime, labour, conservation, population, minorities, and intellectual or religious cooperation, anticipating the non-state-centric perspective that was to emerge thirty years later.

Despite concentration upon social issues, Mander did not place IR in the context of the discipline of sociology. Sociologists themselves were not yet writing mainstream IR texts and generally ventured into the field only marginally. There was one exception: Luther L. and Jessie Bernard had attempted an intellectually broad approach in their *Sociology and the Study of International Relations*.[30] Writers such as Karl Mannheim in *Man and Society in an Age of Reconstruction*[31] and P.A. Sorokin in *Crisis of Our Age*[32] dealt with world society, but hardly from an IR perspective. Aside from these studies, Janowski and Fagen's treatment of the international aspects of German social policies in 1937 and Theodore L. Stoddard's *Clashing Tides of Color*[33] were among the few to suggest possible linkages.

As for other disciplines, some geographers gave an inkling of the role they were soon to play. Along with D.S. Whittlesey in *The Earth and the State*[34] Richard Hartshorn analysed the relationship between the physical environment and political organisation, as well as trying to lend theory to the field of geography. Even before that, in 1938, Charles Colby edited a book of essays by seven leading geographers, *Geographic Aspects of International Relations*.[35] Except for Colby, Samuel Van Valkenburg and James Fairgrieve, most geographers dealt with countries, regions or the planet as a whole, not interstate relations. In economics, analyses of particular problems increased in the 1930s, but only a few endeavoured to cover a broad range of international affairs as had certain of the lawyers, political scientists and historians. The work of R.F. Harrod[36] and Jacob Viner[37] in international economics as such stand out, just as Sonia Z. Hyman,[38] Lionel Robbins[39] and H.B. Butler[40] made notable contributions to an understanding of the relationships between economics, planning, peace and world order. A monograph for the *British Journal of Psychology* by meteorologist L.F. Richardson represented a pioneer effort at statistical analysis.[41] The contributions of Gunnar Myrdal[42] in demography and Tom H. Pear[43] in psychology were beginning to be felt, representing a growing relevance of work in the cultural dimension. The famous *Open Letters* between Sigmund Freud and Albert Einstein, "Why war?" are still of interest,[44] as is Harold Lasswell's *World Politics and Personal Insecurity*.[45] In the passing flood of what we have chosen to call 'apocalyptic' literature, G.D.H. Cole's *Guide through World Chaos*,[46] T. Ishimaru's *Next World War*[47] and George Fielding Eliot's *Bombs Bursting in Air*[48] added to the decade's store of controversial ideas but hardly to the discipline of IR as a science.

In the field of law, general treatises continued to enrich the literature in the mid-1930s before the fabric of law broke down, notably Hersch Lauterpacht's *The Function of Law in the International Community*,[49] Hans Kelsen's weighty and influential *The Legal Process and International Order*[50] and J.L. Brierly's succinct *Law of Nations*.[51] Note the terms 'order' and 'community,' reflective of the same extra-legal concern later to be expressed by another international lawyer, Georg Schwarzenberger.

To give the impression that genuine idealists like Zimmern and especially Toynbee had been totally out of touch with the reality that writers such as Schuman and Carr had grasped, would be grossly to mislead the contemporary student of IR. In one respect, Toynbee was a realist ahead of his time in that he clearly foresaw the coming impact of what is today known as the 'Developing World' upon international politics. Zimmern anticipated the stress now being placed upon values by statesman and scholar alike. Both of them frequently exchanged views with Carr at Chatham House. The basic point is that each wrote within the political context of his times with what he regarded as scientific objectivity. What had changed were the times. The high degree of consensus in the literature of the 1916–1931 phase reflected, with a certain degree of confidence, consensus in the world of politics itself. Now that was not so. Successive editions of Schuman do provide a linkage in that his way of subdividing the subject matter of IR resembles the early model, although his perspective is more akin to the coming stage of consensus based upon power. What is even more useful in terms of the development of the field is the way in which he interpreted shifts in the balance of power. His is the best example of what Fox means by undergraduate texts representing a "prism" through which the authors interpret a changing world.[52]

To summarise, in contrast to the literature of the first modern period of IR as a discipline, when there was agreement on the nature and scope of the subject among the authors of mainstream books, the decade between the basic challenges to the League system starting in 1931 and the extension of the European war to the entire world in 1941 was characterised by widely diverging approaches. The power approach of Schuman, the stress upon economic nationalism of Symonds and Emeny, the theoretical history of Russell, the Marxist critique of Dutt, the thought-action nexus of de Madariaga, the scientific definition of Carr, the inter-disciplinary pragmatism of Brown and his colleagues, the functionalist perspective of Sharp and Kirk, and the welfare paradigm of Mander, all stood in contrast to traditional descriptive expositions and, indeed, from one another. Excessive attention to a new world order had been corrected. Truly interdisciplinary analysis, except possibly for recognition of the necessity to understand historical antecedents, had yet to be achieved by most experts. The essential place of economics had been understood by only a few, notably Simonds and Emeny. There was apparently little discussion even with those few economists, such as Harrod and Ellsworth, who were writing general texts on international economics, so that international political economy had its exponents mainly in the past in Smith, List and Ricardo, or in a distant future which would once again stress international political economy. Similarly, only a few geographers such as Colby and Fairgrieve were attempting to apply the lessons of their well-established discipline to the issues of world politics. Sociologists were, as yet, dealing only with edges of the subjects. Even the broad-gauged contributions of such international lawyers as Lauterpacht and Kelsen must be regarded as exceptions. Hence, after a promising start, there had now to be real doubt whether the literature demonstrated any such thing as agreement in defining a discipline of IR.

Before we leave the interwar period, one other lesson needs to be noted. If we take Carr's definition of the phases in the development of science, both decades take a legitimate and logical place in the growth of the discipline, with the second providing a transition to a new consensus. The apparent contradiction between them may easily be overdrawn, as the return to some of the humane values which so concerned Zimmern and his colleagues in the wake of the carnage of the First World War served to demonstrate.

Anticipating a new consensus

Realism was given a running start into the post-Second World War era by a handful of wartime mainstream books, which managed to surface despite shortages of everything from paper to time to think. About a year after the so-called 'phoney war' came to an abrupt end with the Nazi invasion of Denmark and Norway, one of the last mainstream texts to be written by an international lawyer, Schwarzenberger, was published in London: *Power Politics*. Although he was later to deal extensively with the legal dimension in his *International Law and Totalitarian Lawlessness*,[53] Schwarzenberger now played down this aspect of the subject, sharing with Schuman the belief in the centrality of power. But it was another feature of *Power Politics*, implicit in its subtitle, *A Study of World Society*, which was more unusual and possibly more promising. Schwarzenberger contended that IR constituted "that branch of Sociology concerned with international society."[54] Even the historical sociologist, Harry Elmer Barnes, had in 1930 avoided both the term 'society' and its disciplinary implication for location of the subject matter in the halls of academe. In its actual organisation, however, *Power Politics* proved to be fairly consistent both with mainstream treatment from Buell to

Mowat in the period after Versailles and with Sharp and Kirk at the beginning of the Second World War. For Schwarzenberger, law, organisation and even morality were essentially functions of power. Indeed, instead of citing Grotius as the 'founder' of this new discipline (as might have been expected of an international lawyer), he designated Machiavelli.

Several wartime authors contributed to the discipline's maturity. Based upon childhood experiences in Romania, wartime cooperation in shipping and working for the League, David Mitrany looked beyond the fighting in developing functionalism as the basis for post-war planning. Hitler's war machine was still scoring successes when Robert Strausz-Hupé tried both to explain and to expose its reliance upon a deterministic view of geography: "even if geopolitics were simply the German blueprint for world conquest and nothing else, it would be worth studying," he wrote, "but it is far more than that . . . it remains a challenge to our conception of world policy."[55] A chapter entitled 'Heartland and hokum' attacked the entire approach. Thorsten Kalijarvi, a scholar giving wartime service in the State Department, somewhat apologetically began his anthology, *Modern World Politics* (1943), with the question, "Why another book on international relations when the market is already filled with them?" At one of those times when "the scholar gladly tends to throw off his usual objectivity and detachment in order to preserve his country's stake in the present war," Kalijarvi felt compelled to provide a "detached" presentation of the background of world events.[56] A chapter on world organisation concluded that "the elaborate machinery of the League could not, of itself, keep the peace if States were determined to go to war." His place in the field's development could be said to rest on assenting "in all modesty the distinction" of including military disruption, psychological warfare, espionage, treachery and international secret organisations, unpleasant elements of international relations that could never again be ignored.

Another lasting contribution took the form of an interpretation of the military dimension differing from the dominant pre-war theme of collective security as the means of guaranteeing peaceful change. Edward Mead Earle and his colleagues in *Makers of Modern Strategy*[57] anticipated strategic studies as an integral element in IR. Their interpretation of great military thinkers of the past by prominent thinkers of the present (e.g. Ludendorf by Hans Speier, Jomini by Gordon Craig, Douhet by Margaret Sprout) represented a shift in thinking in the IR community from collective security to grand strategy. A Dutch sociologist turned political geographer, the first Director of the Yale Institute of International Studies (dubbed 'The Power School' within the trade), Nicholas J. Spykman provided both another answer to, and a new expression of, geopolitics. His map-filled *Geography of the Peace*,[58] advancing a counter-theory to Haushofer's distortion of Mackinder's 'Heartland Theory,' the 'Rimland Theory,' followed his more influential volume, *America's Strategy in World Politics*.[59] Representing a logical outgrowth of Mahan's early idea of seapower based upon control of the coasts around the great ocean basins to the east and west of the Western hemisphere, this held great appeal for Pentagon post-war planners. Unfortunately for the development of IR, professional geographers after the war tended to drift towards physical geography, so that strategic thinking profited less from their expertise than might have been desirable; this was the price both disciplines may have paid for having become associated with a subject, or even a 'pseudo-science,' because of what Haushofer and Hitler had done with geopolitics.

As other and more reputable ideas encouraged by the war were finding their way into the literature, one author, W.T.R. Fox, even added a new term to the language of politics, "the Super-Powers." Fox had every reason in 1944 to include Britain as well as the United States and Russia. His short but significant book opened with an apt quotation from the journalist Samuel Grafton relating to a cardinal principle of the emerging international order, "sovereign equality": "even after you give the squirrel a certificate which says he's quite as big as any elephant he is still going to be smaller, and the squirrels would know it and all the elephants will know it."[60]

Fox made no attempt to write a general text at any time in an illustrious career capped by his holding the Bryce Professorship in the History of International Relations at Columbia. The farsighted influence of his essay had already earned him a place in the history of 'the field' (to his dying day, he declined to be drawn into any argument on whether IR is a discipline), even though it was perhaps one of the least of his manifold contributions as an original thinker, teacher and professional counsellor during four decades. Like Thucydides and Machiavelli, Fox described politics 'as it was'; like other wartime writers with the exception of Mitrany, he had little to say about international law and organisation. If it now seems odd that he deemed it necessary to explain why he was writing "in defence of talking about power," since many other observers were now preparing for another post-war era in which, this time with active US participation, world cooperation would at last prove to be a viable alternative to power politics. It would be a recurring phenomenon, as Lasswell's insights should have made clear. To what extent would the new mainstream literature reflect hopefulness?

Four realist authors and their academic hegemony: Niebuhr, Carr, Schwarzenberger and Morgenthau

We are about to enter the period of the academic hegemony of 'a realist' world of 'Power Politics' in its various guises and with its many implications. This was an academic world which responded to the failure of the League of Nations to manage peaceful change through a system of collective security. We shall dwell a little on four major authors, some of whom we have encountered already. Our choice is Niebuhr, Carr, Schwarzenberger and Morgenthau. There are others that we could have chosen, but this quartet reflects individuals who had influence, produced work of high quality and were of considerable standing.

It might be asked why we have not done the same for liberal internationalists. It is not through lack of commanding figures in that tradition, but the nature of the enterprise in the first decades of the twentieth century was different from the 1940s onwards. Liberal inter-nationalists were not writing for a discipline, they were essayists in a time-honoured genre who were writing for an attentive public, to influence public opinion and also government. In Britain, their natural habitat was Chatham House or the Fabian Society rather than an academic profession which in the 1920s already existed. For example, for many years David Mitrany wrote the foreign affairs leaders of the *Manchester Guardian*. There were no aca-demic textbooks of the likes of Schwarzenberger and Morgenthau. There was a whiff of Bloomsbury in the liberal internationalist air. That all changed as in both the United States and in Britain a fully fledged academic discipline was institutionalised. Moreover, the liberal internationalists, whatever their differences, did share a general notion and sense of how the world worked (they were often very experienced in practical politics), or could be made to work. There was no extension of such sharing with the adherents of power politics. This is not to suggest that this gave rise to a great debate. To be sure, the liberal internationalists reviewed and responded to the new climate and particularly to Carr's *The Twenty Years' Crisis*, but this did not constitute a debate.[61] Rather there were intellectual streams and tra-ditions existing side by side. And this coexistence was not limited to internationalists and 'realists.' There was also a continuing concern with imperialism, historically informed stud-ies of the balance of power and the Marxist-Leninist school which was in abeyance, but not dead. It was a rich confluence of ideas, approaches and methods.

The relationship between theory and practice had changed. In the early decades, until the 1930s, conceptual notions had driven policy, whereas from the 1940s until the 1960s conceptual analyses reflected policy. Academics had nothing new to say to practitioners in the realist era because, to a large degree, they thought alike. There was, however, some overlap because although power politics seemed to be effective and necessary in the short term, it could be self-fulfilling and thereby create the very situation that it was trying to avoid.

Power politics was an abdication of a policy for the long term, and most of our quartet recognised that a long-term perspective was vital. Moreover, to survive in the long run required consideration of other ideas and approaches beyond the realist mantra. International approaches in the long term had to go beyond 'power politics in disguise' to purloin Schwarzenberger's subtitle for the second part of *Power Politics*. We begin with Reinhold Niebuhr's *Moral Man and Immoral Society*.[62]

Writing in 1932, after the beginnings of fascism but before Hitler came to power, and with the League of Nations tottering in East Asia, Niebuhr was highly influential in the United States and not least on young German Jewish refugees such as Kissinger and Morgenthau who were to become pillars of the German-American School of International Relations. Niebuhr argued that "a sharp distinction must be drawn between the moral and social behaviour of individuals and of social groups."[63] "What is lacking," he continued, "is an understanding of the brutal character of the behaviour of all human collectives, and the power of self-interest and collective egoism in all inter-group relations."[64] The world is Hobbesian in that:

> [a]ll social cooperation on a larger scale than the most intimate social group requires a measure of coercion. The coercive factor in social life is frequently covert, and becomes apparent only in moments of crisis . . . Yet it is never absent.[65]

Moreover, he argued that "political power has been made more responsible to economic power."[66] But there is a dilemma since "the whole history of mankind bears testimony to the fact that power which prevents anarchy in intra-group relations encourages anarchy in inter-group relations."[67] Thus:

> [e]very group, as every individual, has expansive desires which are rooted in the instinct of survival and soon extend beyond it. The will-to-live becomes the will-to-power . . . As powerful classes organise a nation so powerful nations organise a crude society of nations . . . Thus society is in a perpetual state of war.[68]

Niebuhr, at the end of his essay, appears to take fright at the implications of his own logic:

> A too consistent political realism would seem to consign society to perpetual warfare. If social cohesion is impossible without coercion, and coercion is impossible without the creation of social injustice, and the destruction of injustice is impossible without the use of further coercion, are we not in an endless cycle of social conflict . . . And if power is needed to destroy power, how is this new power to be made ethical? If the mistrust of political realism in the potency of rational and moral factors in society is carried far enough, an uneasy balance of power would seem to become the highest goal to which society could aspire.[69]

But even this, he argued, could be but temporary. And the moralist was just as dangerous because he or she failed to recognise the elements of injustice and covert coercion: "a too uncritical glorification of co-operation and mutuality therefore results in the acceptance of traditional injustices and the preference of subtler types of coercion to the more overt types."[70] The condemnation of the rationalist and moralist is clear as is the type of thinking that Morgenthau, in particular, was to develop. But there were few, if any, answers. The real world and the conceptual world were palpably darkening.

Niebuhr's influence was mainly in the United States although E.H. Carr, the next of our quartet, was aware of Niebuhr's work. Carr was a man of many distinguished parts. Like Mitrany with the *Manchester Guardian* he regularly influenced and often irritated the public and the 'powers that be,' as a regular contributor to *The Times*. Like Mitrany he was also familiar with the corridors of power in the Foreign Office and was, like Keynes, highly critical of the Versailles peace settlement.[71] As an academic he was best known as an historian especially of Soviet Russia, but he probably had greater academic influence through *The Twenty Years' Crisis* and as one of the early holders of the International Relations Chair at Aberystwyth where a Chair now exists in his name.

The conceptual influence of *The Twenty Years' Crisis* is such that it is the earliest book in the academic discipline of IR still read on a regular basis by today's students. Indeed it has provoked three major assessments[72] and a new edition[73] in recent years. Carr himself was somewhat disparaging of IR as an academic discipline. He called it "rag-bag" and the LSE's attempt at professionalisation a "fiasco."[74] More hopefully he called it, "the application of political philosophy to international relations which has hitherto been studied mainly as a part of history and not as a province of political science."[75] Carr had little truck with political science and felt that IR was "simply a study of the best way to run the world from positions of strength."[76] It was the business of the great Powers, and the small Powers were nothing more than a nuisance. For him, the need was to recognise the relative and future political, military and economic strength of the Powers and to draw the appropriate conclusions. Hence his condemnation of Versailles, which left two major Powers out in the cold, and his willingness to accept the logic of appeasement. Britain was a declining Power, the United States was in isolation and therefore Britain should cut its cloth accordingly and accommodate the revived and rising Powers. For this he received a rebuke from Morgenthau that he was "surrendering to the immanence of power."[77]

Many writers have noted Carr's penchant for dichotomous thinking and have used it as a pedagogical talk. The key dichotomy was 'utopia and reality.' How did Carr see this?

> [Realism] places its emphasis on the acceptance of facts and on the analysis of their causes and consequences. It tends to depreciate the role of purpose . . . Realism tends to emphasise the irresistible strength of existing forces . . . and to insist that the higher wisdom lies in accepting and adapting oneself to, these forces and these tendencies . . . there is a stage where realism is the necessary corrective to the exuberance of utopianism, just as . . . utopianism must be invoked to counteract the barrenness of realism. Immature thought is predominantly purposive and utopian . . . Mature thought combines purpose with observation and analysis. Utopia and reality are thus the two facets of political science. Sound political thought and sound political life will be found only where both have their place.[78]

Carr immediately reiterates the theme in his next chapter identifying the antithesis of utopian free will and realist determinism. The utopian is "fixing his eyes on the future," the realist analysing "a predetermined course of development which he is powerless to change."[79] And again, "The radical is necessarily utopian, the conservative realist. The intellectual, the man of theory, will gravitate towards the Left just as naturally as the bureaucrat, the man of practice, will gravitate towards the Right."[80] While Carr inclined strongly to realism he acknowledges that "consistent realism excludes four things which appear to be essential ingredients of all effective political thinking: a finite goal, an emotional appeal, a right of moral judge-ment and a good ground for action."[81] He thus concludes that "any sound political thought must be based on elements of both utopia and reality." But the quest is endless. "Having demolished the current utopia with the weapons of realism, we still need to build a new uto-pia of our own, which will one day fall to the same weapons."[82]

Surprisingly, given his eminence, Carr was not invited to join the first English School International Relations theory group meeting in Cambridge. Neither was Hinsley, who was actually working in Cambridge, nor Manning from the LSE. Carr could not brook the idea of a world-wide community of states held together by a harmony of interests. He argued that the actions of the great Powers were combined to manage structural power and its relative dis-tribution in their collective and individual interests rather than to foster an embryonic world community of globally shared interests and values. At best there could be a *via media* built on short-term realism to provide a stable framework out of which a long-term realistic vision might arise. Until then international politics, international law and ethics would reflect the interests of the powerful. Change would occur and the function of power was to promote this peacefully. In the real word the claims of Germany and Soviet Russia had been grievously mishandled, and Carr pointed to the consequences of this.

Carr acknowledged that from childhood to old age he had lived a comfortable existence according to the norms of the well-to-do middle class in the declining days of Empire and world power. This was hardly the case for our third founding father, Georg Schwarzenberger. He came to Britain in the 1930s chased from his native Germany as a Jew and a socialist. He had, in the end, a good career, but it was slow in coming. In part this was due to his prickly personality and refusal to join the British establishment. He was and remained a continental scholar who never hesitated to be 'brutally frank' as he put it.

Schwarzenberger was not primarily an IR scholar. His prime contribution was as a highly regarded international lawyer. Like the historian Carr, with *The Twenty Years' Crisis*, the lawyer Schwarzenberger nevertheless made a substantial contribution to IR through his massive tome *Power Politics* first published in 1941. It went through several editions and was widely translated but, although a potential textbook, it was overtaken by Morgenthau's *Politics among Nations* after the Second World War. Morgenthau had the advantage of a considerable market as a text not available then in the British system. However, both scholars brought elements of continental thought to an English-language discipline.

Schwarzenberger began his treatise by stating his conception of the field:

> The field of the science of international relations is international society. Its objects are the evolution and structure of international society; the individuals and groups which are actively or passively engaged in this social nexus; the types of behaviour in the interna-tional environment; the driving forces behind the action in the international sphere, and the patterns of things to come on the international plane.[83]

In short, "the study of International Relations is the branch of sociology which is concerned with international society."[84] Schwarzenberger pointed to the distinction between society and community in German sociologist, Ferdinand Tönnies' thought, in which "society is the means to an end, while a community is an end in itself." As he further adds,

> [s]ociety is based on interest and fear, whereas the community requires self-sacrifice and love. The one is founded on distrust, whereas the other presupposes mutual trust – the members of a society remain isolated in spite of the association. The members of the community are united in spite of their individual existence.[85]

Schwarzenberger acknowledged that these were ideal types and that in the real world their existence in undiluted form was unlikely. Nevertheless, in international relations, power politics predominated overtly or in disguise.[86]

Schwarzenberger's analysis is crystal clear and informed by the history of the 1930s. While Carr was reviewed extensively by liberal internationalists such as Toynbee and Zimmern, Schwarzenberger seems not to have made such a mark. But when Morgenthau later made a clear impression on the discipline he was closely following in the footsteps of Schwarzenberger who deserves to be better acknowledged for the contribution he made to the intellectual development of the field. What then did Morgenthau add that was new?

Hans Morgenthau was, like Schwarzenberger, a Jewish refugee from Nazi Germany. Whereas Schwarzenberger came to London, Morgenthau ended up in the United States in 1937 after spells in Spain and Switzerland where the *Institut de Hautes Études Internationales* in Geneva provided an intellectual resting place for several such refugees. Morgenthau was also, like Schwarzenberger, an international lawyer who moved into IR. Morgenthau's first major publication in English was his *Scientific Man versus Power Politics* published in 1946.[87] In 1948 this was followed by a work which has influenced generations of scholars in the field, *Politics among Nations*.[88]

Morgenthau begins by adopting Carr's differentiation between the liberal internationalist belief that reform of the international system was possible and the realists who pointed to a "world of opposing interests," an approach which "appeals to historic precedent rather than to abstract principles, and aims at the realization of the lesser evil rather than the absolute good."[89] As made clear in subsequent editions of *Politics among Nations*, for Morgenthau the essence of political realism is the "concept of interest defined in terms of power."[90] But he goes on to admit that this concept of interest defined as power does not have "a meaning that is fixed once and for all." It is therefore a subjective concept.

> Its content and the manner of its use are determined by the political and cultural environment. Power may compromise anything that establishes and maintains the control of man over man. Thus power covers all social relationships which serve that end, from physical violence to the most subtle psychological ties by which one mind controls another.[91]

Power is an all-embracing concept since "International politics, like all politics is a struggle for power. Whatever the ultimate aims of international politics, power is always the immediate aim."[92] But, as we have seen, this power has no objective content; it is formed by what works on the day. It is as equally difficult to define, in an objective manner, as the notion of interest. So interest defined in terms of power is, because of its subjective nature, hardly a guide for practice or analysis. However, Morgenthau further elaborates that:

> When we speak of power, we mean man's control over the minds and actions of other men . . . Political power, however, must be distinguished from force in the sense of the actual exercise of physical violence . . . Political power is a psychological relation between those who exercise it and those over whom it is exercised.[93]

This highlights again the subjectivity of the concept. Morgenthau then gets to the crucial element in his thought: "it is sufficient to state that the struggle for power is universal in time and space and is an undeniable fact of experience . . . That drive to live, to propagate, and to dominate are common to all men."[94] There is no need for security dilemmas or great Power rivalries to explain power politics, the drive to dominate is enough. There is an eternal struggle between those who dominate and those who are dominated sufficient to guarantee power politics except where there is a Hobbesian 'Leviathan.' Thus:

> [t]he essence of international politics is identical with its domestic counterpart . . . modified only by the different conditions under which this struggle takes place in the domestic and in the international spheres. The tendency to dominate, in particular is an element of all human associations.[95]

Thus there are three basic policies "to keep power, to increase power or to demonstrate power."[96] Missing from the list is the disposition to share power. At best, the balance of power comes to our rescue since it has the capacity to bring a modicum of order and stability, but not peace, if it is seen and acted upon as a prescription for policy.[97]

Morgenthau endorses the notion of a homostatic equilibrium which when "disturbed either by an outside force or by change in one or the other elements composing the system . . . shows a tendency to re-establish either the original or a new equilibrium."[98] The other notion is that of the country 'holding the balance' and able and willing to intervene to preserve stability as Britain did in the nineteenth century.[99] This system worked in the eighteenth and nineteenth centuries, and Morgenthau's endorsement of it laid him open to the charge of nostalgic idealism in wishing to establish anew such a system. But Morgenthau realised that such a system depended on a shared political culture of statesmen willing to play the game, share knowledge of the relative weights of different Powers in the system and a willingness to be flexible in that every state in the system was a potential ally or adversary. Moreover it assumed that the major actors in the system were viable, which by the end of the nineteenth century was no longer the case, as multinational great Powers were under the threat of dismemberment due to the demands of their nationalistic components. While the balance of power system may have revealed tactical flexibility, it could not manage the systemic change rendered inherent by the rise of nationalism.

Politics among Nations is known for its analysis of power politics among nations, but that is not the full story. As Morgenthau points out:

> [n]ot every action that a nation performs with respect to another nation is of a political nature. Many such activities are normally undertaken without any consideration of power, nor do they normally affect the power of the nation undertaking them. Many legal, economic, humanitarian, and cultural activities are of this kind . . . In other words, the involvement of a nation in international politics is but one among many types of activities in which a nation can participate on the international scene.[100]

How then do they fit in? Are they completely separate from power politics? Or, do they influence it and perhaps eventually change its nature, as Mitrany would have it, or are they power politics in disguise, as Schwarzenberger would have it? Or again, do the big Powers in each domain run the show behind the scenes as Carr suggests? Is there a sphere where the harmony of interests is evident and is a basis for institutions? Is it power politics pure and simple or power politics and legitimised cooperative politics as Morgenthau seems to imply? Moreover what of new global structures to replace the imperial world tottering to its formal dissolution? Only Carr really seems to have a clear notion of the powerful effects of structure, but we are still a long way from dependency theory, centre-periphery models and the like. For the present, realism ruled. It had replaced liberal internationalism as the new consensual framework. It made sense because it was simple and seemed to explain a world of rising fascism, the Second World War and the Cold War. But by the 1960s realism no longer was able to 'explain' a new world order in its globalising form.

Notes

1 See Victor-Yves Ghebali: *La Société des Nations Unies et la réforme Bruce, 1939–1940*, Geneva, Centre Européen de la Dotation Carnégie pour la paix internationale, June 1970.
2 Charles Hodges, *Background of International Relations. Our World Horizons: National and International* (New York: Wiley, 1931), p. viii.
3 Cited in S.H. Bailey (ed.), *International Studies in Great Britain* (Oxford: Oxford University Press, 1933), p. 22. This is the official report of the British Co-ordinating Committee carrying out its part of the June 1931 Copenhagen resolution of the Annual Conference of Institutes for the Scientific Study of International Relations.
4 Edith E. Ware (ed.) *The Study of International Relations in the United States: Survey for 1937* (New York: Columbia University Press, 1938), p. xii.
5 Ramsey Muir, *The Political Consequences of the Great War* (New York: Holt, 1931).
6 David Davies, *Suicide or Sanity* (London: Williams and Norgate, 1932).
7 James T. Shotwell, *On the Rim of the Abyss* (London: Macmillan, 1936).
8 Raymond L. Buell and Phyllis A. Goslin, *War Drums and Peace Plans* (New York: The Foreign Policy Association, Incorporated: Grosset & Dunlap, Inc., distributors, 1936).
9 F.L. Schuman, *International Politics*, p. xii.
10 *Ibid.*
11 *Ibid.*
12 Frank Simonds and Emeny Brooks, *The Great Powers in World Politics: International Relations and Economic Nationalism* (New York: American Book Co., 1935).
13 See Chapter 11 of this volume.
14 F.M. Russell, *Theories of International Relations* (New York: D Appleton-Century, 1936).
15 F.M. Russell, *Ibid.*, p. vi.
16 F.S. Marvin, *The Evolution of World Peace* (London: Milford, 1921), vol. 4.
17 Salvador de Madariaga, *Theory and Practice in International Relations* (Philadelphia, PA: University of Pennsylvania Press, 1938), pp. 2–15.
18 Sir Alfred Zimmern (ed.), *University Teaching of International Relations* (Paris: International Institute of Intellectual Cooperation (League of Nations), 1939), p. 16.
19 *Ibid.*, p. 16
20 *Ibid.*, p. 18.
21 *Ibid.*, pp. 332–333.
22 Frances J. Brown, Charles Hodges and Joseph S. Roucek, *Contemporary World Politics: An Introduction to the Problems of International Relations* (London: Chapman and Hall, 1940), pp. viii–ix.
23 E.H. Carr, *The Twenty-Years' Crisis 1919 to 1939* (London: Macmillan, 1942; 5th printing), p. 5.
24 *Ibid.*, p. 9.
25 *Ibid.*, p. 230.
26 W.T.R. Fox, 'E.H. Carr and Political Realism: Vision and Revision.' *Revue of International Studies*, Vol. 11, No. 1, January 1985, p. 1.
27 Frederich Middlebrush and Chesney Hill, *Elements of International Relations* (New York: McGraw-Hill, 1940).
28 Walter R. Sharp and L. Kirk Grayson, *Contemporary International Politics* (New York: Farrar and Rinehart, 1940), pp. vii–viii.
29 Linden A. Mander, *Foundations of Modern World Society* (Stanford: Stanford University Press, 1941).
30 Luther L. and Jessie Bernard, 'Sociology and the Study of International Relations,' *The ANNALS of the American Academy of Political and Social Science* No. 174 (St Louis, 1934), pp. 211–212.
31 Karl Mannheim, *Man and Society in an Age of Reconstruction* (London: Studies in Modern Social Structure, 1940).
32 P.A. Sorokin, *Crisis of Our Age* (New York: E.P. Button & Co, 1941).
33 Theodore L. Stoddard, *Clashing Tides of Color* (New York: Scribner's Sons, 1935).

34 D.S. Whittlesey, 'The Earth and the State,' *Annals of the American Geographers* No. 35, 1939, pp. 1–36.

35 Charles C. Colby, *Geographic Aspects of International Relations* (Freeport: Books for Libraries Press, 1938).

36 R.F. Harrod, *The British Economy* (New York: McGraw-Hill, 1963).

37 Jacob Viner, *International Trade and Economic Development* (Glencoe: The Free Press, 1952).

38 Sonia Z. Hyman, *Economic Security and World Peace* (Madison: League for Industrial Democracy, 1938).

39 Lionel Robbins, 'Interpersonal Comparisons of Utility: A Comment,' *The Economic Journal* No. 48, 1938, pp. 635–641.

40 H.B. Butler, *The International Labour Organization* (Oxford: Oxford University Press, 1939).

41 L.F. Richardson, 'Generalized Foreign Politics,' *British Journal of Psychology, Monographs Supplement*, No. 2 (Cambridge, 1939) cited in Wright, pp. 413, 346.

42 Gunnar Myndal, *Population: A Problem for Democracy* (Cambridge, MA: Harvard University Press, 1938 [Godkin lecture]).

43 Tom H. Pear, *Psychological Factors of Peace and War* (London: Hutchinson, 1950).

44 S. Freud and A. Einstein, *Open Letters* (Paris: International Institute of Intellectual Cooperation, 1933).

45 Harold D. Lasswell, *World Politics and Personal Insecurity* (New York: McGraw-Hill, 1965).

46 G.D.H. Cole, *Intelligent Man's Guide through World Chaos* (New York: Knopf, 1934).

47 Tota Ishimaru, *The Next World War*, trans. by B. Matsukawa (London: Hurst & Blackett, 1937).

48 George F. Eliot, *Bombs Bursting in Air: The Influence of Air Power on International Relations* (New York: Reynal & Hitchcock, 1939).

49 Hersch Lauterpacht, *The Function of Law in the International Community* (1933; repr. New Jersey: The Lawbook Exchange, 2002).

50 Hans Kelsen, *The Legal Process and International Order* (London: Constable & Company Limited, 1935).

51 J.L. Brierly, *The Law of Nations: An Introduction to the International Law of Peace* (Oxford: Clarendon Press, 1955).

52 Correspondence with Olson, July 1988.

53 Georg Schwarzenberger, *International Law and Totalitarian Lawlessness* (London: Cape, 1943).

54 Georg Schwarzenberger, *Power Politics*, 2nd edition, 1951, p. 8.

55 R. Strausz-Hupé, *Geopolitics: The Struggle for Space and Power* (New York: Putnam, 1942), p. xii.

56 T. Kalijarvi, *Modern World Politics* (New York: Thomas Crowell Co., 1943), p. vii.

57 Edward Mead Earle, Gordon Alexander Craig and Felix Gilbert (eds), *Makers of Modern Strategy: Military Thought from Machiavelli to Hitler* (Princeton: Princeton University Press, 1943).

58 Nicholas J. Spykman and Helen R. Nicholl, *Geography of the Peace* (New York: Harcourt, Brace and Co, 1944).

59 Nicholas J. Spykman, *America's Strategy in World Politics: The United States and the Balance of Power* (New Brunswick: Transaction Publishers, 1942).

60 W.T.R. Fox, *The Super-Powers: United States, Britain and the Soviet Union – Their Responsibility for Peace* (New York: Harcourt, Brace and Co, 1944), p. 3. Grafton's sentence appeared in the *New York Post* on November 23, 1943.

61 Lucian M. Ashworth, 'Did the Realist-Idealist Debate Ever Happen?' *International Relations*, April 2002.

62 Reinhold Niebuhr, *Moral Man and Immoral Society* (London: SCM Press, 1963). We have used the British edition published in 1963.

63 *Ibid.*, p. xi

64 *Ibid.*, p. xx.

65 *Ibid.*, pp. 3–4

66 *Ibid.*, p. 15.

67 *Ibid.*, p. 16.

68 *Ibid.*, pp. 18–19.

69 *Ibid.*, pp. 251–252.

70 *Ibid.*, p. 233.

71 See Michael Cox, 'Introduction' to E.H. Carr, *The Twenty Years' Crisis, 1919–1939* (Basingstoke: Palgrave Macmillan, 2001).

72 Cox, *Ibid.*; Charles Jones, *E.H. Carr and International Relations* (Cambridge: Cambridge University Press, 1998); Jonathan Haslam, *The Vices of Integrity: E.H. Carr 1892–1982* (London: Verso, 1999).

73 E.H. Carr, *Twenty Years' Crisis, 1919–1939*. Reissued with a new preface from Michael Cox (Basingstoke: Palgrave Macmillan, 2016).

74 Quoted in Haslam, *op. cit.*, p. 253.

75 Quoted in *Ibid.*, p. 252.

76 Quoted in *Ibid.*, p. 252.

77 David Long and Peter Wilson (eds), *Thinkers of the Twenty Years' Crisis* (Oxford: Clarenden, 1995), p. 311.

78 E.H. Carr, *The Twenty Years' Crisis, 1919–1939* (Basingstoke: Macmillan, 1961), second edition, p. 11.

79 *Ibid.*, p. 11.

80 *Ibid.*, p. 19.

81 *Ibid.*, p. 89.

82 *Ibid.*, p. 93.

83 Georg Schwarzenberger, *Power Politics: A Study of International Society* (London: Stevens, 1951), second edition, p. 3.

84 *Ibid.*, p. 8.

85 In Schwarzenberger's view, "power politics may be defined as a system of international relations in which groups consider themselves to be ultimate ends; use, at least for vital purposes, the most effective means at their disposal and are graded according to their weight in case of conflict." Power is the currency of this system and "may be defined as capacity to impose one's will on others by reliance on effective sanctions in cases of non-compliance . . . The essence of power is the ability to exercise compelling pressure irrespective of its reasonableness" (*Ibid.*, p. 12).

86 *Ibid.*, p. 14.

87 Hans. J. Morgenthau, *Scientific Man versus Power Politics* (Chicago: University of Chicago Press, 1946).

88 Hans. J. Morgenthau, *Politics among Nations: The Struggle for Peace and Power* (New York: Alfred Knopf, 1959), second edition, revised and enlarged.

89 *Ibid.*, p. 4.

90 *Ibid.*, p. 5.

91 *Ibid.*, p. 8.

92 *Ibid.*, p. 25.

93 *Ibid.*, pp. 16–17.

94 *Ibid.*, p. 30.

95 *Ibid.*, p. 31.

96 *Ibid.*, p. 36.

97 *Ibid.*, pp. 155 *et seq.*

98 *Ibid.*, p. 156.

99 *Ibid.*, pp. 175–176.

100 *Ibid.*, p. 26.

6   The second consensus

The quest for power

The nuclear age that emerged from secrecy in the late summer of 1945 transformed the nature of world politics. The usual new configuration of powers that follows wars differed this time in that there were now two giant states engaged almost at once in a confrontation. There was a second attempt at world organisation, this time embracing all the victorious Powers. Just as the 1919 peace settlement and the early promise of the League produced a literature dominated by international organisation, nuclear weapons would give rise to strategic studies.[1] Now the Cold War would take precedence, with its politico-strategic orientation serving to affect nearly every aspect of the study of international relations. Although it became more disciplined in terms of recognition of the need for more of what Thompson termed "rigor of analysis,"[2] it was also dominated more by power than by balance.

However constructive they may have been, the contradictions of the depression decade leading up to the war, which was extended to most of the world in 1941, stood in stark contrast to the hopeful consensus of the relatively prosperous League period. A new, less optimistic level of consensus, anticipated by Schuman and Carr and buttressed by the experience of the war itself, was to be a consensus of power. A new breed of internationalists nevertheless asserted themselves in an earnest outpouring of meetings, resolutions, pamphlets, organisations and pledges of postwar cooperation. If the Charter of the new United Nations was in fact a realistic document,[3] this was not understood as such by many of its most ardent and idealistic supporters. It was realist in that it provided for the mobilisation of power collectively to face aggression, and it did this more effectively than had the Covenant of the League. In neither case did the problem lie in the document, but in its application. Shortly after the UN's founding, the rude awakening provided by Joseph Stalin's speech on 9 February 1946, reaffirming Marxist-Leninist predictions of an inevitable confrontation with capitalism, convinced most observers that, far from being an alternative to power politics, the UN was destined to become its arena.

A new generation of analysis of IR

The centrality – if not the exclusivity – of power had already been stressed by the wartime mainstream writers. An important transitional anthology based upon US Navy officer training courses in universities during the war, *Foundations of National Power* (1945) by Harold and Margaret Sprout, became the first widely used text of the postwar period, stressing national rather than collective security (although successive editions would move towards a more planetary perspective). Soon after, E.H. Carr published the second edition of his *Twenty-Years' Crisis* (1946). In its preface, Carr wrote that, although he had altered nothing of substance, he had departed in two respects from his prewar thinking (actually, there were three, any reference to his controversial defence of the Munich deal now being omitted). One was that the "almost total neglect of the factor of power"[4] by utopians had now been overcome; he even acknowledged that his judgements in 1939 might have been "rather one-sided" in this regard, which confirms the findings earlier concerning the mainstream inter-war literature. The second change was even more interesting (and one wonders whether this would have been written at all had there been a third edition after the Cold War set in): his first edition "too readily and too complacently accepts the existing nation-state, large or small, as the unit of international society."[5] The basic idea was that the unit of analysis in IR should not be the state but, in the tradition of Protagoras, the individual.

While casting his analysis in international societal terms, Schwarzenberger did not change his basic paradigm this far in his 1951 edition. Indeed, he placed an entire new section on the economic, social, educational and other non-political programmes of the UN under the heading of "power politics in disguise." By now it was evident that the old consensus based upon establishing the basis for a cooperative world was not to be restored. Based upon power and coercive capability, the die was cast for a new consensus, although it was within a decade to face challenges which would come not from one but from many different directions. In terms of a second consensus this may have been an advance, but in interdisciplinary terms it must be seen as a retreat, because other disciplines, notably economics, but also diplomatic history and geography, were to be given less emphasis. Another thrust served to 'skew' the way in which the discipline grew, and that was an unstructured 'paper triangle' between academic entrepreneurs, the great foundations and the national security establishment. The principal effect, particularly though not exclusively in the United States, was to stress regional and strategic studies at the expense of universal and functional perspectives.

At the same time, Chatham House reinvigorated its original dual commitment to the systematic analysis of international affairs and to public education, with the new Royal Institute series "Looking forward." *Power Politics* (No. 8) appeared in 1946. In it, Martin Wight, an author usually associated with the 'English School,'[6] dealt with very broad concepts appropriate for responsible, decision-makers and attentive citizens, such as law, geography, the nation, freedom, science, trade, and the UK and the World. Especially in a revised and expanded form published in 1978, it is a classic, rich in historical and philosophical insight: "What we mean by power politics," wrote Wight, "came into existence when medieval Christendom dissolved and the modern sovereign state was born."[7] In discussing 'Beyond power politics,' he carried his perspective into the future:

> In the study of international politics we are dogged by the insistent problem, whether the relations between Powers are in fact more than "power politics" as the popular sense of the term, and whether they can become more. From one point of view, the middle view, the central question is how far Powers can be said to have interest in common . . . But the idea of common interest can never have much vitality if it is separated from the idea of common obligation.[8]

Wight argues that, although there had always been a theory of international politics asserting the primacy of such common ideas as law, right and justice, the tradition of natural law as the basis of international law had now been "eclipsed by the new revolutionary creed of progress." But another tradition, that of the international community, although weakened by colonialism, had never completely faded and "still gleams faintly in the preamble of the Charter."[9] Yet Wight could not be optimistic. He took his place among the new realists creating a second consensus in the discipline.

Shortly after this Royal Institute study was published, a survey prepared for its sister house in New York by Grayson Kirk on the basis of six conferences of IR professors in every part of the United States, provided a quite different basis for judgement. Although not a text, *The Study of International Relations* (1947) was perhaps the closest the Council on Foreign Relations ever came to emulating the Institute's initial objective of scientific analysis, or the *study* of IR along with the study of international affairs *qua* politics. Kirk found that prevailing opinion favoured introducing a course of study with "a general survey of the field," covering:

1   The nature and operation of the state system
2   Factors which affect the power of the state
3   International position and foreign policies of the great powers
4   The history of recent international relations
5   The building of a more stable world order.

Whereas Wight and Carr's contributions served to challenge old paradigms and to raise the intellectual focus of a still relatively new field, Kirk's contributions provided a kind of consensual springboard into the second postwar era. The year following his survey saw one of the most significant events in the history of the field, the inauguration of the journal *World Politics*. It covered ground that the Council's venerable and stately *Foreign Affairs* seemed almost to disdain – the scholarly world of methodology, theory and model-building, appealing to researchers and teachers in academe more than to those in positions of power in banking, government and industry.

Among the authors of the many texts that appeared after Kirk, most undertook at least a brief review of 'the study.' IR was still far from being a well-organised discipline, wrote Norman Palmer and Howard Perkins of the University of Pennsylvania in *International Relations* (1953). Having "emerged from its earlier status as a poor relation of political science and history," it had been plagued more recently by the "extreme" schools of utopianism and a realism emphasising the "virtual inevitability of war." IR is a very inexact science, they concluded, "in fact, it is hardly a science at all."[10] Norman Padelford and George Lincoln disagreed, writing in their book:

> Francis Bacon once spoke of Science as the "endless frontier." Today, the people of this country and other free nations are being increasingly impressed with the fact that international politics is a realm of endless frontier . . . our objective has been to stress those fundamental elements and foundational principles which . . . underlie the policies and actions of nations.[11]

The policy orientation was given further emphasis by Ernst Haas and Allen Whiting, who argued in their text that:

> [t]he ends of foreign policy are qualitatively similar to ends implicit in any other field of politics . . . The scheme of international affairs which emerges is thus a compendium of the ways in which shapers and conditioners of policy view their mutual interrelations . . . The methodological challenge of this approach has been severe.[12]

All seemed to agree that the field had now been established as a distinct, legitimate academic subject, but whether it was a 'science' was another thing. Carr's utopian phase in the development of the science of international relations had long since come to an end, if, indeed, it had ever existed. Others had joined him in the assault upon utopianism, notably the distinguished diplomat George Kennan in *American Diplomacy, 1900–1950* (1951) and the realist theologian Reinhold Niebuhr in *Moral Man and Immoral Society: A Study in Ethics and Politics* (1952). It now remained to be seen whether IR could move ahead into a more mature second phase in the tradition of other disciplines.

The answer was not long in forthcoming. The terms 'science' and 'scientific,' so dear to the early savants of Chatham House Charter,[13] again appeared, now on a somewhat higher level of sophistication. They had apparently meant hardly more than comprehensive, objective and systematic analysis as an antidote to the self-serving, short-sighted propaganda of politicians, publicists and especially governments. To them, science could perhaps be seen as the contemporary historians' answer to a charge that their discipline constituted something of a contradiction in terms; true history would not be written accurately until all the evidence was in, which meant until the diplomatic archives were open. Readers of the *Survey of International Affairs* could not wait that long, so Toynbee and his small band of colleagues had to proceed as systematically as possible in the pursuit of the scientific study of international affairs with what they had. Wright was to point out that "international relations is a field extraordinarily difficult for science to enter."[14] That depends upon how 'science' is defined. The Marxist paradigm, for example, seemed to move from a mastery of an understanding of the inevitability of historical forces, to predictability, to scientific certainty, all based upon an understanding of the politico-economic process that enabled true believers to claim to know what was coming. Carr had suggested more appropriate definitions, and Hans J. Morgenthau, the next major figure to employ the term 'scientific,' exerted an even stronger transforming influence, as we have seen earlier.

In his first postwar contribution, *Scientific Man vs Power Politics* (1946), Morgenthau was engaged in "the search for the general causes of which particular events are but outward manifestations."[15] It is these events that demonstrate the inability of contemporary society to understand and cope with political issues – a "general decay in political thinking" represented most typically in the conviction that science could solve all problems – so the "purpose of this book is to show why this belief in the redeeming powers of science is misplaced."[16]

This was not a rejection of science. "The Science of International Politics" (Part I of *Principles and Problems in International Politics* (1950), an anthology of classical essays, speeches and documents edited with a younger Chicago colleague, Kenneth W. Thompson) represented an attempt to apply a more systematic method of understanding to this science. The authors start with a frank contrast between two schools of thought concerning the proper content of the subject: the eclectic and the systematic. Representative of the first of these was the work of Zimmern. Acknowledging Zimmern's inter-war leadership of the field since his approach at International Studies Conferences seemed to go unchallenged, Morgenthau and Thompson stressed his "extreme vagueness," his "unconcern with methodological problems" and his "aimless humanitarianism."[17] The eclectic school combined all kinds of disparate fields, apparently from agriculture to zoology, "seeing in the qualifying adjective 'international' the common denominator with which to transform this mass of unconnected material into one field of international relations." The second school, which they saw as dominant in institutions of higher learning, "applies a systematic principle of selection to the great mass of phenomena which transcend the frontiers of a particular nation and therefore fall in the general category of 'international' . . . it finds that systematic principle in the power relations of sovereign states."[18]

Power politics as the core

As mentioned in the previous chapter, Morgenthau's more influential and more lasting text, *Politics among Nations*,[19] has gone through several editions. Less openly 'scientific' and more conventional (although in an unconventional manner) than the anthology, it concluded that the only real way to deal effectively with power was through the quality of diplomacy, a concept which led naturally to one of several novel approaches of the following decade: decision-making. Elaborating upon Carr, who had criticised utopianism in general terms, Morgenthau was explicit in attacking three equally ineffective kinds of international efforts to place limitations upon national power. After a classically brilliant interpretation of the first of these – the balance of power – he proceeded to show how uncertain, unrealistic and inadequate it is. Then after noting the frequency with which some kind of world moral consensus is cited, he observed that "as for the influence of that system of supranational ethics upon the actors on the international scene, it is rather like the feeble rays, barely visible above the horizon of consciousness, of a sun which has already set."[20] Similarly, "a world public opinion restraining the international policies of national governments is a mere postulate; the reality of international affairs shows as yet hardly a trace of it."[21] Sometimes mistakenly accused of rejecting the place of moral force in politics (effectively corrected years later in his *Truth and Power*[22] in 1970 as well as in the successive editions of *Politics among Nations*), Morgenthau actually merely insisted that its place be better understood. Universal morality – or internationalism – had lost out to "nationalistic universalism," as a tremendous force in world politics. As for any "psychological unity of the world which in the form of public opinion could or would ever restrain the holders of national power," he simply denied that it existed at the time[23] because of the obstacle of nationalism. Morgenthau regarded international law as a third inadequate limitation on power, but again not in totally negative terms; his delineation of its proper legislative and judicial function is perhaps as good an introduction as can be found. His emphasis upon the central problem of enforceability clarifies what is obscured by both extremes on this issue: those who say, 'it isn't law if it can't be enforced,' and those who appear to believe that just because it is called 'law,' it can.

Possibly encouraged by the notable success of *Politics Among Nations*, texts in IR now began to proliferate, particularly in the United States. No fewer than eight appeared from 1954 to 1956. The acceptance of international obligations, initially under the Charter but very soon within an 'entangling alliance' called NATO, created a political climate in which mainstream IR texts flourished. What did they say and how did they say it?

The period of the second consensus

To define this period of essential agreement, just over twenty standard texts of the realist period of 1945 to 1960 have been compared, including the fourth and fifth editions of the venerable Schuman, still then one of the most widely used and popular of all books ever written on IR. About twenty-five distinct topics were now put forth as constituting principal divisions of the subject matter of IR. Actual chapter titles varied a great deal, although the areas of concern did not, so they are grouped under major substantive categories. Taking those covered by more than two-thirds of the authors and listing them in order of frequency, a composite consensual table of contents of texts during this prolific period might look something like this:

1   Power politics
2   International organisation, the new world order, and peace

3   Sovereignty and international law
4   Strategic studies
5   Nationalism, ideology and propaganda
6   Foreign policy analysis
7   Imperialism or colonialism
8   Economic and technological issues.

Regional topics, particularly in the context of the Cold War, were given prominence by a majority (though less than two-thirds) of the authors. Population was also given major attention. The study of IR as a discipline or at least a separate field now occupied many a preface and even occasionally a substantive chapter. There were many different ways of approaching the same topic; consensus did not require absolute consistency.[24]

Three aspects stand out when this model table of contents is compared with that following the First World War: there was now less emphasis upon diplomatic history, or 'what caused the war' topics; economics played a less prominent role in the analysis of IR; and a preoccupation with power had replaced the concern for peaceful change. Of the authors of these texts, only three were 'British' (Bailey, Carr and Schwarzenberger). Where were the books by their successors from a country (the UK) that had been responsible for more than half the mainstream works of the 1920s? First of all, many of those works had been designed to educate the knowledgeable public, not teach students. Second, a textbook as such was rarely required by British teachers, whose course syllabi were based on extensive library reading lists and whose writing was more specialised than 'IR.' A third reason was, simply, the 'market.' Instead of writing 'required texts,' European authors had to persuade publishers that their books had appeal, not only for pundits of press and pulpit but also for the concerned general reader. But the most notable attempt to do that came from one man, an American, and not through a textbook.

What is still one of the prime intellectual achievements in the discipline's history, *The Study of International Relations*,[25] was published in 1955. It grew out of several years of advanced seminars taught by Wright, who had completed his impressive two-volume *Study of War* thirteen years earlier.[26] Given "all this activity" (in the shape of the proliferation of textbooks, courses and conferences on what is called 'international relations'), Wright impishly began, "there might seem to be little doubt that international relations exists. Yet there is some doubt on this point or, at least, on the sense in which it exists."[27] He then proceeded to deal fairly comprehensively with almost every conceivable sense in which IR might be said to exist.

Wright's opus is divided into five parts: the meaning of international relations, objectives in its study, practical analyses, theoretical analyses and 'towards a unified discipline' of IR, dealing with conceptions, approaches, form and the value of such a discipline. Successfully encompassing this vast range, Wright achieved a combination of generic eclecticism with systematic rigour. Not all of them were convinced; for example, Harold Lasswell, in a basically sympathetic review in *World Politics*, concluded a year or so after its publication that "on the central theme there are grave reservations to be made" regarding the future of IR "as a discernible discipline."[28]

A new round of conferences

C.A.W. Manning and Geoffrey Goodwin of the London School of Economics and Political Science renewed a practice going back to the 1920s in meeting with other IR scholars in various parts of the world. Concentration was upon the teaching of IR in Europe, although countries as distant and divergent as India and the United States participated. Two of the most valuable of these interchanges took place in 1950 and 1954.

The stated purpose of the first of these, which brought together scholars from eight countries, was to discuss "the more important views on the desirability, or otherwise, of making more general provision for the inclusion of International Relations, as an independent discipline, in the curriculum of University students."[29] This faced the issue head on. The General Rapporteur carefully analysed why this was still a problem, citing four possible University responses to growing student interest in IR. The first was wholly negative, involving doubts concerning the subject itself: its very existence, its nature, its social value, its unitary character, its necessity, and even its 'academic merits,' to say nothing of technical feasibility and staffing problems. Most of these reservations could not only be answered but could be directed at other new subjects as well. A second response would simply give somewhat more attention in the curriculum to the international aspects of subjects already being taught, adding no new ones. A third involved grouping portions of modern history, economics and political institutions under a distinctive category of 'so-called' international studies. Finally, there could be genuine acceptance of a new independent discipline of IR.

The conference concluded that there was clearly a "widely felt need for the extension of the study and teaching of international relations." It had "not yet received due recognition," partly because of "structural differences" between universities in different countries. Turning to substance rather than form, it was agreed that what was needed now was "a greater comprehension of the structure and functioning of international society."[30] In other words, the discipline could not and should not ever try to separate itself from the political environment of which it was a part. IR could perform an important synthesising role in overcoming the fragmentation of knowledge, an opportunity being stressed at the same time at Chicago by Wright and his colleagues. Jacob Viner, for example, not only offered international economics for budding economists but also a special course for those in the Chicago IR programme, probably the first in the country at the doctoral level.

Separate reports from five of the participating countries were filed. Only two, the UK and the United States, could demonstrate that progress had clearly been made towards an integrated discipline of IR. Several syllabi from universities in the UK were summarised; for example, at Aberdeen, a one-year course as a subsidiary subject for the MA encompassed the fields of international history (to 1939), public international law, international organisation and the 'study of some contemporary international problems.' Neither economics nor geography was required.

However, as Goodwin pointed out in his summation:

> There is no call to urge teachers of International Relations to agree on a uniform methodology, but perhaps the claims of the subject will gather strength if it can gain in unity and coherence by the development of a more systematised conceptual framework within which the constituent parts can form a better integrated and articulated whole. Such a development is the responsibility of teachers of the subject; it will not be furthered by extravagant doctrinal claims by one teacher or another but rather by a sensitive empiricism on the part of all. Then the very diversity of approach reflected in this note need not be regarded as a reproach but rather as a sign of growing vitality.[31]

In the United States, the professors from several conventional departments which made up the Yale Institute of International Studies provided a prestigious IR masters and doctoral programme (the UK concern was at the undergraduate level not postgraduate degrees). At Yale, requirements were grouped very simply under five headings: diplomatic history, international politics, methods and instruments of control, international economics and regional studies. Ironically, its highly selected graduates often found themselves teaching in a conventional government or political science department in the absence of a separate department specific to the discipline in which they had just been trained. While it mattered little to most, some felt that PhD granting implied a mandate to promote separate departments to which graduates would logically be drawn in future years. Had the Yale Institute not been broken up, it might have advanced to this level of discipline-building. Instead, the field tended more and more to become an especially lively sub-field of political science, although in the UK the interdependent, interdisciplinary nature of IR was never in doubt.

The Paris conference, summarised in a volume in a UNESCO series entitled simply *International Relations*, carried out a 1954 General Conference resolution "to undertake surveys in some countries of the types of consensus and methods of instruction in the social sciences."[32] Contrasting experiences in Egypt, France, India, Mexico, Sweden, the United Kingdom, the United States and Yugoslavia revealed the near impossibility of discovering any consensus at all on any aspect of the inquiry, at least outside the Anglo-American world. For example, the spokesman from India, Dr A. Appadorai, reported that "little headway" had so far been made introducing IR "as an integrated subject" there, and that "such teaching of international relations as exists" is done in courses in history, economics, politics and law. Although one French delegate, V.J. Chevallier, optimistically asserted that "all that is required is to establish a meeting point, a crossroads, a place of assembly, a point of convergence for the several avenues of approach," a colleague was less sanguine. M. Vernant argued that as long as there was no possible liaison in studies between two *groups* of subjects (sociology, anthropology, psychology) and (history, law, economics), there was no way for French universities to set up "in a healthy form, the teaching of International Relations." In Egypt, M.A. Yehia asserted that, even though there were numerous fully qualified teachers in "subdivisions of the field of study prescribed as international relations," the university system with its internal regulations did not permit an interested student to "follow a full course" in IR. Similarly, Karl Birnbaum of Sweden admitted that the prospects of IR achieving independent status in institutions there were "very poor." Even though in Mexico an Institute of High International Studies was established in 1952, "the truth is that, for advanced studies in the field of international affairs, the youth of Mexico have thereafter been, for the most part, obliged to go abroad." And so it went. It may be, as Arnold Wolfers and Laurence Martin suggested in *The Anglo-American Tradition in Foreign Affairs* in 1956, that the two countries shared world views that were not shared by the rest of the world. As we have seen, Grosser of the *Institut d'Etudes Politiques* in Paris (Sciences Po), argued in a paper[33] published that same year, that IR was in fact an American subject, and indeed it would be another generation before the field really took hold in France.

A contrast needs to be pointed out at this juncture between US academic programmes and standard IR texts. As a degree subject, IR was almost invariably interdisciplinary, whereas textbooks tended to be state-centric, generally power oriented, with an emphasis upon foreign policy. Two reasons suggest themselves for this. First, in the absence of a department of IR, a committed student interested in the subject took what he could in a political science department, where economics and other collateral disciplines were secondary if they were brought in at all. Second, textbooks were not only written for the most part *by* political scientists but were designed primarily for use *in* a single political science course on international politics (which might or might not have been part of a broader major in IR), rather than as an introduction to the overall subject. But where Padelford and Lincoln had been explicit in making the distinction, conceiving of their book *International Politics* as covering only *part* of 'international relations,' the two terms tended to be employed interchangeably.[34] On the other hand, to Charles Merriam and his followers in 'the Chicago school of political science,' power was the *integrating* concept in municipal, national and global politics. IR was simply a special case, just as to Frederick Sherwood Dunn (who was responsible for developing the Yale Institute to its one-time position of eminence), IR was "politics in the absence of central authority."[35] Could not one postulate that the difference is that political science is politics *within the context* of an entity with a central authority? But this raises questions about the effectiveness and legitimacy of the central authority. Beyond mature democracies was there always a great difference between the anarchy of the international system and that within states?

One of the most informative interpretations of the stage at which IR had arrived in 1960 was a paper prepared by Annette Baker Fox and William T.R. Fox and first presented at NATO headquarters in Paris at "The Conference on International Relations in the University," and later published by the Institute of International Studies at the University of South Carolina. They predicted that "in the next decade some of the problems which have emerged in the United States will be seen as problems of the extended North American–West European–British Commonwealth family of scholars in international relations."[36] With the realist Max Beloff of Oxford in the chair, twenty-five or so specialists such as Grosser and J.B. Duroselle of France, Manning and P.A. Reynolds of the UK, and Fox and Olson of the United States confronted essentially the same issues as had earlier gatherings, but on a narrower geographical base and one with strategic policy undertones.

Contradictory conclusions can be drawn from these and other postwar conferences. One was that there was an awareness of a *need* in all the countries to develop and integrate the study as a distinct field. The other was that only modest progress had been made towards that end. Most degree programmes were covered, not by separate departments but by teams or committees drawn from the traditional disciplines, such as the long-standing programme at Pomona College in California. Given the unhurried nature of change in universities, where doubts still remained as to whether such an uncertain and contemporary subject belonged there at all, this was not surprising. According to the old saying, war was too important a subject to be left to the generals; it could now be said that both peace and war were too important to be left out of academe. It was this conviction that led President Dwight Eisenhower of Columbia University to invite Fox to establish an 'Institute of War and Peace Studies' in 1950. This served as a reminder of the contribution IR might make to the prevention of the next war (although in some other US contexts, it seemed designed more to help *win* the next war). Indeed, some felt that IR had become a 'Cold War subject.' The stress on power politics rarely went that far, however, and the new consensus it represented, at least its literature, was less a break with the first consensus than a refinement of it.

To what degree did both texts and conferences reflect this second consensus? Several features stand out when compared with the field's first and second decades. First of all, the study of international politics itself now often revealed a recognition or at least a consciousness of the degree to which IR had matured as a discipline. Second, the neglect of power so deplored by Carr and Morgenthau had been overcome. Indeed, power had become the hallmark of the discipline, at least in standard US texts. Third, conventional diplomatic history was given less attention, possibly because the locus of the field had moved from the historically minded UK to a US academic environment dominated by political science. In the fourth place, despite six years of global war followed by the Cold War, major attention was still being given to the original key elements, international law and organisation. Fifth, the distinct treatment of key regions and even countries stood out; indeed, 'area studies' itself was becoming a kind of discipline, some professors (notably J.B. Duroselle of Paris) regarding a global perspective as being too broad to be handled in a systematic manner. Finally, and possibly most importantly for an interdisciplinary perspective, economics was given less emphasis than in either earlier period. Texts were designed for courses in departments of political sciences where economics was regarded as belonging elsewhere.

The dual challenge: behaviouralism and quantification

An entirely new kind of literature was now beginning to present alternatives to mainstream thinking. It had been anticipated by the work of Harold Lasswell on the psychology of propaganda during the First World War and later by Otto Klineberg's notable 'tensions project' for the Social Science Research Council in 1950. The following year saw both psychologist George Kisker's anthology, *World Tension* (1951), and Frederick S. Dunn writing in a similar vein as an international lawyer by training and now Director of the Yale Institute in his *War and the Minds of Men*, a title obviously influenced by Archibald MacLeish's famous preamble to the Constitution of UNESCO. But it was *Decision-Making as an Approach to the Study of International Politics* (Richard Snyder et al.) in 1954 and *System and Process in International Politics* (Morton Kaplan) in 1957 that were the prime examples of a new phase in the development of the discipline. The first of these logically grew out of Morgenthau's reliance on the quality of diplomacy, the second from Quincy Wright's longing for a unified if not quite scientific discipline. Of possibly more lasting impact was *Man, the State and War* by Kenneth Waltz (1959), in which he postulated that there were three "images" upon which answers to the timeless question "where are the major causes of war to be found?"[37] have been based. The first, he argues, lies within man himself ('human behaviour'), the second within separate states ('internal structure of states') and the third within the state system ('international anarchy'). Waltz's book became a major influence in the teaching of IR for a period of a quarter century. The critical contribution of L.F. Richardson needs again to be noted here; in an important work, *Arms and Insecurity* (1960), which correlated armaments and the outbreak of war, the role of mathematics in economics led him to ask, "whether mathematical language can also express the behavior of people in another situation where they act together in large groups, namely in relation to war."[38]

New standard texts continued to appear regularly, but their distinctive role in developing the field of study seemed now to have been exhausted, particularly in evaluating it from a level of explaining the latest headlines. We must turn elsewhere to find the growing points of the discipline, to discover what Klaus Knorr and James Rosenau were to call "contending approaches" to theory in IR. Fox contributed his historic *Theoretical Aspects of International Relations*[39] in 1959. Part of the 'fallout' group from the precipitous breakup of the Yale Institute, Knorr edited *The International System: Theoretical Essays*[40] with Sidney Verba, drawing upon economics less than one seeking an interdisciplinary foundation might have expected to do. Similarly, Stanley Hoffmann's *Contemporary Theory in International Relations*[41] was a well-regarded reader, stronger in philosophy, politics and sociology than in economics. Two years later there finally appeared the long-awaited study of the nature of international society by Manning,[42] capping many years of the intellectual strengthening of the conceptual foundations of the programme of studies at LSE.

Developing trends in thought revealed once again that novel insights rarely totally replace old approaches. They overlap. Some demonstrate more validity, more utility and more resilience than others. A few, like utopianism, disappear completely (or almost completely, for there are always those for whom the silver lining is the only reality). Others, as Annette Fox has pointed out, are essentially new, such as dependency theory, which emerged with the creation of new states in the wake of the breaking up of colonial empires, and integration theory, which has emerged from the creation of the European Community.[43] Still others, saddened perhaps by the barrenness of intellectual squabbling, plead for greater tolerance and mutual advantage from advocates of contending approaches. As Robert North put it constructively:

As research scholars and would-be theorists in international relations we might all derive at least three useful lessons from the old fable about the blind man and the elephant. The first is that the elephant presumably existed; the second is that each of the groping investigators, despite sensory and conceptual limitations, had his fingers on part of the reality; and the third is that if they had quieted the uproar and begun making comparisons, the blind men might – all of them – have moved considerably closer to the truth.[44]

At all events, the second definitional phase was now over. Many singular contributions to theory, often based upon challenges to a consensus based upon power, appeared. Partly in response to a need for a home for the expression of these ideas, the International Studies Association, dedicated to the interdisciplinary advancement of almost any serious approach, was created in the United States in 1960. Hence that year is a logical place to bring to a close any attempt to delineate sequentially the development of ideas.

Basic alternatives to the power politics approach, as it had been set forth by Schuman, Carr and Morgenthau, and confirmed by many others, now demanded attention. The classical state-centric paradigm which had dominated the discipline since its inception was about to encounter the 'world society' and 'global village' approaches, as well as a growing concern with analytical method. A 'paradigmatic debate' was about to take place.

The methodological revolt took two closely related forms, the behavioural and the quantitative approaches to political science. First, just as Marxism had challenged the basic system of political and economic power, behaviouralism now challenged the accepted system of the analysis of power. With aggressive enthusiasm, the behaviouralists adapted relevant methodologies and conclusions from psychology, anthropology and sociology to the analysis of actors on the international stage. As Bruce Russett and Harvey Starr have observed,[45] deductive interpretations of politics such as the balance of power, man's search for the good life or the class struggle were rejected in favour of more inductive definitions based upon scientific analysis of the actual behaviour of human beings. Politics was defined in terms of *observable* 'ranges of action and reaction' instead of more abstract impressions and concepts. Second, the use of mathematics, assisted, if indeed not stimulated, by the increasingly widespread availability of computers, greatly enhanced research capability throughout the social sciences. Like behaviouralism, exponents of quantitative methodology tended to discredit older methodologies based upon historical and legal scholarship, partly because of the promise of results.

The behavioural and quantitative perspectives both promised for a time to engender an entirely new kind of scientific consensus. It featured what many regarded as excessive claims, particularly for predictive capability, and what to the uninitiated was a bewildering array of algebraic formulae. Neither in the end brought about such a consensus, but their contribution to the growth of the discipline was to be unmistakable, if not dominant. Debates such as those which erupted between the 'classical' Hedley Bull of Oxford (who had developed his ideas while still at the Australian National University), and in opposition to those of fellow Australian resident in the UK, John Burton, and the 'scientific' Morton Kaplan of Chicago, served in the long run to stimulate even more than to divide. As Hamid Mowlana has put it, IR was now analytical rather than descriptive, "with new models based on systems, games, bargaining, decision-making procedures, and multifarious other methods of approach . . . the result has been to emphasize the tangible, the formal, and the measurable."[46] Terms like 'post-behaviouralism,' 'structuralism' and 'neo-realism' later signalled a return to classical theory in a new guise. IR would now enter a pluralist phase. This parallel existence of many approaches was appropriately termed "the paradigmatic debate."[47] We now turn to that phase in which the unified theory that Wright sought would be even more remote.

Notes

1 See B. Buzan and L. Hansen, *The Evolution of International Security Studies* (Cambridge: Cambridge University Press, 2009).

2 'The Internationalist's Dilemma: Relevance and Rigor,' *International Studies Quarterly*, Vol. 12, No. 2, 1968, pp. 161–173.

3 See especially Chapter VII of the Charter of the United Nations, 'Actions with respect to threats to the peace, breaches of the peace and acts of aggression.'

4 Carr, *Twenty-Years' Crisis* (New York: St Martin's Press, 1946), second edition, p. vii.

5 *Ibid.*, p. viii.

6 See Tim Dunne, *Inventing International Society. A History of the English School* (Basingstoke: Palgrave, 1998).

7 *Power Politics*, ed. by Hedley Bull and Carsten Holbraad (New York: Penguin, 1979), p. 25. Published for the Royal Institute of International Affairs in 1946, the original work came to only sixty-eight pages and was presumably being expanded for later publication when Wight died in 1972, the editors completing the work from his drafts and notes.

8 *Ibid.*, p. 289.

9 *Ibid.*, p. 291.

10 Howard Palmer and Norman Perkins, *International Relations: The World Community in Transition* (Boston, MA: Houghton Mifflin, 1953), p. 6.

11 N.J. Padelford and G.A. Lincoln, *International Politics: Foundations of International Relations* (New York: Macmillan, 1954), p. v.

12 E. Haas and A. Whiting, *Dynamics of International Relations* (New York: McGraw-Hill, 1956), p. vii, considered by Fox as perhaps the best among the standard texts in providing a distinct contribution to the field (correspondence with Olson, July 1988).

13 Chatham House Charter (July 1926).

14 Wright, *Study of International Relations*, p. 115.

15 H.J. Morgenthau, *Scientific Man vs Power Politics* (Chicago, IL: The University of Chicago Press, 1946), p. v.

16 *Ibid.*, p. vi.

17 Morgenthau with Thompson, *Principles and Problems in International Politics*, pp. 18–19.

18 *Ibid.*, p. vii.

19 Hans Morgenthau, *Politics among Nations: The Struggle for Power and Peace* (New York: Alfred Kopf, 1948).

20 Morgenthau, *Politics among Nations*, p. 195.

21 *Ibid.*, p. 206.

22 Hans Morgenthau, *Truth and Power: Essays of a Decade* (California, CA: Praeger Publishers, 1970).

23 On the complex relation between realist thought and the possibility of a world state, see William Scheuerman, *The Realist Case for Global Reform* (Cambridge: Polity, 2011).

24 Of numerous commentaries on texts, one stands out, Rosenau's 'Of Syllabi, Texts, Students, and Scholarship in International Relations: Some Data and Interpretations on the State of a Burgeoning Field,' *World Politics*, Vol. XXIX, No. 2, 1977, pp. 263–340. Also particularly useful is Kenneth Boulding's review article on several current texts in *The Journal of Conflict Resolution*, Vol. VIII, No. 1, 1964, pp. 65–71.

25 Quincy Wright, *The Study of International Relations* (New York: Appleton-Century-Crofts, 1955).

26 Quincy Wright, *Study of War* (Chicago, IL: University of Chicago Press, 1942), 2 vols.

27 Quincy Wright, *Study of International Relations*, p. vii.

28 H. D. Lasswell, 'Some Reflections on the Study of International Relations,' *World Politics*, Vol. VIII, No. 4, 1956, p. 562.

29 Geoffrey L. Goodwin (ed.), *The University Teaching of International Relations* (Oxford: Blackwell, 1951), p. 5.

30 *Ibid.*, p. 36.

31 *Ibid.*, p. 126.

32 Manning, C.A.W., *International Relations* (Paris: UNESCO, 1954), p. 5.

33 'L'étude des relations internationales, specialité américaine?' *Revue Française de Science Politique*, Vol. VI, No. 3, 1956, pp. 634–651.

34 Quincy Wright, *Study of International Relations*, is particularly useful in defining this distinction (p. ix), as is Schwarzenberger, *Power Politics* (pp. 23–25).

35 Cited by W.T.R. Fox, 'Growing Points in the Study of International Relations,' address at the University of Southern California, October 1, 1966, reproduced in Fox, *The American Study of International Relations*, p. 100.

36 W.T.R. and Annette Baker Fox, 'The Teaching of International Relations in the United States,' *Ibid.*, p. 33.

37 K. Waltz, *Man, the State and War* (New York: Columbia University Press, 1959), p. 36.

38 L.F. Richardson, *Arms and Insecurity. A Mathematical Study of the Causes and Origins of War*, ed. by Nicholas Rashersky and Ernesto Trucco (Pittsburgh, PA: The Boxwood Press, 1960), p. xvii.

39 William T.R. Fox (ed.), *Theoretical Aspects of International Relations* (Notre Dame: University of Notre Dame Press, 1959).

40 Klaus Eugen Knorr and Sidney Verba (eds), *The International System: Theoretical Essays* (Princeton, NJ: Princeton University Press, 1965).

41 Stanley Hoffman, *Contemporary Theory in International Relations* (Englewood Cliffs, NJ: Prentice-Hall, 1960).

42 C.A.W. Manning, *The Nature of International Society* (London: G. Bell and Sons, 1962).

43 Correspondence with Olson, July 1988.

44 'Research Pluralism and the International Elephant,' in Klaus Knorr and James N. Rosenau (eds), *Contending Approaches to International Politics* (Princeton, NJ: Princeton University Press, 1969), p. 218.

45 Bruce Russett and Harvey Starr, *World Politics: A Menu for Choice* (San Francisco, CA: W.H. Freeman, 1981), pp. 3–41.

46 Hamid Mowlana, *Global Information and World Communication: New Frontiers in International Relations* (White Plains, NY: Longman, 1986), p. 177.

47 Part I of Margot Light and A.J.R. Groom (eds), *International Relations: A Handbook of Current Theory* (Littleton, CO: Lynne Reinner, 1985); see especially Michael Banks, 'The Inter-Paradigm Debate,' pp. 7–20 plus references.

Part II
Towards 'now'

7   A pause for reflection

Changes in approach are not usually immediate, wholehearted or effective. Indeed, anomalies are rarely so overwhelming and blindingly obvious that scholars are willing to jettison their intellectual baggage in order to re-equip themselves with a new set, which happens to be conveniently waiting, complete and convincing, ready for an instant switch. Normally it takes time and is the outcome of a messy and confused process. Although realism achieved an acknowledged salience, in the 1950s 'anomalies' began to disturb that remarkable state of intellectual cohesion. Some were red herrings in so far as the intellectual development of the field was concerned, such as behaviouralism, since it became evident eventually, but not until after a fierce intellectual debate characterised by many intemperate *ad hominem* exchanges, that behaviouralism was more a question of methodological proclivities than one of conceptual differences. 'Color It Morgenthau' was the title of a highly influential conference paper,[1] which demonstrated, in an authoritative manner, that most 'behavioural' research was firmly embedded in the realist framework. Other developments were not red herrings, but, although identifying anomalies in realism, they did not propose dispensing with it as a framework, in part because they were only concerned with aspects of the framework and in part because there was no convincing alternative readily available. Progressively, however, other approaches such as world society and structuralism were sketched out and their ancient intellectual provenances explored.

In many subjects there is a well-trodden and well-marked path across the field to the uncertainties of the frontiers of knowledge. In IR there is no such path, but a milling around in a field, the dimensions and shape of which are not known or are in dispute. We are not solving a puzzle with shapes of a fixed dimension and a final picture that is known to exist, we are struggling with a problem in which the shape of the pieces is not clear, neither is it known whether they can constitute a final picture. Indeed, different pieces (of empirical data) suggest different pictures (or conceptual frameworks).

IR is both exasperating and exciting. It is exasperating because there is no conceptual consensus, but also, thereby, exciting, since the search for a new conceptual framework is currently exercising the minds of some of the most talented scholars in IR. There have been fifty years of debate and, more profitably, of discussion since the heyday of realism. The purpose of this part of the book is to point to benchmarks in this literature. As new alternatives emerged, the disciplinary balance between the twin centres of the UK and the United States altered, and new centres are appearing over the intellectual horizon.

Until the 1950s the UK and the United States were the 'Big Two' in intellectual and disciplinary terms where IR was flourishing. There was a separate and isolated Marxist tradition, virtually forgotten but for a few in the Western academic world who mostly ridiculed and despised it. Thereafter, mirroring events in the political world, the relationship between the UK and the United States was by now asymmetrical. In the UK, major contributions to the conceptualisation of world society were made by Mitrany and Burton, although neither was born in the UK and both were controversial figures there. In the realist vein, Martin Wight achieved almost a cult status as much for his teaching as for his writing, and Hedley Bull (like Burton an Australian) made his mark with *éclat* in defence of the traditional approach and, more conventionally, in continuing the Wight tradition and revitalising the 'English School.'

As a body of work, the English School focuses on uncovering "the nature and function of international societies . . . trac[ing] their history and development."[2] Its three main concepts are those of international system, international society and world society. From those three, the concept of international society is the one most directly related to the English School 'brand.' The international system is known as an eminent realist concept – states interact in an anarchical system – and world society, in the English School version, follows from the Kantian tradition and focuses on the individual as the focus of global societal identities. International society accepts the unstable nature of the international relations while accepting that states tend to navigate through that uncertainty by the shared acceptance and promotion of common norms and rules. In that regard, the concept of international society is informed by the normative vision that norms and rules shape states' behaviour. It also accepts that the international realm is evolutionary, which means that norms can become obsolete or be created depending on each historical moment. The international society is, in that sense, a dynamic reality. However, it also an order-setting mechanism that can contribute to regulate conflicts and promote peace. Some states benefit more from it than others, but there is an overall balance between order and justice that is accepted by all of its members that gives stability to a given international society.

The English School aside, for the most part, it was a matter of getting on the US band-wagon or getting nowhere.[3] Moreover, like the Marxist tradition before it, structuralism did not take firm root in the British intellectual climate. Mitrany, Burton and Bull were among the few UK-based scholars to make an academic impact of note beyond the UK in the last decades of the twentieth century, and they did this chiefly through their participation in the academic discourse in the United States.

The reasons for this are not difficult to discern. In the United States the number of scholars and students, the demand for textbooks and monographs, the market for journals and an academic structure based on the 'publish or perish' syndrome, all contributed to the growing asymmetry. Moreover the state, and especially the military and foundations, offered patronage to scholars in the United States undreamed of in the UK. Indeed, UK scholars would hardly have known how to put such resources to good use. The United States was a super Power in more than one sense, but one with an insular mentality. As Holsti demonstrated in *The Dividing Discipline*, the profession in the United States has been less open to outside influences since the late 1980s than previously.[4] Parochialism was rife in the intellectual hegemon, and unjustifiably so. For those in the periphery, it was necessary, and a struggle, to get access to the discipline through the centre, but they had new things to say.

It was, happily, a different story in the structuralist paradigm. Here the intellectual thrust came as much from Scandinavia, Germany and above all from Latin America, as from the United States. Not unnaturally, conceptions of the periphery were often and fruitfully conceived in the periphery, but surprisingly (given the theory), they were taken up by a resolute few in the centre in the United States. Only in recent decades have more exchanges started taking place between regions, languages and culture groups from Australasia to Latin America.[5] Indeed, it is difficult to avoid a suspicion that new frameworks are in the making and old ones are being reformulated. We shall allow ourselves a cautious speculation in our final chapter, but we have a feeling that a consideration of IR may now have a distinctly changed air about it from that which preceded it.

Notes

1 John Handelman, Michael O'Leary, John Vasquez and William Coplin, 'Color It Morgenthau,' ISA Conference Paper, 1973 (mimeo).
2 B. Buzan 'The English School: An Underexploited Resource in IR,' *Review of International Studies*, Vol. 27, 2001, p. 477.
3 As recently as 2001 Barry Buzan, one of its main actors lamented in a *Review of International Studies* article that the English School was "an underutilized research resource and deserves a larger role in IR than it currently has" in *op. cit.*, p. 471.
4 J.K. Holsti, *The Dividing Discipline* (Winchester: Allen & Unwin, 1985), pp. 105–107.
5 See A.J.R. Groom: 'IR Goes Worldwide,' in Fredrik Bynander and Stefano Guzzini (eds), *Rethinking Foreign Policy* (Oxford: Routledge, 2013) and Arlene B. Tickner and Ole Wæver (eds), *International Relations Scholarship Around the World* (Oxford: Routledge, 2009).

8   Breaking the mould

The consensus on the conceptual mould of realism was not shattered by a single revolutionary insight, but by a plurality of approaches that matured in the 1960s and 1970s. As the axioms of power politics were found to be incomplete or wanting, it became necessary to think in terms of the reform of realism or, failing that, of its replacement. Indeed, Morgenthau, him-self, had lamented the decline, in the postwar world, of the conditions most propitious for the proper working of the balance of power – a view echoed cogently by Inis Claude.[1] But the very axioms of power politics were challenged by John Burton[2] and later, from the perspec-tive of political theory, by Charles Beitz, and empirically, in a behaviouralist mode, by John Vasquez.[3] By then an agenda had emerged, which gave emphasis to the questions of the degree of state-centricity in the contemporary world and that of the pervasiveness of power politics.

Various writers began to edge away from the state as the basic unit of analysis. Among these were systems theorists, such as Morton Kaplan and David Easton, and writers in com-parative politics, such as Gabriel Almond, all of whom had a significant influence.[4] However, they did not stray far from a state-centric framework. For Easton and Almond it was a ques-tion of 'states conceived as systems' within which processes were of fundamental importance and interest, while the fertile mind of Morton Kaplan explored a 'system of states' – the international system – in terms of the traditional concerns of power politics, such as the bal-ance of power.

Karl Deutsch, in his innovative work on integration,[5] was looking towards the creation of a state, and in his formulation of a cybernetic model he gave us new insights into how a state might work.[6] But Deutsch also pointed to some nagging anomalies in the realist framework. Peace in the form of a security community did not, he discovered, require a Leviathan, but could be just as efficaciously found, if not more so, through a pluralistic framework involving not only governments but other elites and even the masses. In addition, cybernetics suggested a move from 'power,' based on instinct and drives, to 'steering' based on feedback processes, which could be applied to *any* social organisation. Deutsch therefore opened the way to the challenge to the state as *the* unit of analysis, and this challenge was taken up with alacrity by Burton, who also latched onto the movement from power to steering and applied it to the theory of non-alignment and, later, to problem-solving.

Burton's challenge to state-centricity and realism was not the first to make a mark. David Mitrany had, between the wars and during his war years in the Foreign Office, looked to functional solutions for the creation of a 'working peace system.'[7] With its emphasis on transactions, security by association and the obsolete and dangerous nature of the existing state system, Mitrany's work again became a focus of interest. These ideas did not find particularly fertile ground in the UK. They were more fructuous in the United States and contributed to the flowering of the neofunctionalist school. On the continent, functionalist ideas were adopted in a pragmatic fashion by practitioners such as Jean Monnet, in what was to be the most ambitious (pacific) supranational integration process ever attempted on the international stage, that is the European Union.

James Rosenau edged away from the state, but gingerly. He wrote of penetrated societies, linkage politics and foreign policy as an issue area straining to the limit the very notion of IR in its traditional state-centric mode.[8] While Rosenau described world society and formulated schema for its investigation, it was not until relatively late that he embraced it as a conceptual framework. His approach was incremental and had less impact for that reason. Even the idea of an issue area, later developed by Mansbach and Vasquez,[9] was initially conceived in the context of the comparative study of the foreign policy of states, but it made greater sense when thought of as a system of transactions relating to a particular issue which was the concern of a heterogenous group of actors, drawn from many levels, whose relations could be both conflictual and cooperative. In the United States it was Keohane and Nye, in their early work,[10] who crystallised this approach. However, in neither the UK nor the United States did salient books emerge to fulfil the role of those of Carr, Schwarzenberger and Morgenthau for realism. Only Mitrany's essay *A Working Peace System* approached this status. Nevertheless, an agenda had emerged that clustered around two principal themes – the unit of analysis and the nature of transactions that formed the substance of international relations and, therefore, the study of IR.

The principal unit of analysis for both realists and internationalists was the state. Indeed, the nature of the state and inter-state relations in an environment of anarchy were the justification for the separate status of IR as a discipline. As we have seen, IR owed its formative influence to international history and international law not so much to political science, except to some extent in the United States. There was seen to be a fundamental difference between politics within states and politics between states. Within states, there was deemed to be a high degree of shared values which obviated the security dilemma. Since citizens' behaviour and state institutions (police, courts, and the like) had much in common in terms of their basic values that there was no need to fear the other, so there was no security dilemma. At the interstate level, the level of shared values was much lower, so other states could not be trusted, hence the security dilemma and an anarchical society. The aim of the internationalists was to set the people free through democratic institutions, nation-states and international organisations based on collective security where the harmony of interest would be able to manifest itself. International security would be a mirror image of domestic security. Until that point, IR would be painfully different from national security. But was there such a disciplinary boundary in the nature of politics within states and that between states?

Political, class and ethnic wars could take place within states, and the economic system, and other functional ties, could operate freely across state boundaries reflecting shared value systems. There was no sharp dichotomy. Thus, the debate in the 1960s and 1970s concerned the appropriateness of the state to explain sufficiently that which was deemed important in IR. Are states only affected primarily by what they themselves do, and is only what they do important? In the ensuing discussion many other units of analysis were proposed, which reflected doubts regarding the state-centricity of contemporary world society. The ability to command loyalty, act cooperatively or coercively was no longer restricted to states, and other actors could amass significant resources of all kinds; so, too, could international institutions, both governmental and non-governmental. In many instances states were pushed aside by actors from civil society – but not always.

Behaviouralism in the social sciences generally had its impact on political science and IR, leading *inter alia* to consideration of the individual as the prime unit of analysis. But individuals interact in a framework, so transactions, processes and structure are all relevant. Is process, in the form of transactions, and the resultant structure, which then acts as a constraint upon transactions and socialises individuals and groups, the key? Is the contemporary world such that its interdependencies need to be seen as a single unit of analysis, broken down perhaps into issue areas, regimes or questions? And, if so, should we go beyond the confines of the world society approach to embrace a structuralist notion of the single world system – capitalism – with its centre, semi-periphery and periphery? And what is the role of the state, and of class, in such a conception?

Whatever the answer, the unit of analysis chosen has a significant impact upon the level of analysis at which research is focused. Waltz, in his *Man, the State and War*[11] and David Singer in a justly famous article,[12] had focused attention on this issue. Traditionalists asserted that the international level was the proper one for IR because states interacted there in the full plenitude of their power, and the political processes, due to the international anarchy, were different in kind from national politics. Others responded that states were not always 'in charge,' neither were they always coherent units, and therefore non-state actors, whether operating internationally (e.g. World Health Organisation) or transnationally (e.g. Amnesty International), were relevant. Moreover, the nature of the state and its form varied, and this affected policies. Or should we concentrate on the individual? Was Morgenthau wrong to ascribe a drive to dominate all individuals, but right to identify drives as important, as Burton was later to do with his universal human needs? Or, at the other end of the spectrum, is an ever-contracting and increasingly polluted and overcrowded 'Spaceship Earth' – what we now call the Anthropocene age – to be our principal concern? And if it is to be all or some of these potential units and levels of analysis, how can they be melded together to achieve our goal – a parsimonious explanation of as great a part of the relevant data as possible – especially when whatever the level, question or unit we choose goes a long way towards defining what is relevant?

The second item on the agenda concerned the degree to which all politics is, by nature, power politics. While acknowledging that power politics is common, the world society approach denies that it is ubiquitous. Moreover, it defines politics broadly to include the process whereby values are allocated and roles assigned in a wide variety of dimensions such as the economic, social and cultural systems. This process may be characterised by varying degrees of legitimation, and the interaction and movement between power politics and legitimised processes is complicated and not easy to predict. Should we start from the notion of a harmoniously working, non-coercive legitimised society – a healthy political system – and seek to understand why it works, or should we concentrate on breakdown, and what to do about it, especially when its consequences may be global nuclear war? And what is the relationship between the two? Furthermore, what is the import of such phenomena being evident in every social system – economic, social, cultural and the like? Is the political system something special? Or a chimera? Or a process *within* other systems and thus not separable from them? The agenda, whether concerning units and levels of analysis or the character and form of processes, is broad and exciting. It is to the literature that we must now turn, beginning with the emergence of anomalies that chafed the edges of the realist consensus.

Power politics in question

In his great work codifying the principles of political realism, *Politics Among Nations*, Hans Morgenthau lays emphasis on the concepts of power, interest, imperialism and the balance of power, all of which later became the object of discussion and challenge. The balance of power was perhaps the lynchpin of the realist framework. As a concept, its utility is diminished by the many meanings that have been attributed to it.[13] However, the two dominant meanings are those of a homeostatic equilibrium and a balance of power in favour of the *status quo* Powers. It is also not clear whether a balance of power will emerge automatically or whether it is a prescription. In effect, most writers, including Morgenthau, see it as a prescription. Thus, if the great Powers are in antagonistic competition, Hobbes' state of nature will ensue, with political life being "solitary, poor, nasty, brutish, and short."[14] Each great Power wishes to impose its own world order, which will act as a constraint on all the others. Napoleonic France was a case in point. However, if a Power is unable to do this, it will cooperate with others in order to prevent the most likely dominant state from succeeding in its ambition – hence the balance of power. It is a system predicated on conflict and managed through a degree of cooperation. But this management requires accurate information available to all, a comprehension of and willingness to operate agreed rules of the game, and tactical flexibility – a tall order. Even then, limited wars, as in the Crimea or Korea, may have to be fought to avoid general wars, and the system works only to preserve the role and status of the great Powers. If it is necessary to partition Poland or reassign colonies in the interest of great Power stability, then so be it. Morgenthau himself expressed concern about the system in that it is uncertain in its measurement of relative power capabilities; unreal, since the aim is superiority rather than cooperation; and inadequate, because it depends on a value consensus reflected in an understanding of, and belief in, the rules of a game that no longer existed in a more rigidly ideological second half of the twentieth century. Morgenthau wished, therefore, to diminish the impact of these deficiencies because he set little store by the possibility of collective security or world government and had no desire to see the world relapse into a Hobbesian nuclear nightmare.[15]

In a well written book, Inis Claude likewise expressed his concern at the inadequacies of the realists' prescriptions for the management of power in international relations:

> The crucial fact about the human situation . . . may be simply and starkly expressed: Mankind stands in grave danger of irreparable self-mutilation or substantial self-destruction. The circumstances which underlie this perilous condition may be succinctly described: Humanity is divided into basic units called states; some of these units possess the awesome capacity to destroy others. Once this power is unleashed, there is the high probability of a competitive struggle which may draw the whole world into its devastating vortex . . . the march of military technology is so rapid that it is no longer premature to contemplate the danger of the annihilation of the human race . . . This catastrophe may not occur. In principle, it is doubtless avoidable. But the hard fact is that humanity has developed no means for providing reasonable assurance, let alone confident certainty, that it *will* be avoided.[16]

The balance of power, for reasons that Morgenthau had enunciated, was found wanting in such a context. Moreover:

> [a]ll the fundamental tendencies affecting the political realm in recent generations run counter to the requirements of a workable system of balance of power. There is nothing to indicate that the global setting is likely to become more, rather than less, appropriate to the operation of a balance system . . . today, the balance of power system exists by default.[17]

But the alternatives as Claude saw them – collective security and world government – were no less flawed.

John Burton saw the way out of this dilemma arguing that change, not power, was the central concern. Burton's work went through several metamorphoses. In the 1960s it was concerned with a challenge to the orthodoxy of power politics. Burton argued that neither men nor states were inherently aggressive.[18] Conflict arose out of change. Change, for all actors, was an environmental factor as well as an internal one. In the domain of power politics, change was always likely to lead to violent conflict because its incidence on the interests of the actors would differ, and those who were less well off as a result of change would resist it. Conflict with potential beneficiaries would ensue. But this was not always the case and Burton called for an analysis of "what stimulates passive or non-passive responses, what types of change can be absorbed, what values can be traded, and what types of change provoke aggressive responses."[19] He rejected the idea that the balance of power could manage change since it could not absorb systemic change. For example, the growth of nationalism in the nineteenth and twentieth centuries had disturbing implications for practically all of the major Powers of 1914 regarding their continuing political viability as multinational units. The parameters of the nineteenth-century system were thus breached, and sooner or later the system would collapse under the strain of systemic change. The questions were only 'how?' and 'when?' Burton (and Karl Deutsch) thus began to look to cybernetics and the concept of steering as a means of non-cataclysmic change, which led Burton to explore further the nature of non-alignment as a policy and the possibilities of controlled communication.[20] With power politics now being questioned in a sustained manner, the way was open for a wider debate on the emerging agenda.

Systems thinking

Movements away from the realist consensus occurred along two principal axes – the relaxation of assumptions about the state-centricity of the world and about the pervasive nature of power politics. We shall proceed along the spectrum of declining state-centricity. As for the centrality of power politics, no one can deny its presence in the contemporary world, but the question is the degree and effects of its incidence and its relationship with legitimised politics. Legitimacy is a notion that can be associated with both state-related and non-state-centric perspectives. However, for the sake of convenience, our discussion will follow the spectrum of declining state-centricity without wishing thereby to imply that the question of the relationship between power politics and legitimised politics is secondary. It is not.

In 1957, Morton Kaplan published his *System and Process in International Politics*.[21] The book was important because it brought the notion of system into the mainstream of IR and was thereby instrumental in opening the gates of the field to insights, frameworks and methods from sociology, comparative politics, biology, cybernetics, mathematics and beyond to the philosophy of science. New developments often come late to IR – behaviouralism was a case in point. Historically, the notion of balance entered the lexicon of diplomacy at the time of the Italian city states, later than in science and other social fields. 'Balance' has permeated and impregnated our thought ever since. The notion of system is analogous – coming from science, biology and engineering – but it is now part not only of the behavioural sciences but also of our everyday thought patterns. 'Feedback,' an important notion in systems terminology, was esoteric jargon fifty years ago; it is long since common parlance. Kaplan rightly called his book heuristic and eclectic, but in opening these gates to a new world it was also influential – 'system' and 'process' were notions that were taken up with alacrity.

One of the most frustrating aspects of IR remains the absence of a settled meaning to an agreed terminology – and so it is with systems. There is also the dichotomy between objective and subjective phenomena, which reveals itself in the difference between general systems theory and systems analysis. Kenneth Boulding, in a celebrated article, observed:

> General Systems Theory is the skeleton of science in the sense that it aims to provide a framework or structure of systems on which to hang the flesh and blood of particular disciplines and particular subject matters in an orderly and coherent corpus of knowledge.[22]

In other words, the implication is that all science, indeed the world, is organised along systemic lines with systemic properties that can be revealed by assiduous research. We are back seemingly in the metaphysical world familiar to IR scholars through natural and divine law. Charles McClelland, on the other hand, has a much more subjective notion: "any system is a structure that is perceived by its observers to have elements in interaction or relationships and some identifiable boundaries that separate it from its environment."[23]

Clearly, in this instance, systems are a mental construct, a mechanism for ordering data according to the interests and concerns of the observer. Systems analysis is thus a convenience whereby if one set of transactions 'works' for the observer's purpose, it will be retained, or, if not, it will be dispensed with and another set chosen. It is not a question here of some grandiose 'skeleton of science' that has an objective reality waiting to be revealed that will, *nolens volens*, follow its prescribed pattern of behaviour, thereby affecting outcomes, whether it is perceived or not.

But what is a system? It is a set of patterned interactions between all manner of actors in which behaviour has a rhyme and a reason so that at some level of abstraction general statements can be made about it. Without this belief in regularities, social science would have to shut up shop. Pattern, however, implies duration, and interactions imply structure. Systems, then, are not entirely a matter for the free-floating imagination of the observer. Systems also have boundaries as the world is not a single system. There may be systems at the world level in various dimensions, but there are also sub-systems and sub-sub-systems after the manner of a Chinese box. The boundaries of these systems are marked by significant discontinuities in either the quantity or quality of transactions. Such boundaries are, of course, subject to change as transaction flows vary, but it is a matter of dispute about the extent to which they will vary.

Those writers influenced by Talcott Parsons point to a proclivity towards pattern maintenance in which the structures of a system, and its normative rules that have evolved, combine to set in motion homeostatic processes.[24] In other words, we are stuck with what we have got. Others have a far more dynamic view of systems persistence, evolution, collapse and revolution, as the work of Burton, Easton and Chalmers Johnson attests. In other words, what we get is in some measure what we deserve to get. Systems thinking in the Parsonian mode also carried with it some notion of an intra-systemic harmony of interests in that there is a mutually supporting role differentiation – tasks are functional for the maintenance of the pattern of the system. It is as though everything was for the best in the best of all possible worlds. However, many theorists in political science latched onto systems thinking as a way of explaining political development, by which they meant how the developed state – and its political system – reflected consensus and harmony. The standard of pattern maintenance, integration and the like was thus set for developing countries and world society to emulate. The conservative nature, indeed the arrogance – and the failure – of this approach, have been well catalogued.

"Systems thinking is holistic thinking," wrote Richard Smith Beal and then went on to explain the import of this:

The principle of holism asserts that social reality, to be understood adequately, should be apprehended as a complete, assembled and integrated ensemble. An holistic understanding is vital because (1) the whole is always something different from the mere sum of the parts, (2) parts assume novel properties as a function of their inclusion in the whole, (3) interactive effects modify parts in conjunction in ways undetectable when the parts are disjoined, and (4) the union of the parts is, after all, the most interesting phenomenon because its reality is most unequivocal. In effect, the principle of holism is committed to the idea that many phenomena are simply indivisible. To fragment a given phenomenon, even for the sake of scientific inquiry, is equivalent to losing the rich delineation among the components which made the entity so interesting in the first place.[25]

This idea was uncontroversial among systems thinkers. But what was the whole to be? Easton settled upon the political system of a state, and Johnson on a social system, while Burton and Mitrany laid greater emphasis on transaction systems which were not necessarily state-centric. Moreover, was the international system a system of states or, as in Burton's conception, a world society?

David Easton's work was undoubtedly innovative because he was able to come to terms with this maelstrom of systems ideas and apply his conception of them, with insight and care, to political phenomena in a way that made its impact not only on political science but also on IR. Easton went to considerable trouble before he finally rejected the idea of natural systems as a basis for his research,[26] and he came to the conclusion that "We can simplify problems of analysis enormously, without violating the empirical data in any way, by postulating that any set of variables selected for description and explanation may be considered a system of behaviour."[27] Which set we choose depends upon our interests, but Easton would doubtless agree that it behoves us always to be alive to the implications of our choice. Easton's choice fell upon the political system, which he did not differentiate from a state. However, he did, like the structural-functionalists in sociology and comparative politics, take interactions as the basic unit of analysis as opposed to political structures, which he saw as secondary.[28] Later approaches in this tradition embodied a greater concern for structural constraints.

Easton had to come to terms with the idea of a political system. He commented that "in its broadest context the study of political life, as contrasted with economic, religious, or other aspects of life, can be described as a set of social interactions on the part of individuals and groups."[29] One wonders what a social interaction is that differentiates it from other aspects of life. The comment is not flippant for it raises the question of whether there is a political system, as such, or merely a political process within other systems whereby in each system there can be what Easton called the authoritative allocation of values.[30]

Burton approached this problem in a different manner, which could suggest ways of looking beyond the state as a political system. He suggests that we should map all kinds of transactions in world society:

> The map of this society would appear like millions of cobwebs superimposed upon one another, covering the whole globe, some with stronger strands than others representing more numerous transactions, some concentrated in small areas, and some thinly stretched over extensive areas.[31]

Such systems have relations with each other. States are better regarded as the outcome of the interacting behaviour of systems. Regarding them as systems does not draw attention to the way in which boundaries disturb transaction flows and prejudices. It is not intended to imply that states are no longer significant; on the contrary, their role and range of activities have increased, but it is a role in relation to systems. World society is perhaps best analysed by considering systems first, and then the role of states, which is the reverse of a traditional approach.[32]

There are a number of points to be made in this context. The 'world society' and 'political science' conceptions of Burton and Easton are evidently very different sorts of systems. Burton relates to the international functionalism of Mitrany, which clearly goes beyond the state, whereas Easton is state-centric, but with an emphasis on transactions rather than structure.

How does the question of change, which has always been a central issue in IR and which is often a matter of peace and war, relate to the Eastonian framework? Easton relaxes the Parsonian notion of homeostatic pattern maintenance and, by implication, the equilibrium systems of the balance of power. Although the Eastonian analysis is firmly ensconced in one level of analysis, nevertheless, as Mansbach and Vasquez pointed out:

> [i]t moves the analysis of global politics away from conceptions of power and security and toward the assumption that demands for value satisfaction through global decision making must be at the heart of any theory, and must be the central process that awaits explanation . . . and toward still more basic questions of how dissatisfaction is generated and the processes that respond to it, including the creation of new actors and the disappearance of old ones.[33]

At this point, Chalmers Johnson's treatment of *Revolutionary Change*[34] is apposite since he makes change his central theme and sees it in an Eastonian framework. Johnson argues that when limited change occurs, social systems may be able to cope within their homeostatic capability. But what if this capability is inadequate? It is then up to the leadership to undertake structural change and value adjustment to resynchronise the system. Indeed, this "may occur without disturbing a homeostatic equilibrium so long as the value structure and the environment *change in synchronization with each other* . . . A social system can change its structure and still remain equilibrated."[35] Of course, not all leaderships will be farsighted enough, able or willing to do this in an appropriate manner, and so the dissynchronised system is ripe for revolutionary change in ways that need not concern us here. What is important is that systems change, in whatever its shape and form, is the very stuff of IR, and, although Johnson, Burton and, to a lesser extent, Easton have addressed this problem, many of the Parsonian sociologists who influenced systems thinking did not do so. It is for reasons such as this, and the rejection of the idea of natural systems, at least as a research problem, that general systems theory and Parsonian sociology have not proved to be the 'skeleton of science,' as Boulding had hoped. However, Burton, Johnson and Easton showed that systems analysis is worth taking further. Other systemic approaches have also had an influence upon the evolution of the world society model. In particular, we need to consider other state-related approaches, such as the work of Almond in comparative politics, Deutsch in cybernetics and Rosenau in his issue area formulation before broaching integration theory. Then we shall come to 'world society' proper in the next chapter.

Comparative politics

In the late 1960s, comparative politics seemed to be in a much livelier state of intellectual ferment than IR. This was due to the assimilation of structural-functional ideas culled from anthropologists and sociologists. In the broadest sense, systems thinking, whether of the structural-functional, cybernetic or Eastonian variety, seemed to offer a tool for comparison.

Put simply, all societies, indeed all organisations, need to perform various functions – at least to a minimum level – if they are to survive. There is, of course, no necessary implication that they should survive. Lists of functions varied, but the fundamental ideas were similar. A unit must be able to communicate with, and receive messages from, its social and ecological environment; it must be able to generate a modicum of loyalty – of 'we-feeling'; and finally, it must be able to set goals so that it can put its other attributes to purposeful use, which implies that it has a memory in the form of values and preferences drawn from past experience. These are a necessary requirement for survival at some, perhaps limited, level of cohesion, whether for a village in the highlands of Papua New Guinea, London or the United States. *How* these functions will be performed will vary from setting to setting. In other words, structures and forms may vary, but functional prerequisites for survival remain constant and, as such, constitute a standard for comparison.

Gabriel Almond made structural-functional analysis more acceptable to IR. He replaced terms such as state, powers, offices, institutions, public opinion and citizenship training with political system, functions, roles, structures, political culture and political socialisation.[36] But Almond aspired to more than a cosmetic change. He wished to go beyond parliaments and the like to "*all of the structures in their political aspects*, including undifferentiated structures like kinship and lineage, status and caste groups, as well as anomic phenomena like riots."[37] Nevertheless, all political systems have things in common – political structure, the same functions, substantial multifunctionality, and a mix between modernity and tradition.[38] This led Almond to propose his famous functional categories for comparison: input functions of (1) political socialisation and recruitment, (2) interest articulation, (3) interest aggregation, and (4) political communication. These were followed by the response of government in output functions: (5) rule-making, (6) rule application and (7) rule adjudication.[39]

For Almond, the political system was something special. He acknowledged that the "political system is not the only system that makes rules and enforces them" but, nevertheless, "The political authorities, and only they, have some generally accepted right to utilize coercion and command obedience based upon it."[40] The analysis is still state-centric since, despite an acknowledged concentration on interactions, the emphasis is on the political *system* rather than the political *process* or *function* of the authoritative allocation of values within any system. To move further would require due acknowledgement that political *systems* do not exist, but political *processes* or *functions* are ubiquitous in families, firms or economic systems. Almond and his colleagues were not prepared to look beyond the state-by-another-name. But the work of Almond and his colleagues did have an important influence by bringing structural-functionalism as a means of comparison, potentially between all organisations, to the forefront in political science and IR. The notion of the functional requirements for survival and the importance of interactions were further strengthened by the cybernetic approach.

The cybernetic approach

The cybernetic approach is most frequently, and rightly, associated with the work of Karl Deutsch. Like Almond and Easton, Deutsch put the emphasis on transactions but, ultimately, did not stray far from state-centricity, although the implications for further movement in that direction were implicit in his work. It is, however, important not to forget and to acknowledge fully the second dimension of the world society approach – the movement away from the realist's conception of power politics. As Deutsch put it, "It might be profitable to look upon government somewhat less as a problem of power and somewhat more as a problem of steering . . . steering is decisively a matter of communication."[41] Deutsch devoted his justly renowned *The Nerves of Government* to this seminal idea.

Deutsch brought into the mainstream of political science and IR a new *Weltanschauung* from science and engineering – cybernetics – which is:

> [t]he systematic study of communication and control in organizations of all kinds . . . Essentially it represents a shift in the center of interest from drives to steering, and from instincts to systems of decisions, regulation, and control, including the noncyclical aspects of such systems . . . In other words, the viewpoint of cybernetics suggests that all organizations are alike in certain fundamental characteristics and that every organization is held together by communication . . . It is communication, that is, the ability to transmit messages and to react to them, that makes organizations.[42]

Thus, as with general systems thinking and more especially structural-functionalism, we are given a tantalising means for comparison of all social entities that may have the potential for enabling us to broach the study of world society. Deutsch, however, restricts himself to government, which he likens to the nervous system of the body.

Deutsch's contribution was to suggest that we need to give great attention to each aspect of our daily processes and to their interrelationship. Are we picking up relevant information from the environment? How efficient is our costing procedure and identification of alternatives from our past experience? Do we have a realistic assessment of the operating environment? Above all, are we learning from, and steering according to, our feedback mechanisms? It is from negative feedback that we learn to do things better. This feedback may simply indicate the need for a minor adjustment of method to achieve a given end, say tea rather than coffee for the mid-morning drink, or it may indicate that we should reformulate our goals, for example, to drink less or fewer stimulants. Without feedback, any social unit will drift – ultimately to catastrophe.

Cybernetics is, then, the science of control and communication, of decision-making and interactions. Deutsch, in applying the framework to government, indicated that which was necessary to avoid breakdown – the precise monitoring of accurate negative feedback and a timely ability to take corrective measures.[43] He put the emphasis on processes rather than outcomes, that is, on the domestic environment rather than the operating environment. However, as he acknowledged, they are part and parcel of the same phenomenon.

Further consideration enhances significantly Deutsch's contribution, for it sheds some light on our second dimension – the movement away from power politics. Power, in the Deutschian formulation, is the ability to thrust the burden of adjustment on the environment, that is, on others, by not responding to negative feedback. This notion of steering had a significant influence on Burton in his study of non-alignment as a policy and in the adoption of problem-solving techniques. More generally, it helps us to conceptualise better both power and legitimised politics in the same framework and thereby brings us closer to the real world. But Deutsch's framework is entirely a conceptual one whose potentialities do not seem to have been put fully to the test in an empirical framework. However, his contribution did enable us to think about the nature of government and the relationship between power politics and legitimised politics in a new way. Moreover, it was not the only seminal contribution that Deutsch had to offer.

Deutsch was one of the first in IR to undertake empirical work following the canons of behaviouralism, and he inspired others to do so as well. Indeed, this inspiration, and the work that ensued, is an important part of his legacy. In *Nationalism and Social Communication* and his *Political Community and the North Atlantic Area*, Deutsch demonstrated the virtues of his transactional approach.[44] Neither states nor security communities were henceforth necessarily to be seen as the creatures of coercion. International relations and intranational relations could be conceived fundamentally as collaborative processes. Thus, as Donald Puchala points out, the findings of integration studies in the 1950s and 1960s, inspired and led by Deutsch among others, knocked a sizeable hole in the realist paradigm and did so with the force of empirical research at hand. Orthodoxy was brought into question in a manner that led to theories of transnational relations and interdependence and to a greater prominence being given to international political economy and to negotiating theory as applied to IR.[45]

In a stimulating *Festschrift* for Deutsch, *From National Development to Global Community*, his colleagues and students paid him the compliment not only of praising him but also of criticising him. One area in which this was the case concerns his ideas on social mobilisation and political development.[46] His approach melded ideas previously gleaned from his studies of nationalism and political community with concerns in comparative politics regarding political modernisation. The general idea was a captivating one: as traditional societies unravelled under the impact of modernising forces, a rootless class of landless peasants was created, bereft of organising structures in most dimensions. They were thus ready to be assimilated into modern culture economically, socially and politically. This culture was, of course, much more homogeneous than its traditional predecessors. If mobilisation and assimilation within a modern state structure proceeded *pari passu*, then it was likely to be stability and 'political development.' Indeed, at a wider level, it might even lead to the 'end of ideology' as all industrial societies grow more alike. We could envisage, therefore, the makings of a single world society.[47] However, there are significant reasons to question the central thrust of the argument, especially since ethnic and nationalist politics have proved to be a major phenomenon in both developed and developing societies (for different reasons). Rather than a homogenising world society we seem to be seeing a growth of interdependence *and* diversity. It is a fundamental task of our time, for scholar and practitioner alike, to come to terms with this in both analytical understanding and practical institution building. However, that is a task for the future – a global task – and so are the implications of Deutsch's work, but our concern is primarily IR. By now, however, the innovations of Deutsch, Burton, Easton, Almond, Kaplan and others need to be considered in the context of the traditional confines of the subject.

Foreign policy analysis (FPA)

One of the traditional concerns of IR is the analysis of foreign policy. However, ever since Snyder, Bruck and Sapin[48] offered a new conception of foreign policy decision-making, the study of foreign policy has faced an increasing number of challenging questions.[49] Does it concern formal state-to-state relations and, if so, is it confined to Foreign Offices or does it include other ministries, which may have their own foreign policy? And what of the foreign policy of state enterprises or chartered bodies such as nationalised industries or the BBC? Again, private bodies have foreign policies that are of significant import for official foreign policy, for example the TUC in the ILO. Transnational bodies, whether non-profit making, such as Amnesty International, or profit-making, such as ICI, are far from being irrelevant. Transgovernmental alliances between, say, ministries of agriculture in the EU, further complicate the analysis. And who controls and coordinates all this? Is it in fact controllable? Where is foreign policy? Has it merged into external relations and transnational ties? Yet courses are still taught in it, often as if nothing has happened.

For realists, these questions present no great problem since their conception of the world is state-centric and power political. Their interests suggest a fairly traditional and circum-scribed notion of foreign policy, sometimes to be identified as 'high politics,' which is central to his concerns. In the world society framework, foreign policy is conceived as part of external relations, broadly defined, whereas structuralists give less emphasis to actors and therefore, for them, the question is less acute since states and governments are often seen as being under the control or guiding influence of other actors or subject to powerful structural constraints. Nevertheless, FPA is a core element in the IR curriculum.

Snyder, Bruck and Sapin produced a checklist of factors and actors involved in the for-mulation of foreign policy. Their work attracted a great deal of interest.[50] Karl Deutsch's advocacy of a cybernetic approach, however, continues to exert a powerful influence,[51] as does the legacy from the Sprouts' examination of the man–milieu relationship.[52] The psycho-logical aspects of decision-making were given particular prominence by Kenneth Boulding in *The Image*.[53] Others followed in a similar vein. Robert Jervis devised some important hypotheses on misperception, while Alexander George pointed to the significance of psy-chological factors and the idea of multiple advocacy especially in situations where political leaders had a tendency to fall 'victims of group-think.'[54]

These strands began to be pulled together by various authors, one of whom was par-ticularly salient – James Rosenau. Rosenau had a remarkable ability to stimulate debate. His reader, *International Politics and Foreign Policy*,[55] has been, since its first edition, and remains, a staple part of the literature. But Rosenau, in his pursuit of *The Scientific Study of Foreign Policy*, has delved into its domestic sources, its comparative aspects, the conver-gence of national and international systems and their adaptation – all to stimulating effect.[56] However, the field of FPA has been marked by less cumulative effect than might be expected, a matter put right to some extent, at least in decision-making, by Graham Allison in his *The Essence of Decision*.[57]

Allison applied three different conceptions of decision-making to US policy-making in the Cuban missile crisis: that of the rational actor, organisational processes and bureaucratic politics. Each threw a different light upon that process, thereby suggesting that there is no 'royal road' to understanding. The rational actor model can be given short shrift. In an ideal formulation it assumes that actors will strive to maximise values that are hierarchically organised and not contradictory. The actor will consider the full range of options before choosing, and the decision will be rapidly, faithfully and completely implemented: that is, intended acts by unified governments will be comprehensively implemented in the spirit in which they were conceived. Quite simply, this approach does not correspond with general behaviour. Governments are rarely coherent, hierarchical or maximising. Moreover, infor-mation is often inadequate, either through its paucity or overabundance, analysis is costly and time-consuming, and the criteria of choice are, at best, fuzzy. This suggests that organi-sational processes, in which governments 'satisfice,' in Herbert Simon's phrase, are nearer the mark most of the time.

Braybrooke and Lindblom[58] have coined an inelegant but surprisingly retentive phrase, 'disjointed incrementalism,' to describe the processes of government. Foreign policy, they suggest, is carried forward by an endless sequence of small moves. 'Micro experts' push paper from their in-trays to their out-trays, or into the wastepaper basket, with scant consid-eration or knowledge of the larger policy framework within which they are acting. Their aims are essentially neutral: to keep the wheels turning so that they do not stop in their own patch, and to avoid known pitfalls rather than to seek positive goals. Uncertainty is minimised in the short run, and the long run is at a discount. Organisations break down problems into parts that they can manage and which correspond to their internal structure rather than adapt the organisation to match the problem. The files and archives rule. There is control at the micro level, but not overall. Major change is therefore usually exogenously induced, rare and out of control. It can be catastrophic for the organisation. What holds things together in the normal course of events is the shared values of elites in different domains and socialisation into a shared conventional wisdom. It is drift in the same direction rather than control. Only when the drift looks like going beyond the bounds of the bearable do top decision-makers step in, and then their hands are tied because the range of options has usually been foreclosed, and they have, in effect, little real choice. They can seek either to push out the bounds of the bearable, but this is frequently painful, or, more frequently, to steer back towards the mainstream. In short, top decision-makers are herdsmen looking for lost sheep rather than leaders. They themselves have little time to think; they can only react and rush from one crisis to the next. Politics is usually a retrospective rationalisation rather than a guiding goal and a set of acts designed to achieve that goal in a controlled environment. It is for historians to 'make sense' of chaos and drift, and to give it order.

Morton Halperin expanded upon Allison's third category, that of bureaucratic politics.[59] This approach suggests that problems are not treated on their merits but according to whether they will advance or impede the interests and self-image of the actor considering them. 'Where you stand depends on where you sit,' that is, where you stand on an issue depends on where you sit in a hierarchy, or your location in a bureaucracy will determine reaction to an issue, at least to a significant extent.

All this is not to suggest that rational action never occurs – it does at the micro level – ironically, it may be more likely to do so in a crisis when normal decision-making practices may be held in abeyance. Neither does it rule out the possibility that governments can set clear goals and pursue them single-mindedly, as occurred in Britain's attempt to join the EEC, or that a leader can stamp her values willy-nilly not only on government but on society at large, as Mrs Thatcher did. But these tend to be exceptions rather than the rule. In large complex Western liberal democracies the suggestion is that Parliaments reign but do not rule. Government is a loose confederation of like-minded, semi-autonomous bureaucracies. A twice-weekly Cabinet meeting, for perhaps thirty-five weeks of the year, of more than twenty people, lasting two hours or so, barely has time for mutual greetings and the rubber-stamping of departmental briefs let alone control of an administration, particularly if, as in the United States, the separation of powers is built into the system. Government, in short, is like a dinosaur: it has an enormous weighty body (the bureaucracy) and a very small brain.

For a long time attempts were made, chiefly by scholars in the United States, to develop the comparative study of foreign policy. However, the approach has not fulfilled its promise. But there are intriguing questions to be addressed. Do super Powers have problems in common, as super Powers? Does it make sense to consider middle Powers as a viable category, and in what circumstances, or to what effect? What are the modalities of being a pariah state, a divided state or a mini-state?[60]

At the other end of the spectrum, the psychological and sociological aspects of foreign policy-making continue to exert a fascination. Works by de Rivera, Jervis and Janis,[61] together with those of psycho-historians, hold their place for the insights revealed, as we have seen. Of particular interest, and of some significance, is the work of Robert Axelrod on the *Evolution of Cooperation*.[62] Axelrod highlights the significance of discounting whereby players who weight the future heavily may learn to play cooperatively even in the prisoner's dilemma game. Too often, in the past, IR specialists have discounted the learning process engendered by repetition. Power politics may pay in the short run, and leaders may choose to indulge in it for that reason, thereby leaving their successors to rue their shortsightedness. However, events are rarely, if ever, completely discrete and isolated, so that there is always a long run, although that after a nuclear war does not bear contemplation. Since in the long run cooperative strategies may pay, so FPA should put greater emphasis on the long-term aspects than hitherto – Axelrod's approach is a suggestive one. Consideration needs also to be given to how best the fruits of FPA, and IR more generally, can be brought to the attention of decision-makers.[63]

Over the decades the instruments of foreign policy have changed and require analysis. Diplomacy is no longer what it was in Harold Nicolson's day.[64] In particular, multilateral and conference diplomacy have become much more commonplace,[65] and the social composition and training requirements of diplomats has dramatically changed, for example in the spheres of trade and commerce.

Mansbach and Vasquez offered an issue paradigm based on four assumptions:

(1) Actors in global politics may consist of any individual or group that is able to contend for the disposition of a political stake.
(2) The fundamental causal processes that govern political interaction are the same regardless of whether contention occurs between or within groups. A single theory of politics, domestic and global, is therefore possible.
(3) Politics can be defined as the authoritative allocation of values through the resolution of issues.
(4) The shape of political contention is a function of three general factors – the characteristics of the issues on the agenda, the pattern of friendship–hostility among contending actors, and the nature of the institutional context in which allocation decisions must be made.[66]

The issue is the unit of analysis, and it determines the actors since they are not ascribed but coalesce as a function of the issue, as well as the level of analysis. Of central interest is the nature of the transactions concerning the issue – whether they be conflictual or cooperative.[67] We have in fact arrived at a world paradigm quite distinct from realism on at least two crucial dimensions: those of state-centricity and power politics. This was a framework compatible with another major area of research that blossomed in the late 1950s and 1960s, namely integration theory.

Integration theory

The anarchical society of classical political theory may be anarchical, but it is still a society which implies some measure of integration, as indeed does any form of organised activity at whatever the level.[68] Integration, we would argue, has two complementary aspects: it is a state of affairs and a process. A state of affairs implies criteria setting a standard which, if met, constitutes integration. As a process, there is movement towards (or away from in the case of disintegration) collective action based upon consensual values for the achievement of common goals, in which the parties have long-term expectations of mutually compatible and acceptable behaviour. The process is self-maintaining, and, unlike imperialism, which is an enforced integration, it is not based on coercion. Since no actor exists in total isolation, integration is ubiquitous.

While a conception of global integration is not an important characteristic of world society in so far as realism is concerned, the conscious process of integration in Europe in the decades after the Second World War, and theorising about it, provided a major challenge to the prevailing orthodoxies of the 1950s.[69] The process of decolonisation, too, focused attention on integration, whether within states such as India or Nigeria, or between states, as in the West Indies or East Africa. The mixed record suggests that insufficient attention was given to processes of disintegration from unitary states towards autonomy, federation, devolution, association or secession, despite the prevalence of disintegration in both the developed and developing worlds.

At the other end of the scale, the contemporary world was increasingly described as 'one world' or a 'shrinking world.' This is not inaccurate: 'one world' issues abounded in the 1960s and 1970s, such as population, food, environment and development.[70] The shrinking world was reflected in the prodigious movement and interdependence of goods, services, ideas and people. How can and should such developments be conceptualised? The literature of this period is heavily weighted in favour of certain integration theories – in particular neofunctionalism, regionalism and federalism – to the neglect of other approaches such as anarchism, cooperation or harmonisation. Moreover, disintegration has only recently been taken seriously as something other than an anomaly or a pathological state.

The literature on integration can conveniently be placed into three categories: that which has, as its essential function, to take advantage of opportunities, or deal with problems, within the ambit of the existing state system; that which envisages the rebuilding of the existing state system; and that which goes beyond or escapes from either the existing or a refurbished state system.[71]

Within the existing state system there is a variety of ways in which a greater degree of integration can be sought without substantial structural impact. At the lowest level, *cooperation* involves an agreement to undertake a specific task without any thought of task expansion or spillover into other areas. Where there is a process of continuous adjustment by governments, through a process of intensive consultation within an international institution designed to serve important goals that can only be achieved together, then *coordination* results, while *harmonisation* involves the joint setting of standards and goals, again, frequently, in an institutional framework. However, this is not usually the case in *parallel national action*, where complementary or compatible legislation and practices are instituted separately but in a coordinated manner by different actors in order to reduce the impact of frontiers. *Association*, on the other hand, is usually more formal and has greater structural implications. Paradoxically, it can enable both integration and separation to be pursued at the same time, promoting integration in certain domains but restricting it in others, thereby denying the 'functional imperative' of task expansion and spillover. Donald Puchala has suggested that an amalgam of these processes can form a 'concordance system.'[72] In such a system, governments remain important actors, but so do actors from the subnational, transnational and supranational arenas. However, there is no fixed relationship between such actors in terms of hierarchy or the like. Nevertheless, there is a strong institutional framework and bureaucracy concerned with and reflecting "ordered, standardised, planned, efficient problem-solving in relations."[73] But this need not be done centrally, neither is it necessarily obligatory. Attitudes of the actors tend to be pragmatic and characterised by a high degree of mutual sensitivity and responsiveness, with a willingness to acknowledge, and act to promote, the greater good of the whole. Moreover, a concordance system depends, for its successful operation, upon a large degree of popular support – a permissive climate. However, the concordance system, and the 'menu' set out earlier, does not lead to an irrevocable derogation of sovereignty. It can also be seen as a practical basis for multilateralism with its sense of confidence in acceptable long-term behaviour through thick and thin, giving rise to notions of legitimacy and solidarity.[74]

Regionalism, however, is a hybrid, which may stay within the bounds of the existing state structure (its conception in the UN Charter) or become the embryo for a new state system.

Region is a geographical concept, and the doctrine of regionalism implies that geographical variables are a prime influence on behaviour. While the notion of region may be helpful in individual dimensions such as transport or the environment, it does not appear to be the great organising principle when considering multidimensional phenomena. This much is evident from Bruce Russett's work.[75] The subject has not excited much comment for some time, but there is now a renewed interest, especially in inter-regional relations.

Neofunctionalism, as a means to regional integration, goes beyond the conception of regionalism enshrined in the UN Charter in its implications for sovereignty, especially in the context of a regional or putative federal body coming to possess authority over national sub-systems, function by function. The end-goal of neofunctionalism is in fact a federation.[76] It is more than a process but a *finalité*. We have now gone beyond the confines of the existing state system into the realm of rebuilding the state system in a new form, in which the former units are arranged or otherwise changed so that they no longer have the attributes of sovereign independence. The establishment of federations is a case in point. In *federalism*, the stress is upon a constitutional instrument setting out the relationship and competence of the federal and local bodies within defined territorial areas. *Consociation*, which may have greater relevance in the contemporary world, avoids the creation of strong central institutions in an endeavour to encourage joint and consensual decision-making, avoiding any possibility of the tyranny of the majority. It is appropriate for units with deep cleavages such as language, religion or ethnicity, which nevertheless wish to establish or maintain an element of political unity. They aspire to be united but not unitary. This can be achieved by establishing a 'grand coalition' of representatives of the segments, each of which in effect maintains a veto. Although con-sociation is more typical within states such as Switzerland, or as 'power sharing' in Northern Ireland, it is relevant between states, for example, in the European context.

As we will see in some more detail in the next chapter, the neofunctionalists undoubtedly owe much to Ernst Haas. Influenced by Mitrany, but aspiring to a more rigorous methodology, he pioneered the study of European integration[77] before expressing doubts about the whole neofunctionalist enterprise.[78] Incidentally, his approach has been recovered in the last few decades as a mid-level theory that helps explain parts of the European integration process – mostly related to the European Single Market. Although less ambitious in terms of its potential application, neofunctionalism remains a relevant theoretical approach at least for European studies.

Notes

1 Inis L. Claude, *Power and International Relations* (New York: Random House, 1962).
2 J.W. Burton, *International Relations* (London: Cambridge University Press, 1967).
3 Charles R. Beitz, *Political Theory and International Relations* (Princeton, NJ: Princeton University Press, 1977), and John A. Vasquez, *The Power of Power Politics* (London: Frances Pinter, 1983).
4 Morton Kaplan, *System and Process in International Politics* (New York: Wiley, 1957); David Easton, *A Framework for Political Analysis* (Englewood Cliffs, NJ: Prentice-Hall, 1965); David Easton, *A System Analysis of Political Life* (Chicago, IL: University of Chicago Press, 1979); Gabriel A. Almond and James S. Coleman (eds), *The Politics of Developing Areas* (Princeton, NJ: Princeton University Press, 1960); Gabriel A. Almond and G. Bingham Powell Sr. (eds), *Comparative Politics* (Boston, MA: Little, Brown, 1966).
5 Karl W. Deutsch, *Nationalism and Social Communication* (London: MIT Press, 1966); Karl W. Deutsch et al., *Political Community and the North Atlantic Area* (Princeton, NJ: Princeton University Press, 1957).
6 Karl W. Deutsch, *The Nerves of Government* (London: Collier-Macmillan, 1963).
7 David Mitrany, *A Working Peace System* (Chicago, IL: Quadrangle, 1966).

8 James N. Rosenau (ed.), *The Domestic Sources of Foreign Policy* (New York: Free Press, 1967); Rosenau, *The Scientific Study of Foreign Policy* (London: Frances Pinter, 1980); Rosenau (ed.), *Comparing Foreign Policies* (New York: Wiley, 1974); Rosenau (ed.), *Linkage Politics* (New York: Free Press, 1969).

9 Richard W. Mansbach and John A. Vasquez, *In Search of Theory* (New York: Columbia University Press, 1981).

10 Robert O. Keohane and Joseph S. Nye Jr. (eds), *Transnational Relations and World Politics* (Cambridge, MA: Harvard University Press, 1971).

11 Kenneth N. Waltz, *Man, the State and War* (New York: Columbia University Press, 1959).

12 J. David Singer, 'The Level of Analysis Problem in International Relations,' in Klaus Knorr and Sidney Verba (eds), *The International System* (Princeton, NJ: Princeton University Press, 1961).

13 Ernst B. Haas, 'The Balance of Power: Prescription, Concept or Propaganda?' *World Politics*, July 1953.

14 Thomas Hobbes, *Leviathan* (London: Penguin 1987 [1651]), p. 186.

15 See especially Hans J. Morgenthau, *Politics among Nations* (New York: Knopf, 1959), second revised and enlarged edition, chapter XIV.

16 Claude, *Power and IR*, pp. 3–4.

17 *Ibid.*, pp. 92–93.

18 Burton, *International Relations*.

19 *Ibid.*, p. 54.

20 See J.W. Burton, *Conflict and Communication* (London: Macmillan, 1969).

21 Kaplan, *System and Process in International Politics*.

22 K.E. Boulding: 'General Systems Theory: The Skeleton of Science,' *General Systems*, Vol. 1, 1956, p. 17, quoted in J.W. Burton, *Systems, States, Diplomacy and Rules* (London: Cambridge University Press, 1968).

23 McClelland, *Theory and the International System*, p. 20.

24 Parsons stresses that four functional prerequisites must be performed if societal equilibrium is to be maintained: (1) pattern maintenance, which is the ability of a system to ensure the reproduction of its own basic patterns, values and norms; (2) adaptation to the changing environment; (3) goal attainment; and (4) integration of the various functions and sub-systems into a coherent whole. For Parsons it is important to maintain such an equilibrium.

25 Richard Smith Beal, 'Theoretical Innovations in Systems Theory in International Relations,' in K.P. Mishra and Richard Smith Beal (eds), *International Relations Theory* (New Delhi: Vikas, 1980), p. 83.

26 Easton, *A Framework*, pp. 26 ff.

27 *Ibid.*, p. 30.

28 *Ibid.*, p. 49.

29 *Ibid.*, p. 49.

30 Easton discusses this in David Easton, *The Political System* (New York: Knopf, 1953), pp. 130 ff., and Easton, *A Framework*, pp. 50 ff.

31 J.W. Burton, *Systems, States*, p. 8.

32 *Ibid.*, pp. 8–10.

33 Mansbach and Vasquez, *In Search of Theory*, p. 29.

34 Chalmers Johnson, *Revolutionary Change* (London: Longman, 1983).

35 *Ibid.*, pp. 57–58.

36 Almond and Coleman, *The Politics of Developing Areas*, pp. 34–36.

37 *Ibid.*, p. 8.

38 *Ibid.*, p. 11.

39 *Ibid.*, p. 17.

40 Almond and Powell, *Comparative Politics*, p. 18.

41 Deutsch, *The Nerves of Government*, p. 9.

42 *Ibid.*, pp. 76–77.

43 *Ibid.*, pp. 221 ff.

44 See note 6.

45 Donald J. Puchala: 'Integration Theory and the Study of International Relations,' in Richard L. Merritt and Bruce M. Russett (eds), *From National Development to Global Community* (London: Allen & Unwin, 1981), p. 148.

46 Karl Deutsch, 'Social Mobilization and Political Development,' *American Political Science Review*, September 1961.

47 For an explanation of Deutsch's approach and some criticisms of it, see the articles in his *Festschrift* by William J. Foltz and Michael C. Hudson, in Richard L. Merritt and Bruce M. Russett (eds), *From National Development to Global Community* (London: Allen & Unwin, 1981).

48 R.C. Snyder, H.W. Bruch and B. Sapin, *Foreign Policy Decision-Making* (New York: Free Press, 1962), earlier versions of which circulated in the mid-1950s.

49 See A.J.R. Groom: 'Foreign Policy Analysis: From Little Acorn to Giant Oak?' *International Studies*, Vol. 44, No. 3, 2007.

50 G.D. Paige, *The Korean Decision* (New York: Free Press, 1968) is a notable exception.

51 A.V.S. de Reuck and Julie Knight (eds), *Conflict in Society* (London: J. & A. Churchill, 1966); John Steinbruner, *The Cybernetic Theory of Decision* (Princeton, NJ: Princeton University Press, 1976).

52 Harold and Margaret Sprout, *Man–Milieu Relationship Hypotheses in the Context of International Politics* (Princeton, NJ: Princeton University, Center of International Studies, 1956).

53 Kenneth Boulding, *The Image* (Ann Arbor, MI: University of Michigan Press, 1961).

54 Robert Jervis, *Perception and Misperception in International Politics* (Princeton, NJ: Princeton University Press, 1976); Robert Jervis and Thierry Balzacq, 'Logics of Mind and the International System,' *Review of International Studies*, Vol. 30, No. 4, 2004; Alexander L. George and Juliette L. George, *Woodrow Wilson and Colonel House: A Personality Study* (New York: Dover, 1964); Irving L. Janis, *Victims of Groupthink* (Boston, MA: Houghton Mifflin, 1982).

55 James N. Rosenau (ed.), *International Politics and Foreign Policy* (New York: Free Press, 1961, 1969).

56 James N. Rosenau, *The Scientific Study of Foreign Policy; The Domestic Sources of Foreign Policy; The Study of Political Adaptation* (London: Frances Pinter, 1980); Rosenau (ed.), *Comparing Foreign Policies*; Rosenau (ed.), *Linkage Politics*.

57 Graham Allison, *The Essence of Decision* (Boston, MA: Little, Brown, 1971).

58 David Braybrooke and Charles Lindblom, *The Strategy of Decision* (New York: Free Press, 1970).

59 Morton H. Halperin, *Bureaucratic Politics and Foreign Policy* (Washington DC: Brookings, 1974).

60 M.R. Singer, *Weak States in a World of Powers* (New York: Free Press, 1972); Michael Handel, *Weak States in the International System* (London: Frank Cass, 1981); Christor Jonsson, *Superpower* (London: Pinter, 1984); Carsten Holbraad, *Middle Powers in International Politics* (New York: St Martin's Press, 1984); Sheila Harden, *Small is Dangerous* (New York: St Martin's Press, 1985).

61 J. De Rivera, *The Psychological Dimension of Foreign Policy* (Columbus: Charles E. Merrill, 1968); Robert Jervis, *The Logic of Images in International Relations* (Princeton, NJ: Princeton University Press, 1970); Robert Jervis, *Perception and Misperception in International Politics* (Princeton, NJ: Princeton University Press, 1976); I.L. Janis, *Victims of Groupthink* (Boston, MA: Houghton Mifflin, 1982).

62 Robert Axelrod, *The Evolution of Cooperation* (New York: Basic Books, 1984).

63 Robert Rothstein, *Planning, Prediction and Policy Making in Foreign Affairs* (Boston, MA: Little, Brown, 1972); Lincoln P. Bloomfield, *The Foreign Policy Process* (Englewood Cliffs, NJ: Prentice-Hall, 1982); A.J.R. Groom, 'Academics and Practitioners,' in Michael H. Banks (ed.), *Conflict in World Society* (Brighton: Wheatsheaf, 1984), p. 8.

64 Harold Nicolson, *Diplomacy* (Oxford: Oxford University Press, 1963).

65 Paul Taylor and A.J.R. Groom (eds), *Global Issues in the United Nations' System* (London: Macmillan, 1989). See A.J.R. Groom, 'Conference Diplomacy,' in Andrew F. Cooper, Jorge Heine and Ramesh Thakur (eds), *The Oxford Handbook of Modern Diplomacy* (Oxford: Oxford University Press, 2013).

66 Mansbach and Vasquez, *In Search of Theory*, pp. 68–69.

67 In an earlier work, Mansbach and colleagues came up with the astonishing finding, 'The more conflictual the behaviour, the less the state-centric model can explain; the more cooperative the behaviour, the more the state-centric model can explain!' R.W. Mansbach, Y.H. Ferguson and D.E. Lampert, *The Web of World Politics* (Englewood Cliffs, NJ: Prentice-Hall, 1976), p. 278.

68 See Hedley Bull, *The Anarchical Society* (London: Palgrave, 2012 [1977]) and A.J.R. Groom and Alexis Heraclides, 'Integration and Disintegration,' in Margot Light and A.J.R. Groom (eds), *International Relations: A Handbook of Current Theory* (London: Frances Pinter, 1985), on which this section draws liberally.

69 See Donald Puchala, in Richard L. Merritt and Bruce M. Russett, *From National Development*.

70 See Paul Taylor and A.J.R. Groom (eds), *Global Issues*.

71 This framework is that used in A.J.R. Groom and Paul Taylor (eds), *Frameworks for International Cooperation* (London: Pinter, 1990). This volume contains a chapter on each of the approaches mentioned, with appropriate reference to the literature.

72 Donald J. Puchala, 'Of Blind Men, Elephants and International Integration,' in M. Smith, R. Little and M. Shackleton (eds), *Perspectives on World Politics* (London: Croom Helm, 1981), pp. 238 ff.
73 *Ibid.*, p. 240.
74 See A.J.R. Groom: 'Multilateralism as a Way of Life in Europe,' in Edward Newman, Ramesh Thakur and John Tirman (eds), *Multilateralism under Challenge* (Tokyo: UNU Press, 2006).
75 Bruce N. Russett, *International Regions and the International System* (Westport, CT: Greenwood, 1975).
76 For an overview, see A.J.R. Groom, 'Neofunctionalism: A Case of Mistaken Identity,' *Political Science*, July 1978.
77 Ernst Haas, *The Uniting of Europe* (London: Stevens, 1958).
78 Ernst Haas, *The Obsolescence of Regional Integration Theory* (Berkeley, CA: University of California, Institute of International Studies, 1976).

9 Transnational, global and world society approaches

Two of the most important forebears of IR as a discipline were international law and diplomatic history. International law, as an organic element of the state system, is likely to be important as long as the state system functions. Indeed, it may outlast that system by becoming the legal component of various world society approaches or transnational regimes. Moreover, international law can be seen in many guises.[1] For example, the notion that law is the sovereign's command and is only law so long as it is backed by an effective sanction fits well into the realists' schema. Moreover, the historical derivation of international law must not be forgotten: it arose out of the Christian Commonwealth of Europe and was imposed by the rising European Powers on the rest of the world, whether they liked it or not. It reflected European values of Christianity and capitalism – the prevailing social and economic system – and it became a world system through colonialism and, where necessary, through coercion.

International law can also arise out of a jural community reflecting genuinely shared values and be based upon reciprocity, convenience, coordination or a high degree of normative consensus. Then, law is not coercive, but consensual. As such, it is a good predictor of behaviour because it reflects behavioural patterns emanating from freely shared values. Where no such consensus exists, where the dispute is over basic values rather than within a consensus on values, law tends to become a weapon of propaganda to be used by those who benefit from the status quo against those who wish to change it to reflect different value systems and conceptions of world order. It acts then not as a constraint or a guide to and predictor of behaviour but as a normative stick with which to beat an adversary.

International lawyers, who played such an important and fructuous role in fashioning the great consensus in IR in the first decade of our discipline, and before, viewed law as a positive reflection of the progressive elements of free democratic nation-states associating themselves in a League of Nations to create a better international community. Law would henceforth reflect a genuine jural community rather than the power of states, and as such the need for sanctions would be rare. The goal was to build an international community based on collective security, in a manner similar to that of national communities. We have seen how, in political relationships, they failed and realism returned to rule the roost. But they did not fail in economic and social matters – the functional dimensions – as the Bruce Report on those aspects of the League's activities attested in a clear and forthright manner. Thus, there were lessons to be learned from both the successes and the failures of the League, as we shall see in the discussion of functionalism as a prescriptive approach to world order and as a description of world society. But what of the second great intellectual forebear of IR as a discipline – international history?

In a sense we have law and history with us always because any sort of order implies some form of law, and it is rare indeed, if not impossible, for there to be no hint of a collective memory. But what we choose from that memory is influenced by what we are trying to do as well as having its influence on our goals. We use history for a purpose, but in part history shapes what that purpose will be. There can be realist history or structuralist history, for all history is selective. Many of the early holders of chairs in IR were historians, especially in the UK, and their attitude to their old calling was ambivalent because diplomatic history tended to be imbued with the tenets of realism and was thus out of focus with the new spirit of the times, both in terms of philosophy and method, for example, the desire to be 'scientific.' However, old methods prevailed, and the intellectual and methodological baggage of the new discipline was, in its first decades, clearly reflective of its legal and historical forebears – but not entirely so, as the names of Lewis Richardson and Quincy Wright suggest, and these were both concerned with central aspects of the new field, that is, the study of war. Another name comes to mind in this context, that of Arnold Toynbee, for long a stalwart of Chatham House and an historian of civilisations. Both of his historical fortes, that of contemporary international history and the study of the grand sweep of civilisation, are part of IR now and they are not restricted to any particular framework or paradigm. A Toynbeean grand sweep of history can be found in the work of George Modelski, Immanual Wallerstein and Michael Mann, all of whom bear consideration, and it is to Mann that we turn before considering other pluralist approaches – those of Mitrany's functionalism, the *IO* network, global approaches and Burton's world society framework. All go beyond the state system and think in terms of patterns of transactions across state boundaries.

The domination of Europe as a process

Modelski, Wallerstein and Mann are all concerned with the rise of the Eurocentric world, not so much as a chronology of a particular set of human beings but as a social process. Mann's views are set out in the first volume of a longer study. However, in his history of social power to 1760, Mann gives us the central thrust of his argument.

Mann's approach stems from two statements, of which the first is that "Societies are constituted of multiple overlapping and intersecting sociospatial networks of power."[2] Societies are therefore neither unitary, nor social systems, nor totalities:

> Because there is no whole, social relations cannot be reduced "ultimately," "in the last instance," to some systemic property of it – like the "mode of material production," or the "cultural" or "normative system," or the "form of military organization" . . . Because there is no social system, there is no "evolutionary" process within it. Because humanity is not divided into a series of bounded totalities, "diffusion" of social organization does not occur between them. Because there is no totality, individuals are not constrained in their behaviour by "social structure as a whole," and so it is not helpful to make a distinction between "social action" and "social structure."[3]

Mann, unlike many of his fellow sociologists and others, does not conceive of society as an "unproblematic, unitary totality," neither does he take politics or states as the 'society' or unit of analysis. He puts it bluntly: "I would abolish the concept of 'society' altogether."[4]

Mann's second position accounts for societies, their structure and their history "in terms of the interrelations of . . . the four sources of social power: ideological, economic, military, and political relationships."[5]

For Mann, ideological power has two distinct meanings:

First it offers a *transcendent* vision of social authority. It unites human beings by claiming that they possess ultimately meaningful, often divinely granted, common qualities ... The second means of ideological power is what I called *immanence*, the strengthening of the internal morale of some existing social group by giving it a sense of ultimate significance and meaning in the cosmos, by reinforcing its normative solidarity, and by giving it common ritual and aesthetic practices.[6]

Economic power likewise has two components, the first of which involves coordination (often coercive) in the exploitation of nature to produce goods, and the second concerns commerce and consumption. The means of military power are what Mann calls "concentrated coercion"[7] whereas the "first means of *political power* is *territorial centralization*."[8] But Mann maintains that "autonomous state powers are precarious" because human societies are not unitary systems but varying conglomerations of multiple, overlapping, intersecting networks of power. But where state powers are enhanced, then 'societies' become more unitary, more bounded, more separated from one another, and more structured internally:

Additionally, their interrelations raise a second means of political power, *geopolitical diplomacy*. No known state has yet managed to control all relations travelling across its boundaries, and so much social power has always remained 'transnational' ... But an increase in territorial centralization also increases orderly diplomatic activity ... Where centralization is proceeding in more than one neighbouring territorial area, a regulated multistate system will develop.[9]

We are back in the familiar territory of IR as traditionally defined. And Mann does not baulk at the question of change and what "types of power configuration have pioneered jumps in world-historical collective social development."[10] He suggests that there are two:

1   *Empires of domination* combined military concentrated coercion with an attempt at state territorial centralization and geopolitical hegemony ... The principal reorganizing role is here played by a mixture of military and political power, with the former predominating.

2   In *multi-power-actor civilizations*, decentralized power actors competed with one another within an overall framework of normative regulation. Here extensive powers were diffuse, belonging to the overall culture rather than to any authoritative power organization. Intensive powers were possessed by a variety of small, local power actors, sometimes states in a multistate civilization, sometimes military elites, sometimes classes and fractions of classes, usually a mixture of all of these. The predominant reorganizing forces were here economic and ideological, though in varied combinations and often with political and geopolitical help.[11]

The relevance of Mann's observation is clear and cheering, at least to those in the world society approaches who point frequently to the fundamental problems of the contemporary world such as nuclear war, ecology, the global and national economic divide, racism and the like, and the need for change. But they oscillate between the world and the individual as the unit of analysis. Mann's second model suggests that a spurt or a breakthrough is possible while encompassing both of these units. An empire of domination or the attempt to achieve one is not necessary to achieve a breakthrough. There are other ways. Where it will come from, Mann can only hint. He suggests that as a power centre develops it tends to lift its neighbours, "who learn its power techniques but adapt them to their different social and geographical circumstances"[12] – in often less confined and constrained circumstances. Here the interplay of the four sources of power may have greater scope and something new may be generated. Where it might be now, Mann does not surmise, but a modish view would be to suggest that it is outside the European and North American 'centre.' Other regions are likely to be the starting point, as the struggles in Central Asia, the Near East and in North Africa suggest.

Mann's work and that of other historical sociologists has led us back to vistas that we cannot and should not ignore. Indeed, some would argue that our subject is as much the political sociology of IR as it is anything else more narrowly or differently defined. However, historical sociologists differ among themselves, and the sweep of history can be seen in economic or more purely political terms, as we shall see. It is because Mann puts the emphasis on the changing interactions of four different forms of social power, which overlap and intertwine but do not coalesce into a coherent whole, that he sets a suitable historical backcloth to approaches to world society from within IR that share some of these same characteristics.

Functionalism

International functionalism as an approach to world order owes much to the work of David Mitrany.[13] Mitrany was, of course, one of many writers in this approach, but his work has achieved such a salience that we can take it as an exemplar – perhaps an extreme one – much in the manner that Morgenthau's *Politics among Nations* is taken as an exemplar of realism. Mitrany was a practical man of affairs in journalism, business and international organisation as well as in transatlantic academic life. His *A Working Peace System*[14] grew out of Mitrany's practical experience in his native Balkans and his role in a Foreign Office think tank on the future of international organisation during the Second World War. It was republished in 1966, whereafter Mitrany's conceptions again excited interest.[15]

Mitrany sought to devise a strategy to create and sustain a 'working peace system.'[16] He was not offering a panacea for world government, the idea of which was completely alien to his thought. His premise was that form should follow function so that the institutional element would reflect and promote the activity being performed without any constitutional hindrance and, in particular, without attempting to organise the activity around state actors or state boundaries.

But not all systems of transactions are appropriate, according to the proponents of functionalism. Only those systems that reflect human needs and maximise welfare are truly functionalist because they have not been 'corrupted' by state actors pursuing state and institutional values at the expense of human values. Indeed, it is precisely because the state is unable to guarantee such basic needs as social security and the maximisation of welfare, as evidenced by the world wars and the Great Depression, that functional institutions are needed. In a functional institution, problems will be dealt with in an open participatory manner by the relevant experts and concerned public on the basis of the best technical knowledge, and felt needs, free from the pressures of power politics and state chancelleries. Gradually, as more activities are organised along such lines, a working peace system will evolve, bringing people together in a positive manner to resolve problems and maximise welfare, rather than keeping them fearfully and miserably apart.

To achieve such a working peace system, state sovereignty and national loyalties will not be attacked frontally but will be rendered harmless and obsolete, to the extent that they have no continuing functional rationale, by the growth of other institutions based on systems of transactions that maximise welfare. To this extent the state will 'wither away.' For Mitrany, the starting point lies in the economic and social welfare spheres. This is thought to be separate from the power-ridden high politics of interstate relations. Individuals, peoples, groups, and even in some circumstances governments, will be working together to solve their common problems and maximise welfare. Gradually they will develop a sense of community, and common interests will arise out of interests previously held in common.

This will take place through a twofold learning process of task expansion and spillover in which cooperation will deepen in existing areas and spread to new domains. As such, cooperative habits are established and nurtured, and when a realisation of the benefits of such cooperation becomes more widespread, power politics will be tamed and then transformed. After individuals and groups join the diverse functional bodies, the institutions of the state are held to lose their salience and significance and cross-national ties will develop, which will be both instrumental and attitudinal. The greater the number and diversity of ties the less likely is war to occur, since any war is likely to disrupt such ties and thereby diminish welfare. War will quickly be rejected as a policy of cutting off the nose to spite the face. Thus, instead of separate states, the repositories of loyalty and inefficient sources of welfare, crashing into one another like balls on a billiard table, the world will evolve towards a myriad of actors concerned with a variety of topics organised along lines best suited for the management of matters of common concern to the parties involved. In short, it will no longer resemble the billiard ball analogy, but that of a cobweb.

Scientists, businessmen, students, workers and the like will develop their functional loyalties in addition to, and then instead of, their national loyalties. Moreover, superordinate goals will be identified and sought after, goals which, while desired by all, can only be attained through cooperation. The achievement and enjoyment of such goals will buttress peace and form an important element in the working peace system. In time, the barriers to relationships caused by state boundaries and loyalties will be circumvented and lifted, and welfare, participation and peace will be maximised. Security will depend not upon deterrence and threat systems but will arise out of association, that is, through playing roles in systems of transactions that are valued and valuable to all the parties concerned on the basis of criteria acceptable to them. In short, it will be a working peace system.

The functionalist approach purports to be both a description and a prescription. It claims to describe aspects of contemporary world society in which there is a variety of effective actors besides states and in which levels of analysis are clearly intertwined. Moreover, while government has got bigger and has penetrated into many new facets of the activities of groups and individuals, it also become functionalised. Departments, boards, ministries go their own way with little coordination or control. Government is no longer monolithic but is made up of semi-independent, functionally based components. As a prescription, the belief is that functional organisation will bring about a working peace system, that it should facilitate the participation of all those relevant, and that it will maximise welfare by dealing with activities on the basis of expert advice on the merits of the question, and not in a context of the pursuit of power interests.

Unfortunately, it is difficult to envisage how a functionally organised world would be a conflict-free world. Conflict, after all, is endemic in the sense that separate decision-making centres, which do not have perfect knowledge, are likely to embark upon incompatible policies. This phenomenon can arise, presumably, irrespective of whether the actors concerned are functional institutions, actors within them, or states. The relevant question concerns reactions when these incompatabilities have been recognised by the parties concerned. Are there appropriate and legitimised mechanisms available for handling the conflict, for steering in a cybernetic sense, or will parties persist in their courses, the one trying to impose the burden of change on the other? The functionalist asserts that institutional flexibilities, participatory decision-making and cross-cutting ties augur well for the development of legitimised conflict-handling mechanisms. A functionally organised world society would not eliminate conflict, but it would act as a prophylactic and possibly alter the form of conflict, by putting the stress more on non-violent forms of coercive activity.

The functionalist is hard pressed to justify her faith in the notion of technical decision-making by experts on the merits of the question. First, he has to provide for the desired degree of participation by non-expert actors in the system. Second, a question can be decided on its technical merits only if there is a prior consensus on the values to be applied in deciding upon what constitutes merit. Corrupting political pressures may be kept at bay once the rules of the game have been decided upon: technical expert decision-making may then hold sway. But what if a functional institution, and relations between such institutions, is not based upon a value consensus? Then we are back to power politics. Functional institutions may facilitate the legitimisation of the decision-making process and relationships, but they cannot guarantee them.

The transfer of loyalties from outmoded, power-maximising state institutions to welfare-maximising functional institutions is also an open question. Humankind is well known for its proclivity to bite the hand that feeds it. Empirical evidence is not clear about the relationship between affective ties and the satisfaction of utilitarian needs. Thus, even if a functional institution maximises welfare and is fully participatory, there is no guarantee that it will attract the sort of loyalty that presently resides with national entities, the more so since such affective ties will be dissipated among a range of institutions. Once again, therefore, the central role of the learning process, and the functionalist's sanguinity in regard to it, comes to the fore. Yet it is precisely this learning process that the neofunctionalists latched onto when surveying the tenets of functionalism in their search for an explanation of integration, and particularly of Western European integration.

The differences between functionalists and neofunctionalists are marked. The neofunctionalists' unit of analysis is the state, and not a system of transactions, and their approach is teleological – a single decision-making centre for a newly integrated territorially based unit. Functionalists abhor such regional integration, in the form of state-building, unless it is based on coterminal systems of transactions, which in Europe, and elsewhere, is not the case. Thus, while the interests of both may coincide when restricted to a single functional dimension, such as the European Coal and Steel Community, they diverge radically in a multidimensional analysis. Functionalism, in Mitrany's conception, is a way to a world society that is beyond the state system, rather than an attempt to rebuild it on a regional basis. It is not a theory in any strict sense but an argument pointing to a possible way to a better world. Rather than being a panacea, it is a sense of direction reflecting a set of (liberal) values. And the alternatives have been found wanting in the achievement of its goals of peace, welfare and participation. Mitrany is more a forerunner of Burton than of Haas and the neofunctionalists. But, before we turn to Burton, we must consider other related approaches – transactionalism and complex interdependence on the one hand, and world order modelling on the other.

The International Organization (IO) network

For nearly five decades, *IO* has been the vehicle for a *coterie* or network of scholars to express their ideas and publish their research. Their contribution has been highly influential, as well as agenda setting.[17] One of the great contributions that this network has made has been to investigate notions of transnationalism, complex interdependence and regimes. They have done so with an eye to the two dimensions of state-centricity and power politics. And they have been careful to undertake accompanying empirical work. To generalise, Keohane,

Nye, Krasner and others are fully aware of the arguments regarding declining state-centricity and the changing nature and means of power politics, which they certainly do not consider as ubiquitous. They see the need to explain these phenomena, but they approach them from the perspectives of state-centricity and power politics. Mitrany, Burton, Mansbach and Ferguson approach the phenomena from the perspective of world society and legitimised politics. It is as though each is regarding the same phenomena from opposite ends of the telescope. The emphases differ considerably, but there is much in common. The special issue of *IO* on transnational relations, edited by Keohane and Nye, is a case in point.

Transnational Relations and World Politics is an impressive work.[18] Keohane and Nye commissioned a number of studies on a variety of areas involving different actors such as multinational enterprises, transnational revolutionary movements, the Ford Foundation and the Roman Catholic Church. They focused on what they anticipated would be:

> [f]ive major effects of transnational interactions and organizations, all with direct or indirect consequences for mutual sensitivity and thereby for interstate politics . . . (1) attitude changes, (2) international pluralism, (3) increases in constraints on states through dependence and interdependence, (4) increases in the ability of certain governments to influence others, and (5) the emergence of autonomous actors with private foreign policies that may deliberately oppose or impinge on state policies.[19]

In their conclusion, the editors reject the realists' idea that the state-centric model can *grosso modo* accommodate transnational relations simply because, in direct confrontation with transnational actors, governments prevail and that transnational relations, which have always existed, do not affect significantly the great issues of security, status and war.[20] They go on to state that:

> [t]he state-centric paradigm provides an inadequate basis for the study of changing world politics. Transnational actors sometimes prevail over governments . . . But it is theoretically inadequate to use the exogenous variables of the environment to account for outcomes in the interaction of various actors in world politics. State-centric theories are not very good at explaining such outcomes because they do not describe the complex patterns of coalitions between different types of actors . . . We hope that our "world politics paradigm" will help to redirect attention toward the substance of international politics, in which the major theoretical as well as practical questions can be found, and away from the relatively unenlightening application of subtle reasoning or sophisticated methodology to problems that have been narrowly defined by a limited theoretical outlook or the wrong units of analysis . . . The "world politics paradigm" does not provide scholars with an instant revelation, but it does provide them with at least one path toward relevance.[21]

It was a path that Keohane and Nye trod with circumspection, as *Power and Interdependence* revealed.[22]

Keohane and Nye refer, by interdependence, "to situations characterized by reciprocal effects among countries or among actors in different countries."[23] Such situations do not always result in mutual benefit since "Our perspective implies that interdependent relationships will always involve costs, since interdependence restricts autonomy: but it is impossible to specify a priori whether the benefits of a relationship will outweigh the costs."[24] It may be that everyone will gain, but not in what they perceive as an equal or equitable manner, and so there may be "distributional conflict."[25] This distributional conflict is likely to be structured by the relative degrees of sensitivity and vulnerability of the parties concerned. Sensitivity involves the speed and the extent to which changes in one country entail costly changes in another. Vulnerability concerns the relative availability and cost of alternatives to having to accept the burdens imposed by the sensitivity of the second country. If the effects of changes in one country are immediate, great and costly for the second country, and there is no alternative available, then that country may be at a disadvantage *vis-à-vis* its interdependent partner. Of course, such disadvantages could be nullified by the initial country avoiding the damaging change – steering in Deutsch and Burton's terminology in an example of legitimised politics – or by attempting to cope with the costly effects jointly in a problem-solving manner. On the other hand, the initiating country could thrust the burden of change on its partner by refusing to change in a power response. Keohane and Nye give greater attention to the latter. If "Power can be thought of as the ability of an actor to get others to do something they otherwise would not do (and at an acceptable cost to the actor) . . . [and] can also be conceived in terms of control over outcomes,"[26] then complex interdependence is an interesting concept to be explored along the power politics' spectrum.

The notion of complex interdependence, which Keohane and Nye see as challenging the precepts of realism, conceives of "a world in which actors other than states participate directly in world politics, in which a clear hierarchy of issues does not exist, and in which force is an ineffective instrument of policy."[27] However, distributional conflict can still exist so that power politics in forms other than force can be prevalent, although its presence in one issue area does not necessarily presage its spread to, or its presence in, other areas. If the balance of power conceives of cooperation in a world of conflict, complex interdependence depicts conflict in a world of cooperation. The case studies in which Keohane and Nye explore distributional conflict concern complex interdependence in oceans and monetary policy involving the United States in its relationships with Canada and Australia. The case studies are not entirely apposite because, although they concern issue areas, they nevertheless create parameters for their analysis by bringing in the 'United States,' 'Canada' and 'Australia.' Thus, the study had a predeliction towards power politics and state-centricity – the all-pervasive influence of which it purported to deny. A way of thinking that might avoid this tendency is to think in terms of regimes – a subject to which the *IO* network paid considerable attention.

Stephen Krasner was the editor of the special issue of *IO* devoted to regimes.[28] His definition of regimes has been widely accepted. Regimes are:

> [s]ets of implicit or explicit principles, norms, rules, and decision-making procedures around which actors' expectations converge in a given area of international relations. Principles are beliefs of fact, causation, and rectitude. Norms are standards of behaviour defined in terms of rights and obligations. Rules are specific prescriptions or proscriptions for action. Decision-making procedures are prevailing practices for making and implementing collective choice.[29]

Regimes, of course, are not new phenomena. They have a nineteenth-century ring to them, either of a colonial nature, as in the case of European Powers supervising the finances of some unfortunate debtor government or establishing an international enclave, or, more benignly, international public unions for the standardisation of weights and measures and the like. In their modern guise they can be construed to bear a strong resemblance to Mansbach and Vasquez's issue areas, Burton's systems and Mitrany's functional bodies.

Regimes can come into being in various ways. Some may emerge spontaneously, as a perception of common interest and interdependence grows; others may be arrived at by negotiation, particularly when an important issue is in a state of flux; but some may be imposed by a hegemonic actor or group of actors. However, regimes do not exist in themselves; they have to be perceived to exist. Moreover, once in existence they can wax, wane, transform themselves or collapse. But usually they are evolutionary phenomena, although they can be overthrown, or even created, in a revolutionary manner. And they can proceed in various ways, ranging from loose coordination to a single policy.[30]

In a particularly perceptive essay in the *IO* volume, Donald Puchala and Raymond Hopkins stress several features, including their subjective nature, in which "participants' understandings, expectations or convictions about legitimate, appropriate or moral behaviour" are important.[31] As we have seen, their decision-making processes can vary considerably, as can the standing of actors who range from governments, including bureaucratic units and individuals therein, to international, transnational and subnational organisations. Puchala and Hopkins also point out that "a regime exists in every substantive issue-area in international relations where there is discernibly patterned behaviour."[32] We are, in other words, back in the systems framework so characteristic of world society and transactional approaches. And the transactions in the system may be under the tight coercive control of a hegemon or emanate from the voluntary consensus of all the participants characteristic of legitimised politics.

Puchala and Hopkins invite us to consider various characteristics of regimes – whether they be specific or diffuse, formal or informal, given to evolutionary or revolutionary change (after the manner of Chalmers Johnson) – and to note their distributive bias since they generally favour the interests of the strong, particularly if they are imposed by a hegemon. But in the latter case they may be shortlived.[33] Nevertheless, a hegemon does not have to impose a harsh coercive regime, it can also act in a benign manner by providing an appreciated collective good for the benefit of the regime as a whole, itself included. On any account, regimes are not overly state-centric, or necessarily power political.[34] Frequently they outlive the particular concatenation of events that led to their gestation and go on, often *faute de mieux*, providing a guiding framework when there are no obvious reasons that they should continue to do so. Perhaps, as Puchala and Hopkins point out, it is because they "mediate behaviour largely by constraining unilateral adventurousness or obduracy . . . and during transitions of power." Compliance with the rules and procedures of a regime "depends largely upon the consensus or acquiescence of participants . . . Usually it is self-interest, broadly perceived, that motivates compliance."[35] But that self-interest, being broadly perceived, can also include notions of community interest, otherwise the regime may have difficulty in surviving.

If we accept that the world is interdependent in a complex manner, then regime theory is a useful way of coming to terms with it because it can accommodate a wide range of actors in a transactional framework, enabling us to investigate empirically process and structure in an open-minded way. There is no *a priori* reason why a regime should be state-centric and power political – or the converse to a lesser or greater extent. The burden is on us to find out how and why this may be so and how and why it may or may not change. Complex interdependence may expand the capacity of actors to play power politics with each other, but it may also, and perhaps the more, lessen their desire to do so. Regime theory is, therefore, a useful tool for our understanding of international politics. But it is not the only one. Regimes may be worldwide, but they are not global.

Global approaches

In some ways, it is only in the last fifty years that we have had global politics and globalisation in international relations. Before that, issues may have been worldwide, but they were usually not truly global. The Second World War is a case in point. The increasing globalisation of some aspects of world politics has given added impetus to global approaches far more sophisticated than previous schema for world government, which were often the pipedreams of well-meaning international lawyers. The global approach can refer to questions such as nuclear annihilation or the global ecosystem, but it can also take us back to the individual.

In the early 1970s a new *genre* of intellectual exercise captured the imagination of the attentive public in IR – global modelling. The Report of the Club of Rome, entitled *Limits to Growth*,[36] reached some highly disturbing, if subsequently very contested, conclusions:

1   If the present growth trends in world population, industrialization, pollution, food production, and resource depletion continue unchanged, the limits to growth on this planet will be reached sometime within the next one hundred years.

2   It is possible to alter these growth trends and to establish a condition of ecological and economic stability that is sustainable far into the future.

3   If the world's people decide to strive for this second outcome rather than the first, the sooner they begin working to attain it, the greater will be their chances of success.

These conclusions are so far-reaching and raise so many questions for further study that we are quite frankly overwhelmed by the enormity of the job that must be done.[37]

Several other models were to follow, often using sophisticated modelling techniques, and their results were in some cases contradictory. Moreover, there was "the relative lack of *explicit* political and social content [which] is widely recognized by modelers as a weakness."[38] However, some political figures did come together in various commissions[39] to give a practical politicians' input to discussion of this range of issues, both then and subsequently.

In the narrower perspective of IR literature the greatest impact was the World Order Models Project (WOMP). Since the initial meeting in New Delhi in 1968, many studies were published. WOMPers sought to relate their starting point – world peace and security – to a new, but classic, agenda of issues. The issues concerned problems of ecological balance, population, basic needs such as food, and unbalanced development, but they came down to some classic questions of political life – equity, participation and justice – without which there can be no peace and security. Like Mitrany and Burton, WOMPers saw the existing state system as part of the problem, and their vocation was to be radical in changing it. As in the Club of Rome report, there is a context of emergency, and the perspective is globalist. They were not seeking the 'fixes' of technocratic futurism but "comprehensive value realization"[40] for all, but first and foremost for the oppressed. They accepted the challenge of doing away with the "avoidable evils"[41] of hunger, war, repression and environmental decay. In short, they saw their task as threefold:

(1) a *diagnostic/prognostic* task of describing present world order conditions and trends, (2) a *modelling* task of designing preferred futures, and (3) a *prescriptive* task of mapping a transition process, including concrete steps and an overall strategy.[42]

Their critics contended that they knew where they wanted to go, and why, but they did not know how to get there. Nevertheless, we shall not find out without trying. Moreover, setting goals has an important benefit for the mundane affairs of day-to-day politics: preferred future worlds, likely future worlds and undesirable future worlds, as distinct models, may give a hint in response to the question 'how do I go about today's work in such a manner as to make the first more likely and last less so?' Moreover, modelling of ideal types can be very heuristic in requiring us to specify independent variables which we might not have wished, or thought, otherwise to consider.

Andrew Scott would probably share these sentiments. His *Dynamics of Interdependence* is a thoughtful and provocative book.[43] It has long been evident that we are broaching the problems of the twenty-first century with the tools of the nineteenth century. Whereas in the past scientific and technical change, and its implications, may have proceeded at a rate that did not outstrip the rate of adjustment of political, social, economic and cultural mores, ideas, institutions and processes, this is manifestly no longer the case. Moreover, as Scott points out, while some global problems did exist in the past they were largely unperceived, and the more devastating for that reason, for example, deforestation of lands around the Mediterranean.

Scott (like Wallerstein) makes much of Braudel's history of the Mediterranean world, in which Braudel works at three levels, that of geographical time and social time which set slow-moving apurposive processes within which there is individual time during which princes and politicians enter onto the stage.[44] But their role is circumscribed by these deeper processes, even though they may have been unaware of it. The long-term processes of change are not the stuff of politicians' daily fare. Harold Wilson is reputed to have remarked that a week is a long time in politics. Nowadays, the political clock is set by continuous news bulletins and social media.[45]

The global approaches considered here have all had a strong orientation towards action. They share a sense of a worsening predicament about which something must be done if catastrophe is to be avoided. And it is difficult to remain sanguine in the face of this *oeuvre*. Thus, the call to action is clear, and in a subsequent chapter we shall address it. We turn now to a statement of a world society approach, drawn from the writings of John Burton and a group of scholars associated with him mainly, but not exclusively, in the UK.

Burton's 'world society' approach

We have the benefit of hindsight. In his magisterial survey of the field in 1955, Quincy Wright exhibited an enviable degree of foresight:

> It is not only the nations [to] which *international relations* seeks to relate. Varied types of groups – nations, states, governments, peoples, regions, alliances, confederations, international organizations, even industrial organizations, cultural organizations, religious organizations – must be dealt with in the study of international relations, if the treatment is to be realistic . . . Is not the subject matter of *international relations* really the history, organization, law, economy, culture, and processes of world community? Should we not conceive of the human race as a community which, while divided into numerous geographic, functional, cultural, racial political, economic, and other subgroups, is becoming integrated into a society with the progress of technology and the growth of population bringing the members of all sub-groups into closer and closer contact with one another?[46]

Such sentiments express the rationale of world society approaches. The formulation of one variant of this theme owes much to the thought and influence of John Burton. But there can be other formulations, with differing emphases.

In the first place, the role of states is treated as an empirical question rather than as being axiomatic. States may, on significant occasions, be the most important actors, but this is not necessarily and always so. Neither are state boundaries necessarily the fundamental dividing line between intrastate consensus and interstate anarchy. Intrastate relations can be anarchical and interstate relations highly consensual. States are not alone in having effective means of self-help and the self-arrogated right to make use of them. Moreover, important systems of transactions, both qualitatively and quantitatively, both of a coercive and legitimised nature, transcend state boundaries in ways that are not amenable, actually or potentially, to governmental control, even as a 'gatekeeper.' Furthermore, states themselves, and especially their governments, frequently do not act as cohesive, hierarchically organised, well-integrated units commanding the full loyalty of their citizens. Indeed, even government departments may frequently be at odds with each other, and even seek alliances with like-minded departments of other governments in a network of transgovernmental relationships such as can be seen between treasuries, defence ministries and foreign offices in NATO countries or similar phenomena in organisational settings such as the European Union. Non-governmental organisations (NGOs) can also play an important world role, and even intergovernmental institutions can, usually through their secretariats, have an impact that escapes the control of their member-states. Greenpeace, Amnesty International, Bob Geldof and Band Aid, the International Olympic Committee, and the World Council of Churches – to name a random selection – illustrate, in contemporary world politics, the active and frequently independent role of NGOs, and many of them operate in an aterritorial manner. So, too, do many multinational corporations, whose ability to mobilise financial, technical and human resources may rival or surpass that of many governments. A range of such actors can come together to form a regime that thereafter acts as a constraint on their behaviour. In short, the state is a penetrated society. It can be *a* nodal point, *an* actor, *a* potential gatekeeper, but when, and the extent to which it is so, must be an empirical question and cannot be assumed.

But if the state is not necessarily a basic unit of analysis, what can take its place? In the world society model, the emphasis is put on transactions so that the notion of system – a set of patterned interactions – is the basic unit of analysis. In this approach the level of analysis is not crucial (interstate, intrastate, individual), neither is the status of actors. To analyse a phenomenon, it may be necessary to include the activities of actors as widely disparate as a particular individual and the UN Security Council. Since an adequate explanation cannot be given at one particular level, say interstate relations, it is necessary to go beyond that level. By mapping transactions related to a particular phenomenon, and determining where marked discontinuities occur, both qualitatively and quantitatively, a systems analysis emerges. Such systems develop properties that have a durable and independent existence (as, in their different ways, regime theorists, structural-functionalists and general systems theorists would argue), but the world society approach is, in general terms, a systems approach, which does not necessarily imply far-reaching normative consideration or 'deep structure.' It can be conceived mainly in descriptive terms, although it frequently goes beyond this and develops a strong normative orientation, as in WOMP or in Burton's concern with legitimacy.[47] Yet if international relations goes beyond the interstate system, where does it stop? Does world society include everything? Surely not, for then it would be of little analytical use.

The starting point in the world society framework is a question, a problem or phenomenon to be explained, and the approach to it is the mapping of transactions in a systemic framework. This gives an added dimension to the conceptualisation of social science. Confining the analysis to one level, such as the interstate, is too constraining, and so too is a limitation to one facet of behaviour, be it economic, legal, sociological or political. Interdisciplinary research, therefore, became fashionable because few questions, problems or phenomena are exclusively, say, economic or could reasonably be treated as such. Hybrids came to the fore, or reappeared, such as political anthropology, political psychology, political sociology or political economy, throughout the social sciences. Interdisciplinary research teams and centres were established. But the results were often disappointing. The reason for this lay frequently in the non-cumulative nature of the work of members of the team: an economist would look at the problem from the perspective and within the paradigm of economics, and others likewise from their differing paradigms. These paradigms or frameworks were not easily made compatible and therefore interdisciplinary research did not cohere – it lacked a discipline.

A solution to this problem is to reverse the process of proceeding from a discipline or a level of analysis to a problem by making the problem, question or phenomenon itself the starting point. Moreover, the choice of starting point is clearly impregnated with normative implications. However, themes such as conflict, security, integration, participation, identity and the like cut across both levels of analysis and academic disciplines. Conflict, for example, has economic, legal, psychological and other disciplinary dimensions. It manifests itself at different levels between individuals, between states, in industry and across all these levels. But conflict (and the other themes) also has a coherence of its own so that, whatever the idiosyncracies of level and discipline, general statements can usefully be made. The problem, question or phenomenon in the world society framework is located within, and acts as the fulcrum of, three dimensions – level of analysis, discipline and theme (Figure 9.1).

Besides suggesting that the world is increasingly non-state-centric in character, adherents of world society approaches suggest that humans are not driven primarily by an instinct to dominate. Thus, aggressive behaviour at all levels results usually from other factors, notably as a learned response in certain environmental conditions. Peace, in the sense of being more than the mere absence of overt violence, is therefore possible. Indeed, transactions in any social system can be located on a spectrum between a pole of power politics and one of legitimised politics.

Realists view all politics as being necessarily power politics. Even ostensibly cooperative relations are merely "power politics in disguise," in Schwarzenberger's phrase, because there are inevitably asymmetries in relationships that can be manipulated to the benefit of

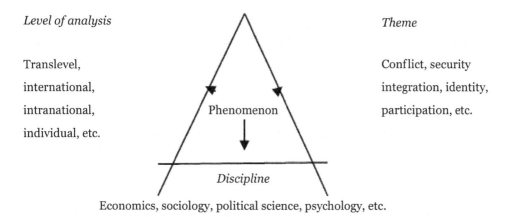

Figure 9.1 World society framework

some and to the detriment of others, a view echoed later by Keohane and Nye in *Power and Interdependence*.[48] Since the parties know this, they take it into account even in the 'cooperative' behaviour. Thus, realists do not view transactions within the purview of international relations as being situated on a spectrum between power politics and legitimised politics. In so doing they limit themselves unnecessarily since some degree of legitimisation must always exist as it is difficult to coerce most of the people most of the time. Moreover, the idea of a continuum between a pole of power and a pole of legitimacy, rather than the realist's usual sharp distinction between intrastate and interstate politics, may be a more accurate reflection of the empirical world even during the Cold War. Prescriptions based on such a sharp distinction could therefore give rise to self-defeating policies. However, the notion of a continuum requires a criterion by which the transactions can be situated along it. This is the degree of acceptability of the transaction to all the parties concerned. The parties concerned are determined by their potential capability and likely willingness to 'spoil' a given set of transactions. If a transaction is acceptable to all concerned, then it is legitimised; if it is not, then it is situated towards the power end of the spectrum.

As a rule of thumb, a legitimised relationship is one in which the behaviour of the actors is based on criteria fully and freely acceptable to them without coercion, either overt, latent or structural. The essential element is not overt behaviour but motivation. Motivation, that is acceptance by actors of the criteria on which their behaviour is based, can only be free and without coercion if, among other things such as a low opportunity cost whenever the behaviour is

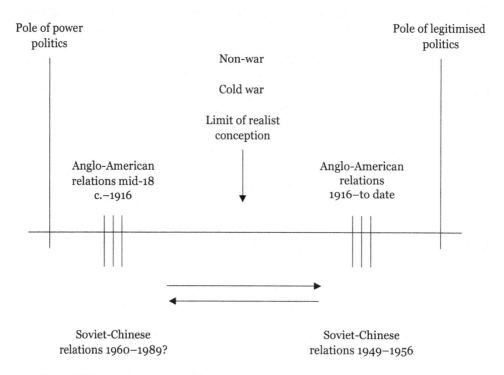

Figure 9.2 From peace to war and back

rejected, the actors have 'perfect knowledge' of the range of possibilities. Without that knowledge the actors may be the victims of structural violence. Of course, transactions rarely fall at either extreme end of the spectrum. Transactions can cluster consistently towards one or the other end of the spectrum. Consider Franco-German relations from 1870 to 1950 at the power end or, towards the other end, Nordic country relations. The realist, however, would deny that the spectrum could venture much further from the power pole than a situation of non-war or Cold War. The conception in world society approach, on the other hand, envisages the full spectrum and tries to account for a basic shift along it. Why, for example, did Anglo-American relations have such a shift towards the pole of legitimised politics after 1916 or Soviet-Chinese relations move in the contrary direction (Figure 9.2)?

For the world society approach, a degree of power or legitimacy is simply a label to indicate the nature of a transaction. Because power relations tend to be dramatic and traumatic, they monopolise the attention, but without the all-pervasive fabric of legitimisation there is little chance of a stable social order. Moreover, even theorists who see the struggle for power as being universal in time and space usually accept some socialisation of this instinct in the form of a limited degree of consent.

The world society model acknowledges that the political function may be perceived in power terms, but it does not allow that this need necessarily be so. The reasons for this lie in a different conception of the nature of man. Behaviour is a rational response to the environment as the actor sees it, so that changing the environment can elicit different, more cooperative behaviour from that postulated by the realists. It is the old story of the predominance of either nature or nurture. The realist points to the ground rules being set by the former, and the world society analyst sees them as a function of the latter.

This statement of *a* conception of the world society approach can act as a navigation point through the debates, discussions, confusions and controversies of the last three decades of the twentieth century. It reflects the views of Burton and his colleagues, but Burton himself became a somewhat erstwhile advocate of the world society framework. For him, the solution is to go back to the individual as the unit of analysis since, in his view, paradoxically, we can only reach global processes through the needs of the individual.

Needs theory

Burton is not the only scholar to return to the individual as a unit for the analysis of international relations and world society. Waltz, in *Man, the State and War*,[49] devoted part of his analysis to such theories and, in a well-known paper, Sidney Verba drew our attention to assumptions and theories about individual decision-making in models of the international system.[50] Later, Chadwick Alger gave much thought to innovative and exciting ways of bridging the micro and the macro in IR research.[51] Alger quoted Singer and Galtung to the effect, in Singer's case, that "no theory which ignores the single person is scientifically adequate or morally defensible,"[52] and in Galtung's, that the empowerment of *all* people in world affairs through "a plurality of revolutions at the micro level" is desirable.[53] Alger argued that this involves breaking with the state as the unit of analysis and the removal of constraints regarding the conduct of 'foreign policy' by all manner of local groups: "From this perspective, research would extend beyond studying the individual as object and instead contribute to activate the individual as subject, or as purposeful actor."[54] To some degree the Green movement, stressing cultural identity, self-reliance, social justice and ecological balance, is a practical response moving in that direction.[55]

For Burton, the basic principles of the needs approach are:

1   There are certain human needs and desires that are specific and universal.
2   These *will* be satisfied, even at the cost of social disruption and personal disorientation.
3   Some structures and institutions that have evolved over time, as a result of differentiation of power and of socialisation, do not necessarily, either in the short or the long term, reflect these needs and desires and frequently frustrate them.
4   Disruptive behaviour is the consequence of interaction between the pursuit of human needs and the institutional framework created by power differentiation.

Thus, "the individual must be the unit of analysis, because it is individual human needs that ultimately have to be catered for in the interests of public policy at all levels."[56] Moreover:

> We are asserting that if there were to be discovered a definite set of human needs on the basis of which societies could be harmonious, major methodological problems in behavioural sciences and in policy-making would be avoided. If there were agreement as to human needs then there would be a logical starting point of behavioural analysis for there would be a scientific basis for determining goals.[57]

It is a view shared by others. The starting point is that the individual is adopted as the basic unit of analysis for all of social science from individual psychology to the study of world society. While institutions of all types, at all levels and in all dimensions have a considerable effect, outcomes, it is argued, are significantly related to individuals acting as individuals out of role but in nature. In the hoary argument over whether nature or nurture 'maketh man,' Burton comes down heavily in favour of nature. Indeed, since individual behaviour is fundamentally grounded in an unchanging nature, then social science knowledge can be objective and constitute a set of navigation points for practitioners.

Burton, with others, points to the "genetic drive to learn"[58] about a set of universal basic human needs "such as stimulus, security, identity, consistency of response and the need for control by the person of his/her environment as a means of pursuing these needs."[59] Since these drives are of a genetic origin, then they will be pursued come what may. The only constraints are "values attached to relationships."[60] If institutions obstruct the fulfilment of such needs, then conflict will result. However, the individual will prevail, for even if one, or many, are crushed, others will (because they will have to) pursue similar goals. However, conflict is not inevitable because the needs being pursued are not necessarily in short supply.

Everyone can be stimulated, secure, have a sense of identity and the like, although there is no guarantee of this in practice. Security, for example, can be defined so that it is thought by others to engender insecurity for them, whereupon conflict will ensue. But it can also be defined in such a way that it does not threaten others. The same can be said of identity, participation, development and other similar basic needs. Indeed, it is the job of the practitioner to ensure that basic needs are fulfilled in such a manner that conflict does not ensue, and Burton suggests the process of problem-solving to ensure that dysfunctional policies are changed.

Basing himself on a number of needs theorists, Burton stresses Sites' notion that "The individual's most fundamental drive [is] . . . to attempt to control his environment in order to meet his needs"[61] whether by societally acceptable means or otherwise. If society is not able to offer the individual acceptable relationships, then there will be no constraints on the forms of the pursuit of needs. If society offers relationships cherished by the individual, he or she will not prejudice them by anti-societal behaviour. The individual and his or her needs therefore provide "objectively determined guides to policy – bases on which goals and policies could be assessed and predictions made as to success or self-defeating consequences."[62]

However, some groups and individuals are likely to engage in the defence of privileges that they feel can be rendered secure in the short term. But society, and especially world society in a nuclear age, may thereby find itself jeopardised in the long term in a possible clash between the inexorable pursuit of individual needs and a tenacious role defence in a world vulnerable to breakdown.

Such a controversial but potentially important argument requires examination. For example, are there genetically based universal needs? While needs theorists have offered some empirical data, Burton quotes Sites to the effect that such hard empirical data is unnecessary:

> In using the need concept we must ever be conscious that we are operating at an abstract conceptual level and that in the last analysis the actual basis of the need is tied up with certain psycho-physiological processes which are in interaction with the environment and which are not at this point in our scientific development directly observable. The fact that these processes are not directly observable, however, should not prevent us from working with the need concept if it allows us better to understand and to explain human activity.[63]

Abduction is after all a respectable way of establishing causes from effects. Burton follows Peirce in arguing that the hypothesis is an end in itself: it is the hypothesis and the process through which it is derived (abduction or retroduction) that is all-important, rather than its falsification. But we still need to see this process demonstrated, and in this Burton and other needs theorists are not as forthcoming as they might be.

In embracing so wholeheartedly the case of 'nature,' Burton and needs theorists may well have played down overly the role of 'nurture.' Even if there are basic universal human needs genetically implanted which act as the motor for learning and an explanation of behaviour, their expression takes place in a social environment. The social environment differs for each individual, and the experience of the search for the fulfilment of basic needs feeds back into a specific environment – that of each individual and group. While society may not be able, in the last resort, to mould humankind so as to turn it from their basic needs, it can engage in a dialogue with an individual and influence substantially the way in which those needs will manifest themselves. Moreover, society is not homogeneous. Basic needs, therefore, are mediated by culture – *different* cultures. The process of mediation may make the end result significantly different in terms of concrete expression. Thus, even if the starting point is universality, the end point is heterogeneity. This makes things difficult for the practitioner – for he or she is dealing with the heterogeneous concrete manifestation of basic universal human needs. For him or her, it is no great consolation to know that there was universality before culture and nurture got to work to present him or her with his or her daily fare of very different-looking problems. Difficulties in the operationalisation of the needs approach therefore face the practitioner. Here, however, Burton has been especially innovative in his development of 'controlled communication' and 'problem-solving,' and through problem-solving techniques the cultural factors can receive their proper due.[64]

Are we thus back to what has been considered traditionally as 'the proper study of humankind,' namely 'humans?' This is not a view that all advocates of the world society approach would accept, at least not in Burton's formulation. World society approaches are non-state-centric, on that there is agreement, and some form of systems or issue approach has been the most favoured unit of analysis, with stress on the importance of processes and interactions. Nevertheless, while the structuralists have made both realists and world society analysts more aware of structural factors, Burton and others have argued that structures may be a part of the problem in the sense of denying basic human needs. It is an individual's relationship with the environment that is crucial in determining behaviour and outcomes, which takes us back to the question of legitimacy and power politics. For some, 'the relationship' is therefore the most appropriate unit of analysis.[65]

Cogito ergo sum was Descartes' famous formulation. 'I relate, therefore I am' might be a reformulation appropriate to the world society approach, particularly in the UK. Although, as Mitchell points out, 'relationship' can have many meanings, in the world society context it is usually considered as an exchange, a transaction or an interaction, which may give rise to the sense of belonging to the same set.[66] Within such a set, relations can be legitimised both in terms of transactions and the distribution of roles. Role differentiation may involve inequalities, but not a sense of inequity. The relationship and role structure is freely and non-coercively accepted as 'right' in full knowledge of the circumstances. Difficulties arise when either the transactions or the role distribution are not considered to be 'right,' or if actors extraneous to the system intrude upon it coercively, or if some relevant actors are likewise excluded. Then, power politics ensues because one or other party has refused to steer, in a Deutschian sense, by putting the burden of adjustment on others. To do this is to deny the legitimacy of a relationship, but it is the 'values attached to relationships,' as Burton has argued, that provide stability in society. If a relationship is denied, it is, in this sense, a denial of worth to the individual or group, who may begin, therefore, to feel absolved of societal restraint. The business of politics, at any level – family or firm, system or state – is thus to promote the degree of legitimacy by responding to basic needs. Even for those sceptical of claims to universality, the fulfilment of basic needs makes a reasonable set of navigation points for a harmonious society. Failure to do so is to invite endless confrontation. Conflict may be endemic, but particular conflicts can be resolved, even protracted deep-seated conflicts, in a self-sustaining manner. They will be so resolved when the degree of legitimisation of relationships is high, or so the conflict researchers in the world society paradigm assert, not without reason.[67] And Burton's basic needs are a good starting point for legitimacy.

Mitchell points to a difference between what we might call the 'British world society' and the 'American or *IO* complex interdependence' approaches in that:

> [t]he world society approach begins by assuming that legitimised relationships should be regarded as a "norm," in both a statistical and a prescriptive sense. In other words, in contemporary global society it is usual to find networks of relationships that are accepted by those involved and are thus both functional for the elements interacting, and self-supporting because of the mutually recognised benefits conferred by the transactions involved. The legitimised relationship is the norm, in the sense that the sheer number of such relationships far outweighs non-legitimised relationships involving power and coercion.[68]

It is thus power politics that requires explanation. The *IO* network seems to start from the other end of the stick: the question is why power politics and state-centricity do not prevail. Both acknowledge the existence of a power-legitimacy dimension and a state-centric–non-state-centric dimension, and assume that behaviour falls permanently at neither pole but oscillates between them. Nevertheless, the starting point distorts perception of the spectrum – from either end – and this also colours prescription. As Mitchell comments:

> [t]he world society approach also posits that legitimised relationships are the norm in a prescriptive sense; that is to say, the search for peace and a harmonious global society can best begin by rejecting the conception that stability and absence of violence can

most surely be assured by the use of threats, coercion and deterrence. What is needed is a search for ways of changing existing coercive relationships into those acceptable to elements involved. This would remove the need for threat systems to ensure continuation, or "stability," to use the polite euphemism. In the best of all possible worlds, relationships would be entirely legitimised and durable because of this fact.[69]

It is not an argument saying that the world will be 'good' when the world is good. Degrees of legitimacy can be measured. Burton has suggested ways in which legitimacy can be enhanced and procedures for achieving this. But they are in no sense a panacea.[70]

In short, realism seems to be too simple and stark, and it may be wrong. World society and other transnational approaches are complex and confused, and not yet quite right. But what of structuralism?

Notes

1 For an overview, see David Armstrong, Theo Farrell and Hélène Lambert, *International Law and International Relations*, second edition (Cambridge: Cambridge University Press, 2012).
2 *Ibid.*, p. 1 (italics deleted).
3 *Ibid.*, pp. 1–2.
4 *Ibid.*, p. 2.
5 *Ibid.*, p. 2 (italics deleted).
6 *Ibid.*, p. 519.
7 *Ibid.*, p. 520.
8 *Ibid.*, p. 521.
9 *Ibid.*, pp. 521–522.
10 *Ibid.*, p. 531.
11 *Ibid.*, pp. 533–534.
12 *Ibid.*, p. 539.
13 Mitrany was a Romanian who went to LSE as a postgraduate student in 1912. Among other things he was the foreign affairs leader-writer for the *Manchester Guardian* in the great days of C.P. Scott, and was a part of the interwar Bloomsbury set. He served on the Board of Unilever from the end of the Second World War until his death in 1975, aged 87, although latterly in an honorary capacity. See his autobiographical note in Mitrany, *Functional Theory*.
14 David Mitrany, *A Working Peace System* (Chicago, IL: Quadrangle, 1966).
15 See David Mitrany, *The Functional Theory of Politics* (London: Martin Robertson, 1975); A.J.R. Groom and Paul Taylor (eds), *Functionalism Theory and Practice in International Relations* (London: University of London Press, 1975).
16 The paragraphs that follow draw upon A.J.R. Groom, 'Neofunctionalism: A Case of Mistaken Identity,' *Political Science*, Vol. 30, No. 1, 1978.
17 K.J. Holsti, *The Dividing Discipline* (London: Allen & Unwin, 1987).
18 Robert O. Keohane and Joseph S. Nye Jr (eds), *Transnational Relations and World Politics* (London: Harvard University Press, 1971).
19 *Ibid.*, p. xvii.
20 *Ibid.*, p. 371.
21 *Ibid.*, p. 386.
22 Robert O. Keohane and Joseph S. Nye Jr, *Power and Interdependence* (Boston, MA: Little, Brown, 1977).
23 *Ibid.*, p. 8.
24 *Ibid.*, p. 9.
25 *Ibid.*, p. 10.
26 *Ibid.*, p. 12.
27 *Ibid.*, p. 24.
28 *International Organization*, Spring 1982.
29 Stephen Krasner, *International Organization*, Spring 1982, p. 186.

30 Ernst B. Haas, 'Why Collaborate? Issue Linkage and International Regimes,' *World Politics*, April 1988.

31 Donald J. Puchala and Raymond F. Hopkins, 'International Regimes: Lessons from Inductive Analysis,' *International Organization*, Spring 1982, p. 246.

32 *Ibid.*, p. 247.

33 *Ibid.*, pp. 248ff.

34 Stephen Haggard and Beth A. Simmons (in 'Theories of International Regimes,' *International Organization*, Summer 1987) suggest that there are four 'families' of regime: structural, game-theoretic, functional and cognitive (p. 498). "Most structural, game-theoretic, and functional theories of regimes are state-centred, presuming unified rational actors, even if the assumption is relaxed to gain explanatory leverage" (p. 499). Haggard and Simmons argue that the cognitivists have a "radically different research program. Focusing on the intersubjective meaning structures that bind actors together, they necessarily see a looser fit between structural constraints, interests, and choices. Where functional theories see regimes as more or less efficient responses to fixed needs, cognitive theories see them as conditioned by ideology and consensual knowledge and evolving as actors learn" (p. 499).

35 Puchala and Hopkins, *International Organization*, Spring 1982, p. 271.

36 Donella H. Meadows et al., *The Limits to Growth* (London: Pan, 1974).

37 *Ibid.*, pp. 23–24.

38 Barry B. Hughes, 'World Models: The Bases of Difference,' *International Studies Quarterly*, March 1985, p. 81. In this useful survey of models, Barry Hughes points to two important world views that underpin world models and future studies – those of political economy and political ecology.

39 Such as the Brandt and Palme Commissions. The Brandt Commission, *North South* (London: Pan, 1980) and *Common Crisis* (London: Pan, 1983). The Palme Commission, *Common Security* (London: Pan, 1982).

40 Richard Falk and Samual S. Kim, 'World Order Studies and the World System,' in William R. Thompson (ed.), *Contending Approaches to World System Analysis* (London: Sage, 1983), p. 207.

41 *Ibid.*, p. 208.

42 *Ibid.*, p. 211.

43 Andrew M. Scott, *The Dynamics of Interdependence* (Chapel Hill, NC: University of North Carolina Press, 1982).

44 *Ibid.*, p. 42.

45 *Ibid.*, p.60.

46 Quincy Wright, *The Study of International Relations* (New York: Appleton–Century–Crofts, 1955), p. 6.

47 Burton first set out his conception of world society in three works: J.W. Burton, *Systems, States, Diplomacy and Rules* (Cambridge: Cambridge University Press, 1968); *World Society* (Cambridge: Cambridge University Press, 1972) and, with A.J.R. Groom, C.R. Mitchell and A.V.S. de Reuck, *The Study of World Society: A London Perspective* (Pittsburgh, PA: International Studies Association, Monograph No. 1, 1974). His more recent views stressing the role of the individual as the basic unit of analysis can be found in *Deviance, Terrorism and War* (Oxford: Martin Robertson, 1979); *Dear Survivors* (London: Frances Pinter, 1983) and *Global Conflict* (Brighton: Wheatsheaf, 1984). For a brief overview, see his 'World Society and Human Needs,' in Margot Light and A.J.R. Groom, *International Relations* (London: Frances Pinter, 1985).

48 Robert O. Keohane and Joseph S. Nye. Jr., *Power and Interdependence* (Boston, MA: Little, Brown, 1977).

49 Kenneth Waltz, *Man, the State and War* (New York: Columbia University Press, 1950), p. 60.

50 Sidney Verba, 'Assumptions of Rationality and Non-Rationality in Models of the International System,' in Klaus Knorr and Sidney Verba (eds), *The International System* (Princeton, NJ: Princeton University Press, 1961).

51 Chadwick Alger, 'Bridging the Micro and the Macro in International Relations Research,' *Alternatives*, Winter 1984–1985.

52 *Ibid.*, p. 324.

53 *Ibid.*, pp. 324–325. See Johan Galtung, *The True Worlds* (New York: Free Press, 1980).

54 *Alternatives*, Winter 1984–1985, p. 325.

55 *Ibid.*, p. 335. Alger quotes the Swedish economists Friberg and Hettne, who neatly characterise 'Blue' (market, liberal, capitalist) and 'Red' (state socialism, planning) as well.

56 John Burton, *Dear Survivors*, p. 216.

57 Burton, *Deviance*, p. 63.
58 Burton, *Dear Survivors*, p. 34.
59 *Ibid.*, p.16.
60 *Ibid.*
61 *Ibid.*, p. 35.
62 *Ibid.*, p. 36.
63 Paul Sites, quoted in Burton, *Deviance*, pp. 66–67.
64 See J.W. Burton, *Conflict and Communication* (London: Macmillan, 1969), Edward E. Azar and John W. Burton (eds), *International Conflict Resolution* (Brighton: Harvester, 1986) and J.W. Burton, *Resolving Deep-Rooted Conflict* (Lanham, MD: University Press of America, 1987).
65 C.R. Mitchell: 'World Society as Cobweb,' in M. Banks (ed.), *Conflict in World Society*, pp. 64 ff.
66 *Ibid.*, pp. 65–67.
67 See A.J.R. Groom, 'Paradigms in Conflict,' in *Review of International Studies*, April 1988.
68 Mitchell, *op. cit.*, p. 71.
69 *Ibid.*
70 Burton, *Deep-Rooted Conflict, op. cit.*

10 Structural approaches to international relations

In some ways the first approach to IR as an academic study in modern times was structuralist. The great debate on imperialism in the late nineteenth century and the early decades of this century marks the advent of the discipline. But, apart from Hobson, it was a debate that had its intellectual roots in Central and Eastern Europe and was somewhat alien to the intellectual climate of the English-speaking world. Moreover, it was an approach that later became associated with a particular state – the USSR – which was treated as a diplomatic pariah, and it lay at the basis of a political doctrine – Marxism-Leninism – which was feared, denigrated and reviled by Western elites. Structural approaches, especially those of a Marxist derivation or ethos as well as those of a geopolitical nature, were, for the most part, beyond the pale in the Anglo-American tradition, as the discipline became established in the 1920s and 1930s not to mention the Cold War.

There are many structural approaches to IR, but structuralism, as an approach, does not originate in IR. On the contrary, it has flowered in French and German thought to an extent far greater than in the Anglo-American traditions that have governed IR as a discipline. Considerations of structure take us back to the epistemological division between a methodological individualism which, if everything is reduced to units, does not easily give rise to explanation, and holism, with its emphasis on autonomous laws. Structural approaches are holistic, but they are vulnerable to the charge that they are deterministic, and to a significant extent absolutist because there is only one all-pervading structure. Certainly structural approaches bring an element of grand theory to IR.

The use of the term structuralist in IR is confusing. It evokes overtones of a French-inspired grand theory. Frequently it alludes to a more overt structuralism in the Marxist tradition, referring to the social relations of production, the world economic order and the role of the state therein. Or again, it may reflect a concern with political structure. Behind the many stipulative definitions lies a hint of some conception of grand theory, and this is not necessarily linked to any political position of left or right, although its emphasis on structure as opposed to actors does suggest some kind of 'anti-humanism.'[1] While structuralists give us new insights by asking questions different from those of other approaches, they do have a wide range of varying emphases among themselves in their approach to IR. We shall attempt to simplify this, albeit in a crude manner, by concentrating first on economic theories derived largely from the Marxist tradition, then on political theories and the debate between the advocates of economic or political underpinnings of structure, before considering the extent to which the geopolitical approach can be considered usefully in a structural light.

In each of these three categories of structural approach – economic, political and geopolitical – there is an element in common. Structure is independent of the actors which form part of it. While structure is affected by the activities of actors within it, it also has a determining effect on the behaviour of actors and the outcome of social processes. An emphasis must be given to the whole since this has an impact greater than the sum of its parts. It must therefore be taken into consideration in any empirical theory of behaviour at whatever level. As Richard Little put it:

> Structuralists assume that human behaviour cannot be understood simply by examining individual motivation and intention because, when aggregated, human behaviour precipitates structures of which the individuals may be unaware.[2]

Structure thus takes on a life of its own and becomes a social fact that moulds future behaviour so that individuals (or states) find it difficult either to escape from such constraints or to create new ones more to their liking.

This simple notion is now clearly acknowledged in the other two principal paradigms in IR. The structural realists or neorealists, as we shall see in greater detail in the next chapter, have rediscovered the structuralist wheel, or at least its terminology. Even Morgenthau himself, while formulating his six principles of political realism from an actor's perspective, did consider the structure of the international diplomatic system and regretted the movement from multipolarity to bipolarity in the postwar period. Systems thinkers, for their part, came easily to thinking in terms of wholes since it is implicit in the very nature of their basic unit of analysis and endeavour. The resurgence of structuralism has had the happy effect of inducing them to consider more carefully the durable aspects of systems' structures.

More generally, structuralists have had a significant impact upon the conceptual, empirical and prescriptive agendas and discourse to the extent that we are all to some degree impregnated with structuralist ideas. The interdependence of politics and economics is now widely recognised, if not enough by economists, and theories of *dependencia*, and centre–periphery models have a cogency and relevance for the understanding of historical and contemporary international relations. Wallerstein and Modelski, among others, have postulated a single world system that emerged in the fifteenth century and which continues to this day, thereby bringing to the forefront not only structural factors but also a heightened awareness of the need for historical depth. More recently, the notion of a single world system has been extended backwards in time to a 5,000-year world system.[3]

In the last chapter we have already noted the importance of historical sociology for contemporary IR, by referring to the work of Michael Mann. We shall, in considering both economic and political structural approaches to IR, make reference to the work of structural historians. These historians give salience to the very long-term evolution of the world system, to the rise and fall of successive international orders and the waves in economics and war at the heart of the world system.[4] What is the driving force at a particular time – economics, political factors or culture – is a matter of fierce debate, but it is a debate about emphasis because few structuralist historians would advocate one factor to the exclusion of others. We shall consider this debate, using the writings of Wallerstein and Modelski as exemplars.

Structural approaches, by nature of their emphasis, force us to think in grand terms. But the application of structural thought to economic, political, historical or cultural issues incites controversy because it is difficult to be authoritative in demonstrating the play of grand theory in day-to-day events and processes and in the behaviour of actors. What, at one level, seems to be plausible is difficult to discern in the minutiae of daily life and, given the practical and pragmatic turn of mind of practitioners and most academics in IR, this constitutes an additional barrier to the proper consideration of structural approaches to the field. Why, then, and how, did IR begin to give structural factors their due?

One starting point is the intellectual effervescence generated by post-behaviouralism in the United States and in parts of Europe, notably Germany and Scandinavia. Associated with this was the revisionist school of international historians of the Cold War and US foreign policy. This leads us into a consideration of the Marxist tradition of structural analysis, which takes capitalism as the basic structure. In contrast to the centre–periphery and *dependencia* theorists and the world-system approach of Wallerstein and his colleagues, Modelski espouses an analysis of long cycles, which is primarily political, not economic, in orientation. The debate is then joined about the relationship between economic and political factors in the world system. But it is not the only approach to world structure. The long-standing geopolitical tradition has its contemporary formulation in the work of those studying ecopolitics, such as the Sprouts,[5] and the notion of lateral pressure developed by Choucri and North,[6] which has been taken up by Ashley.[7]

Post-behaviourism in international politics

'The New Revolution in Political Science' was the title of David Easton's presidential address to the American Political Science Association in September 1969.[8] In it, Easton urged his colleagues to come to terms with the post-behavioural revolution. Post-behaviouralists sought to go beyond the arid and hopeless quest for a value-free, positivistic social science to recognise that social scientists are not political eunuchs, but political actors, and that they should take cognisance of this. "Its battle cries are *relevance and action*," Easton reported. Moreover, it is "future oriented."[9] Easton then proceeded to spell out the credo of post-behaviouralism:

> It is more important to be relevant and meaningful for contemporary urgent social problems than to be sophisticated in the tools of investigation . . . Behavioral science conceals an ideology of empirical conservatism. To confine oneself exclusively to the description and analysis of facts is to hamper the understanding of these same facts in their broadest context . . . Political science unwittingly purveys an ideology of social conservatism tempered by modest incremental change . . . The task . . . is . . . to help political science reach out to the real needs of mankind in a time of crisis . . . Science cannot be and never has been evaluatively neutral . . . Hence to understand the limits of our knowledge we need to be aware of the value premises on which it stands and the alternatives for which this knowledge could be used . . . To know is to bear the responsibility for acting and to act is to engage in reshaping society . . . Contemplative science was a product of the nineteenth century when a broader moral agreement was shared. Action science of necessity reflects the contemporary conflict in society over ideals and this must permeate and color the whole research enterprise itself . . . Politicization of the professions is inescapable as well as desirable.[10]

Easton himself went a considerable way towards espousing this credo, and the line of thought takes us directly to critical theory with its strong criticism of positivism. But the jump was not immediate.

The intellectual effervescence of post-behaviouralism reflected the political and social context in the United States at the time. The Vietnam War, the revolt of the black community, nuclear issues, radical politics on the campus and abroad, May 1968 in Paris, were the context in which a new generation of scholars in the United States and on the Continent of Europe sought to lend their science and intellect to the building of a better world. The entry onto the political stage of a considerable number of 'third world' states and the consequent placing of development issues high on the international agenda was instrumental in sparking an academic interest in the political and economic issues of development. By the late 1960s comparative politics and political development had lost some of their intellectual cutting edge and were losing salience to *dependencia* studies.

The theories of *dependencia* integrated political analysis into an economic framework and, for the first time, a major academic thrust in Western IR came not from the UK or the United States, but from Latin America. Quickly, the nature of capitalism became central to the analysis and, while dependency studies continued to be fuelled by developing world scholars joined by their intellectual followers in the UK, North America and on the Continent, such studies were only partial theories of international political economy. Wallerstein, inspired by the ideas of Braudel, took the argument further by taking the capitalist world system from the late fifteenth century as his unit of analysis. The post-behavioural revolution had started a process that led to a metamorphosis of the intellectual agenda. There was now a structuralist world-system approach to rival world society and other pluralist conceptions (discussed in Chapter 9). Moreover, the structural realists or neorealists likewise began to give serious consideration to structural variables, but of a political nature, and in the case of Modelski, to do so in the same historical context as Wallerstein.

While the agenda was thus broadened and given greater historical depth, the post-behavioural spirit of critical thought also broached a traditional area of IR – that of foreign policy. In particular that of US foreign policy in the twentieth century, seen as the policy of the principal power of capitalism, the hegemon in the world system be it conceived economically or politically. Most of the radical writers conceived the world system in economic terms. They saw US policy from Wilsonian internationalism to beyond the Vietnam War as being one to make the world safe for capitalism, and in particular US capitalism, if necessary at the expense of the old declining imperialist Powers. While conservative historians could agree on this central thrust of US policy, the radicals went on to express their conviction that capitalism was necessarily imperialistic and exploitative. Thus, many of the ills of the world could be laid at the United States' door. Particular attention by radical historians was paid to US policy in negotiating the postwar political and economic framework after the two world wars.[11] In this, the United States was deemed largely to have been successful in achieving its aims after the Second World War, even at the cost of provoking the Cold War. For the radical historians, the deepening North–South problem was evidence enough of the plausibility of their thesis. Ironically, two of the most cogent and well-written statements of the radical case, even after due (but unnecessary) allowance has been made for bias, or of selective perception by the setting up of straw men, are made by writers in strong disagreement with the radical thesis. Robert Tucker's *The Radical Left and American Foreign Policy* and Benjamin Cohen's *The Question of Imperialism* are important contributions to the debate.[12]

For Tucker, the core of the radical historians' approach lay in their unwillingness to see the growth to, and conduct of, world power by the United States in terms other than economic: "The essence of the radical critique is not simply that America is aggressive and imperialistic but that it is so out of an institutional necessity . . . the institutional structure of American capitalism."[13]

As Harry Magdoff has so simply and starkly put it, "imperialism is not a matter of choice for a capitalist society; it is the way of life of such a society."[14] Aggressive expansion cannot be explained by security needs, chance or the machinations of a bureaucracy since these are all subservient to the capitalist imperative.[15] This, Tucker saw as central to the radical analysis. It was a national policy driven by a transnational economic and social structure. Politics was merely the instrument of this drive. Tucker does not deny that "America's economic war aim was to save capitalism at home and abroad," as Kolko put it, but he does question the assertion that this was the sole or overriding war aim.[16] For Tucker, political and security questions have an autonomous validity, and they are not necessarily subservient to economic questions. Moreover, with Cohen, and like Hobson before him, Tucker rejects the notion that imperialism is a necessary and organic part of capitalism.

Cohen's thesis was that, although trade, investment and raw materials in developing world countries are important to developed countries, they are not necessary for the developed countries, and, therefore, contrary to the radical thesis, economic imperialism is not an inevitable concomitant of capitalism:[17] "As important as trade and investment connections may be for the rich, they are not decisive."[18] They may be important for particular firms, sectors or countries, but they are not a structural requirement for the system as a whole: "They are simply a convenience – the path of least resistance to profits, prosperity, and growth. Of course, even convenience may be sufficient excuse to take advantage of the poor countries – to distort their growth and exploit them."[19]

Thus, Tucker and Cohen were not inclined to make a difference in degree become a difference in kind. Their argument was not to deny some aspects of the radical case – US policy was to make the world safe for (US) capitalism, which could exploit the developing world – but these were not organic to, or necessary for, capitalism. This can be seen in their acceptance of Magdoff's thesis:

> The reality of imperialism goes far beyond the immediate interest of this or that investor: the underlying purpose is nothing less than keeping as much as possible of the world open for trade and investment by the giant multinational corporations . . . When all these factors are taken into account, it will be seen that attempts to explain isolated actions in "bookkeeping" terms make no sense . . . the expenditure of vast sums of money are not balanced in the eyes of US policy makers against profitable business opportunities; rather they are weighed according to the judgement of military and political leaders on what is necessary to control and influence, in order to keep the entire area within the imperialist system in general, and within the United States sphere of influence in particular.[20]

For Cohen and Tucker, this sphere was as much a politico-security sphere as an economic one.[21] Indeed, it was an integrated whole of the three elements.

One aspect of the radical critique that should not be ignored is the Leninist one, of the imperial rivalry of the major capitalist Powers that, as Fred Halliday argued, is still with us:

> Inter-imperialist conflict lay at the origins of both the First and Second World Wars, and despite US predominance, it has continued to fuel major international tensions in the post-war epoch. After two decades of relative harmony, emphasis on the increased level of conflict between major capitalist states began to be noticeable from the late 1960s onwards, as the rivalry between the USA on the one side, and Europe and Japan on the other, gathered force. It was an emphasis found in the analyses of both left and right.[22]

Radical historians were not alone in noticing the degree to which the United States took the UK's economic place in Latin America, as well as the Middle and Near East, and not always in the most gentle of manners.[23] The Marshall Plan was, of course, warmly welcomed by Western European governments and most of their people, but it did give US business a red carpet *entrée* into the European economy, and it was only in the 1970s that a dependent relationship began to become an interdependent one in trans-Atlantic terms. It still remains to become so to all parties' satisfaction across the Pacific. Rival blocs are not unthinkable as protectionism grows apace. What was the 'engine of growth' could become the 'apple of discord,' to mix the metaphors. It is clear, therefore, that the Leninist thesis of inter-capitalist competition has both advocates and relevance today. Since the structuralist approach owes much to its Marxist-Leninist heritage, it is to that heritage that we now turn.

The Marxist heritage

As Tony Thorndike pointed out in an insightful essay, "in International Relations, Marxism is primarily treated as an *ideology* in the formation of the foreign policies of particular states."[24] Unhappily, those bad old days are not entirely behind us. Indeed, too many students of IR would now, on reflection, deny the importance both of structural approaches and of the historic and present debt such approaches owe to the Marxist tradition in part because of the current seeming eclipse of Marxist thought. Marx argued that the superstructure of political and social ideas, institutions and, indeed, social consciousness, was a reflection of and derived from the substructure of economic and production relations. In our time, and that of Marx, these relations are, to a lesser or greater degree, capitalistic. In such a situation the state and its servants are deemed to act in defence, and to further the interests, of the capitalist ruling class. But these interests are not immutable: they evolve. Neither are they always complementary within the capitalist class. Moreover, mistakes can be, and are, made. Nevertheless, while a state may have a degree of relative autonomy, it is not the starting point for fundamental analysis. The unit of analysis is class.[25]

At the world level, capitalism is seen to be a progressive force because it was instrumental in the downfall of feudalism and it will itself succumb to its own internal contradictions as the proletariat overthrows the bourgeoisie to establish a socialist, and later, a communist classless society. Capitalism, therefore, has its uses as an engine of change. But for the most part Marx concentrated on class relations within state and societal structures. It was Lenin, among others, who added a global dimension by postulating that imperialism was organic to and, indeed, the highest stage of capitalism. Imperialism, too, had its contradictions between the imperial Powers each seeking to establish a single monopoly position in all aspects of the global economic system. Their global struggle would become the death knell of capitalism. Again, there was a sense of progress, of stages on the way to a different and better world. However, more recently, this sense of movement, indeed progress, has been challenged by *dependencia* and world-system theorists, who see a much more static system in which the present world is witnessing a greater accentuation of different levels of development and of exploitation. Indeed, the system has been stable structurally for 500 years. In short, they are far less sanguine than Marx and Lenin about the degree and rapidity of progress that the contradictions of capitalism are likely to engender.

We have seen how in the late nineteenth and early twentieth centuries the debate on imperialism revitalised the Marxist tradition and provided one basis for the academic study of international relations. This tradition was ignored until the 1970s in so far as the mainstream of IR in Western academia was concerned. A new interest in economic theories of IR, which reflect the Marxist heritage, came not only from the revisionist historians but more centrally from scholars in Latin America, whose principal concerns were the causes of underdevelopment and the processes of development of what came to be known as the 'developing world.' They came to the conclusion that structural considerations were of great moment in this and, in particular, the nature of capitalism as a global structure. As they articulated their ideas in theories of *dependencia*, they were absorbed into the mainstream of IR by scholars whose intellectual awareness had been heightened by the tenets of post-behaviouralism and the need to understand the post-colonial world and its concerns. Thus, IR returned to its roots, or one aspect thereof – capitalism as a structure.

Capitalism as a structure

We have mentioned earlier those Marxists who saw historical evolution in teleological terms with an inevitable progress towards communism. For them, as for Marx himself, the spread of capitalism was to be welcomed as a movement towards that goal. Others, however, were not so sanguine. Paul Baran, in his *Political Economy of Growth*,[26] argued that the developing countries were not just 'behind' in this global forward movement but different in kind from developed capitalist countries. They needed, therefore, to be considered separately as fitting into capitalism in a different and especially disadvantaged way. Starting from different premises, a group of Latin American economists working for the UN Economic Commission for Latin America (ECLA), led by Raoul Prebisch, began to come to not dissimilar conclusions. In his clear and helpful survey on development and dependency Chris Brown suggests a threefold division of the literature: that is, *dependencia*, centre–periphery analysis and world-system analysis, which we shall adopt.[27]

ECLA analysts soon came to question the conventional wisdom of development theory in the 1950s and to suggest that the lack of development was due not only to deficiencies or mistaken policies in the developing countries themselves but, more importantly, to the terms of trade that, after the boom of the Second World War and the Korean War, were moving against exporters of primary products. This was a long-term trend, the remedy for which was deemed to be import substitution in which protected industries would be set up locally to obviate the need for so many increasingly expensive imports (in terms of their costs in exports necessary to finance the imports). The strategy of import substitution did not resolve the problem, and writers in the *dependencia* school suggested that this was so for a number of reasons:

> [b]ecause the internal market for consumer goods is too limited and the nature of demand is determined by elite tastes oriented to the products of the developed world and because it tends to be based on capital-intensive industries, which have low employment effects and therefore do little to create demand. Moreover, it is based on imported capital goods, components and materials which, therefore, does little to assist the balance of payments and may even cause crises, and it increases dependence on multinational capital and on foreign technology.[28]

The remedy, the *dependencia* school suggested, would have to be found elsewhere in the context of centre–periphery relations. It was not just a question of economic relations, which had been the main concern of the ECLA and *dependencia* analysts, but the structure within which these relations were embedded.

Andre Gunder Frank stresses the centre–periphery relationship or, in his terms, the metropolis–satellite structure of the capitalist system, both now and in the past. The metropolis exploits the satellite, a process which started in Latin America with the Spanish and Portuguese conquests, and it keeps the surplus, which is then used to develop the metropolis. Development in the satellite is thus hindered and choked so that there is the 'development of underdevelopment' in the satellite. This is a wilful process in contrast to the notion of 'underdevelopment' – the state of affairs before capitalist penetration occurred. Frank notes that when the metropolis was cut off from the satellite, as in the case of Latin America in the world wars or when, as with Japan, no metropolis existed, the development of underdevelopment ceased, and genuine development began. However, Frank's analysis needs to come to terms with the autonomous development in the periphery of NICs (newly industrialising countries) and a new stage in the international division of labour whereby MNCs invest and establish manufacturing subsidiaries in developing world countries. Nevertheless, in Frank's view, the problem was structural and so, therefore, would have to be the solution. Other writers laid different emphases, for example Emmanuel and Amin,[29] but the trend was clear: the issue of development was leading to a questioning of structure, and especially centre–periphery relations. But centre–periphery relations were not only an economic phenomenon, they could be seen as a multidimensional form of contemporary imperialism. Johan Galtung saw them as such.[30]

Galtung's concern was about centre–periphery relations both within and between states. These relations constitute, in their ensemble, a modern form of imperialism. The centre of a state in the developed world draws into it 'the best' of society, not only in terms of the fruits of industry but cultural institutions, advanced hospitals and the like, which are supported by the wider society but enjoyed in a disproportionate manner by the centre, as thoroughly explored by Immanuel Wallerstein.

The world as a system

The *oeuvre* of Wallerstein must surely be among the most talked about, the most quoted – and the least read in their totality – in the Marxist tradition since those of the master himself. Wallerstein says that the world-system perspective was inspired by five rejections. The first was a denial of a single or multidisciplinary approach. Second, the state was rejected as a primary unit of analysis and the "state–society antinomy was a misleading premise for enquiry." Political action was seen as being "inside *all* social action." Third, there was a rejection of both cyclical and evolutionary theories of history. "Instead, insofar as any historical system existed, there were within it repetitive patterns (cycles), for as long as the particular system existed." The fourth rejection was that of the notion of the sequential development of comparable subunits because "The dynamic of the system not only was the sum of all the forces contained in it but also affected all its zones at every moment."[31] The final rejection was that of "formulating concepts as essences rather than as processes."[32] Thus, Wallerstein had cleared the decks ready for his thesis.

Wallerstein's basic unit of analysis is the world system, or, to be more precise, the contemporary world system of capitalism, which began with the establishment of a capitalist world economy, without the accompaniment of a world empire, in about 1500. The world economy is:

> [a] single division of labor within which are located multiple cultures . . . but which has no overarching political culture. Without a political structure to redistribute the appropriated surplus, the surplus can only be redistributed via "the market," however frequently states located within the world-economy intervene to distort the market. Hence the mode of production is capitalist.
>
> A capitalist mode is one in which production is for exchange; that is, it is determined by its profitability on a market in which each buyer wishes to buy cheap (and therefore that which is, in the long run, most efficiently produced and marketed) but in which each seller wishes to sell dear (and therefore is concerned that the efficiencies of others are not permitted to reduce his sales).[33]

Let us note in passing that Modelski would assert that, although there was no world empire in the cycles of the world system, there was most certainly an efficacious global political structure – a subject to which we shall return. Since Wallerstein does not accept this he is surprised that the new world economy did not collapse, as similar such economies had before, when sub-systems drifted away because there was no political authority to arrest the drift and impose and maintain the unity in the form of a world empire. However, once surviving, it aroused three questions in Wallerstein's mind: those of its genesis, once consolidated that of its *modus operandi*, and its secular trends.[34]

Wallerstein argues that feudal Europe had "'exhausted its potential' in its great socioeconomic spurt of 1100–1250." The real income of the ruling states was falling, due to the rising of real wages caused by demographic disasters, peasant revolts and the internecine warfare of the ruling strata.[35] There was no world empire to stop the rot. Instead there was a sort of creative leap of the imagination on the part of the ruling strata. It involved trying an alternative mode of surplus appropriation, that of the market, to see whether it might serve to restore the declining real income of the ruling groups. This involved geographical expansion, spatial economic specialisation, the rise of the 'absolutist' state – in short, the creation of a capitalist world economy.[36] It should be noted that in his work Wallerstein goes into detailed historical analysis, but not always without controversy.

The *modus operandi* of the system revolved around two struggles – between bourgeoisie and proletariat, and between core and periphery:

> The genius, if you will, of the capitalist system, is the interweaving of these two channels of exploitation which overlap but are not identical and create the political and cultural complexities (and obscurities) of the system. Among other things, it has made it possible to respond to the politico-economic pressures of cyclical economic crises by rearranging spatial hierarchies without significantly impairing class hierarchies.[37]

This it has done by outward expansion for, unlike in Modelski's conception, Wallerstein's world economy grew piecemeal and it did not become truly global, in all its aspects, until after 1917. However, there is within this expansion a cycle of repression (necessary to enable the maintenance of unequal distribution) becoming more costly, and 'reform,' to make that cost less onerous. A little of the surplus is used to 'buy off' the rising class, but this can then result in "depriving the top strata of a prize high enough to be worth struggling for. This is the 'failure of nerve' that is setting in."[38] This may lead to changes within the core, Holland giving way to the UK, movement from periphery to semi-periphery, core to semi-periphery or the reverse: that is, the spatial dimension acts as a stabilising factor for the class dimension. But eventually that may not be enough, and in the fullness of time – a long time, Wallerstein insists – the capitalist world economy will give way to a socialist world government.[39]

Wallerstein lays particular stress on the semi-periphery as a factor likely to enable the smooth running of the world economy. While repression by state forces has its efficacious uses and there is a "pervasiveness of an ideological commitment to the system as a whole" by "the staff or cadres of the system . . . [it] is the normal condition . . . to have a three-layered structure [core, semi-periphery, periphery]. When and if this ceases to be the case, the world-system disintegrates."[40] The semi-periphery countries are given a cut of the surplus to prevent revolt, but they are denied political rights to make them "constantly vulnerable to confiscatory measures whenever their economic profits become sufficiently swollen so that they might begin to create for themselves military might."[41] They are a political device to stop polarisation, rather than an economic necessity. The semi-periphery is both exploiter and exploited.

The state is one means by which reallocations within the core, semi-periphery or periphery or between them can take place. It can interfere in the market in such a way as to deflect normal market forces and secure a non-market rate of exploitation or distribution of surplus.[42] But there is not always agreement as to how this should be done, its extent and in favour of whom, among the bourgeois world class and their attendant states.[43] They may use states to intervene for the smooth functioning of the system in the general class interest, or they may use the state to steal a march on their 'class colleagues.' And beyond states there are cultural communities that have a potential to muddy the waters since "the formation and disintegration of cultural communities do form a fundamental set of processes in their own right."[44]

As Giddens has pointed out, "for Wallerstein the existence of separate states seems to be a largely historical residue of the fact that capitalism came into being within a pre-formed state system."[45] In Wallerstein's conception, states are there to be used or not, as the case may be, usually to meet the functional needs of the system. Indeed, there are strong functional elements of a sociological kind in Wallerstein's thought.

Wallerstein's position is a very clear-cut one in the Marxist debate between those who argue that the core-periphery division of labour of the capitalist world economy leads to unequal exchange relations in favour of the core and others, who "argue that relations of production (class relations) precede economic exchange, making class relations the determinate social relation of world capitalism."[46] The latter is the classical position in a debate that we have broached before – it is a debate about whether to emphasise class relations within societies or exploitation between core and periphery. It also raised the question of the relationship between the two struggles. Bergesen argues that since most of the global means of production are under the control of the core, this makes "the core-periphery relation a class relation rather than an unequal exchange relation,"[47] at least in its essence. But Wallerstein's thought makes it difficult to square the circle in this way. His emphasis is on the spatial aspects of exploitation – the physically separate core and periphery – which could lead him to be more regionally or even state-oriented than he is wont to admit.[48]

Wallerstein's emphasis on the core and core states suggests that politics is important and that the world system may not only have an economic rationale or logic but also the makings of a political logic as well – as is Modelski's contention. It is also easy to see why so many Marxists reject Wallerstein's work. Chris Brown has commented that, "Although Wallerstein uses much of the language of Marxism his notions are actually very unmarxist in their denial of 'progress,' their stress on distribution/exchange rather than production, and their lack of interest in the law of value."[49]

The plenitude of nuclear weapons (and other weapons of mass destruction), capable of destroying the world as we know it, is, of course, a powerful balancing factor on the side of an important political logic. The inability and inappropriateness of market forces to deal effectively with the 'green' agenda and other 'one world' problems also points to the imperative for political intervention. Moreover, exploitation gives rise to a contested distribution that is, in its nature, political, although its substance may be economic. In addition, the distribution of resources and the inequalities that arise therefrom again suggest a spatial and political factor. It also suggests that neither an economic nor a political theory of structure alone is likely to be as rich as an integrated theory of both. As Zolberg has remarked:

> In an analysis of global transformation, it depends very much on the investigator's starting point whether culture or social structure, politics or economics, is considered causally dominant. That starting point itself is dictated by the investigator's inclination toward one or the other intellectual tradition, by his position in contemporary political controversies, or merely by his field of academic specialization.[50]

The emergence, and now perhaps the demise, of the world system of states and the growth of alternative world political structures, as well as that of capitalism, is an empirical phenomenon, the explanation of which is worthy of the intellectual heavyweights of structuralism. Wallerstein has made a start but so, too, in a more political conception of global structure, has Modelski, an author who seems to have lost part of his salience but not his relevance in contemporary IR, and whose work was fundamental to the development of the discipline in the 1980s.

Long cycles in a global structure

Just as Wallerstein has become pre-eminent in the economic field, so have George Modelski and his associates in the political field. It is, therefore, to Modelski's work that we can turn to get the essence and flavour of this approach.[51] Modelski's argument captures the imagination. It is not exclusive since it includes economic and cultural elements as well as the political, although the latter clearly dominate. For this reason, and his concern with governance in an anarchical society with emphasis on the concomitant prevalence of power politics, Modelski is clearly in the realist tradition. But his starting point is structure, or at least the five centuries of world history at the global level, so he fully merits (if that is the right word) the appellation of a structural realist.

World-system approaches, such as those of Modelski and Wallerstein, have several characteristics in common.[52] They acknowledge the existence of a single world system, on a global basis, for at least the last five centuries, which has political, economic and cultural components at the global level. They cannot agree on which component dominates or on the interaction between the components – the debate about which we shall discuss later. Nevertheless, there is a consensus that a fruitful starting point, and basic framework, is the notion of a world system. It is within this framework, or so it is contended, that other phenomena are likely to fall into place. Their importance is not minimised but put into an historico-structural perspective. That perspective is no blind structure: it is enlivened by cycles as the processes of life manifest themselves. Such cyclical processes have, by their very nature, a predictive capacity. In short, there is the essential 'holism' of the structural approach: historically, in the sense of a major portion of recorded human history, in terms of dimension, be it political, economic or cultural and in approach, since the traditional boundaries of discipline are set aside in a new fusion. And this is important, as Thompson points out:

> World system analysis emphasizes structures and processes that, while not altogether ignored in the past, have never received adequate and integrated attention. To the extent that world system arguments prove to be well supported by the evidence, a respectable proportion of social science knowledge will require considerable revision. In the process, our understanding of world history will undergo equally extensive revision . . . Finally, the potential of world system analyses for reintegrating a large number of frustratingly separate fields of study and levels of analysis is unusually promising.[53]

The stakes are indeed high. Modelski's starting point is the long cycles, which in his view are "a conservative process of repetition" but also a "dynamic phenomena that embody evolutionary development through strategic innovations."[54] The interaction between political and economic factors is an important element in Modelski's thought, which thus differs markedly from Wallerstein's in this regard. In their respective explanations of the world system, Modelski gives politics a primacy whereas Wallerstein gives capitalism a near exclusivity. As Modelski explains:

The long cycle is the process of change in the structure of politics at the global level; its essence has been the rise of nation-states to a position of world leadership and the competition that has followed. Running in tandem with it over the past five hundred years has also been the process of emergence, and subsequent decline, of lead economies. While the rise of world powers has been central to world politics, and the formation of lead economies has been fundamental to world economics, the relationship of these two processes to each other . . . has rarely been subject to sustained analysis . . . At the global level, generation-long periods of fundamental political innovation alternate with those of change in the industrial structure. The coordinating mechanism seems to reside in the sustained movements in prices known as the Kondratieff waves.[55]

Modelski denies the absence of governance and vaunts the existence of leadership at the global level.[56] On these grounds Modelski has cast doubt over the very foundations of the realist world – anarchy, separateness, self-help and, as we shall see in Kenneth Waltz's neo-realist conception, no functional differentiation. Modelski's rejection of anarchy stems from his acknowledgement of a "global political system," which "is the topmost political structure of the world."[57]

Within this 'topmost political structure,' leadership is exercised by a particular power, "but such a nation-state does not rule the world (or other nation-states) in an imperial manner nor exercise 'world-wide domination'; rather, it orders aspects of global problems in a manner at the time regarded as legitimate." This leads to the distinction between leadership and hegemony. For Modelski, that differentiation is based on the application of two criteria: common interest and legitimacy. According to him:

> When a leading state acts in the public interest and its actions are thought legitimate, then its behaviour cannot be described as hegemonial. On the other hand, we need not assume that nation-states in positions of world leadership can never act other than in the common interest or legitimately. All we do is not to adopt an initial presumption of hegemonial, that is, in the classical style, tyrannical, behaviour.[58]

Modelski asks of what the services provided by the leading Power consist and responds, "They are, in respect of global politics: (i) agenda formation, (ii) mobilisation, (iii) decision-making, (iv) administration, and (v) innovation."[59] Agenda formation "concerns the clarification and definition of global problems and the assignment of priorities." It is thus "a function of knowledge and values, and is the product of debates."[60] Mobilisation refers to the ability to build a coalition of support for the existing global system, whereas decision-making arises out of the ability to prevail in a systemic war and thus make "a basic decision about the political direction of the global system for a significant period ahead." This decision needs to be administered and an "active economy is a basic precondition for such administration." Innovation, by definition, is unpredictable, but what Modelski has in mind is "Britain launching the Industrial Revolution, that moved and reorganised the world and achieved more than a strictly political transformation."[61]

The changing balance between legitimised and power politics is what Modelski identifies as the long cycle, of which in the present world system there have been five, during which the following Powers exercised world leadership: Portugal (sixteenth century), the Netherlands (seventeenth century), Britain (eighteenth century), Britain again (nineteenth century) and the United States (twentieth century). Portugal established the system although Venice could be considered a forerunner, and, like its successors, it went through the long cycle:

Each contains the same characteristic sequence of events: *a global war*; a worldwide struggle of major proportions and consequences; an era of political and economic consolidation (*world power*); a mid-course period of political unsettlement and possible innovation (delegitimation); and a final sequence of rivalry and competitive disruption (deconcentration), setting the stage for another global conflict.[62]

That there were serious rivals for such a position of world leadership, and Spain, France, Germany and the Soviet Union immediately sprang to mind, Modelski readily admits, but they did not ultimately prevail because they lacked, in masterful plenitude, the capacities necessary for the task. These are:

(i) a secure platform from which to observe and debate the state of the world system and its problems; (ii) a society capable of coalitioning, that is coherent and stable, hence worth aligning with, but one that is also open to the world and pluralistic in its internal arrangements; (iii) a political system with effective forces for global reach . . . ; (iv) an economy that is of world significance in its lead industries and foreign trade; and (v) capacity to innovate and respond to emerging world problems. As this list makes abundantly clear, leadership in this context does not bestow upon its holders the licence to govern other national states or to intervene in their domestic or local politics.[63]

And what of economics? A 'lead economy' is an important requirement for political leadership. Modelski has a clear idea of what constitutes a 'lead economy':

[w]e emphasise not size . . . but the creation of leading sectors and the relative size of the industrial economy, and participation in world trade, both qualitatively . . . and quantitatively . . . The linkage between world power and lead economy is not really surprising. A lead economy requires the political stability and international protection afforded by the services of the quality and the dimensions afforded by the world power . . . On the other hand, world power is also costly and cannot be maintained without the support of an active and growing economy. Hence a lead economy built upon a global flow of activities becomes a sine qua non of world power.[64]

In his view, "the significance of the world powers has not been in their size but in their capacity to accomplish global functions."[65] And it is this ability to fulfil *global* functions that resolves the apparent anomaly whereby the world leader might not necessarily be the principal regional Power. Indeed, until the United States, that was never the case. But the leader could survive in its region *and* perform global functions, whereas rivals might have the edge at the regional level, often through sheer size, but they were found wanting in comparative global capacities. Nineteenth-century Britain and France are a case in point.

Modelski gives a principal, but not the predominant, place to economics in a symbiotic relationship between the political and economic systems. But what is the basis of this linkage? Is there a cycle of general expansion and a slowing down in both systems, or is there an alternance between political growth and economic expansion? Modelski favours the latter because it is likely to be simple and require less coordination. However simplistically, this at least enables some handle to be obtained on world culture, a notion the importance of which Modelski acknowledges but finds difficult to accommodate in his framework. Prices are linked to values, which in turn are grounded in culture, which is also tied to politics and ideology: "It could be, therefore, that both global politics and global economics 'listen to the same drummer': coordinated by the same value-price-priority system, both being affected by, and both responding to, the same movements in social valuations."[66]

This explains Modelski's interest in Kondratieff cycles of prices, in which Kondratieff identified long-term movements of prices of thirty years' length. Modelski attempts to match these with his century-long world leadership cycles, not with unmitigated success. Nevertheless, despite this, and the more general difficulty of operationalising and incorporating the notion of world culture in his framework, Modelski's schema has a plausible ring. He can provide convincing examples and explain away sensibly counter-examples. His work has an authentically intuitive rightness to it in its grand lines.

Modelski's schema not only inspires the historical imagination by shedding a pale and fitful light where there was little before, it also alerts us to our current predicament. We seem, as we would expect, to be in the period of the delegitimation of the world leadership of the United States, both politically and economically. However, Modelski is quick to point out that this is so only if we assume the 'constancy' of the modern world system, a constancy which "may indeed need to be questioned."[67] Modelski alludes to transnationalism and the sorts of considerations that are important in the world-society approach discussed in Chapter 9.

Modelski has explained a linkage between political and economic factors, but he is noticeably unconvincing on incorporating cultural including ideological factors. Wallerstein and the Marxist tradition give undisputed pride of place to economic structure. Yet there has been little debate between these two opposing conceptions. There has been a vigorous affirmation of position by the leading advocates of the two approaches, but beyond that little more than a dialogue of the deaf or an intellectual turning away of one from the other rather than a joining of debate. Perhaps this is understandable since such grand theories, while attractive, exciting and seductive, are weak on prescription for the affairs of today or tomorrow, and such issues are, for most of us, our daily lot. This is not to deny the wealth of detailed historical evidence sifted by both Wallerstein and Modelski, but history is, perforce, personal and selective – it is a plausible fairy tale. In effect, it reinforces rather than closes an argument, which lends it an intriguing fascination. But an historical argument is more than a charade. It can provide context to current events and point us in new directions. In this Modelski and his colleagues provide us with great contextual relevance and point to more exciting vistas, precisely because of the fusion between political, economic and cultural factors. Equally to the point is their ability to broaden their horizon from the axioms of power politics to a conception of legitimised politics. Long cycles can be managed in concert through cooperation – or is this merely wishful thinking? Can capitalism evolve or must it be destroyed? Is a global war 'inevitable' no matter how catastrophic it might be? It cannot be gainsaid that those who study global structures, be they economic or political, are relevant. But these structures can also be conceived in other ways. It is to the geopolitical and geoecological conception of structure that we now turn.

Geopolitics and meta-rationality approaches

In Chapter 3 mention was made of geopolitical theorists who were prominent in the years when IR was coming to the point of being an academic discipline. Mackinder had a great intellectual influence and Alfred Thayer Mahan an enormous practical influence and popularity in the UK, the United States and Germany. Ironically, Mackinder (UK) was the theorist of land power, while Mahan (US) that of sea power, when the United States was still principally a continental state in the making. But geopolitics also flourished on the Continent of Europe. The Swedish scholar Rudolf Kjellen and the German geographer Friedrich Ratzel both made noteworthy contributions, as did Yves Lacoste and the *Herodote* group in France.[68] Geopolitics at that time was concerned with the 'science' of the development and configuration of states, "an expression of Social Darwinism and imperialist rivalry" or a strategic doctrine with normative implications.[69] There is an element of holism in geopolitics. Parker defines geopolitics as "the study of the international scene from a spatial or geocentric viewpoint, the understanding of the whole – what Ritter called *Ganzheit* – being its ultimate object and justification."[70] But it was the practical application of geopolitical analysis that led to a dramatic decline in the respectability of geopolitics, although analysts such as Nicholas Spykman continued to write in geopolitical terms and the wartime 'grand strategists' were also largely practitioners in the same *genre*. The occasion of the 'downfall' of geopolitics was its use by Nazi geographers, especially Karl Haushofer's school at Munich, in an attempt to provide a scientific rationale for Hitler's claim that the German *Volk* had need of *Lebensraum* (living space) in central and eastern Europe, giving them the scientific justification to create a new international order in the course of Hitler's *Drang nach Osten* (drive to the East). The terrible consequences of this policy did no good for the respectability, academic or otherwise, of geopolitics.

The approach did not really surface again in IR until Harold and Margaret Sprout began to take a serious theoretical interest in the 'man–milieu' relationship. They circulated an essay in 1956, which elicited a wide and interested response.[71] A decade later they published *The Ecological Perspective in Human Affairs*, which surveyed a range of geopolitical themes, from environmental determinism to environmental possibilism, and brought attention to the interaction between the psychological environment and the operational environment in determining outcome.[72] The approach had similarities with what Deutsch was developing in *The Nerves of Government*.[73] They succeeded not only in giving back the topic some respectability and reinserting it in the mainstream of discussion but also in making a significant contribution to it. The work of the Club of Rome and the WOMP school, discussed in Chapter 9, was also instrumental in the climb back to respectability. The geopolitical approach has a clear structural emphasis, if we consider the work of Robert North, Nazli Choucri and Richard Ashley on 'lateral pressure.'[74]

Meta-rationality

Richard K. Ashley's *The Political Economy of War and Peace* is brimming with ideas, reflecting wide, if eclectic, reading, strongly reminiscent, in its spirit, of the work of the young Galtung two decades previously (see note 30). Like Choucri and North, Ashley presents an empirical analysis as an exemplification of his approach – in his case that of the United States, the Soviet Union and China locked in a security *problématique*, while Choucri and North concentrated on the decades before the Great War. Ashley adopts the Choucri-North notion of lateral pressure – a notion not alien to the ideas of Gilpin, Modelski and Wallerstein on the process by which expansion occurs. However, lateral pressure has specific roots in the inter-relationship between growth in population, the economy and technology, which results in external expansion. Growth in any of the three induces the proclivity for like movement in the other two. But this may not be possible on the basis of the existing resource base. Can enough food be grown for a rising population, can the economy sustain it, is there a technological fix? Does the size of the market give the economies of scale for a technological breakthrough? The pressure is on to expand, and this lateral expansion quickly becomes politicised both within the expanding society, because it is seen as a justified pursuit of a better life, and externally, because it may run up against similar 'legitimate' tendencies on the part of others, either in bilateral confrontation or a multilateral balance of power system. Choucri and North show how these long-term processes of lateral expansion shed light on the structural aspects of the conflictual relations between the European great Powers between 1870 and 1914.

Ashley examines the dynamics of rivalry in the context of China, the United States and the USSR in the decades until 1980. While Ashley is aware that blind rivalry is not the necessary outcome, since there are possibilities for upgrading the common interest, it is the most common outcome. In attempts to rise above this, he takes his readers into the realm of critical theory. But, in the meantime, "The progression from growth through rivalry to balance of power, then, is a creative progression, and what it creates and recreates is the modern security *problématique*, to this day from the 'dawn of absolutism' in Europe."[75] And this is because "lateral pressure represents a generic, timeless social process, potentially evidenced by all living systems at all levels."[76] But it is a dangerous process because:

> [i]n a finite world of finite resources, its expansion cannot go on forever. War and conquest are among the mechanisms of its transformation once the limits of its growth are reached, approached, or become too costly to overcome . . . This logic applies so long as technical rationality prevails.[77]

Lateral pressure can create what has now become, potentially, a structure of doom.

In the preface to his book Ashley warns us that his "is a story of human beings behaving quite rationally to gain and extend mastery over nature and creating an irrational global state of nature that masters humans and threatens their destruction." Moreover, "humankind is caught in the most tragic of traps . . . the trap is made through a long, cumulative history of false technical-rational solutions, and . . . the search for technical-rational solutions can never set us free."[78] Hence the need "'to get out of' this restrictive grammar of thought"[79] and this by means not of technical rationality but 'rationality proper':[80]

> [A] technical-rational grammar of thought needs to conceive of life as consisting of so many more or less discrete problem situations; and problem situations are defined in terms of certain given purposes or needs, certain obstacles to or limits on the realization or satisfaction of these, and certain means by which the obstacles and limits can or might be overcome. Accordingly, such a grammar tends to take for granted hence disregard those slowly changing aspects of life that, relative to immediate purposes or needs, are too costly to manipulate. It tends also to leave unquestioned the boundaries of the immediate problem, how obstacles and limits might be given form by choices and actions in other sectors of life, and how attempts to solve the immediate problem might reverberate through time and impact upon other sectors. Most importantly, it takes purposes and needs for granted.[81]

For Ashley, critical theory can take us beyond this. We will then no longer need to pretend that we are 'in control,' by making false puzzles out of real problems in order to make them amenable to technical-rational solutions, the long-run logic and cumulation of which are potentially of disastrous consequences:

> Where technical rationality seeks to focus knowledge and skills on specific, bounded problem situations, rationality proper starts from the premise that knowledge and skills so focussed are not and cannot be autonomous of the historical processes giving the problem situation its manifest form. This attempt is made, not by invoking the assumption

that there exists some fixed, final, and potentially knowable structure predominating over the whole of reality, but through the attempt to engage, criticize, and synthesize competing vantage points associated with other aspects of reality as these do or might relate to the specific problem situation . . . rationality proper embeds and subordinates technical rationality within a richer logic.[82]

The relationship with the environment is no longer zero sum – conquer or submit – in a way that disenfranchises creative thought. Rather it must be one of critical engagement. It must be based on the realisation that we are not freely autonomous in relation to our environment, but we are an integral part of it. But, as we will see in greater detail in Chapter 13, the relationship is one of continuous, constructive and critical engagement in order to transform it.

Notes

1 We are grateful to Chris Brown for this point.
2 Richard Little, 'Structuralism and Neo-Realism,' in Margot Light and A.J.R. Groom (eds), *International Relations: A Handbook of Current Theory* (London: Frances Pinter, 1985), p. 76.
3 See Andre Gunder Frank and Barry K. Gills (eds), *The World System* (Oxford: Routledge, 1993). We shall be more modest and for the sake of argument adopt the 500-year benchmark for the present world system.
4 See Joshua Goldstein, *Long Cycles: Prosperity and War in the Modern Age* (London: Yale University Press, 1988), p. 289.
5 Harold Sprout and Margaret Sprout, *The Ecological Perspective in Human Affairs* (Princeton, NJ: Princeton University Press, 1965).
6 Nazli Choucri and Robert C. North, *Nations in Conflict: National Growth and International Violence* (San Francisco, CA: W.G. Freeman, 1975).
7 Richard K. Ashley, *The Political Economy of War and Peace* (London: Pinter, 1980).
8 David Easton, 'The New Revolution in Political Science,' *American Political Science Review*, December 1969.
9 *Ibid.*, p. 1051.
10 *Ibid.*, p. 1052.
11 On the First World War, see N. Gordon Levin Jr, *Woodrow Wilson and World Politics* (New York: Oxford University Press, 1968) and Arno J. Mayer, *Politics and Diplomacy of Peacemaking* (London: Weidenfeld and Nicolson, 1968). On the later period, other important works besides those mentioned in the text include Gabriel Kolko, *The Roots of American Foreign Policy* (Boston, MA: Beacon, 1969) and W. Appleman Williams, *The Tragedy of American Diplomacy* (New York: Dell, 1972).
12 Robert W. Tucker, *The Radical Left and American Foreign Policy* (London: Johns Hopkins Press, 1971) and Benjamin D. Cohen, *The Question of Imperialism* (London: Weidenfeld and Nicolson, 1980).
13 Tucker, *The Radical Left*, p. 12.
14 Harry Magdoff, *The Age of Imperialism* (London: Monthly Review Press, 1969), p. 26.
15 Tucker, *The Radical Left*, p. 71.
16 *Ibid.*, pp. 94–95. See also Joyce Kolko and Gabriel Kolko, *The Limits of Power* (London: Harper and Row, 1972), p. 2.
17 Cohen, *The Question of Imperialism*, p. 132.
18 *Ibid.*, p. 134. Cohen's data, like that of Magdoff, who argues to the contrary, is from the period until the late 1960s.
19 *Ibid.*, p. 141.
20 Magdoff, *The Age of Imperialism*, pp. 14–15.
21 Cohen, *The Question of Imperialism*, pp. 250–251.
22 Fred Halliday, *The Making of the Second Cold War* (London: Verso, 1983), pp. 174–175.
23 See A.J.R. Groom, 'Conflict and Collaboration in Anglo-American Relations,' *Arès*, Vol. XX11, Fascicule 2, No. 57, November 2006.
24 Tony Thorndike, 'The Revolutionary Approach: The Marxist Perspective,' in Trevor Taylor (ed.), *Approaches and Theory in International Relations* (London: Longman, 1978), p. 57.

25 See Anthony Brewer, *Marxist Theories of Imperialism* (Oxford: Routledge and Kegan Paul, 1980), pp. 14–15.

26 Paul Baran, *The Political Economy of Growth* (New York: Monthly Review Press, 1957).

27 Chris Brown, 'Development and Dependency,' in Margot Light and A.J.R. Groom (eds), *International Relations*, p. 63. A good survey of the theorists is Anthony Brewer, *Marxist Theories*, and a judicious selection of their writings can be found in Michael Smith, Richard Little and Michael Shackleton (eds), *Perspectives in World Politics* (London: Croom Helm, 1981).

28 Brown, 'Development and Dependency,' in Light and Groom (eds), *International Relations*, pp. 63–64.

29 See Brewer, *Marxist Theories*, for summaries of their positions.

30 Galtung developed a penchant for writing articles entitled 'A Structural Theory of...,' which included aggression, imperialism and integration. They can be found in his collected essays: Johan Galtung, *Essays in Peace Research* (Copenhagen: Christian Ejlers, 1975–9), five volumes.

31 Immanuel Wallerstein, 'An Agenda for World-System Analysis,' in William R. Thompson (ed.), *Contending Approaches to World System Analysis* (London: Sage, 1983), p. 300.

32 *Ibid.*, p. 301.

33 Immanuel Wallerstein, *The Capitalist World Economy* (London: Cambridge University Press, 1979), p. 159.

34 *Ibid.*, pp. 160–161.

35 *Ibid.*, p. 161.

36 *Ibid.*

37 *Ibid.*, p. 162.

38 *Ibid.*, p. 163.

39 *Ibid.*, p. 164.

40 Immanuel Wallerstein, 'The Rise and Future Demise of the World Capitalist System,' in Michael Smith et al., *Perspectives in World Politics*, p. 376.

41 *Ibid.*, p. 376.

42 Wallerstein, *Capitalist World Economy*, pp. 223, 274–275.

43 *Ibid.* p. 277.

44 Terence K. Hopkins, Immanuel Wallerstein et al., *World System Analysis Theory and Methodology* (London: Sage, 1982), p. 43.

45 Anthony Giddens, *The Nation-State and Violence* (Cambridge: Polity Press, 1985), p. 167.

46 Albert Bergesen, 'The Class Structure of the World-System,' in W. R. Thompson (ed.), *Contending Approaches*, p. 43.

47 *Ibid.*, p. 50.

48 James Lee Ray, 'The "World-System" and the Global Political System,' in Pat McGowan and Charles W. Kegley Jr (eds), *Foreign Policy and the Modern World-System* (London: Sage, 1983), p. 19.

49 Chris Brown, private communication, November 12, 1988.

50 Aristide R. Zolberg, 'Origins of the Modern World System,' *World Politics*, January 1981, pp. 275–276.

51 See George Modelski, *Long Cycles in World Politics* (London: Macmillan, 1987) for an overall statement of his position. Several volumes of empirical data are now appearing, by Modelski and others. Modelski's ideas were first put into general currency in a series of articles: George Modelski, 'The Long Cycle of Global Politics and the Nation-State,' *Comparative Studies in Society and History*, April 1978; George Modelski, 'Long Cycles, Kondratieffs, Alternating Innovations and Their Implications for U.S. Foreign Policy,' in C.W. Kegley Jr and P.J. McGowan (eds), *The Political Economy of Foreign Policy Behavior* (Thousand Oaks, CA: Sage, 1981); George Modelski, 'Long Cycles and the Strategy of United States International Economic Policy,' in W.P. Avery and D.P. Rapkin (eds), *America in a Changing World Political Economy* (New York: Longman, 1982); George Modelski, 'Long Cycles of World Leadership,' in William R. Thompson, *Contending Approaches*. The Thompson volume does for world-system analysis what Robert Keohane (ed.), *Neorealism and Its Critics* (New York: Columbia University Press, 1986) does for structural realism or neorealism. Each is an essential *vade mecum* for the respective debates.

52 William R. Thompson (ed.), *Contending Approaches*, pp. 8ff.

53 *Ibid.*, p. 11.

54 Modelski, *Long Cycles in World Politics*, pp. 1–2.

55 Modelski in W.P. Avery and D.P. Rapkin (eds), *America in a Changing World Political Economy*, p. 97.

56 Modelski in W.R. Thompson (ed.), *Contending Approaches*, pp. 121–122.

57 Modelski, *Long Cycles in World Politics*, p. 9.
58 Modelski in W.P. Avery and D.P. Rapkin (eds), *America in a Changing World Political Economy*, p. 98.
59 Modelski, *Long Cycles in World Politics*, p. 14.
60 *Ibid.*
61 *Ibid.*, p. 15.
62 Modelski in W.P. Avery and D.P. Rapkin (eds), *America in a Changing World Political Economy*, p. 100.
63 Modelski, *Long Cycles in World Politics*, p. 16.
64 Modelski in W.P. Avery and D.P. Rapkin (eds), *America in a Changing World Political Economy*, pp. 104–105.
65 *Ibid.*, p. 106.
66 *Ibid.*, p. 109.
67 Modelski in W.R. Thompson (ed.), *Contending Approaches*, p. 136.
68 For an excellent summary, see a review article by Oyvind Osterud, 'The Uses and Abuses of Geopolitics,' *Journal of Peace Research*, June 1988, and especially one of the books reviewed, Geoffrey Parker, *Western Geopolitical Thought in the Twentieth Century* (London: Croom Helm, 1985).
69 Osterud, *ibid.*, p. 191.
70 Quoted in *ibid.*, p. 192.
71 Harold and Margaret Sprout, *Man–Milieu Relationship Hypotheses in the Context of International Politics* (Princeton, NJ: Center of International Studies, Princeton University, 1956).
72 Harold and Margaret Sprout, *The Ecological Perspective in Human Affairs* (Princeton, NJ: Princeton University Press, 1965).
73 Karl Deutsch, *The Nerves of Government* (New York: Free Press, 1963).
74 Nazli Choucri and Robert C. North, *Nations in Conflict: National Growth and International Violence* (San Francisco, CA: W.H. Freeman, 1975) and Richard K. Ashley, *The Political Economy of War and Peace* (London: Frances Pinter, 1980).
75 Ashley, *Political Economy*, p. 47, italics deleted.
76 *Ibid.*, p. 248.
77 *Ibid.*, p. 255, italics deleted.
78 *Ibid.*, p. xii.
79 *Ibid.*, p. 207.
80 *Ibid.*, p. 208.
81 *Ibid.*, p. 210.
82 *Ibid.*, pp. 216–217, italics deleted.

11 Old wine in new bottles?

Structure and change in international relations

The 1980s was a period of structural change in world politics. Thatcher and Reagan consolidated their power and dramatically redrew the role of the state and its relation with its citizens. The US indirect response to the Soviet military intervention in Afghanistan opened the door for Osama bin Laden and radical Islamism. In Europe, the Berlin Wall crumbled, by the end of the decade, while the European integration project expanded and showed the world that other forms of international governance were possible. On the academic front, it was a period of great innovation, with many authors and theories nowadays seen as part of IR's canon developed during this period. Some had the ultimate aim of reinforcing the *status quo*; others clearly focused on challenging it.

One could argue that Kenneth Waltz's *Theory of International Politics* published in 1979 could be 'blamed' for much of this. Waltz's "elegant theory" that explained "a small number of big and important things"[1] rocked the discipline. Waltz's simplification and update of realist thought in line with the scientific language of the 1970s became "the most influential [book] in the history of the discipline,"[2] leaving behind works of equal value published at the time, such as Robert Gilpin's *War and Change in World Politics*.

Theory of International Politics is a quirkish and eclectic essay that, in relatively short compass and an easy style, reviews the contribution of various writers such as Hobson, Lenin, Rosecrance, Hoffman and Kaplan, takes a controversial position on the stability of bipolar and multipolar systems of the balance of power, and purports to present a structural theory of international politics. Waltz starts in a conventional manner, familiar from that of the systems' theories discussed in Chapter 10. In *Man, the State and War*, published in 1959, Waltz defended the existence of three images that explained international politics: human nature, state behaviour and the international system.[3] In *Theory of International Politics*, he focuses on only one of them, the third. A theory of international politics should explain how that area functions, in the same way as microeconomics explains the functioning of markets. We only understand price fluctuation and consumer behaviour by looking at the structure – in this case at the market – as a whole.

For Waltz, structures are defined by their ordering principle, the functions of their units and by the distribution of capabilities. According to his theory, the anarchical system is the key explanatory factor in international politics, the eternal structure that explains the units' behaviour, in this case, that of states. Unlike domestic politics, characterised by hierarchical structures in which units are formally differentiated according to their authority and function, international politics is characterised by horizontal relationships in which all states are functionally equal due to the principle of sovereignty. The system is defined by the arrangement of its constitutive units, by "how they stand in relation to one another"[4] and not by how they relate to each other. The specific attributes of each unit are not particularly relevant, as they are functionally equivalent. That means, "leaving aside questions about kinds of political leaders, social and economic institutions and ideological commitments states may have."[5]

In international politics, the system is anarchical as there is no overarching sovereign entity. This also means the units cannot rely on anything other than themselves – it is a self-help world. Whereas the functional differentiation of the units determines the structure of the system, it does not explain the power dynamics within it. For that, it is necessary to look into the distribution of capabilities (mostly military) that determine the polarity of the system. In Waltz's view, "if there is any distinctively political theory of international politics, balance-of-power theory it is."[6] In the attempt to provide a more rigorous and potentially consensual theory, Waltz argues that a proper balance of power theory starts with the assumption that states "are unitary actors who, at a minimum, seek their own preservation and, at a maximum, drive for universal domination."[7] After accepting this assumption, it is necessary to define its operative condition:

> [t]hat two or more states coexist in a self-help system, one with no superior agent to come to the aid of states that may be weakening or to deny to any of them the use of whatever instruments they think will serve their purposes.[8]

Once both the key assumption about the units and the operative condition are accepted, the theory will then "describe the constraints that arise from the system that those [state] actions produce, and it indicates the expected outcome: namely, the formation of balances of power."[9]

The bipolar system is, in principle, the most stable as both actors know the ropes and can have a proper basis of accurate information on which to manage their relationship. They are likely, therefore, to be vigilant since they know what the danger is and from whom and whence it comes. In a multipolar system, the waters are much more likely to be muddied. There is no proper basis of accurate information regarding capabilities, actual or potential alliances and the likelihood of their implementation. This induces instability, born of the fear engendered by uncertainty.

For Waltz, power acquires an instrumental role, rather than being an end in itself as portrayed by classical realists: "power is a possibly useful means, and sensible statesmen try to have an appropriate amount of it. In crucial situations, the ultimate concern of states is not for power but for security."[10] As he adds, "this is an important revision of realist theory."[11] In reality, Waltz departs from classical realist authors such as Hans Morgenthau in (at least) two important ways. First, he does not consider the motivations of political leaders or states' interests as causal variables in the international system. Second, he does not attempt to explain the individual behaviour of states. It is not, in that regard, a theory of foreign policy: "by depicting an international political system as whole, with structural and unit levels at once distinct and connected, neorealism establishes the autonomy of international politics and thus makes a theory about it possible."[12] Until then, the best authors could aim for was to develop approaches to foreign policy, often mere guidelines of how states should behave than actual theories.

This approach obviously had important consequences in terms of what the theory was able to explain. The focus on the structure meant that issues related to how processes unfold in international politics or why states behave in a specific way were not under consideration. Kenneth Waltz had no problem admitting it. In his view, the distinction between processes and structure was essential for it to be possible to study their mutual effects, but the absence of a detailed analysis of processes did "not imply their unimportance." This leaves the door open for others to be concerned with issues such as "tradition and culture, analysis of the character and personality of political actors, consideration of the conflictive and accommodative processes of politics, [or the] description of the making and execution of policy."[13]

Waltz and his critics

Waltz's *Theory of International Politics* is one of the most important, but also a highly criticised book in the history of IR. As mentioned earlier, much of its popularity can be attributed to his critics. An important criticism, which, as we will see, Gilpin addresses more competently than Waltz, has to do with the issue of change in international politics. John Ruggie, who is generally favourably disposed towards Waltz, suggests that the failure to acknowledge functional differentiation has quite profound implications for the theory because it means that the dimension of change is missing from Waltz's conception.[14] As Ruggie points out, "The problem with Waltz's posture is that, in any social system, structural change itself ultimately has no source other than unit-level processes . . . Waltz's theory of 'society' contains only a reproductive logic, but no transformational logic."[15]

Waltz suggests that changes in systems are relatively easy to achieve, but he concedes that, though possible, changes of systems are hard to imagine.[16] In part, this is because Waltz is himself a reductionist owing to his "understanding of system structures as only constraining the agency of preexisting states, rather than . . . as generating state agents themselves . . . system structures cannot generate agents if they are reduced to the property of agents in the first place."[17] Gilpin also disagrees with Waltz's emphasis on the distribution of power. In his view, "the most important factor for the process of international political change is not the static distribution power in the system (bipolar or multipolar) but the dynamics of power relationships over time." In this regard:

> [i]t is the differential or uneven growth of power among states in a system that encourages efforts by certain states to change the system in order to enhance their own interests or to make more secure those interests threatened by their oligopolistic rivals.[18]

Siding with Gilpin, William C. Wohlforth, argues that "Waltz's book is not really a theory of international politics. It does not address in any explicit way most of the phenomena that are encompassed by that term."[19] The parsimony and elegance of the theory, which for some is its strongest asset, is here taken as an inevitable show of its weakness.

As mentioned earlier, *Neorealism and Its Critics* was instrumental in providing Waltz with a quasi-paradigmatic status. In the introduction to the volume, Robert Keohane argues that the importance of Waltz's theory lies "in his attempt to systematize political realism into a rigorous, deductive system theory of international politics."[20] Keohane's compliments were to be accompanied by a number of criticisms in a subsequent chapter.[21] There, Keohane criticises – among other realist approaches – Waltz's balance of power theory, where he identifies a number of problems associated with it. First, he highlights the difficulties in predicting the conditions of change, particularly in terms of alliances. Second, his theory is so general that it is all but impossible to test it. Finally, Keohane highlights the ambiguity in Waltz's theory regarding rationality and interests. Waltz argues that it is irrelevant whether actors are rational or not in terms of international politics, as the structure of the system will determine their success and failure. However, Waltz also argues that states tend to be less reckless in bipolar systems, which leads Keohane to conclude that "Waltz does rely on the rationality argument."[22] As for interests, Waltz assumes that states seek survival, a necessary condition for the balance of power to succeed, while following the realist credo that in some cases states might aim to maximise power. As Keohane points out, this is a fundamental contradiction in realist thought – which would lead to the division between defensive and offensive realists – that Waltz only reinforces in his work. All in all, Keohane concludes, "the ambitious attempt of Structural Realist theory to deduce national interests from system structure via the rationality postulate has been unsuccessful."[23]

In 'The Poverty of Neorealism,' initially published in *International Organization* in 1984 and reproduced in *Neorealism and Its Critics*, Richard K. Ashley adopts a critical tone, referring to the "orrery of errors"[24] of Waltz's theory. His critique, however, goes beyond Waltz's work. It is an accusation against the turn of the decade realist literature. Although it claims to side with the victors in two US revolutions – the realist revolution against idealism and the scientific revolution against traditionalism – it in fact betrays both. It betrays the former's commitment to political autonomy by reducing political practice to an economic logic, and it neuters the critical faculties of the latter by swallowing methodological rules that render science a purely technical enterprise. From realism, it learns only an interest in power, from science it takes only an interest in expanding the reach of control, and from this selective borrowing it creates a theoretical perspective that parades the possibility of a rational power that need never acknowledge power's limits. What emerges is a positivist structuralism that treats the given order as the natural order, limits rather than expands political discourse, negates or trivialises the significance of variety across time and place, subordinates all practice to an interest in control, bows to the ideal of a social power beyond responsibility, and thereby deprives political interaction of those practical capacities which make social learning and creative change possible. What emerges is an ideology that anticipates, legitimises and orients a totalitarian project of global proportions: the rationalisation of global politics.[25]

Ashley's concerns are also with the extent to which structural realism is in fact structural at all in the sense that:

> The structuralist posits the possibility of a structural whole-a deep social subjectivity-having an autonomous existence independent of, prior to, and constitutive of the elements. From a structuralist point of view, a structural whole cannot be described by starting with the parts as abstract, already defined entities, taking note of their external joining, and describing emergent properties among them.[26]

Ashley castigates structural realism for being 'silent' about "four dimensions of history . . . process, practice, power, and politics."[27] As a process, structural realism is not open-ended, but circumscribed and limited. In its practice "people are reduced to some idealized *Homo economicus*, able to carry out, but never to reflect critically on, the limited rational logic that the system demands of them,"[28] a charge just as applicable to Gilpin as to Waltz. Both seem to deny the relevance of critical theory – explored in Chapter 14 – and of "the social basis and social limits of *power*."[29] Finally, "neorealist historicism denies politics . . . [because] it reduces politics to those aspects which lend themselves to interpretation exclusively within a framework of economic action under structural constraints."[30] While politics, in this sense, of a technical rationality for solving 'puzzles,' is also a characteristic of economic reasoning, the essence of politics, which is the realisation of 'problems' and their resolution, is lost.

Waltz had the opportunity to respond to his critics in the last chapter of the volume. In it, he regrets very little and when he does, it does not change any of the points he makes in *Theory of International Politics*. For instance, when responding to Robert Keohane, he acknowledges he (Keohane) "is correct" in that his (Waltz) definition of power is "insufficient" as he "did not carry the definition very far"[31] but, not only power is in itself a contested term, as his definition of power as "who affects whom more strongly" is "a move in the right direction."[32] Moreover, Waltz quickly turns his attention to, first, the issue of power fungibility where he is able to defend his ground against Keohane's accusations and then to the issue of power maximisation. He concurs with Keohane that some realists defend that states always seek to maximise power but that he was not part of such group, as he contends that states are first and foremost looking to achieve their own security above else. We can study it by looking at the consequences of the states' actions, even if it does not tell us the full story. To do so would require a theory of domestic politics. Nonetheless, he defends the position that such is not always the case and that the balance of power theory can, on its own, explain many of the dynamics in the international system.

Before Keohane, Waltz had already addressed some of John Ruggie's comments, particularly regarding interaction between units and structure. After a long discussion of Emil Durkheim's definition of society, Waltz concludes that "through all of the changes of boundaries, of social, economic, and political form, of economic and military activity, the substance and style of international politics remain strikingly constant."[33] If Ruggie's advice was to be followed, instead of theory we would have "rich and dense description"[34] as the definition of structure had to offer too much detail about the characteristics of the units and their interactions.

Moving from the theory to its application, Waltz engages with the argument that his theory is, basically, unfalsifiable. Not only does he reject the idea that the validity of a theory depends on it not being falsified.[35] He also points out that theories gain or lose credibility in multiple ways, of which falsification is one them: "theories gain credibility in a variety of ways – by unsuccessfully attempting to falsify, by successfully attempting to verify, by demonstrating that outcomes are produced in the way the theory contemplates, and by the intellectual force of the theory itself."[36] This goes back to the point raised in *Theory of International Politics* that a theory must contain "at least one theoretical assumption" that is not factual ("one therefore cannot legitimately ask if they are true, but only if they are useful"), can only "be evaluated in terms of what they claim to explain," and that a theory "as a general explanatory system, cannot account for particularities."[37] Ultimately, returning to Waltz's response to his critics, a "theory applies only so long as the conditions it contemplates endures in their essentials."[38]

In the last part of his response, Waltz discusses the voices from critical theory. He takes no issues with the idea that his is a 'problem solving theory' – "Ashley and Cox would transcend the world as it is; meanwhile we have to live in it"[39] – but he struggles to address Ashley's comments, which he finds "difficult to deal with"; a maze in which he is constantly lost. He does not understand in what way the balance of power theory *produces* sovereign states, nor why history matters to his theory ("how can one incorporate history in the type of theory I constructed?"[40]). Ashley's criticisms do not tell him much about how he should create a better theory.

For all the criticism, there are multiple aspects of Waltz's theory that are often misunderstood, or knowingly misarticulated. In an excellent piece published in *International Relations*, Ole Wæver sets out to clarify Waltz's stance on positivism and theory – two of the most contentious issues in his work. Regarding the former, as Wæver points out, "Waltz has been labelled a positivist, a Popperian, a pragmatist and a scientific realist. 'Positivist' is by far the most common, and also by far the most mistaken."[41] Waltzians rather than Waltz are to blame for such an association. As Wæver reminds us, Waltz never saw himself or his theory as positivist. Although he had a difficult relation with testing,[42] his understanding of the philosophy of science (which he studied thoroughly) and of what a theory should be – a number of abstractly created theoretical concepts that define a model, and principles that need to be understood in relation to that model[43] – clearly indicate that Waltz's work needs to be interpreted under a different light; one less focused on positivist reinterpretations of *Theory of International Politics*, and more in line with what Waltz's theory actually states.

What it was, and what it could have been

Waltz's work was a defining moment for the discipline in the United States, for what it created, for the criticism it generated, but also for what it inadvertently prevented from happening. According to William C. Wohlforth, "had Robert Gilpin's War and Change in World Politics been given equal billing, international relations research would have unfolded quite differently over the past three decades."[44] As late as 1984, Gilpin and Waltz were treated on equal terms, in works from Robert Keohane[45] and Richard Ashley.[46] For Wohlforth, Keohane's edited volume *Neorealism and Its Critics* was key in helping Waltz' work "trump all others as the definite modern restatement of realism."[47] As a consequence, Waltz became the 'successor' of Morgenthau in the realist canon (to be followed by John Mearsheimer), whereas Gilpin was "recognized as a major figure, but one whose work does not quite seem to fit."[48]

Discussing the reasons for this, Wohlforth points to three main 'contextual factors' that help to explain the centrality of Waltz's role in the discipline. First, the historical context. The Cold War was dominated by the Soviet military intervention in Afghanistan and the rise to power of Ronald Reagan, a period in which international reality seemed to be better explained by Waltz's ever-lasting (anarchical) structural features of the international system when compared to Gilpin's attention to change. Second, Waltz's elegant theoretical conceptualisation was more appropriate for the 'scientific' language of the day: it offered a clear research programme, "comprising a hard core of assumptions and a related set of scope conditions and specific propositions."[49] Finally, it was a more attractive theory for other scholars to both build on and criticise. As a theory with a limited scope, it opened the door for many to explore unwritten dimensions of the theory – foreign policy, for instance – and multiple case studies testing Waltz's theory. As argued by Wohlforth, without *Theory of International Politics* "it is hard to see what contribution all these books and articles made."[50]

Whereas Waltz's theory rests on the possibility of conflict, Gilpin's focuses on the probability of conflict.[51] Gilpin rejects Waltz's "assertion that wars are caused by uncertainty and miscalculation." On the contrary, "it is perceived certainty of gain that most frequently causes nations to go to war."[52] Thus:

> Both bipolar and multipolar structures contain elements of instability . . . the most important factor for the process of international political change is not the static distribution of power in the system (bipolar or multipolar) but the dynamics of power relationships over time. It is the differential or uneven growth of power among states in a system that encourages efforts by certain states to change the system in order to enhance their own interest or to make more secure those interests threatened by their oligopolistic rivals. In both bipolar and multipolar structures, changes in relative power among the principal actors in the system are precursors of international political change.[53]

States will behave according to the context and not necessarily as 'security maximisers.' As a result, the international system is, in Gilpin's theory, much less stable than what Waltz portrayed. That gives a much more dynamic dimension to Gilpin's theory. Both domestic and international factors contribute to this. Political, economic and technological conditions lead to a frequent "redistribution of power in the system."[54] While acknowledging that "economic and sociological approaches must be integrated to explain international political change,"[55] Gilpin puts greater emphasis on economic and rational-choice theory. Gilpin argues this notion can be used to develop an understanding of international political change, because structures will change when the interests and relative power of states change.

In this quest, Gilpin rests his argument on five assumptions:

1   An international system is stable (i.e. in a state of equilibrium) if no state believes it profitable to attempt to change the system.
2   A state will attempt to change the international system if the expected benefits exceed the expected costs (i.e. if there is an expected net gain).
3   A state will seek to change the international system through territorial, political, and economic expansion until the marginal costs of further change are equal to or greater than the marginal benefits.
4   Once an equilibrium between the costs and benefits of further change and expansion is reached, the tendency is for the economic costs of maintaining the status quo to rise faster than the economic capacity to support the status quo.
5   If the disequilibrium in the international system is not resolved, then the system will be changed, and a new equilibrium reflecting the redistribution of power will be established.[56]

Gilpin agrees with the Marxist notion that revolutionary or structural change occurs when there are "differential rates of change in major components composing the social system," otherwise "there would be incremental evolution of the system."[57] For Marx, however, the engine of change is in the economic system, whereas for Gilpin it is in the political system. States, because international society is anarchic, must always be expansive for otherwise they risk being the victims of the expansion of others. This, Gilpin suggests, sets in motion a cycle of expansion, consolidation, challenge and decline (Gilpin's work is part of what the literature calls 'rise and fall realism'[58]). Eventually the initial expansion, originally fuelled by economic surplus, meets countervailing forces and the returns to expansion diminish after the initial enjoyment of the economies of scale. An equilibrium is then reached, and:

> [t]here is an erosion of the original élan that supported an aggressive and expansionist foreign policy. the society grows conservative, less innovative, and less willing to run risks . . . society becomes less willing to pay the costs . . . associated with political and economic expansion.[59]

But, owing to the decline of the marginal returns to expansion, the costs of maintaining even the *status quo* rise, while the will to make sacrifices falls. Consumption, rather than savings, is the order of the day, and comparative advantage declines:[60]

> These rising states, on the other hand, enjoy lower costs, rising rates of return on their resources, and the advantages of backwardness. In time, the differential rates of growth of declining and rising states in the system produce a decisive redistribution of power and result in disequilibrium in the system.[61]

At this point, the rising state can seek to change the rules of the international system in its favour.[62] War, in particular hegemonic war, is the "principal mechanism of change throughout history,"[63] thus always the probable outcome of changes in the stability of the system.

Hegemonic wars can, in Gilpin's view, be defined by three main characteristics. First, it must be a conflict between the dominant Power(s) and those that attempt to challenge the *status quo*. Second, the conflict is about the "nature and governance of the system."[64] Finally, the means employed are potentially unlimited.

According to Gilpin, these wars tend to take place once the space available for the main Powers to dominate is reduced, and "interstate relations become more and more a zero-sum game."[65] This must be associated with a generalised perception that history is changing and therefore, the dominant Power(s) needs to secure its position whereas the challenging Powers attempt to maximise their gains. Finally, events will unfold at a rate that becomes out of control for the main actors involved.

Rather than focusing on the eternal structures of international politics, Gilpin's approach is thus much more concerned with the potential signs of change. This leads Wohlforth to argue that "had Gilpinian realism been more prominent at the time, the field would have been better prepared intellectually for rapid power shifts and major geopolitical change,"[66] such as the end of the Cold War.

Another important distinction between Waltz and Gilpin is that whereas the former based the rest of his career on his *Theory of International Politics*, Gilpin built on his *War and Change in World Politics*, also known as the 'red book,' producing, a few years later, what became known as the blue book. In *Political Economy of International Relations*, published in 1987, Gilpin attempts to assess the "accumulated knowledge of how international politics and international economics interact and affect one another."[67] As recognised by Gilpin himself,[68] this work was part of a bourgeoning literature on international political economy (IPE)[69] that was trying to "focus attention on the inevitable tensions and continuing interactions between economics and politics."[70] The modern state and the market, the two predominant forms of social organisation, evolved together, to the extent to which "their mutual interactions have become increasingly crucial to the character and dynamics of international relations in our world."[71] After all, this was a time in which the trade wars between Japan and the United States were frequently taking the spotlight from the Cold War confrontation. Economically, this was already a time of transition from the predominantly state-focused international politics, to the increasingly visible importance of multinational corporations and the opening of international markets. Globalisation, which will be discussed in the next chapter, was overtaking the Cold War as the predominant factor of change and action in international relations.

In his *The Political Economy of International Relations*,[72] Gilpin attempts to "develop in a more systematic way" what he calls "the three ideologies of political economy": realism ("or economic nationalist perspective"), liberalism and Marxism.[73] The evaluations of their strengths and weaknesses are, in Gilpin's view, important "to illuminate the study of the field of international political economy." The US decline is an issue very much present in this work, particularly its loss of the economic leadership role. Gilpin considers it to be one of the three major developments in IPE by the end of the twentieth century. The shift of the world economy's core from the Atlantic to the Pacific (albeit with Japan rather than China as the leading nation) would constitute the second major development. Finally, Gilpin predicted the "increasing integration" of the Japanese and US economies, "to a degree that is unprecedented for sovereign nations,"[74] which in hindsight never materialised to the extent that it was predicted in the 1980s.

Basing himself on the work of Max Weber, Gilpin identifies the contradiction between the aims of the state and that of the market as "the crucial problem in the study of political economy." In his view, "for the state, territorial boundaries are a necessary basis of national autonomy and political unity. For the market, the elimination of all political and other obstacles to the operation of the price mechanism is imperative."[75] Each of the three ideologies identified by Gilpin treat this relationship differently. In general (and as Gilpin recognises, liberalism is a broad church), liberals believe in the appeasing effects of trade and economic intercourse and have had the upper hand in promoting an international political system that materialises that ideal. This view differs from the nationalist perspective that ascribes to the primacy of the state and therefore believes "that economic activities are and should be subordinate to the goal of state building and the interests of the state."[76] Finally, Marxism, which also comes in different tones and shapes, believes "that the state is ultimately the servant of the dominant class."[77] This dominant class determines not only the functioning of each particular society but also that of the international system. As a result, "war, imperialism, and the state [are] evil manifestations of a capitalism that will disappear with the communist revolution."[78]

The clash between these three ideologies is responsible for three main controversies in IPE, which Gilpin's book seeks to address: the causes and consequences of the rise of the market economy; the mutual relation between economic and political change; and, finally, the domestic impacts of the world economy.[79] After carefully addressing each of these ideologies and each of these issues, Gilpin concludes that the mid-1980s – at the time of his writing – was a transition period between the post Second World War US hegemony and a new system in which states were more forcefully asserting their presence in the international economy. Gilpin also points to the paradox that the rise of protectionist barriers in the name of national interest in the United States coincided with privatisation and economic deregulation at the domestic level. This phased transition was marked by a very high level of uncertainty and moderate optimism. Gilpin's major concern, however, was that the victory of a mercantilist, nationalistic approach would lead to the overall deterioration of the world economy. Looking back with the benefit of hindsight, it is now clear that Gilpin's concerns did not materialise and the 1990s was a period of unprecedented liberalisation. In that regard, Gilpin's book is better at explaining how we got to the IPE of the 1980s, than to anticipate its future.

The book's analysis based on the comparative assessment of the three main ideologies deserves to be mentioned. It results from the ontological conviction that these three ideologies coexist in the international system, and that "they define the conflicting perspectives that individuals have with regard to the implications of the market system for domestic and international society."[80] The acceptance of this coexistence (and the reference to the international society) is very much in line with what we find in the so-called English School. The fact that Hedley Bull was a reference for Gilpin[81] might help to explain such a pluralist stance. The focus on ideologies, however, was an important methodological approach that linked theoretical concerns with the practice of power politics and the international economy, whose connection has been more or less disregarded by the post-Cold War IR literature.

IPE and its critical voices

It could be argued that most of the innovative work in IR during the 1980s was produced in the bourgeoning field of IPE. Despite starting as a sub-discipline "defined by the topics that it investigated, such as trade, finance, raw materials politics, and multinational corporations,"[82] progressively became organised around different theoretical perspectives. The surge of interest gave rise to a demand for textbooks or surveys, and Brett and Spero,[83] among others, have met this need in a satisfactory manner, while Robert Keohane in addition to Gilpin, has taken stock in a broader manner. Keohane, building on his work with Nye, discussed in Chapter 9, has examined the situation *After Hegemony* from the point of view of the United States and the vestiges of the Bretton Woods system created by the United States and the UK at the end of the war.[84] In his ambition to "use concepts from economics to develop a political theory about cooperation and discord in the world economy,"[85] Keohane developed a sophisticated analysis of power, wealth cooperation and hegemony in IPE, highlighting the prospects of a more rigorous scientific study of the interrelation between economics and politics. Starting from an institutionalist position, his book shows "how adaptive strategies of institution-building can also change reality, thereby fostering mutually beneficial cooperation."[86] Unlike what is defended by those promoting the hegemonic stability argument – such as Gilpin or Kindleberger[87] before him – for Keohane, "there is little reason to believe that hegemony is either necessary or a sufficient condition for the emergence of cooperative relationships."[88]

The work of these authors was, as seen before, linked to the *International Organization* project. They were – and, to an extent are – the gatekeepers of IPE; their orthodoxy. Working "outside of, and in many instances in opposition to"[89] this orthodoxy was Susan Strange and also Robert Cox. Susan Strange's contribution to IR was substantive but often "unacknowledged." Her work challenged the realist cannon, while also contributing to it. She explained the rise of multilateralism, offered a different theory of power (structural power) and a different understanding of diplomacy (trilateral diplomacy). She included other actors in the analysis of international relations, including the Mafia and insurance companies, and she was highly critical of the international financial system, which she saw as an integral part of IR's object of study.[90] Strange – just as Cox – had a previous life, as a journalist working for the *Observer* (among others) while keeping connections with academia via UCL. It was her spell at Chatham House in the 1960s that led her to engrain more thoroughly in the academic world of IR. Robert Cox's biography was slightly different, working for the International Labour Organization for twenty years before becoming an academic. In both cases, their 'real-world' experience shaped their approach to academia, and helped consolidate IPE and diversify IR.

Susan Strange was particularly instrumental in terms of the former. Her 'International Economics and International Relations: A Case of Mutual Neglect' published in 1970 in Chatham House's *International Affairs*, had, in the words of her friend Robert Cox, "the appearance of a manifesto,"[91] calling for the creation of IPE as an academic discipline. She would then be instrumental in the creation, one year later, of the International Political Economy Group (which still exists as one of the Working Groups of the British International Studies Association). Before that, as Katzenstein, Keohane and Krasner recognise, "no independently recognized field for studying the international political economy existed."[92]

We would argue that it was 'Cave! Hic Dragones: A Critique of Regime Analysis' that brought her to the limelight of the discipline. In this incisive piece, published in the gatekeepers' realm – *International Organization* – Strange criticised regime theory as an "'imprecise,' 'woolly,' 'value-based,' 'distorting,' 'narrowminded' fad of the time."[93] Embracing the concept would lead, in Strange's view, to two major consequences. First, it would make the study of world politics the study of the *status quo*, ignoring "the vast area of nonregimes that lies beyond the ken of international bureaucracies and diplomatic bargaining."[94] Second, it would continue, in Strange's view, the negative trend in IR of trying to rely on 'grand theories' that offer neat, simplified explanations of the world. As she concludes, "the dynamics character of the 'who-gets-what' of the international economy . . . is more likely to be captured by looking not at the regime that emerges on the surface but underneath, at the bargains on which it is based," and these are not necessarily between states. Once "the factors contributing to change in bargaining strength or weakness" have been duly analysed "it will be easier . . . to proceed to look at the outcome with less egocentric and value-biased eyes,"[95] as is the case with regime theory.

Strange would go on to publish a number of important books that became part of the IPE framework, and even of the IR canon: *Casino Capitalism* (1986), *State and Markets* (1988),

The Retreat of the State (1996) and *Mad Money* (1998). Her critique of the international system, and of how the IR mainstream only captured a small part of the real dynamics in world politics, was instrumental in opening up the discipline, but they were also rather premonitory, particularly regarding her views on the centrality of credit, the decoupling of the financial sector from the real economy and the inevitable prevalence of periodic financial crises as eventually happened in 2007.

Arguably, the concept of 'structural power' was Strange's biggest contribution to the discipline. In her view, there are two kinds of power in IPE: relational and structural. Strange associates relational power with the power as described by realists, i.e. "the power of A to get to B to do something they would not otherwise do."[96] Structural power, on the other hand, "is the power to shape and determine the structures of the global political economy within which other states, their political institutions, their economic enterprises and (not least) their scientists and other professional people have to operate."[97] It is in that regard much more important than relational power in terms of shaping the behaviour of the actors: it "confers the power to decide how things shall be done, the power to shape frameworks within which states relate to each other, relate to people, or relate to corporate enterprises."[98]

Strange's understanding of structural power was based on what she thought to be the basic values of society: security, production, finance and knowledge. Security is about controlling violence whereas production is about being able to "decide and control the manner or mode of production of goods and services for survival." Finance relates to the control over credit, which, in return, determines the purchasing within a given society (including the international one). Finally, knowledge is, among other things, central to the decision-making process that leads to the attribution of credit.[99] Understanding it was crucial, however, as power "determines the relationship between authority and market,"[100] which is fundamental for the study of IPE. Power results from the articulation between these elements and not from the control over one of them. They are four sides of a pyramid. Structural power is then the control over the pyramid. This makes power more complex to assess in international relations. It also dilutes the difference between political and economic power as they often overlap in these four categories. Another important conclusion from this – which somewhat contradicts Robert Gilpin's – is that when applying the model to the United States in the late 1980s:

> [t]he United States government and the corporations dependent upon it have *not* in fact lost structural power in and over the system. They may have changed their mind about how to use it, but they have not lost it. Nor, taking the four structures of power together, are they likely to do so in the foreseeable future.[101]

This understanding of structural power also differs from that of Robert Cox. According to Strange, Cox's understanding of structural power is based on the Marxist concept of the ownership of means of production in which the state "is the embodiment in political terms of the authority of the class or classes in control of the production structure,"[102] which is less complex than the four-faceted triangular pyramid offered in her model. Although indeed focusing on the means of production, Cox's work goes much beyond.

Robert Cox became a leading figure in IR critical theory in the early 1980s. His articles, 'Social Forces, States and World Orders,' and 'Gramsci, Hegemony and International Relations,' from 1981 and 1983 respectively, highlighted a new dawn for radical thought in the discipline. Much of his thought would then be consolidated in a number of monographs, of which we would highlight *Production, Power and World Order*, in which Cox seeks approaches to power and production as the two key concepts in world politics. According to him:

Production creates the material basis for all forms of social existence, and the ways in which human efforts are combined in the productive processes affect all other aspects of social life, including the polity. Production generates the capacity to exercise power, but power determines the manner in which production takes place.[103]

Moreover, "to assert the centrality of production . . . leads directly to the matter of social classes."[104] Cox, however, argues that the state is important because "the principal structures have been, if not actually created by the state, at least encouraged and sustained by the state,"[105] be they competitive capitalism and the liberal state, central planning and the Bolshevik state or state corporatism, and the fascist state. Indeed, for Cox, "production has been more shaped by the state than shaping of it."[106] Moreover, "class and party are the channels of encounter between production and the state. They explain where the balance of influence lies, whether it comes primarily from the social forces generated in the production process or from the state." The class structure determines for the state's servants what is possible and what is precluded: it acts as a constraint.[107] But so does the particular world order that is, in its turn, reflective of the dominant mode of production. Where there is a hegemonic world Power, there tends to be a linkage between social classes in different states and connections in production giving rise to a world economy. Thus, "an incipient world society grows up around the interstate system."[108] Such linkages do not flourish in non-hegemonic world orders. In those cases, states "advance and protect the interests of particular national social classes and production organizations, using all the political, economic, and military means at their disposal as necessary."[109]

Of the three levels of enquiry, the most important one for Cox is the state, as it "determine[s] the whole complex structure of production from which [it] extracts sufficient resources to continue to exercise its power."[110] Cox does not deny that when applies to the international system, states are constrained by their position and power, but they have, in his view, a certain level of autonomy that does not make them entirely reliant on the structure of the system.

When comparing Gilpin and Cox's work, Stephen Gill argues that the latter's "is the more original and imaginative" as "it offers an avenue towards a reflexive, broad-ranging and consistent theory of international political economy."[111] Both Cox and Strange end up offering alternative views to that of the US decline as portrayed by Gilpin by highlighting the forms (structural power for Strange, the consolidation of the neoliberal historical bloc first and then the move towards some sort of hyper-liberalism in the 1980s) in which that power has been produced and reproduced. More than providing alternative answers, Strange and Cox have set different questions for IR to answer; questions that lead to a more complex, fluid and dynamic grasping of the field, crucial in comprehending the world as it entered the 1990s.

Notes

1 Kenneth N. Waltz 'Reflections on Theory of International Politics: A Response to My Critics,' in Robert O. Keohane (ed.), *Neorealism and Its Critics* (New York: Columbia University Press, 1986), p. 329.
2 Ole Wæver, 'Waltz's Theory of Theory,' *International Relations*, Vol. 23, No. 2, 2009, p. 201.
3 Kenneth N. Waltz *Man, the State and War* (New York: Columbia University Press, 2001 [1959]).
4 Kenneth N. Waltz, *Theory of International Politics* (Boston, MA: McGraw-Hill Higher Education, 1979), p. 80.
5 *Ibid.*
6 *Ibid.*, p. 117.
7 *Ibid.*, p. 118.

8 *Ibid.*

9 *Ibid.*

10 *Ibid.*

11 Kenneth N. Waltz 'Realist Thought and Neorealist Theory,' *Journal of International Affairs*, Vol. 44, No. 1, 1990, p. 36.

12 Kenneth N. Waltz, 'Realist Thought and Neorealist Theory,' p. 21.

13 Waltz, *Theory of International Politics*, p. 82.

14 John Gerrard Ruggie, 'Continuity and Transformation in the World Polity,' *World Politics*, January 1983.

15 *Ibid.*, p. 285.

16 Kenneth Waltz, 'A Response to My Critics,' in Keohane (ed.), *Neorealism*, p. 328.

17 Alexander E. Wendt, 'The Agent-Structure Problem in International Relations,' *International Organization*, Summer 1987, p. 342.

18 Gilpin, *War and Change*, p. 91.

19 Wohlforth, p. 502.

20 Robert O. Keohane, 'Realism, Neorealism and the Study of World Politics,' in Keohane (ed.), *Neorealism*, pp. 15–16.

21 Robert O. Keohane, 'Theory of World Politics: Structural Realism and Beyond,' in Keohane (ed.), *Neorealism*, pp. 158–203.

22 *Ibid.*, p. 173.

23 *Ibid.*, p. 190.

24 Richard K. Ashley, 'The Poverty of Neorealism,' *International Organization*, Vol. 38, No. 2, 1984, p. 226.

25 *Ibid.*, p. 228.

26 *Ibid.*, p. 255.

27 *Ibid.*, p. 258.

28 *Ibid.*, p. 258.

29 *Ibid.*, p. 259.

30 *Ibid.*, p. 260.

31 Kenneth Waltz, 'A Response to My Critics,' in Keohane (ed.), *Neorealism*, p. 333.

32 *Ibid.*

33 *Ibid.*, p. 329.

34 *Ibid.*, p. 330.

35 *Ibid.*, p. 334.

36 *Ibid.*, p. 336.

37 Kenneth N. Waltz, *Theory of International Politics*, pp. 117–118.

38 Kenneth N. Waltz, *Theory of International Politics*, p. 340.

39 *Ibid.*, p. 338.

40 *Ibid.*

41 Ole Wæver, 'Waltz's Theory of Theory,' p. 203.

42 As Wæver recognises, "Waltz is misleading or at least ambiguous, when he – after criticising previous tests of realism – claims that tests are easy when finally you have a real theory," *Ibid.*, p. 211.

43 *Ibid.*, p. 207.

44 William C. Wohlforth, 'Gilpinian Realism and International Relations,' *International Relations*, Vol. 25, No. 4, 2011, p. 499.

45 Robert O. Keohane, 'Theory of World Politics: Structural Realism and Beyond,' in Ada Finifter (ed.), *Political Science: The State of the Discipline* (Washington DC: American Political Science Association, 1983).

46 Richard K. Ashley, 'The Poverty of Neorealism,' *International Organization*, Vol. 38, Spring, 1984, pp. 225–286.

47 Wohlforth, p. 500.

48 *Ibid.*, p. 501.

49 *Ibid.*

50 *Ibid.*, p. 503.

51 *Ibid.*

52 Gilpin, *War and Change*, p. 91.

53 *Ibid.*, p. 91.
54 Robert Gilpin, *War and Change in World Politics* (Cambridge: Cambridge University Press, 1981), p. 9.
55 *Ibid.*, p. xiii.
56 *Ibid.*, pp. 10–11.
57 *Ibid.*, p. 48.
58 Colin Elman and Michael A. Jensen 'Introduction,' in Colin Elman and Michael A. Jensen (eds), *Realism Reader* (Oxford: Routledge, 2014), p. 9.
59 Gilpin, *War and Change in World Politics*, p. 154.
60 *Ibid.*, pp. 156–157, 184–185.
61 *Ibid.*, p. 185.
62 *Ibid.*, p. 187.
63 *Ibid.*, p. 15.
64 Gilpin, *War and Change in World Politics*, p. 46.
65 Gilpin, *War and Change in World Politics*, p. 200–201.
66 Wohlforth, p. 505.
67 Robert Gilpin, *The Political Economy of International Relations* (Princeton, NJ: Princeton University Press, 1987), p. xiv.
68 Gilpin, *The Political Economy of International Relations*, p. 3.
69 It must be said that this was not Gilpin's first incursion into IPE. In 1975 he published *U.S. Power and the Multinational Corporation*, where he first expressed his concerns regarding the decline of the United States as a great Power, which would eventually lead to *War and Change in World Politics* (1981).
70 Gilpin, *The Political Economy of International Relations*, p. 3.
71 *Ibid.*, p. 4.
72 Which was to be followed by the *Global Political Economy* in 2001 (Princeton, NJ: Princeton University Press).
73 Gilpin, *The Political Economy of International Relations*, p. xiii.
74 *Ibid.*, p. 6.
75 *Ibid.*, p. 10.
76 *Ibid.*, p. 31.
77 *Ibid.*, p. 43.
78 *Ibid.*, p. 43.
79 *Ibid.*, pp. 13–14.
80 *Ibid.*, p. 25.
81 *International Relations* (2005), 'Conversations in International Relations: Interview with Robert Gilpin,' *International Relations*, Vol. 19, No. 3, 2016, p. 366.
82 Peter J. Katzenstein, Robert O. Keohane and Stephen D. Krasner 'International Organization and the Study of World Politics,' *International Organization*, Vol. 52, No. 4, 1998, p. 646.
83 E.A. Brett, *The World Economy since the War* (London: Macmillan, 1985); Joan E. Spero, *The Politics of International Economic Relations* (London: Allen & Unwin, 1982).
84 Robert O. Keohane, *After Hegemony* (Princeton, NJ: Princeton University Press, 1984).
85 Robert O. Keohane, *After Hegemony: Cooperation and Discord in the World Political Economy* (Princeton, NJ: Princeton University Press, 2005 [1984]), p. 12.
86 *Ibid.*, p. 30.
87 Charles P. Kindleberger, *The World in Depression, 1929–1939* (Berkeley, CA: University of California Press, 1973).
88 Keohane, *After Hegemony*, p. 30.
89 Roger Tooze, 'Susan Strange, Academic International Relations and the Study of International Political Economy,' *New Political Economy*, Vol. 5, No. 2, 2000, p. 281.
90 Ronen Palan, 'Susan Strange 1923–1998: A Great International Relations Theorist,' *Review of International Political Economy*, Vol. 6, No. 2, 2011, p. 122.
91 Robert W. Cox, '"Take Six Eggs": Theory, Finance and the Real Economy in the Work of Susan Strange,' in Robert W. Cox (with Timothy Sinclair) (ed.), *Approaches to World Order* (Cambridge: Cambridge University Press, 1996), p. 174.
92 Peter J. Katzenstein, Robert O. Keohane and Stephen D. Krasner, 'International Organization and the Study of World Politics,' *International Organization*, Vol. 52, No. 4, 1998, p. 652.

93 Susan Strange, '*Cave! Hic dragones*: A Critique of Regime Analysis,' *International Organization*, Vol. 36, No. 2, 1982, p. 479.
94 *Ibid.*, p. 480.
95 *Ibid.*, p. 496.
96 Susan Strange, *States and Markets* (London: Continuum, 1988), p. 24.
97 *Ibid.*, p. 25.
98 *Ibid.*
99 *Ibid.*, pp. 27–28.
100 Susan Strange, *States and Markets* (London: Continuum, 1988), p. 23.
101 *Ibid.*, p. 28.
102 *Ibid.*, p. 26.
103 Robert W. Cox, *Production Power and World Order* (New York: Columbia University Press, 1987), p. 1.
104 *Ibid.*, p. 2.
105 *Ibid.*, p. 5.
106 *Ibid.*
107 *Ibid.*, p. 6.
108 *Ibid.*, p. 7.
109 *Ibid.*, p. 8.
110 *Ibid.*, p. 399.
111 Stephen Gill, 'Two Concepts of International Political Economy,' *Review of International Studies*, Vol. 16, No. 4, 1990, p. 369.

12 A new world order and the effects of globalisation

When does a new world order emerge? It is often when the old system has collapsed either through being overthrown by a rising military Power, therefore by the use of force, or has simply collapsed from internal or external pressures. We tend to identify these turning points by the name of a treaty or set of negotiations with particular dates, but in reality they result from processes of change, such as Westphalia in 1648, Utrecht in 1713, Vienna in 1815, Versailles in 1919, or new post-Second World War order which emerged between 1945–1951 and lasted until the collapse of the Soviet Union and the end of the Cold War followed by the reunification of Germany in 1991.

If we take the last four of these periods – that is 1815 with the Congress of Vienna, 1919 with the Congress of Versailles, 1945–1951 with the peace settlements, and 1989–1991 with the end of the Cold War and the collapse of the Soviet Union – then there are some lessons to be learned. A pattern emerges. In three of the cases, after a period of retribution, there followed a change of policy by the victors to that of reconciliation and the creation of a new world order which satisfied both the victors and the vanquished. France was accommodated after the Napoleonic Wars while Germany, Japan and Italy were accommodated after the Second World War. Finally, the East European states, and to a lesser degree, and initially at least, Russia, were accommodated after the end of the Cold War. The one case which stands out as a disaster was the Treaty of Versailles whereby Germany was treated in a very harsh fashion. It lost territory in Europe; it lost its colonies; it found itself forced to admit war guilt; economic reparations were imposed which were impossible to fulfil; the Kaiser was forced to abdicate and fled to the Netherlands; and the Germans were not allowed to join the newly founded League of Nations, thereby undermining the concept of collective security. In short, the whole question was a *Diktat*. It is for such reasons that two eminent British academics resigned from their role in Versailles in order to warn of the likelihood of creating a situation in which a new war would spring from the settlement of the old war. E.H. Carr and John Maynard Keynes both resigned and published articles and monographs as to why they felt that the peace settlement of 1919 was in fact only a transient settlement and not a resolution of the conflict. The period 1989–1991 saw the emergence of another world order. The Soviet Union had collapsed and together with the Western Powers oversaw the reunification of Germany. The Cold War was at an end, and the United States saw this as a victory and proudly embraced the notion of a unipolar world. There was, however, a countervailing power in each of the major dimensions of a super Power's behaviour – military, economic, cultural, that of legitimacy and acceptance by others of political leadership.

Such a major change excited a great deal of analysis and publications throughout the 1990s. In order to get a feel for the debates, we shall concentrate on the works of five different authors. The first is John Mearsheimer.[1] His views were expressed in an article entitled

'Back to the Future: Instability in Europe After the Cold War.' Our second author took a very different point of view but equally caught the imagination of the attentive public. He is Francis Fukuyama,[2] who points to *The End of History and the Last Man*. Our third writer takes a long historical view. He is Paul Kennedy, a UK but US-domiciled historian, writing on *The Rise and Fall of Great Powers*.[3] His work leads into a discussion of unipolarity and the future which faces us now in terms of global leadership in the face of global problems. Later we shall also consider the contributions of academic and practitioner Joseph Nye and foreign policy expert John Ikenberry.

But the globalisation decade was also about military interventionism, which changed character with 9/11 and shifted the focus from humanitarianism to national security concerns, associated with terrorism. Whereas the first phase led to the re-emergence of the so-called English School, the second phase was central for the partial re-emergence of realism, including its classical form, as we will see in the last part of this chapter.

The process of globalisation

This process is associated with the spread of capitalism over the last 500 years, and it has resulted in a single market and now a worldwide economy which includes states which formerly did not participate, such as China. But it is not merely an economic phenomenon; it has side-effects which are political, cultural, social and ideological.

Globalisation is associated with the notion of complex interdependence and the growth of interconnection so that what affects one actor often has an impact for all. It has elements of governance without being a government. It has weakened the primacy of the interstate system, but on the other hand it has used it for the creation of regulatory procedures. It has stimulated but only partially caused global problems which affect everyone and which can only be managed together. Such problems are environmental degradation, the question of nuclear weapons, weak institutional frameworks, the growing role of civil society, the revolution in communications, and in the handling and storing of data.

There is considerable discussion about how long this process has been active. The common assumption is that it began sometime around half a millennium ago with the establishment of capitalism and its spread. A conventional periodisation would be the establishment around 1500 lasting until the mid-nineteenth century, a second period from the mid-nineteenth century until 1960, and a third period from 1960 to date. The latter date, 1960, was the year in which the global economy had recovered from the Second World War. It was a period of nuclear plenty for the first time; there was a growth of environmental issues and of weak institutions for the handling of such issues. However, this easy chronology has been challenged in a volume of collected essays edited by André Gunder Frank and Barry K. Gills.[4] Their argument is that there has only ever been one global system, and it reaches back 5,000 years.

Others are more modest in their claims, such as Janet Abu-Lughod, who cites the fourteenth century as the point of lift-off for the current network of globalisation. The Frank–Gills book is particularly helpful in that it encompasses essays espousing all points of view including those of Immanuel Wallerstein. Views as to the positive or negative nature of globalisation vary enormously. For some, it is "an anonymous, actorless process."[5] Again, the same authors argue that globalisation has "even challenged the very idea of human agency, be it individual or collective."[6] Not all authors see the phenomenon of globalisation in such dramatic terms.

There are many monographs and collected volumes of essays on globalisation which cause the shelves in libraries to creak under their weight, and two in particular stand out. One is Jan Aart Scholte in his volume simply entitled *Globalisation*.[7] In his book, Scholte points out that many of the developments associated with globalisation are a continuation of pre-existing trends, and therefore nothing is new except the extent of the spread of globalisation and its deep penetration in numerous areas of economic and other aspects of activity. The one big difference is that globalisation has increased cosmopolitan links on a non-territorial basis. It not only builds up but it builds down to smaller identity units, some of which are territorially based, some of which are not. Indeed, the striking point that Scholte makes is that the time-space ratio has been annihilated in terms of how quickly effects are felt globally from wherever they come in the global system. But, on the whole, change is within continuity and not a revolutionary break.

A reader with the same title, edited by George Ritzer, is a well-balanced collection[8] and contains a summary of the views of a major scholar in the area, Anthony McGrew. McGrew identifies various forms of globalisation such as the liberal transformationalist, which he entitles *defensive globalism.*[9] There is a justification for this liberal interpretation in that poverty may be reduced unequally but democracy is strengthened, and the problem is one, therefore, of uneven distribution of goods. To transform it has structural consequences in multiplying complexity in societies and transnational problems such as climate change.[10]

A way forward is to differentiate clearly between what is rational for an individual and what is rational for a collectivity, in this instance the world. Can global problems such as we have mentioned bring a new rationality, or are we going to hang separately if we cannot hang together individually? Many of these questions remain unanswered today, but by the end of the Cold War there were some strong positions regarding where we were heading.

A shifting world: from Mearsheimer to Ikenberry

As seen in the previous chapter, Kenneth Waltz's (as well as Gilpin's) work contributed to the revitalisation of realism in the 1980s, after a period in which both the liberal and Marxist voices, with their predominant focus on the economy, seemed to gain the upper edge. In the United States, the debate between defensive and offensive realists (concentrated round John Mearsheimer) would take centre-stage. Defensive realism came more as an attempt to 'improve' Waltz's theory (whose work is often put in the defensive realist category), than to dramatically change it. In that regard, there are three main differences between defensive realism and its predecessor. First, defensive realism offers a sole explanation for state behaviour – rational choice – whereas neorealism is quite open in terms of why states behave in a certain way (other than they try to guarantee their security). Second, for defensive realists, states tend to make those rational decisions based on an offence-defence balance approach in which they tend to opt for a cautious behaviour as the risks associated with power projection and expansionist policies are often too great. Finally, as a result of the previous two points, defensive realists tend to defend the *status quo* over systemic change.[11] For neorealists, both points two and three are open to discussion as states make their decisions based on a multiplicity of reasons and may or may not prefer the *status quo*.

For offensive realists, the international system is much more brutal and ruthless than what is depicted by defensive realists. For offensive realists, such as John Mearsheimer, power is the ultimate security guarantor in the international system. States will therefore do whatever they can to acquire increasing levels of it. This means that, following Kenneth Waltz, the existence of a bipolar system offers the best guarantees of stability. Multipolarity generates a higher risk of miscalculations, misperceptions and, therefore, war.

John Mearsheimer's controversial piece 'Back to the Future: Instability in Europe After the Cold War,' published a decade before his now classic *The Tragedy of Great Power*

Politics, applies offensive realist thought to the emerging post-Cold War geopolitical context in Europe. His argument is that the prospects for major crises in Europe are likely "to increase materially if the Cold War ends." He goes on to state that:

> [t]his pessimistic conclusion rests on the argument that the distribution and character of military power are the root causes of war and peace. Specifically, the absence of war in Europe since 1945 has been the consequence of three factors: the bipolar distribution of military power on the Continent; the rough military quality between the two states comprising with two poles in Europe, the United States and the Soviet Union; and the fact that each super power was armed with a large nuclear arsenal.

In short, the situation in central Europe with the absence of the two super Powers would lead to a multipolar system with all the problems inherent therein "and would therefore be more prone to instability."[12]

Four scenarios were postulated by Mearsheimer. First, a scenario in which Europe is free from nuclear weapons, "thus eliminating a central pillar of order in the Cold War era." Second, a scenario in which the European states do not expand their arsenals to compensate for the departure of the super Powers' weapons. In a third scenario, nuclear proliferation takes place, but is mismanaged; no steps are taken to dampen the many dangers inherent in the proliferation process. In the fourth "least dangerous scenario, nuclear weapons proliferate in Europe, but the process is well managed by the current nuclear powers."[13]

Mearsheimer defines three possible counter-arguments to this "pessimistic set of predictions of Europe's future." First, that the liberal international economic order will ultimately guarantee peace in the continent. Second, the democratic nature of states in Europe, and subsequent democratisation of Central and Eastern Europe, will make "wars still less likely." Finally, the argument that Europeans have learned from their costly mistakes (i.e. two world wars) and have realised that war is no longer an option.[14]

These arguments are all swiftly rejected by Mearsheimer. The liberal economic argument cannot explain the absence of strong economic ties between the West and the Soviet Union during the Cold War. The same applies to the democratic argument. The cost of war, more persuasive, still falls short when looked at from an historical perspective, as it should have prevented the Second World War, and it did not. Mearsheimer then ends with three principal policy prescriptions:

> First, the United States should encourage a process of limited nuclear proliferation in Europe. Specifically, Europe will be more stable if Germany acquires a secure nuclear deterrent, that proliferation does not go beyond that point. Second, the United States should not withdraw fully from Europe, even if the Soviet Union pulls its forces out of Eastern Europe. Third, the United States should take steps to forestall the re-emergence of hypernationalism in Europe.[15]

Mearsheimer used some traditional realist arguments to justify his position by referring to a security dilemma for states. He also stressed that states seem to give greater importance to relative gains rather than to absolute gains. Finally, even in a system of close economic cooperation, states are still vulnerable to the actions of the other and will need to be able to counter any vulnerability.

This article – which was also an attack against neoliberal institutionalism – was much criticised at the time both for its theoretical stance and for its analysis of Europe's geopolitics. In a series of articles and letters published in *International Security* in the months following its publication, authors such as Stanley Hoffman and Robert Keohane offered a dire indictment of Mearsheimer's views. Stanley Hoffman's letter to the Editors was certainly the harshest in terms of language: "Back to the Future" was "almost a caricature of neo-realism," dogmatic and without much relevance to the real world.[16] His critique is one against Mearsheimer as much as it is one against Waltz: "in anarchy, any structure can lead either to peace or to war; it depends on the domestic characteristics of the main actors, on their preferences and goals, as well as on the relations and links among them."[17] Mearsheimer's analysis does not take into sufficient consideration the European integration experience and assumes Europeans did not learn anything from the past. As he concludes, "mediocre theory leads to bad analysis."[18]

Robert Keohane was more moderate, but equally critical of Mearsheimer's analysis. Keohane reaffirmed the importance of institutions in shaping state expectations and how that plays a role in Europe. In his view, "avoiding military conflict in Europe after the Cold War depends greatly on whether the next decade is characterized by a continuous pattern of institutionalized cooperation," including the future of NATO, (then) CSCE and the European Community.[19]

In a reply to both authors, John Mearsheimer suggests that Stanley Hoffman can only fully challenge his theory by offering an alternative of his own, which (understandably) did not fit in a two-page letter. For Mearsheimer, Hoffman's critique is not theoretically clear and thus does not refute his analysis. At the time, the 'systemic change' was just beginning. Hence, one could not expect significant alterations in terms of state behaviour in Europe.[20] Regarding Robert Keohane's critique, Mearsheimer addresses not only his comments but also some of the points included in Keohane's *After Hegemony* (discussed later). Mearsheimer dismisses Keohane's arguments as lacking sufficient "historical evidence." As for the concrete case of Europe, Mearsheimer reasserts that the EC only flourished as a result of the Cold War environment and that "if the Cold War ends and the stable order it produces collapses, the EC is likely to grow weaker, not stronger with time."[21]

Twenty years later, Mearsheimer was invited to give a keynote lecture at the ECPR conference, later published in *European Political Science*. Unrepentant, Mearsheimer reaffirmed his prognosis, stating:

> I am sure that some of you do not find my argument convincing and instead think that there is no serious chance of war in Europe and thus there is no need for the United States to maintain its continental commitment. The truth is that we cannot know whether you are right or I am right until US troops are pulled completely out of Europe and NATO is disbanded. If Europe remains at peace after an American withdrawal, you will be proved right. But if serious security competition breaks out, I will be proved right.

In his view, peace in Europe would be determined by three critical issues: the future of out of area missions, the US pivot to Asia (and subsequent reduction in its European presence) and, rather prophetically, the future of Russia-Ukraine relations.[22] Ultimately, however, Europe's fate remains, in Mearsheimer's view, in the hands of the US 'pacifier.'

In his keynote address, Mearsheimer also took the opportunity to praise the work of another scholar that rose to polemical prominence in the 1990s: Francis Fukuyama and his *End of History*. As he argued in his ECPR address: "I do not know of anybody who seriously argued that he [Fukuyama] was wrong about the triumph of liberal democracy in Western Europe."[23] It is to Fukuyama's work that we now turn our attention.

The end of history or the beginning of the end?

Francis Fukuyama, in *The End of History and the Last Man*,[24] has no such qualms about the security aspects of liberal international democratic frameworks. In the introduction to this monograph, Francis Fukuyama refers to an article on the same subject that he wrote for the journal *The National Interest* in the summer of 1989. He summarised his own analysis in the following manner:

> I argued that a remarkable consensus concerning the legitimacy of liberal democracy as a system of government had emerged throughout the world over the past few years, as it conquered rival ideologies like hereditary monarchy, fascism, and most recently, communism. More than that, however, I argued that liberal democracy may constitute the "end point of mankind's ideological evolution" and the "final form of human government," and as such constituted the "end of history." That is, while earlier forms of government were characterised by grave defects and irrationalities that led to their eventual collapse, liberal democracy was arguably free from such fundamental internal contradictions . . . these problems were ones of the incomplete implementation of the twin principles of liberty and equality on which modern democracy is founded, rather than of flaws in the principles themselves . . . the *ideal* of liberal democracy could not be improved on.[25]

Fukuyama went on to state that his understanding of history was that of a "single, coherent, evolutionary process, when taking into account the experience of all peoples in all times."[26] As if to underline the point, Fukuyama argues that,

> Liberal democracy remains the only coherent political aspiration that spans different regions and cultures around the globe. In addition, liberal principles in economics – the "free market" – have spread, and have succeeded in producing unprecedented levels and material prosperity, both in the industrially developed countries and the countries that had been, at the close of World War Two, part of the impoverished third world.[27]

Fukuyama goes further in stating that:

> The unfolding of modern natural sciences had a uniform effect on all societies that had experienced it . . . technology confers decisive military advantages on those countries that possess it . . . Second, modern natural science establishes a uniform horizon of economic production possibilities. This process guarantees an increasing homogenisation of all human societies, regardless of their historical origins or cultural inheritances. When they must unify nationally on the basis of a centralised state, urbanised, replace traditional forms of social organisation. Such societies have become increasingly linked with one another through the global markets and the spread of a universal consumer culture.[28]

Nevertheless, Fukuyama does concede that "in many cases, authority and states are capable of producing rates of economic growth unachievable in democratic societies."[29] He notes that "we have trouble imagining a world that is radically better than our own, and a future that is not essentially democratic and capitalist."[30]

Three decades after the publication of his polemical *The National Interest* article, the world seems far from the perspectives and forecasts of Fukuyama at the time. There are the travails of liberal democracy, with a growth of voting for far-right political parties, and pressure groups. There is the economic crisis and the collapse of the banking system and the imposition of austerity, bringing with it poverty and hardship. Moreover, the efficacy of traditional military force is brought into question by the defeat of one of the super Powers in long-term military wars in Afghanistan and Iraq. Above all, in various parts of the world, there is an alarming spread of fundamentalist ideologies. In an essay published in the *Atlantic* in 2014, Timothy Stanley and Alexander Lee argued "History isn't over and neither liberalism nor democracy is ascendant."[31] Fukuyama himself would recognise the limitations of his theory when applied to our current times. In an interview reported in the *Washington Post* in February 2017, he recognised that "Twenty five years ago, I didn't have a sense or a theory about how democracies can go backward . . . I think they clearly can."[32]

The beginning of the end

Like Mearsheimer and Fukuyama, Paul Kennedy's work evoked a wide response within and beyond academia. He fits nicely into the tradition of world history and long cycle theory, as exemplified by Modelski and William Thompson. When considering the rise and fall of great Powers over the past five centuries, his argument is that "there exists a dynamic for change, driven chiefly by economic and technological developments, which then impact upon social structures, political systems, military power, and the position of the individual states and empires."[33]

His second major argument, as he puts it, is that "this uneven pace of economic growth has had crucial long-term impacts upon the relative military power and strategical position of the members of the state system."[34] Kennedy goes on to emphasise that:

> [t]he fact remains that all the major shifts of the world's *military-power* balances have followed alterations in the *productive* balances; and further, that the rising and falling of the various empires and states in the international system has been confirmed by the outcomes of the major great power wars, where victory has always gone to the side with the greatest material resources.

Kennedy points out that, in the end, all great Powers fall. Henceforth:

> [i]n the largest sense of all, therefore, the only answer to the question increasingly debated by the public of whether the United States can preserve its existing position is "no" – for it simply has not been given to any one society to remain *permanently* the head of all the others, because that would imply a freezing of the differentiated pattern of growth rates, technological advance, and military developments which have existed since time immemorial.[35]

So much for unipolarity, which was truly a moment rather than a decade. It was the moment from the concern of the European Powers for German reunification to the end of the Soviet Union, a period of, at best, five years. When the United States did seek to act in a unipolar manner, it found that although it felt itself bound to lead, others did not feel themselves bound to follow, which takes us into the notion of leadership at the global level and the nature of soft power.

In raising the question about whether or not the United States was fit for purpose in this leading role, Joseph Nye, a leading academic and practitioner, emphasised the importance of legitimacy and what he termed soft power. In a series of monographs and articles over a twenty-year period, he developed the concept for judging the degree to which the United States or anybody else for that matter is fit for purpose as a global leader; and the prime aim of the global leader would be to ensure that we hang together rather than hang separately when faced by global problems.

As Nye puts it:

> [s]oft co-optive power is just as important as hard command power. If a state can make its power legitimate in the eyes of others, it will encounter less resistance to its wishes. If its culture and ideology are attractive, others will more willingly follow. If it can establish international norms that are consistent with its society, it will be less likely to have to change. If it can help support institutions that encourage other states to channel or limit their activities in ways that the dominant state prefers, it may not need as many costly exercises of coercion or hard power in bargaining situations. In short, the universalism of a country's culture and its ability to establish a set of favorable rules and institutions that govern areas of international activity are critical sources of power.

From Nye's point of view, the United States was bound to lead, and soft power was one of the ways more likely to induce others to be bound to follow.[36] At least that seemed to be the case until 9/11 . . .

The post-globalisation world: terror, interventionism and decline

One of the great changes that was brought about by the end of the Cold War, or at least revealed by the end of the Cold War, was the changing nature of conflict. No longer was it tank battles on the scale of the Second World War or even trench warfare, as in the First World War. Such phenomena still occurred, as, for example, in the confrontation between Eritrea and Ethiopia, but by and large, conflicts were now intra-state and transnational rather than inter-state wars or conflicts. The tactics used also meant that the balance had changed between military losses and civilian losses, with the latter now being predominant. Such wars were people's wars in an entirely new sense. They also altered the nature of military capability. Leviathans tended to become muscle-bound, and although the United States, for example, could, with the UK's help, overthrow regimes in Iraq, Afghanistan and Libya, it could not win the peace.

That was very clearly recognised by Joseph Nye, who a decade after promoting his soft power concept, readjusted his thesis in the face of what now was a world dominated by the global war on terror. Whereas soft power was still central, it only worked as long as the United States remained an attractive proposition in the eyes of the rest of the world and that was now being questioned with the invasions of Afghanistan and Iraq: "attraction can turn to repulsion if we act in an arrogant manner and destroy the real message of our deeper values."[37] Whereas soft power could explain the success of the 1990s, the United States would now have to embrace the 2000s by trying to bring together its formidable hard power and its fast declining soft power in what Nye would call 'smart power,' which is neither hard nor soft, being a suitable dosage of both.[38] Smart power, in Nye, is defined as "the ability to combine hard and soft power resources into effective strategies." Differently from soft power, the smart version "is an evaluative as well as a descriptive concept. Soft power can be good or bad from a normative perspective, depending on how it is used. Smart power has the evaluation built into the definitions."[39]

Like Joseph Nye, John Ikenberry analysed the problems of establishing a new world order and the role of the United States therein. Both were rather sanguine about the continuing role of US leadership and thought that, given good sense and practical policies on the part of the United States and others, this could be managed. Ikenberry is more state-centric than Nye, whereas Nye emphasises the element of legitimacy from civil society in establishing a post-world war order. We shall concentrate on two of Ikenberry's many writings, namely *After Victory*[40] and *Liberal Leviathan*.[41]

A winning Power or coalition has three options at the end of a war according to Ikenberry: one is to dominate, the second is to abandon and the third is to transform the existing relationship after the conflict into a new world order. The United States opted for abandonment after the First World War and for transformation of the situation in 1945 into a world order to its liking after the Second World War. The question both Nye and Ikenberry ask is whether or not this can continue after the end of the Cold War. While Nye stresses the notion of legitimacy, Ikenberry refers to a transformation of the post-war situation into a new constitutional world order whereby the dominant victorious Powers would give up some benefits in order to gain others. It is a case of *reculer pour mieux sauter*. The United States did this by being a hegemonic Power but one which was building a constitutional order through multilateralism, which reflected, or so Ikenberry argues, both the interests of the United States and those subject to its hegemonic leadership.[42] Ikenberry writes that:

> Constitutional orders "limit the returns to power." Limits are set on what actors can do with momentary advantages. Losers realize that their losses are limited and temporary, and that to accept those losses is not to risk everything or to give the winners a permanent advantage.[43]

Again, Ikenberry argues that:

> [a]n international order with strong constitutional characteristics is one in which the power capabilities of the relevant states are highly constrained by interlocking institutional and binding agreements . . . Seen in this way, constitutional order can be contrasted with balance-of-power and hegemonic orders. The balance-of-power order is one in which the restraints on state power are maintained exclusively by countervailing coalitions of states. Hegemonic power is effectively unrestrained power. Weaker and secondary states cooperate with the hegemon because of threats and inducements.[44]

Ikenberry goes on to make the rationale abundantly clear:

> In general, a leading state will want to bind weaker and secondary states to a set of rules and institution of post-war order – locking in these states to predictable patterns of behavior – that remain unbound itself, free of institutional constraints and obligations. But to get the willing participation and compliance of other states, a leading state must offer to limit its own autonomy and ability to exercise power arbitrarily. The willingness and ability of states to offer and enter into these self-binding bargains hinge on the types of states involved and the character of post-war power disparities. Democracies are better able to do so, but are also often unwilling.

Ikenberry goes on again to stress the importance of far-sightedness by the dominant Power, by asking the question:

> Why would a new lead powerful state want to restrict itself by agreeing to limits on the use of its power? Because it has an interest in conserving its power. A leading state gives up some freedom on the use [of its power] in exchange for agreed-upon principles and institutional processes that ensure a durable and predictable post-war order.

In short, the nail is driven home when Ikenberry writes:

> In sum, the constitutional development involves a bargain: the leading state gets a predictable and legitimate order based on agreed-upon rules and institutions. It attains the acquiescence in this order by weaker states, which in turn allows it to conserve its power. In return, the leading state agrees to limits on its own actions and to open itself up to a political process in which the weaker states can actively press their interests upon the more powerful state. The hegemonic or leading state agrees to forego some gains in the early post-war period in exchange for rules and institutions that allow it to have stable returns later, while weaker states are given favorable returns upfront and limits on the exercise of power. Institutions play a two-sided role: they must bind the leading state when it is initially stronger and the subordinate states later when they are stronger.[45]

While the United States may have played this role in the period of institution building in economic and military and political affairs after the Second World War, could it do likewise after the end of the Cold War, which was also a period of construction of a new world order?

The response of John Ikenberry in his book on the *Liberal Leviathan: The Origins, Crisis, and Transformation of the American World Order* is an emphatic 'yes.' In his view, the United States could still lead through 'rules' and look for ways to renegotiate hegemonic bargains with other states.[46] The notion of liberal hegemony is seen by Ikenberry as being in contrast with another ideal type of international order, namely empire. He comments that:

> Each offers a distinct logic of hierarchy. In an imperial order, the dominant state operates unilaterally and above the rules and institutions. In a liberal hegemonic order, the lead states establishes agree-upon rules and institutions and operates – more or less – within them. The lead state negotiates rather than imposes order. In an imperial order, the lead state rules through command and, ultimately, coercion. In a liberal hegemonic order, the lead state rules by shaping the *milieu* in which states operate. The character of domination and authority varies accordingly.[47]

Ikenberry then goes on to examine the impact of unipolarity on questions of leadership and foresees three possible pathways:

> [t]hat lead away from the current era of American-led liberal hegemonic order. One pathway is simply a renegotiated American-led system . . . A second pathway is really the move to a post-American liberal international order . . . Finally, a third pathway is toward a more fragmented system of rival spheres or blocs.[48]

It is true that the United States has colossal military power in a formal sense, but to what extent is this still a valuable tool in global politics? And could not those resources be better used in creating a sense of legitimacy after the depredations on the standing of the United States during the Bush administration? To be sure, there was an element of unipolarity, or a moment at least, in the period from the collapse of the Soviet Union to the unification of Germany. But it is clear the United States has difficulty in coercing allies and equal difficulty in convincing them to follow the US lead. Of all the three pathways proposed by Ikenberry, the first one seems the least likely to be followed in the coming decades.

Realism as a normative voice

Before we turn to more critical voices and how they are reshaping IR, it is worth pointing out that this post-globalisation world has also – surprisingly one could say – seen the emergence of an alternative take on 'classical' realism that moves closer to what is seen as international political theory.[49] Michael Williams, one of the authors at the forefront of this 'back to classics' movement, aims to bring the political element back to realist thought, both analytically and normatively. In his view, not only realism should have political and ideological elements in much stronger consideration when looking at international politics as they should be normatively engaged with the issues and problems at hand.[50] That dimension became quite evident with the post-9/11 security context and the unfolding global war on terror, particularly once it became clear the United States was about to embark on an interventionist campaign of a slighter different kind from what it had done in the 1990s, when humanitarian concerns dictated interventions in places such as Somalia, Bosnia and Kosovo. The current interventionist project was to be potentially global in scope and without a clear end line in sight.

This had three main consequences in the realist coterie. First, it led to the creation of a movement in the United States that brought together academics from all theoretical angles, but with a clear predomination of realist authors. The Coalition for a Realistic Foreign Policy published in the first half of the 2000s a number of letters and op-eds in major US outlets arguing against the creeping imperialism in US foreign policy, particularly after 9/11. As they wrote in an op-ed published in 2004, "We can persist in imperial policies that are sacrificing our soldiers every day and heightening antagonism all over the world, or we can embrace an approach that combines democratic values with a more responsible understanding of our national interest."[51]

Second, it led to some of those authors actively and publicly opposing some of George W. Bush's policies from an academic position. They recovered a realist tradition of public critique that was quite clear when not only Hans Morgenthau but also Kenneth Waltz were active in criticising the US involvement in Vietnam. This was more than op-eds showing intelligent arguments against the Global War on Terror, it was a concrete application of realist thought to the current political situation. Two cases were particularly illuminating in that regard: Kenneth Waltz's chapter on Al-Qaida arguing against an excessive concentration of attention on a threat that was far from existential to the United States, and, more emphatically, John Mearsheimer and Stephen Walt's *Foreign Policy*[52] piece on why invading Iraq was not in the interests of the United States, and that, ultimately, Saddam Hussein was a rational actor whose historic track record had always been "to stay alive" and "to remain in power."[53]

Finally, it contributed to the above-mentioned revival of classical realism. Authors such as Michael C. Williams,[54] William E. Scheuerman and Richard Ned Lebow,[55] revisited the post-Second World War literature in order to find new ways of dealing with the expansion of emergency powers, the redefinition of national interest and the need for a renewed ethics of international politics that moves away from interventionism as a default option.

Notes

1 John Mearsheimer, 'Back to the Future: Instability in Europe after the Cold War,' *International Security*, Vol. XV, No. 1, 1990.
2 Francis Fukuyama, *The End of History and the Last Man* (London: Penguin, 1992).
3 Paul Kennedy, *The Rise and Fall of Great Powers* (London: Unwin, 1998).
4 André Gunder Frank and Barry K. Gills (eds), *The World System* (Oxford: Routledge, 1993).
5 Nathalie Karagiannis and Peter Wagner (eds), *Varieties of World-Making* (Liverpool: Liverpool University Press, 2007), p. 3.
6 *Ibid.*, p. 4.

7 Jan Aart Scholte, *Globalisation: A Critical Introduction* (London: Macmillan, 2000).
8 George Ritzer (ed.), *Globalisation* (Oxford: Blacknell, 2002).
9 Anthony McGrew, 'Globalization in Hard Times,' in *Ibid.*, p. 35.
10 McGrew, in *Ibid.*, pp. 31–37.
11 Colin Elman and Michael A. Jensen 'Introduction,' in Colin Elman and Michael A. Jensen (eds), *Realism Reader* (Oxford: Routledge, 2014), p. 7.
12 Mearsheimer, *op. cit.*, p. 7.
13 *Ibid.*
14 *Ibid.*, pp. 7–8.
15 *Ibid.*, p. 8.
16 Stanley Hoffman, 'Correspondence,' *International Security*, Vol. 15, No. 2, 1990, pp. 191–192.
17 *Ibid.*, p. 192.
18 *Ibid.*
19 Robert O. Keohane, 'Correspondence,' *International Security*, Vol. 15, No. 2, 1990, p. 192–194.
20 John Mearsheimer, 'Correspondence,' *International Security*, Vol. 15, No. 2, 1990, p. 194–199.
21 Mearsheimer, *idem*, p. 198.
22 According to Mearsheimer "Russia does not have good relations with Ukraine and there is no reason to expect them to improve in the foreseeable future, especially since Ukraine wants the Russian militarily to leave the Crimean Peninsula when its lease expires in 2017, while Russia will surely want to remain there," In John Mearsheimer 'Why Is Europe Peaceful Today?' *European Political Science*, Vol. 9, 2010, p. 396.
23 *Ibid.*, p. 392.
24 Francis Fukuyama, *op. cit.*
25 Francis Fukuyama, *op. cit.*, p. xi.
26 *Ibid.*, p. xii.
27 *Ibid.*, p. xiii.
28 *Ibid.*, pp. xiv, xv.
29 *Ibid.*, p. xv.
30 *Ibid.*, p. 46.
31 Timothy Stanley and Alexander Lee, 'It's Still Not the End of History,' *The Atlantic*, 1 September 2014. Available at: www.theatlantic.com/politics/archive/2014/09/its-still-not-the-end-of-history-francis-fukuyama/379394/.
32 In Ishaan Tharoor, 'The Man Who Declared the "End of History" Fears for Democracy's Future,' *The Washington Post*, 9 February 2017. Available at: www.washingtonpost.com/news/worldviews/wp/2017/02/09/the-man-who-declared-the-end-of-history-fears-for-democracys-future/?utm_term=.a08cc5774dd0.
33 Paul Kennedy, *op. cit.*, p. 439.
34 *Ibid.*
35 *Ibid.*, p. 533.
36 Joseph S. Nye, *Bound to Lead* (New York: Basic Books, 1990), pp. 32–33.
37 Joseph S. Nye, *Soft Power* (New York: Public Affairs, 2004), p. x.
38 *Ibid.*, p. xiii.
39 Joseph S. Nye, *The Future of Power* (New York: Public Affairs, 2011) p. 23.
40 G. John Ikenberry, *After Victory* (Princeton, NJ: Princeton University Press, 2005).
41 G. John Ikenberry, *Liberal Leviathan: The Origins, Crisis, and Transformation of the American World Order* (Princeton, NJ: Princeton University Press, 2011).
42 Ikenberry, *After Victory*, *op. cit.*, p. 4 *et seq.*
43 *Ibid.*, p. 6.
44 *Ibid.*, pp. 36–37.
45 *Ibid.*, p. 57.
46 *Ibid.*, p. xiv.
47 *Ibid.*, p. 67.
48 *Ibid.*, p. 281.
49 That search for the politics and political ethics of classical realism overlaps with the research undertaken by what is now known as international political theory. International political theory sits between international relations theory and political theory, focusing on normative theory. This goes right to one of the main issues associated with the development of the discipline, Martin Wight's 1960 article 'Why Is There No International Theory?' where Wight contrasts political theory as being mostly about the good life in domestic politics with IR as being merely about survival.

50 Michael C. Williams 'In the Beginning: The International Relations Enlightenment and the End of International Relations Theory,' *European Journal of International Relations*, Vol. 3, 2013, pp. 647–665.
51 Coalition for a Realistic Foreign Policy (2004), 'The Perils of Occupation,' October 2004. Available at: www.realisticforeignpolicy.org.
52 John Mearsheimer and Stephen Walt, 'An Unnecessary War,' *Foreign Policy*, Vol. 134, No. 1, 2003, pp. 50–59.
53 *Ibid.*, p. 59.
54 Michael C. Williams, *The Realist Tradition and the Limits of International Relations* (Cambridge: Cambridge University Press, 2005).
55 Richard Ned Lebow, *The Tragic Vision of Politics: Ethics, Interests and Orders* (Cambridge: Cambridge University Press, 2003).

13   The construction of international reality

Richard K. Ashley[1] and Robert Cox's[2] critiques of Kenneth Waltz's neorealism had already announced the beginning of a new era in IR: the strong rationalist focus of the 1970s and early 1980s was now progressively opening up to something new. As had often been the case since the origins of the discipline, the theoretical and conceptual innovations of the 1990s were imports from other disciplines, mostly social theory, but also cultural studies, anthropology and linguistics. The disciplinary oligopoly of law, history and economics was now giving way to different disciplines and new contributions. Many of those developed within what the disciplinary orthodoxy decided to label as 'radical' approaches – critical theory, feminism, poststructuralism and postcolonialism (the next chapter will delve into some of those innovations). A clear and slightly less 'radical' mark in the discipline's evolution, however, was the centrality that social constructivism, building on the social theory works of Berger and Luckmann,[3] John Searle[4] and Anthony Giddens[5] as well as on the linguistic approaches put forward by J.L Austin[6] in the late 1960s, assumed in the discipline. Nicholas Onuf,[7] Peter Katzenstein,[8] Alexander Wendt[9] and Friedrich Kratochwil[10] were among the IR pioneers in that regard. They were soon to be followed by an impressive list of authors, such as Martha Finnemore,[11] Stefano Guzzini,[12] Karin Fierke[13] and Jutta Weldes.[14] Some journals, such as the *European Journal of International Relations* became strongholds for the constructivist 'cause,' and by the end of the 1990s it was already clear that Europe and to a lesser extent the United States had embraced these authors' ideas.

Although constructivism has been widely adopted on both sides of the Atlantic, the intellectual context in which it took place was significantly different. Whereas in the United States, despite the effort of constructivist authors, the debate was set as one research project against the other,[15] in Europe the conversation was more in terms of how constructivism could contribute to pre-existing research programmes, such as in security studies or when discussing international society, both of which were revitalised with this sociological turn in the discipline.

Constructing constructivism

Nicholas Onuf's work was, to a large extent, the precursor of what was to become a much more accentuated trend in the post-Cold War world of IR. Rationalist approaches had largely failed to predict the outcome of the bipolar confrontation. In the words of Alexander Wendt, it "caught scholars on all sides off guard but left orthodoxies particularly exposed."[16] How was it possible that the two countries that were responsible for over four decades of tension, proxy wars and the fabrication of endless electoral results across the world, were now effectively partners in a new world order? Few rationalist approaches could explain such a drastic change. To rationalism's individual ontology, constructivism would respond with intersubjectivity. International relations were, to a very large extent, the result of social interactions and patterns of sociability. These were in stark contrast with Waltz's focus on the position of the units (states).

Influenced by the works of authors such as Anthony Giddens and Jurgen Habermas – "particular sources of inspiration"[17] – Onuf introduced constructivism in IR not to offer a new theory of how states behave, but rather to provide "a large and sturdy framework from the diverse 'theoretical' materials of many disciplines";[18] a theoretical approach that could be interpreted as "a way between positivist social science and assaults on modernity then rampant."[19] Constructivism emerged as a *via media*, advocating a distinct ontology – depicting "the social world as intersubjectively and collectively meaningful structures and processes,"[20] but opening spaces for all sorts of epistemological and methodological approaches. In his view, constructivism does not prescribe a specific theoretical approach, being compatible with rationalism, quantitative methods and most forms of qualitative analysis.[21] In practice, Onuf opened the door for the development of new theories about how the world works. And that is precisely what Alexander Wendt did, as we shall see in the next section.

Constructivism's premise is rather simple and not that dissimilar from what authors writing in the mid-century had already argued,[22] albeit not in such a consistent way: reality is a social construction and international relations are the result of social interactions. We thus cannot speak of an objective world or objective social relations, as they are the product of intersubjective knowledge of social facts. Meaning is established by the interaction of subjects. Therefore, understandings are not purely individual and subjective, but shared, and contextually accepted.

According to constructivist authors, intersubjectivity leads to an understanding of social phenomena as based on dialogical relations.[23] It is due to the existence of that context that discourses, practices and actions have 'sedimented' meanings that can change over time, but that are temporarily stable. As a result, structures are not deterministic features of everyday life, but rather limiting and temporary boundary setting, formed from the stabilisation of certain meanings.[24] Structures open the way for the agent's autonomous decision-making, which in turn can lead to the change of the structure. In that sense, the structure is not seen as the insurmountable barrier that defines how the world interacts, but rather as a mediator between human agency and social dynamics. Following the structurationist approach of Anthony Giddens,[25] human agency is situated in relation to structural properties. Structure and agency are mutually constituted, and one only has meaning through the other,[26] which implies that "people are both socialized into their situations and capable of transformative actions."[27] With this claim constructivism makes an important ethical claim: political actors are ultimately responsible for their political decisions.

According to Ted Hopf, five main features could broadly define constructivism. First, actors and structures in the international system are mutually constituted "through the media of norms and practices" as "in the absence of norms, exercises of power, or actions, would be devoid of meaning."[28] Onuf and Friedrich Kratochwil have certainly popularised this focus on norms. We could even argue that it was through norms that constructivism made its way into IR. Second, and as result of the first, anarchy is an imagined community that has no material existence; it is a social fact, as Alexander Wendt clearly highlighted in his work. Third, identities and interests are interrelated in world politics: interests reflect identity constructions and these identity constructs are essential "in order to ensure at least some minimal level of predictability and order."[29] Fourth, practices are fundamental to understanding international relations due to their "capacity to reproduce the intersubjective meanings that constitute social structures and actors alike."[30] Finally, through social practices, it becomes clear that "change in world politics is both possible and difficult."[31] Alexander Wendt elaborated on these points, advancing what according to him was the first social constructivist theory of international politics. In that regard, it is fair to acknowledge that if Onuf, Kratochwill and others introduced constructivism to IR, Alexander Wendt consolidated its stance in the discipline, offering a social theory based on its core premises.

Alex Wendt and the consolidation of social constructivism

First in a series of articles (including the now classical 'Anarchy Is What States Make of It'), and then in his 1999 *Social Theory of International Politics*, Wendt delineated what was to be an alternative reading of the world. His aim was to "build a bridge between these two traditions . . . by developing a constructivist argument, drawn from structurationist and symbolic interactionist sociology, on behalf of the liberal claim that international institutions can transform state identities and interests."[32] Using Kenneth Waltz's work as the springboard for his own theory, Wendt quickly concluded that anarchy and the distribution of power were insufficient factors to explain how international relations work. Neorealism had failed to consider in sufficient depth what was a fourth crucial element in international relations – ideas.

In his view, ideational structures shape the way actors define themselves through processes of socialisation. Wendt would claim that ideational structures and actors co-constitute and co-determine each other. Therefore, anarchy only exists if states believe it does. Unlike what Waltz and others would argue, "it is through ideas that states ultimately relate to one another."[33] As a result, "self-help and power politics are institutions, not essential features of anarchy"[34] and institutions are a "relative stable set of 'structure[s]' of identities and interests."[35] In the 1999 book, Wendt was particularly interested "in the structure and effects of states (or 'international') systems, which means that I will be taking a 'systems theory' approach to IR."[36]

Wendt's constructivism does not entirely reject neorealism, which has often been at the basis of the criticisms against his theory,[37] as we will have the opportunity to explore further in the following section. Wendt's constructivism requires the acceptance of states as central actors in the international system endowed with "(1) an institutional-legal order, (2) an organization claiming a monopoly on the legitimate use of organized violence, (3) an organization with sovereignty, (4) a society, and (5) territory,"[38] States are, in his view, still at the core of the international system. Any systemic change at the international level needs to occur through these actors. Furthermore, "it makes no more sense to criticize a theory of international politics as 'state-centric' than it does to criticize a theory of forests for being 'tree-centric.'"[39] As states tend to believe that we live in an anarchical system, "there should continue to be a place for theories of anarchic interstate politics, alongside other forms of international theory." To that extent, he considers himself to be "a statist and a realist."[40] In his 1995 article 'Constructing International Politics' he had already revealed his sympathy for the offensive realist John Mearsheimer:

> I share all five of Mearsheimer's realist assumptions: that international politics is anarchic, and that states have offensive capabilities, cannot be 100 percent certain about others' intentions, wish to survive and are rational. We even share two more: a commitment to states as units of analysis, and to the importance of systemic or third image theorizing.[41]

That said, Wendt provides ample arguments that allow him to distance himself from realism and thus sustain the specificity of his constructivist theory. In *Social Theory of International*

Relations, Wendt identifies three main problems with realism,[42] some of which he had already identified in previous works. First, realism cannot explain structural change. It cannot explain why states change their behaviour or why the international system went from bipolarity to unipolarity at the end of the Cold War. Using the demise of the Soviet Union as an example, Wendt argues that "what is so important about the Gorbachev regime is that it had the courage to see how the Soviets' own practices sustained the Cold War, and to undertake a reassessment of Western intentions." He further adds that, "this is exactly what a constructivist would do, but not a realist, who would eschew attention to such social factors as naive and as mere superstructure."[43]

Second, neorealism, as a theory, is too general even to generate falsifiable hypotheses. The scope of analysis is so broad and the temporal frame so generous that it is difficult to understand, for instance, what can constitute a balancing approach in international politics. For any specific change in the system that potentially falsifies the theory, a neorealist can always suggest that it is too early to say. In that regard, neorealism as a theory can never be falsified. Finally, although neorealism only intends to explain a "small number of big and important things,"[44] Wendt questions whether it is able to do so. Even if we were to take neorealism's explanation at face value, state behaviour could still not be explained by the anarchical structure of the system. States balance in the international system, not because the structure is anarchical, but because they want to survive: it is security rather than anarchy that explains their self-help behaviour. The problem is that self-help is not a constant feature of state behaviour: "Sometimes states are egoists and other times they are not, and this variation can change the 'logic' of anarchy."[45] Therefore, the process resulting from state interaction might lead to an anarchical system, but not the other way around.[46] Wendt's ideas distance him further away from neorealism when he explains how those interactions occur. Here we delve into the realm of ideas, identities and interests.

According to Wendt, ideas lead to the constitution of identities – "relatively stable, role-specific understandings and expectations about self"[47] – through interactionist processes. The self is a reflection of an actor's socialisation with other actors: "If repeated long enough, these 'reciprocal typifications' will generate stable concepts of self and other regarding the issue at stake in the interaction."[48] In his view, "identities are the basis of interests. Actors do not have a 'portfolio' of interests that they can carry around independent of social context; instead, they define their interests in the process of defining situations."[49]

Although stable, these patterns can change. That is why in IR we always have the possibility of friends becoming enemies and vice versa. According to Wendt's theory, this is done in three steps. First, there must be an end to the consensus around the terms of the relationship. This might happen for myriad different reasons, but the most frequent is when an actor behaves differently from what it usually does. That unexpected behaviour leads to the end of the consensus and, consequently, to the de-naturalisation of both identities. That de-naturalisation will eventually open the possibility for new identity constructions, which usually happens (step three) through altercasting practices, that is, when one side starts to interact with the other as if that other had already changed its identity. Enemies can thus become friends and friends can become enemies.

In short, relationships between actors in the international system evolve over time as results of historical processes of interaction. These interactions are conditioned by specific intersubjective processes, but the conditions of possibility are greater than the material constraints to which particularly neorealist authors would point. Wendt's example of the two aliens (alter and ego) that meet for the first time having to decipher each other's communication signs from analogy with previous experiences and having from their interaction to set the path for amicable or inimical relations, shows the constructed dimension of social relations. Before that moment of interaction, "'the state of nature' is characterised by the existence of two elements: materiality, which for states means 'an organizational apparatus of govern-ance' and a desire for survival."[50]

The possibility of change and the constructed character of the international system does not translate into a necessarily 'malleable' system, due to the reification of the interactions within that system and to the stability of identities and interests that its members seek to achieve. They have a desire for certainty, stability and "to avoid the expected costs of breaking com-mitments made to others – notably domestic constituencies and foreign allies in the case of states – as part of past practices."[51] Moreover, it does not entail that international relations should be understood as solely being about ideas. The predominant tendencies of a given system will pressurise states to internalise specific identities and interests, as rivals, enemies or friends.[52] Ultimately, it is up to each individual state to accept that internalisation process.

For Wendt, these identities, interests and roles interplay in three different cultures of anarchy, which he labels as Hobbesian, Lockean and Kantian, in a clear reference to Martin Wight's typology.[53] In a Hobbesian culture, states are mostly concerned with self-help and survival. This is based on a rather 'crude reading' of authors such as Hobbes, Carr and Morgenthau[54] that places states in a context of constant violence, the balance of power and relations of enmity.[55] Wendt's Lockean anarchy is very much in line with Hedley Bull's anarchical society.[56] In such a context, rivalry rather than enmity is the base of inter-state relations. Conflicts and violence are constrained by the mutual rec-ognition of sovereignty. Finally, in the Kantian culture states move beyond a self-help system, embracing a collective security culture. As summarised by Wendt:

> The "sauve qui peut" egoism of a Hobbesian anarchy has a different logic from the more self-restrained egoism of a Lockean anarchy, which differs still from the Kantian anarchy based on collective security interests, which is no longer "self-help" in any interesting sense.[57]

As ideal types, these cultures correspond to different stages of state behaviour that change according to the evolution of ideas, experiences and socialisation processes. In that regard, these three cultures are useful conceptual tools to understand how states oscillate between relations of enmity, the fulfilment of international norms and the membership of collective defensive arrangements. These oscillations happen at three different levels: chronologically, in the evolution of relations between two or more states; geographically, as states can simul-taneously engage in enmity, rivalry and amity relations depending on the state(s) with which they are interacting; and sectorially, as states will behave differently depending on the issue at stake. They may, for example, adopt a normative position in environmental issues and a survival discourse when it comes to migration issues.

Alexander Wendt's work helped to consolidate the role of identities in the discipline, offering a richer account of how they were formed and reproduced; certainly richer that what was offered by neorealism. Ted Hopf summarised these differences in very clear terms: "Whereas constructivism treats identity as an empirical question to be theorised within a his-torical context, neorealism assumes that all units in global politics have only one meaningful identity, that of self-interested states."[58]

Looking outside the ivory tower, identity conflicts were a central feature of IR in the 1990s, when Wendt developed his theory: from the Balkans to Southern Africa, ethnic and religious motives were responsible for multiple humanitarian disasters. While not focusing directly on these, Wendt offered a conceptual toolbox that allowed IR better to understand the role identities play in the constitution of interests. However, it was, as highlighted by a significant number of critics, a significantly flawed one.

Wendt's critics

As in all theoretical endeavours that attempt to establish a *via media*, the tendency is always to be attacked by both ends of the bridge one is trying to build. It is not different with Wendt's theory. By accepting the possibility of a rationalist epistemology and a social ontology through his scientific realism, Wendt opened the gates for major criticism from both those outside constructivism,[59] but also, from those labelling themselves as constructivists.

As mentioned earlier, constructivism is far from being a consensual field. It could, broadly speaking, be divided between those that accept the premises of Wendt's theory (conventional constructivism) and those that see it as inherently flawed and inconsistent (critical constructivism according to Risse[60] and Ted Hopf[51] or consistent constructivism if we followed Karin Fierke's definition[62]). Wendt himself, in the acknowledgment section of his book, argues that the "thicker constructivisms" of the "Minnesota School" (Michael Barnett, Mark Laffey, Rhona Leibel and Jutta Weldes) "should not be identified with the thin one on offer below," that is, in his *Social Theory of International Politics*.[63]

For Emanuel Adler, that division is slightly more complex and encompassing. For him there are four different constructivist approaches: modernist, modernist linguistic, critical and radical constructivism. Modern constructivists include authors such as Michael Barnett, Martha Finnemore, Peter Katzenstein, John Ruggie, Alex Wendt and Adler himself. Despite minor differences, they all try to "uncover the causal social mechanisms and constitutive social relations that make IR more intelligible."[64] Modernist linguists – such as Friedrich Kratochwil, Nicholas Onuf, Karen Fierke and Jutta Weldes – emphasise the role of discourse in the construction of social reality, with a particular emphasis on rules and norms. Radical constructivists combine "a radical turn to language" with "a dissident emancipatory or deconstructivist attitude toward knowledge in general."[65] Authors such as Richard Ashley, James Der Derian and David Campbell fit this category. Finally, critical constructivists bring together objective hermeneutics and a "dissident interest in the emancipatory effects of knowledge."[66] Andrew Linklater and Robert Cox are among the authors that fit this category, according to Emanuel Adler. Although encompassing and thought provoking, this typology is arguably too broad, overlapping constructivism with other theoretical contributions, such as poststructuralism and critical theory. Rather than becoming a *via media*, constructivism becomes an all-inclusive intellectual project difficult to define. In that regard, we prefer the simpler definition between conventional and critical constructivism.

In Hopf's view, conventional and critical constructivism share a number of positions: "mutual constitution of actors and structures, anarchy as a social construct, power as both material and discursive, and state identities and interests as variables."[67] Already in this definition one can see the seeds for intra-constructivist disagreement, as many constructivist authors would receive with scepticism the idea that identities and interests could be seen as 'variables.' Conventional constructivism is delimited by the full acceptance of a rationalist ontology (conventional constructivists are already open to a positivist epistemology), whereas critical constructivism is delimited by a more radical poststructuralist agenda in which understanding is replaced by interpretation and intersubjectivity by subjectivity. In that regard, conventional constructivism is much closer to rationalism[68] than to poststructuralism. It is thus not surprising that critical authors such as Maja Zehfuss find that attempts such as Wendt's "to address the social construction of the world without abandoning the idea of scientific explanation as it is commonly constructed in International Relations"[69] run the risk of missing the contingent aspects of central concepts such as identity by excessively adhering to the rigid compartmentalisation demanded by conduct of 'rigorous' scientific research. Wendt's treatment of identity politics becomes even more problematic, in Zehfuss's eyes, when taking into account Wendt's state-centrism. According to her:

> Wendt's anthropomorphic concept of the state cannot cope with identities which are unstable in themselves. Identity change is merely about shifting from one relatively stable identity to another. States are unitary actors with minds, desires and intentions. Wendt's recognition that domestic politics influence state behaviour and state identity fails to address the complexity of the issue at hand.[70]

In addition to the complex treatment of identity and the theory's unhelpful state-centrism, Wendt is also accused by critical constructivists and poststructuralists alike of not giving language a more central role in his theory. For Guzzini and Leander, Wendt's theory is a "curious type of constructivism where language is very much out of the picture."[71] In these authors' views, conventional constructivism disregards the role of language as central to the understanding of law and norms. If we bring together identity and discourse, it is clear that by excluding the latter Wendt jeopardises the understanding of the former. In the absence of discourse, we can only understand the constitution of a given identity through the actor's behaviour. Hence, "if an identity matters only in its realization in certain types of behaviour, then it is difficult to see what should justify calling it 'identity' rather than 'behaviour.'"[72] For Onuf, this is a strategic decision as Wendt and other conventional constructivists are simply playing the game in US academia where positivism dominates mainstream research. As a result, "any concern with language was left to the dissidents."[73] Dissidents who, according to Karin Fierke, offer a more consistent constructivism, as they bring together social ontology and epistemology, "which has the analysis of language and processes of interaction between multiple actors at its core."[74]

Following this perspective, discourse is a constitutive feature of our world, not just an expression of it. According to Jennifer Milliken,[75] there are three main theoretical claims linked to discourse analysis. The first claim tells us that discourses are systems of signification, that they are "structures of signification which construct social realities."[76] The second claim tells us that discourses produce, reproduce and define things, meanings and knowledgeable practices. Finally, discourse analysis entails the study of "dominating or hegemonic discourses and their structuring of meaning as connected to implementing practices and ways of making these intelligible and legitimate."[77] Language describes our world embedded in other discourses and dependent on an ever, even if slowly, changing context.

By embracing social epistemology and consequently the importance of language in the constitution of international reality, critical constructivists were able to identify important potential flaws in Alexander Wendt's theory. The insignificant role that discourse plays in his theory limits our understanding of identity and identity construction, which is a fundamental concept for the theory to work. By making it a state-prerogative and understanding the latter as the basic unit of analysis in IR, it excludes other actors from the intersubjective constructions that operate at the international level.

Alexander Wendt has replied to some of those criticisms. In 'On the Via Media: A Response to the Critics,' Wendt engages with multiple criticisms, including the accusation that his work is ontologically "confusing, inconsistent, and contradictory,"[78] his treatment of reasons as causes, his privileging of explanation over understanding and his state-centrism.

The first accusation takes him to the separation between ideas and material conditions: they are "separate but inevitable linked phenomena."[79] As Wendt further adds, "if we focus on how material forces and ideas are articulated in concrete situations then we can have the best of both worlds. Reality will be judge."[80] As for the accusation that he treats reasons as causes, Wendt argues in defence that there is little that he can add from what he had already made clear in his *Social Theory of International Politics*. He concludes after reasserting his case that "the proper criticism, if it be that, of the causal approach is not that reasons are not causes, but that they are not only causes, and that research focusing on their constitutive aspect is therefore important in its own right."[81] In that regard, they are – just as explanation and understanding – complementary, both "parts of a complete science."[82]

Regarding the accusation of state-centrism Wendt is quite adamant in his defence of his position. The state has to be reified (and he accepts that this is the case) as the question he tries to answer in his book is about the understanding of the social construction of the state *system* and not of the state. In his concluding words, Wendt returns to the issue of the division between rationalism and constructivism, arguing once more that IR should accommodate both as "for students of international politics, philosophy should be the servant, not the master."[83]

As mentioned earlier, both strands of constructivism share, despite their differences, many similarities. Interestingly they are both accused of not being sufficiently normative.[84] With the exception of a few authors, such as Andrew Linklater and Cynthia Enloe, whose connections with constructivism are (contrary to Emanuel Adler's view), tenuous at best, constructivists are often accused of not engaging in normative debates or in actively promoting social and political change. Blending normative theory with explanatory theory is, in Emanuel Adler's view, one of the main problems constructivism needs to face.[85] There is indeed very little indication from constructivist work of how to answer the question "how should we act?"[86] and it is clear most constructivists do not have an explicit normative approach in their research.[87] Interestingly, the same accusation is, despite their multiple differences, often put forward against poststructuralism.

Poststructuralism: so close and yet so far

Poststructuralism challenges the IR orthodox canon in more than one way. Postructuralism is not a theory, not even a particularly homogenous school of thought. Following Lene Hansen, it could be said that poststructuralism:

> [p]ursues a particular set of research questions, centered on the *constitutive significance of representations of identity for formulating and debating foreign policies*, and it argues that *adopting a non-causal epistemology does not imply an abandonment of theoretically rigorous frameworks, empirical analyses of "real world relevance," or systematic assessments of data and methodology*.[88]

Their starting point is not in the Anglo-Saxon tradition but in the social and cultural theory of Michel Foucault, Jacques Derrida, Jacques Lacan or Julia Kristeva. As put by Jim George, these are influences that were, until not long ago, rather 'foreign' to IR as a discipline. Authors such as James Der Derian, Michael Shapiro or R.B.J. Walker have, since the late 1980s, embarked on a 'translation' process of those works to the realm of international politics, bringing with them innovative (for IR) approaches such as discourse analysis, intertextuality and genealogy.[89]

If on one side of the rationalist-reflectivist spectrum, constructivism borders the mainstream rationalist approaches in IR, on the other side it 'borders' poststructuralism. As is often the case when two approaches have so much in common, differences seem to be more important than similarities. Constructivists such as Nicholas Onuf are resolute in pointing out constructivism's specificities in the face of poststructuralism. In David Campbell's view, although the distinction between poststructuralism and (particularly) critical constructivism "is difficult to make and contentious to suggest"[90] an ethical argument could be made in which poststructuralism "contains within it a necessarily affirmative moment through which existing identity formations are denaturalized and alternative articulations of identity and political are made possible," whereas critical constructivism "can appear hesitant to pursue this radical logic to its ultimate conclusions, preferring instead to secure some dimensions of identity as a way of anchoring analysis."[91]

Poststructuralist authors point out that despite the supposedly post-foundational dimension of (critical) constructivism, their analyses remain very much grounded in some form of 'reality' – international for Wendt, everyday for Kratochwil and raw material for Nicholas Onuf.[92] As argued by Maja Zehfuss that is particularly problematic from a poststructuralist perspective as "reality cannot be known other than through representations."[93] As mentioned earlier, poststructuralists and constructivists necessarily have a distinct understanding of the role of language: "for constructivists performativity depends on the words spoken by the agents; for poststructuralists language itself is the performance."[94] For the latter, meaning is constantly being (re)constructed through discursive practices.[95] There is less opportunity for words to sediment: "language is . . . an inherently unstable system of signs."[96]

Hence, if there is no external dimension to discourse beyond other discourses, then any material dimension is only relevant once it has been framed discursively, including in foreign policy:[97]

> [m]aterial facts do not exist, but rather they are produced by and inserted into foreign policy discourses. For facts to become politically salient and influence the production and reproduction of foreign policy discourse there must be human and discursive agency; individuals, media and institutions who collect, document and distribute them.[98]

Using Julia Kristeva's intertextuality in which "the inimitability of every individual text is always located within a shared textual space and all texts make references, explicitly or implicitly, to previous ones,"[99] together with the ideas of other leading poststructuralists – such as Michel Foucault and Jacques Derrida – Lene Hansen discusses in her *Security as Practice* how discourse, identity and foreign policy are intimately connected and crucial for the understanding of IR. According to the Danish author, "identity is a relational concept, given through reference to something it is not"[100]; it is always constructed through a process of differentiation – a self in opposition to one or multiple others. This construction is always discursively articulated, with identity and differentiation being part of the same process. In that regard, "identity is not something that states, or other collectivities, have independently of the discursive practices mobilized in presenting and implementing foreign policy,"[101] they are "ontologically inseparable"[102] and they always imply a process of differentiation, even if that is not done against a radical other. When looking at the EU, Ole Wæver argues that the EU and the European ideal have been constructed against its own terribly devastating past, rather than against a different 'other.'[103] This poststructuralist view has two consequences in terms of foreign policy: first, that foreign policy is always a discursively constructed policy of exclusion and, second, that such construction is never completed; it is always in need of constant reproduction.[104] From this results the more general conclusion that "states are never finished as entities"; they are constantly "in a process of becoming."[105]

The constant engagement in 'othering' foreign policy activities, the definition of threats, enemies and dangers is more than a result of what the responsibility of the state is; it defines its very "condition of possibility."[106] Thus the incentive is for states to focus on boundary-creating foreign policies rather than bridge building.[107] This leads Campbell to distinguish between two types of foreign policy. The first type creates the space of differentiation in which the second type, foreign policy (the official one) operates. The latter "serves to *reproduce* the constitution of identity made possible by 'foreign policy' and to *contain* challenges to the identity that results."[108] Foreign policy as the official state policy is already the result and the promoter of (further) exclusionary practices. In short, states' (and state system) existence depends on the perpetual continuation of relations of differentiation (foreign policy).

Reconfiguring the discipline: links with critical theory

Poststructuralism brought to IR alternative approaches and theories to the study of world politics, with a particular focus, as mentioned earlier, on the connection between identity and foreign policy. But poststructuralism has also shed considerable light on the study of IR in itself, as a discipline cut across by hidden (and less so) power relations and long-lasting exclusionary practices. As with any other discipline, IR is defined by key authors, debates, theories and schools of thought. Most importantly, it is defined by a small number of disciplinary narratives that attribute more importance to some texts over others, that establish specific authors as 'founding fathers' or simplify often complex and nuanced perspectives in order to fit specific disciplinary silos. What poststructuralism has done and does is to reveal the contingent nature of all of those hallmarks of an academic discipline; to put in simple words, "how great texts are readings, one narrative among many other possibilities."[109] As Jim George writes in the Preface to his *Discourses of Global Politics*, as a discipline, IR "reduces a complex and turbulent world to a patterned representation of post-Renaissance European historical experience, articulated in orthodox Anglo-American philosophical terms."[110] As such, IR should be seen as a "discursive process, a process by which identities are formed, meaning is given, and status and privilege are accorded – a process of knowing *as* power."[111] In his now classic *Inside/Outside: International Relations as Political Theory*, R.B.J. Walker discusses how the fundamental basis of IR as a discipline has within it a politicised notion of time. Unlike political theory, it invokes an "eternally absent community between modern sovereign states."[112] Within it, "the principle of state sovereignty expresses a historically specific articulation of the relationship between universality and particularity in space and time."[113]

Despite sharing a strong commitment to introduce alternative voices to the discipline, different methodologies and new topics, poststructuralism and critical theory in IR have kept what Jim George calls "a kind of intellectual apartheid."[114] They have both "been palpably concerned with systematic injustices, evils and human wrongs that cause grave and avoidable suffering,"[115] but poststructuralism's default scepticism towards the possibilities of human emancipation and the merits of cosmopolitanism makes it difficult to relate to some critical theory approaches. More deeply, whereas critical theorists share with rationalists the acceptance of fixed understanding of terms, for poststructuralism (particularly the key) terms in international politics are political; always involving "a struggle for power, and a process for constructing social life."[116] For Jenny Edkins, poststructuralism offers an important shift in the axis of analysis, from politics to the political, reproducing a long-standing discussion in political theory that goes back to authors such as Carl Schmitt, and reintroduced by poststructuralist authors such as Ernesto Laclau and Chantal Mouffe.[117]

So what does poststructuralism offer beyond the dismantling of acquired knowledges? First and foremost, it contributes through different authors and methodologies to a culture of reflexivity within IR which allows for a more open and plural understanding of the discipline. Second, it gives us important tools to question some of the key concepts and assumptions in the discipline, such as the idea of anarchy, sovereignty or security. As R.B.J. Walker argues regarding the latter:

> [t]o speak of security is to engage in a discourse of repetitions, to affirm over and over again the dangers that legitimize the sovereign authority that is constituted precisely as a solution to dangers. But it is important to remember that this discourse of dangerous affirmations of a self-constituting danger, they simultaneously exclude the possibility of admitting the presence of other subjectivities, most obviously of those of class, race, gender, and humanity.[118]

Finally, by dismantling those above-mentioned acquired knowledges that translate into power relations, poststructuralism enables us to uncover the practices of exclusion that contribute to the reinforcement of specific regimes of truth. This then opens the space for other alternative and transformative approaches. This arguably is poststructuralism's most evident ethical contribution to IR.

Poststructuralism does not go without its critics, and they are many. One of the major criticisms has to do with the fact that poststructuralist research lacks 'grounding.' As argued by Fred Halliday in a critique of R.B.J. Walker's work, it lacks "anchorage in either social reality or ethical and historical necessity."[119] Other authors, such as Jan Selby, criticise the silo mentality of poststructuralism in IR, particularly regarding the use of Michel Foucault's work. His critique is both to poststructuralism and to IR as a discipline: "that Foucault has been employed so narrowly within IR is perhaps testimony to the theoretical greenness of a discipline which only during the 1980s discovered the joys of social theory."[120] In his view there are three main problems with the use of Foucault in IR. First, there is a problem of *translation* of Foucault, as he was "primarily a historian/theorist of the domestic realm of liberal capitalist societies."[121] Applying his work to IR is not always possible or adequate.[122] Second, partially as a consequence of the previous point, there is a problem of *representation*. Many works use Foucault more as a label than as an author, as a form of fitting in within the *Foucauldians*. Finally, there is a problem of *over-consistency* as Foucault is always put together with other poststructuralist authors, even when – as is the case with Derrida – there were significant tensions with the works of these other authors. In Selby's view, the works of some of the main poststructuralist authors, such as R.B.J. Walker, Richard Ashley or Jim George, owe much more to Derrida than they do to Foucault.[123]

The problems identified by Selby could potentially be applied to other social theorists and philosophers whose work has been applied to IR by specific 'schools of thought.' The paradox in this case is that for all the contestation of the hidden powers of the discipline, poststructuralism in IR follows the same patterns and (disciplinary) practices of other schools of thought.

Notes

1 Richard K. Ashley, 'The Poverty of Neorealism,' *International Organization*, Vol. 38, No. 2, 1984, pp. 225–286.
2 Robert W. Cox, 'Social Forces, States and World Orders: Beyond International Relations Theory,' *Millennium: Journal of International Studies*, Vol. 10, No. 2, 1981, pp. 126–155.

3   Peter Berger and Thomas Luckmann, *The Social Construction of Reality* (New York: Anchor Books, 1966).
4   John Searle, *The Construction of Social Reality* (New York: Free Press, 1995).
5   See *Central Problems in Social Theory* (Berkeley, CA: University of California Press, 1979); *The Constitution of Society* (Berkeley, CA: University of California Press, 1984); *The Nation-State and Violence* (Berkeley, CA: University of California Press, 1985).
6   J.L. Austin, *How to Do Things with Words* (Oxford: Oxford University Press, 1962).
7   Nicholas Onuf, *World of Our Making* (Columbia, SC: University of South Carolina Press, 1989).
8   Peter Katzenstein ed., *The Culture of National Security* (New York: Columbia University Press, 1996).
9   Alexander Wendt, 'Anarchy Is What States Make of It: The Social Construction of Power Politics,' *International Organization*, Vol. 46, No. 2, 1992, pp. 391–425.
10 Friedrich Kratochwil, *Rules, Norms, and Decisions* (Cambridge: Cambridge University Press, 1989).
11 Martha Finnemore, *National Interests in International Society* (Ithaca, NY: Cornell University Press, 1996).
12 Stefano Guzzini, 'A Reconstruction of Constructivism in International Relations,' *European Journal of International Relations*, Vol. 6, No. 2, 2000, pp. 147–182.
13 Karin Fierke, *Changing Games, Changing Strategies. Critical Investigations in Security* (Manchester: Manchester University Press, 1998).
14 Jutta Weldes, *Constructing National Interests: The United States and the Cuban Missile Crisis* (Minneapolis, MN: University of Minnesota Press, 1999).
15 For Peter Katzenstein, Robert Keohane and Stephen Krasner, writing for the 50th anniversary issue of *International Organization*, the future of the discipline would be determined by the debate between rationalists and constructivists.
16 Alexander Wendt, *Social Theory of International Politics* (Cambridge: Cambridge University Press, 1999), p. 4.
17 Nicholas Onuf, 'Worlds of Our Making: The Strange Career of Constructivism in International Relations,' in D.J. Puchala (ed.), *Visions of International: Assessing an Academic Field* (Columbia, SC: University of South Carolina Press), p. 128.
18 *Ibid.*, p. 139.
19 *Ibid.*, p. 128.
20 Emanuel Adler, 'Constructivism and International Relations,' in Walter Carlsnaes, Thomas Risse and Beth A Simmons (eds), *Handbook of International Relations* (London: Sage, 2002), p. 100.
21 *Ibid.*, p. 136.
22 For example, E.H. Carr wrote in his 1946 edition of *The Twenty Years' Crisis* that what he calls a world community is a social construction: "It has already been shown that there is in fact a wide-spread assumption of the existence of a world-wide community of which states are the units and that the conception of the moral obligations of states is closely bound up with this assumption. There is a world community for the reason (and no other) that people talk, and within certain limits behave, as if there were a world community," p. 162.
23 Karin Fierke, 'Critical Methodology and Constructivism,' in Karin Fierke and Knud Erik Jorgensen (eds), *Constructing International Relations: The Next Generation* (London: M.E. Shape, 2001), p. 117.
24 Audie Klotz and Cecelia Lynch, *Strategies for Research in Constructivist International Relations* (London: M.E. Sharpe, 2007), p. 24.
25 Anthony Giddens, *Sociology* (Cambridge: Polity, 2001).
26 Vivienne Jabri, *Discourses on Violence : Conflict Analysis Reconsidered.* (Manchester: Manchester University Press, 1996), p. 70.
27 Klotz and Lynch, *Strategies for Research in Constructivist International Relations*, p. 59.
28 Ted Hopf, 'The Promise of Constructivism in International Relations Theory,' *International Security*, Vol. 23, No. 1, 1998, p. 173.
29 *Ibid.*, p. 178.
30 *Ibid.*
31 *Ibid.*, p. 181.
32 Wendt, 'Anarchy Is What States Make of It,' p. 394.
33 Wendt, *Social Theory of International Politics*, p. 372.

34 *Ibid.*, p. 395.
35 *Ibid.*, p. 399.
36 Wendt, *Social Theory of International Politics*, p. 11.
37 Stefano Guzzini and Anna Leander (eds), 'Wendt's Constructivism: A Relentless Quest for Synthesis,' in *Constructivism and International Relations: Alexander Wendt and His Critics* (Oxford: Routledge, 2006), p. 77.
38 Wendt, *Social Theory of International Politics*, p. 202.
39 *Ibid.*, p. 9.
40 Wendt, 'Anarchy Is What States Make of It,' p. 424.
41 Alexander Wendt, 'Constructing International Politics,' *International Security*, Vol. 20, No. 1, 1995, p. 72.
42 Wendt, *Social Theory of International Politics*, pp. 17–18.
43 Wendt, *'Constructing International Politics,'* p. 80.
44 Kenneth Waltz, 'Reflections Theory of International Politics: A Response to My Critics,' in Robert O. Keohane (ed.), *Neorealism and Its Critics* (New York: Columbia University Press, 1986), p. 329.
45 Wendt, *Social Theory of International Politics*, p. 18.
46 *Ibid.*, p. 21.
47 Wendt, 'Anarchy Is What States Make of It,' p. 397.
48 *Ibid.*, p. 406.
49 *Ibid.*, p. 398.
50 *Ibid.*, p. 402.
51 *Ibid.*, p. 411.
52 Wendt, *Social Theory of International Politics*, p. 259.
53 Wendt, *Social Theory of International Politics*, p. 247.
54 Alan Chong, 'The State Has a Mind: Alexander Wendt's Social Theory of International Politics,' in Henrik Bliddal, Casper Sylvest and Peter Wilson (eds), *Classics of International Relations. Essays in Criticism and Appreciation* (Oxford: Routledge, 2013), p. 219.
55 Wendt, *Social Theory of International Politics*, p. 266.
56 *Ibid.*, p. 283.
57 *Ibid.*, p. 18.
58 Ted Hopf 'The Promise of Constructivism in International Relations Theory,' *International Security*, Vol. 23, No. 1, 1998, p. 175.
59 Chong, 'The State Has a Mind: Alexander Wendt's Social Theory of International Politics,' p. 221.
60 Thomas Risse, 'Social Constructivism and European Integration,' in Antje Weiner and Thomas Diez (eds), *European Integration Theory* (Oxford: Oxford University Press, 2004), p. 160.
61 Hopf, 'The Promise of Constructivism in International Relations Theory,' p. 185.
62 Karin Fierke, 'Constructivism,' in Tim Dunne, Milja Kurki and Steve Smith (eds), *International Relations Theories. Discipline and Diversity* (Oxford: Oxford University Press, 2007).
63 Wendt, *Social Theory of International Politics*, p. xiv.
64 Emanuel Adler, 'Constructivism and International Relations' in Walter Carlsnaes, Thomas Risse and Beth A Simmons (eds), *Handbook of International Relations* (London: Sage, 2002), p. 98.
65 *Ibid.*
66 *Ibid.*
67 Hopf, 'The Promise of Constructivism in International Relations Theory,' p. 185.
68 Wendt, *Social Theory of International Politics*, p. 367.
69 Maja Zehfuss, 'Constructivism and Identity: A Dangerous Liaison,' in Stefano Guzzini and Anna Leander (eds), *Constructivism and International Relations: Alexander Wendt and His Critics* (Oxford: Routledge, 2006), p. 116.
70 Maja Zehfuss, 'Constructivism and Identity: A Dangerous Liaison,' *European Journal of International Relations*, Vol. 7, No. 3, 2001, p. 335.
71 Stefano Guzzini and Anna Leander, 'Wendt's Constructivism: A Relentless Quest for Synthesis,' p. 86.
72 Maja Zehfuss, 'Constructivism and Identity: A Dangerous Liaison,' p. 327.
73 Onuf, 'Worlds of Our Making: The Strange Career of Constructivism in International Relations,' p. 129.
74 Fierke, 'Constructivism,' p. 182.
75 Jennifer Milliken, 'Discourse Study: Bringing Rigor to Critical Theory,' in Karin Fierke and Knud Erik Jorgensen (eds), *Constructing International Relations: The Next Generation* (London: M.E. Shape, 2001), p. 138.

76 *Ibid.*
77 *Ibid.*, p. 139.
78 Alexander Wendt, 'On the Via Media: A Response to the Critics,' *Review of International Studies*, Vol. 26, No. 1, 2000, p. 166.
79 *Ibid.*, p. 167.
80 *Ibid.*, p. 169.
81 *Ibid.*, p. 171.
82 *Ibid.*
83 *Ibid*, p. 180.
84 Christian Reus-Smit, 'Constructivism and the Structure of Ethical Reasoning,' in Richard M. Price (ed.), *Moral Limit and Possibility in World Politics* (Cambridge: Cambridge University Press, 2008), p. 72.
85 Adler, Emanuel, 'Constructivism and International Relations,' p. 110.
86 *Ibid.*, p. 53.
87 *Ibid.*, p. 72.
88 Lene Hansen, *Security as Practice. Discourse Analysis and the Bosnian War* (Oxford: Routledge, 2006), p. 5. Italics in original.
89 Jim George, *Discourses of Global Politics: A Critical (Re)Introduction to International Relations* (Boulder, CO: Lynne Rienner Publishing, 1994), p. 191.
90 David Campbell, *Writing Security. United States Foreign Policy and the Politics of Identity* (Manchester: Manchester University Press, 1998 [1993]), p. 223.
91 Campbell, p. 223.
92 Vincent Pouliot, 'The Essence of Constructivism,' *Journal of International Relations and Development*, Vol. 7, 2004, p. 321.
93 Quoted in Pouliot, 'The Essence of Constructivism,' p. 322.
94 Pouliot, *op. cit.*, p. 325.
95 George, *Discourses of Global Politics*, p. 156.
96 Hansen, *Security as Practice. Discourse Analysis and the Bosnian War*, p. 17.
97 *Ibid.*, p. 34.
98 *Ibid.*, p. 32.
99 *Ibid.*, p. 55.
100 *Ibid.*, p. 6.
101 *Ibid.*, p. 1.
102 *Ibid.*, p. 27.
103 Ole Wæver, 'The EU as a Security Actor: Reflections from a Pessimistic Constructivist on Post-Sovereign Orders,' in Kelstrup, Morten and Williams, Michael (eds), *International Relations Theory and the Politics of European Integration: Power, Security and Community* (Oxford: Routledge, 2000), pp. 250–294.
104 Campbell, *Writing Security*, p. 12.
105 *Ibid.*
106 Campbell, *Writing Security*, p. 13.
107 *Ibid.*, p. 51.
108 *Ibid.*, p. 69.
109 George, *Discourses of Global Politics*, p. 192.
110 *Ibid.*, p. ix.
111 *Ibid.*, p. 216.
112 R.B.J. Walker, *Inside/Outside: International Relations as Political Theory* (Cambridge: Cambridge University Press, 1993), p. ix.
113 *Ibid.*, p. 176.
114 *Ibid.*, p. 164.
115 *Ibid.*, p. 97.
116 Anthony Burke, 'Security as Ethics,' in Peter J. Burgess (ed.), *The Routledge Handbook of New Security Studies* (Oxford: Routledge, 2015), p. 96.
117 Ernesto Laclau and Chantal Mouffe, *Hegemony and Socialist Strategy: Towards a Radical Democratic Politics* (London: Verso, 1985).
118 R.B.J. Walker, 'The Subject of Security,' in Keith Krause and Michael Williams (eds), *Critical Security Studies* (London: UCL Press, 1997), p. 73.

119 Fred Halliday, 'Book Review: R.B.J. Walker, Inside/Outside: International Relations as Political Theory,' *Millennium: Journal of International Studies*, Vol. 22, 1993, pp. 362–365, p. 364.
120 Jan Selby 'Engaging Foucault: Discourse, Liberal Governance and the Limits of Foucauldian IR,' *International Relations*, Vol. 21, No. 3, p. 325.
121 Selby, 'Engaging Foucault,' p. 338.
122 *Ibid.*, p. 334.
123 *Ibid.*, p. 328.

14 Beyond the *status quo*

IR has, since its inception, been a discipline of exclusions. Wealth and (a certain understanding of) power consistently defined who could speak and for whom they could speak. This means that the daily experiences of millions of people across the world were consistently subsumed under myriad 'more relevant' considerations that became the guiding points in a discipline made by and for privileged white men with a concern over sovereignty, national security and economic growth. With some exceptions, issues of race, class and gender became progressively part of the agenda, and as we moved into the 1990s, these voices became organised in recognisable alternative approaches to the mainstream. Having just discussed the merits and flaws of constructivism and poststructuralism (developed as part of those alternatives), what now follows is an overview of three approaches and schools of thought that give voice to the above-mentioned subaltern subjects of IR: critical theory, feminism and postcolonialism.

Critical views

Critical theory in IR came to life with the works of authors such as Robert Cox,[1] Richard K. Ashley and Andrew Linklater.[2] Of all the three, Robert Cox is the most often and most directly associated with critical theory, despite his own doubts about the label. Ashley's work is at the intersection of critical theory and poststructuralism, and Andrew Linklater is also rather taken up with the English School.

Critical theory in IR is strongly influenced by the works of Karl Marx,[3] Antonio Gramsci,[4] as well as – for obvious reasons –the so-called Frankfurt School (although, interestingly, that does not seem to apply to Robert Cox[5]). From Marx, critical theory took a shared starting point that production – and with it class relations – is a central feature in the analysis of the social, whether domestically or at the international level. The unfairness of the prevailing relations of production is, in that sense, at the basis of critical theory's call for the transformation of the international system. The work of the Italian thinker, Antonio Gramsci, has also been co-opted under the 'critical' label. Cox's work is seen as a direct application of Gramsci's thought to IR, whose concepts such as 'hegemony' and 'historic bloc,' are very much central to the work of this Canadian scholar.

Finally, the Frankfurt School, whose name is given to the authors from the Institute of Social Research in Frankfurt, advocated some sort of a post-Marxist view of politics and society. The Frankfurt School distanced itself from Marxism both in terms of the centrality of the proletariat as the revolutionary guiding light and in terms of the positive understanding of technology as a force for social and economic development.[6] It was its founder and director – the German thinker Max Horkheimer[7] – who originally developed the term 'critical theory' into social theory, by contrasting it with 'traditional' theory. According to him, traditional theory was concerned with the separation between object and subject, understanding science as value-free with a mere explanatory value. On the other hand, critical theory understood theory as part of social and political life, with the possibility of promoting the emancipation of the individual through knowledge.

For Mark Hoffman,[8] Horkheimer's approach to critical theory had three main driving forces behind it. First, the belief that the society of his time – the 1930s – needed radical transformation and not just reform. Second, that theory had always had a particular social context from which it could not and should not be separated. Finally, Horkheimer rejected the idea that social sciences could have independent objective theories. All theorists associated with the school were "seeking to illuminate the question of emancipation in world politics."[9]

However, as rightly put by Richard Wyn Jones, not only the Frankfurt School label encompasses a wide range of different ideas and authors, often at loggerheads with each other. Therefore, "the connection between critical international theory and the Frankfurt School, is far from consistent," and is "at times even tenuous."[10] Rather than focusing on closely following specific theoretical allegiances, Wyn Jones suggests – in a different text – that we should look at three major strands of theory within the school: the development of theory as 'critical' theory, which he defines as "a broad framework within which the insights of the traditional social science disciplines can be integrated with and through Marxian theory to produce an analysis of society that aims, eventually, to facilitate and support a process of emancipatory social transformation"[11]; the study of the failure of the emancipatory change promised by the Enlightenment project; and the Habermasian work on communicative action, which strongly influenced the works of Andrew Linklater and Mark Hoffman.

Within IR, critical theorists are particularly sceptical of some of the key assumptions on which mainstream theories are based, starting with its state-centric tendencies. They understand the state as an historically situated social construction whose main goal is to maintain and reproduce a specific order by defining clear boundaries between who is inside and who is outside. In that regard, the state functions as a mechanism of inclusion and exclusion. Unlike constructivism (and even poststructuralism), critical theory is explicitly normative, in the sense of advocating alternative world-views. The urge for transformation and promotion of some sort of social emancipation guides the works of many of the authors classified as 'critical.' In that regard, critical theory asks questions about the normative, sociological and praxeological conditions of emancipation, that is, its meaning, conditions and means.[12]

Updating critical theory

Decades after Horkheimer's distinction between traditional and critical theory, Robert Cox introduced a similar distinction into IR as a criticism of Kenneth Waltz's neorealism. According to him, Waltz's theory fits into what could be defined as a 'problem-solving' theory, that is, a theory that "takes the world as it finds it."[13] In Cox's view, the problem with Waltz's approach is that it neither questions those conditions of existence of what it is looking at, nor does it consider the possibility of change beyond the existing structure. Besides, it does not take into consideration that theories are "always *for* someone and *for* some purpose [original italics]."[14]

Contrary to this, 'critical' theory questions the prevailing order, how that order came into existence and what are its underlying processes of historical change. In contrast to problem-solving theories, critical theories are constantly adjusting to the changing concepts and the objects they seek to explain.[15] Moreover, they are open to normative approaches that favour the change of the standing order: they are potentially normative in that sense. Such openness is, however, limited by the feasibility of that alternative order, constrained "by the comprehension of historical processes."[16]

The key distinction between problem solving and critical theory is in the role theory must have in understanding the world. In that sense, problem-solving theory explains the world as 'it sees' it, whereas critical theory attempts to go beyond that, asking questions about why it is seeing the world in a certain way. This inquisitive, often self-reflexive attitude thus marks the essence of the distinction between problem solving and critical theory.

Andrew Linklater explains how the distinction between problem solving and critical theory can help us to understand the difference between Robert Cox and Kenneth Waltz's theories. In his view, they differ in four main areas: in terms of the purpose of social inquiry, methodology, object of analysis and disciplinary scope.[17] In terms of the purpose of social inquiry, as mentioned earlier, critical theory focuses on an emancipatory agenda, of a normative stance, whereas Waltz's theory is ethically concerned with the avoidance of war, in what could be seen as a lowest common denominator approach. As for methodological questions, Cox adopts a radical-dialectical approach that focuses on finding the possibilities of transformation out of patterns of interaction and conflict; Waltz's theory follows an approach much closer to positivist concerns.[18] The object of analysis is also different: for Cox it is about the articulation between the modes of production, state structures and world order, whereas for Waltz it is about power politics. This leads to the last point – the scope of the discipline – with Waltz arguing for a clear delimitation of competencies (very much in accordance with the realist tradition) between international politics and other areas, whereas Cox advocates a broader approach that is closer to Gramsci's historical materialism – in which power dynamics cut across sectors and societies.[19]

There have been many critical voices of Cox's work[20] and in particular of his critical credentials,[21] but very much like Kenneth Waltz, the capacity to generate criticism reflects the quality and the importance of his work. As concluded by Michael G. Schechter, the criticism against Cox, "is almost always accompanied by praise for his sophistication, his courage and his accomplishment in expanding the space for intellectual dialogue, discussion and debate."[22]

In a recent interview, Robert Cox elaborated on this notion of critical theory by adding that "the role of critical theory is to examine current proposals and doctrines and to . . . show how they have originated, what are the things that they protect and, if you are hoping for change, what possibilities exist within them."[23] Andrew Linklater is more ambitious in that regard, advocating that critical theory's main task is "to understand how human beings learn to include some in and exclude others from their social arrangements."[24] In his view, the state plays a central role in this, by generating a clear distinction between insiders and outsiders, between those that belong to a given community and those that do not; but also by directly and indirectly legitimising other forms of exclusion: "various systems of exclusion which are confronted by subordinate classes, women, racial minorities and sub-national groups are interwoven with the practices of state exclusion."[25] For all the criticism, Robert Cox reminds us, the state still is, "the focal point," particularly for those "who feel deprived in society and that look for recourse and rectification of their situation. The state is the closest thing able to do something."[26] From a critical theory perspective the state is part of the problem but also a necessary entity to attenuate the dramatic negative consequences, for instance, a pure capitalist system would have on individuals.

The solution in Linklater's view is not in the replacement of the state with another form of sovereignty, but rather in the progressive transformation of political communities, by bringing to the fore the cosmopolitan elements that link them all, something Marxism got wrong by thinking that such transformation could be reduced to the reconstruction of property relations.[27] The aim is not to transform the state, but to transform international relations thus "realising the promise of the post-Westphalian era."[28] Europe, with its largely successful and unique integration process and post-Westphalian understanding of European citizenship would be ideally placed to take a leading role in this area. Looking at Europe almost two decades after the publication of Linklater's *Transformation of Political Community*, that no longer seems so certain.

That uncertainty results, in part at least, from a legitimacy crisis to which Robert Cox already alluded in 2002 in *The Political Economy of a Plural World*. In the Preface to the volume, Cox wonders how to construct "an alternative order, on alternative principles, and with a new basis of popular legitimacy."[29] In his view, there are two sources for an alternative order: the first lies in the "revitalization of civil society" and the second "in the prospect of a coexistence of civilizations" that replaces "the globalization project of one single all-encompassing civilization gradually absorbing and homogenizing what is left of the cultural diversity of the world."[30] These two interrelated sources derive from bottom-up approaches that should bring citizens alienated by individualism, globalisation and 'ideological sectarianism' closer to the public decision making in a process that "will inevitably reflect the diversity of material conditions, historical experience, mentalities and aspirations prevail among the world's people." As civilisations express "the inter-subjective meanings common to a large group of people as to what is natural, just and desirable," this legitimacy project will "take form through a number of civilizations."[31] In his view, civilisations as ideational constructs offer different understandings of legitimacy that need to be heeded and accepted if we are to have a more legitimate, plural world. Feminist and postcolonial approaches certainly share some of Cox's ambitions (even if not necessarily his solution – starting with the problematic concept of civilisation).

Gender matters

From the standpoint of feminism[32] to the most recent queer theory, gender has, similarly to critical theory, assumed a progressively important role within IR. This is particularly remarkable (but not necessarily surprising) when one considers that the first widely acknowledged feminist works in the discipline only emerged in the late 1980s, much later than in other social disciplines. It is even more so, as it is clear how feminism has had a significant impact on the practice of international politics, with gender streamlined into international organisations as a policy priority and with women assuming key roles in the daily affairs of states and organisations. And yet, as of August 2015, only twenty-one women served as Head of Government or State and only 22 per cent of all national parliamentarians were female.[33] As Ann Tickner concludes, "in spite of the presence of some women in foreign and defense policy leadership positions, the term 'woman' is still antithetical to our stereotypical image of a 'national security specialist.'"[34]

Within IR, feminism is now a vibrant and broad community. Feminist studies have had a section in the International Studies Association (ISA) since the early 1990s, in the Feminist Theory and Gender Studies (FTGS) section. The same applies to other regional organisations, including BISA, in the UK, with its Gendering International Relations Working Group. Despite the growing importance of feminism in IR, its coverage remains less relevant than that of realism, liberalism and constructivism. A study conducted by Elizabeth Matthews and Rhonda Callaway concluded that out of eighteen IR textbooks, feminism was never explored extensively, and its coverage lagged behind even that of Marxism.[35] As recognised by Lucian M. Ashworth, even if feminism is now part of the IR canon, "resistance to [its] insights is still worryingly common."[36] It is true that feminism is a relatively recent theoretical approach in IR, a discipline – as many other – historically dominated by white men. It is no less true that feminist works *avant la lettre*, from inter-war period authors such as Helena Swanwick[37] had been marginalised by the discipline's historiography, suitably forgotten in the idealist box of ideas.

In terms of its contribution to the discipline, we would argue there are three elements that cut across most feminist approaches. First, feminism has strongly contributed to affirming the centrality of the social in IR, in contradistinction to the more rationalist approach that still is quite common in the United States. In the words of Ann Tickner, feminism "comes out of an ontology of social relations, particularly gender relations, which starts at the level of the individual embedded in hierarchical social, political, and economic structures."[38] Second, feminism has made important methodological contributions, be it through the adaptation of previously existent approaches, such as discourse analysis,[39] or the incorporation of methods common in other disciplines, such as ethnography. Finally, feminism has reinforced the normative credo that was at the basis of the creation of the discipline and that was abandoned by a good part of IR scholars during the 1960s and 1970s. Feminism is "explicitly normative and often emancipatory." It aims to promote the transformation of international politics. It believes "that theory cannot be separated from political practice."[40]

Those common features and contributions do not hide the different forms and shapes that feminism can assume. Liberal feminists, for instance, focus on gender as an explanatory variable, highlighting the benefits of considering "integrating women into the governance and economic structures of the existing order,"[41] whereas constructivist feminists highlight the role gender has in shaping and being shaped by global politics and the importance of changing the norms that define gender relations. Finally, poststructuralist feminists adopt a language-based approach, focusing on "how and why gender-based dichotomized linguistic constructions such as strong/weak, rational/emotional, and public/private, serve to empower masculinities and devalorize femininities."[42] To this, we could also add postcolonial feminists, who "see false claims of universalism arising from knowledge that is based largely on experiences of relatively privileged Western women."[43] Chandra Talpade Mohanty was among the feminist authors that in the 1980s started criticising feminism for subsuming women's experiences under the same label. As she argued, "the discursively consensual homogeneity of 'women' as a group is mistaken for the historically specific material reality of groups of women."[44]

Gender has, to an extent (and not without its controversy as we shall see later), replaced 'women' as the centre of feminist research. Indeed, most feminists aim to understand the reasons behind gender discrimination in IR – both as a discipline and as a practice and "to use this understanding to advocate on behalf of those who, because of their gender, are rendered insecure or oppressed by the prevailing order."[45] According to Cynthia Enloe, a gender analysis implies, first, a mapping exercise of where man and women are (and how they got there) in a given context, and, second, an investigation into "each and every manipulation . . . of ideas and practices of both masculinities and femininities."[46] The often subtle role gender plays in ordering the international was the focus of Enloe's now classic *Bananas, Beaches and Bases: Making Feminist Sense of International Politics*.

Pocahontas, Carmen Miranda and the birth of a feminist classic

Cynthia Enloe's *Bananas, Beaches and Bases*, published in 1989, is seen as feminism's first major work[47] in IR, one that "marked the irreversible entry of feminism and gender theory into the study of IR."[48] Enloe starts by analysing the life experiences of two names rarely mentioned in an IR book until then: Pocahontas and Carmen Miranda. The more she focused on the lives of these women, the more she realised that we "had been missing an entire dimension of international politics," one that explains "how relations between governments depend not only on capital and weaponry, but also on the control of women as symbols, consumers, workers and emotional comforters."[49] In the concrete case of Pocahontas and Carmen Miranda, they were instrumental in, respectively, opening the door for the British colonisation of America, and the US domination of Latin America for most of the twentieth century.[50] In that regard, understanding the place of women in IR, Enloe argues, is not just a normative concern but one with explanatory value. In her view:

> [i]gnoring women on the landscape of international politics perpetuates the notion that certain power relations are merely a matter of taste and culture. Paying serious attention to women can expose how much power it takes to maintain the international political system in its present form.[51]

Enloe's work touches on a number of traditional IR topics – nationalism, diplomacy, military interventionism or international debt. But in each case, it does so from an original perspective. It looks at nationalism (and colonialism) by focusing on the supposed traditional role of women in maintaining the power relations between the centre and the periphery; at diplomacy through the eyes of the wives of career diplomats; at military interventionism through the prism of the women that live, work (particularly sex workers) and demonstrate around military bases; and at international debt by looking at the role of women at the receiving end of austerity cuts and underpaid jobs. Cynthia Enloe's work takes gender as a tool for understanding IR, as well as being a tool for conceptual and practical change. The articulations between the public and private, masculinity and femininity, north and south, run deep in the constitutive fabric of international politics. That the life of a Sri Lankan domestic servant is as important to understanding international dynamics as the opinion of a long-serving diplomat is arguably one of Cynthia Enloe's biggest contributions to the discipline. As she argues:

> [i]nvestigations of how international politics rely on manipulations of masculinity and femininity suggest that the conventional approaches to making sense of inter-state relations are superficial. Conventional analysis stops short of investigating an entire area of international relations, an area that women have pioneered in exploring: how states depend on particular constructions of the domestic and private spheres.[52]

In that regard, the control of women's lives is frequently about the optimisation of the control over men in their multiple international roles, such as migrant workers, soldiers, diplomats and bankers.[53]

Bananas, Beaches and Bases does not have significant theoretical ambitions. It does not offer a feminist 'theory' that can be applied to multiple cases – which in itself would be a reductionist understanding of theory. It does, however, offer a fresh approach to international politics and raises the prospect that, "every time a woman explains how her government is trying to control her fears, her hopes and her labor, such a theory is being made."[54]

Following in Enloe's footsteps, Ann Tickner published *Gender in International Relations* in 1992, where she intended to start a conversation on "how the discipline of international relations might look if gender were included as a category of analysis and if women's experiences were part of the subject matter out of which its theories are constructed."[55] As argued by

Tickner, placing gender at the centre of the discipline illuminates the inequalities in the discipline of IR and the eschewed understanding of national security as a concept. Overcoming these differences, inequalities and insecurities demands the inclusion of experiences that go beyond those of (white) men: "Only through analysis that recognizes gender differences but does not take them as fixed or inevitable can we move toward the creation of a nongendered discipline that includes us all."[56]

Cynthia Enloe and Ann Tickner were part of a group of feminists responsible for placing gender and feminism on the IR agenda. Equally important, at least on the European side of the Atlantic, was the conference on 'Women and International Relations' organised at the London School of Economics in 1988, and later turned into a special issue of *Millennium: Journal of International Studies*.

Taking (regular) stock of feminism

Published shortly before Cynthia Enloe's *Bananas, Beaches and Bases*, the 1988 Special issue in the *Millennium* journal on 'Women and International Relations' clearly contributed to mark the affirmation of feminism in IR.[57] This stocktaking exercise is now a regular feature of this journal. It has had editions in 1998 and, in a more reduced version, in 2008.

In its first instalment, Fred Halliday hoped that the Special issue contributed to overcome "the 'invisibilisation' of women [in IR],"[58] which, in his view, was due to three main reasons. First, it was due to institutional inertia that privileges mainstream over novelty; second, to the 'insulation' of IR from other social sciences that prevented the former from reaping the intellectual benefits feminism was making visible in other disciplines; third, and finally, to the definition of issues that are seen to be relevant, or 'high politics' and therefore worth studying, which by default tend to 'hide' women and gender-related issues from the discussion.

For Sarah Brown, writing in the same Special issue, both feminist and international theory were to blame for that invisibility: the former for failing "to theorise about international relations" and the latter for failing to "theorise gender."[59] She highlights the works of those feminists that historically trace the invisibility of women in international politics, not as being in need of being made visible and brought into the discipline but as already "embedded in the theory and practice of international relations."[60] As she concludes, "the appearance of separation between the development of international theory and the development of feminist thought conceals the way in which gender – a relation of inequality – has been constructed and maintained in international relations at large." Therefore, "a feminist international relations that is genuinely emancipatory will take gender difference as its starting point," but its ultimate aim should be "to explain how gender has been constructed and maintained in international relations and if and how it can be removed."[61] The article reflects on the challenges feminism brings to the distinction between private and public, a topic that is then problematised at length in Philip Windsor's piece 'Women and International Relations: What's the Problem?' By digging into the fundamentals of Western political thought, Windsor argues that "to discuss the role of women in international relations" is also "to question the cultural and intellectual assumptions of which our very [Western] thought was born."[62] In his view, this is something we need to do, but that we need to acknowledge comes as an historical novelty.

J. Ann Tickner's contribution to the Special issue, later reproduced in her book *A Feminist Voyage through International Relations*, was to become one of the most widely read feminist pieces in IR. Entitled 'Hans Morgenthau's Principles of Political Realism: A Feminist Reformulation,' Tickner's piece is, as indicated, a feminist critique of Morgenthau's famous six points. She argues that the importance of these points to the discipline derives from a certain view of international politics as "a man's world, a world of power and conflict in which warfare is a privileged activity."[63] If we were to adopt a feminist understanding of central concepts such as power (act in concert) and security (in interdependent terms), we would value different aspects of international politics. In such a case, those six points would be reformulated to contain the following:

1   Objectivity is culturally defined according to specific understandings of masculinity. Therefore, the objective laws of human nature that Morgenthau mentions are "based on a partial masculine view of human nature."[64] Instead, we should try to construct a view of humanity that is both masculine and feminine and that results, according to Tickner, in a sort of dynamic objectivity that prevents the definition of eternal laws.
2   This results in the national interest being "multidimensional and contextually contingent,"[65] more dependent on cooperation than on power relations.
3   Power needs to be redefined as a concept (in order to include "the possibility of collective empowerment"[66]), and it cannot be taken to be universal.
4   From a feminist perspective, it is not possible to separate morality from political action.
5   Nations should strive to find common elements that enable the de-escalation of conflicts and the development of cooperative relations.
6   The political is not autonomous. Understanding it as such is a masculine and ultimate partial interpretation of the political realm.

Ten years later, the 1998 Special issue was a time for an initial reflection of what feminism as a fully incorporated approach within the IR canon had achieved by then. Fred Halliday, in his introductory piece, highlighted improvements and problems feminism faced in the previous decade.[67] On the positive side, he underlined the proliferation of new journals, books and the influence of gender in shaping public policy at the international level. On the negative side, the gendered character of globalisation and information technology, the rise of conservative ideologies, the collapse of state socialism and the use of gender as a tool of war (particularly in ethnic conflicts during the 1990s) constituted a negative backlash in terms of the feminist agenda.[68] In his view, there had been five main developments within feminism in IR. First, the move from debating women to debating gender. Second, the introduction to IR of the debate on sexualities, including the development of queer work, as discussed in the next section. Third, the development of a body of literature on feminism and international law which highlights the gendered dimension of norms in IR but also raises the importance of issues normally seen as part of national agendas, such as domestic violence. Fourth, the consolidation of a feminist international political theory that addresses key concepts in the discipline, such as citizenship and identity. Finally, the emerging work on gender and development.[69] Overall, Halliday paints what he says to be a 'mixed picture,' in which advancements and backlashes unfolded hand in hand.

In another piece in the same 1998 Special issue, Marysia Zalewski questioned the move from the position of 'the woman in IR' to a focus on gender as a positive development.[70] This move, together with the exclusion from some important edited collections, or the dismissive attitude of key (male) authors in the field, was part of an attempt to minimise the disruptive impact of feminism in the discipline.[71] If that was the plan, it certainly did not work.

In the introduction to what was just a special section – rather than a Special issue – on 'Gender, Feminism and International Relations,' Kimberly Hutchings looked at both the 1988 and 1998 Special issues as a stocktaking exercise.[72] In her view, whereas the concerns in the late 1980s were about highlighting the gendered dimension of IR and the impact the incorporation of a feminist and gendered perspective could have in the discipline, ten years later, those two aspects had more or less been taken for granted. Instead, they were more concerned in problematising both the concepts of 'gender' and 'masculinity.' From a perspective of showing its relevance to the discipline, the debate moved to a conceptual debate that now also included notions of Eurocentrism and cultural imperialism (Spivak's article[73] was particularly important in that regard). Similar to Fred Halliday, Kimberly Hutchings also points to the direction of a mixed record, tending more towards the positive developments of the previous twenty years.

During a roundtable later reproduced in the special section, seven authors[74] previously associated with the 1988 or 1998 Special issues discussed the status of feminism and its future within IR. As the first speaker, Marysia Zalewski, questioned the relevance of asking whether feminism is or is not at the margins of IR, whereas Ann Tickner focused on the directions of feminist research, highlighting its contribution to "making women more visible"[75] as well as the introduction of new issues and methodologies to the discipline. Another prominent feminist author, Christine Sylvester, considered that since 1988 the field of IR had changed substantially, to the point where "there is no real mainstream any longer, margins are disappearing, and no topic is forbidden to it,"[76] which is positive but also contributed to increased divisions along sub-disciplinarian sectarianisms of which feminism is not immune. Also speaking of contributions, Vivienne Jabri focused on what feminism can tell about the international and the political, and Jabri concluded that different forms of feminism bring different answers, which means that the "contest is no longer one of feminism and the rest, but rather lies within feminism itself."[77]

In a recent review of her work, Cynthia Enloe highlighted how when engaged in the update of her now classic work, she was "struck again by how, amid all the admittedly important changes that had occurred during that last twenty-five years, the patriarchal dynamics of international politics have persisted."[78] We would add, that in many instances, some of those dynamics have deteriorated with the conservative and nationalist agendas popping up across the world: from Asia to Latin America but also including Europe and the United States. It is in this complex political environment that queer theory has been making some inroads since the late 2000s.

Gender beyond feminism

One could argue queer studies problematise gender beyond feminism. Despite its increasing visibility in cultural studies, IR has until recently been more or less silent regarding queer studies, particularly to what Cynthia Weber calls Global Queer Studies (GQS). According to the author, only six GQS-related articles have been published in the top twenty IR journals between 2003 and 2013, and only one book was published or commissioned by a top IR series in the same period.[79] In her article, 'Why Is There No Queer International Theory?' Weber problematises that absence and criticises the standards against which theory is judged and accepted within what she labels as Disciplinary IR. Weber went on to address that gap by publishing multiple articles in top IR journals on issues related to queer studies, as well as a monograph 'Queer International Relations' in one of the best IR collections.[80] In her book, Weber addresses the connection between a central issue in mainstream IR – sovereignty – from the perspective of sexuality, and how their meanings remain intertwined way more than both IR and queer studies care to acknowledge. On the way she also firmly places queer studies as a conceptual and methodologically sound approach to the study of IR.[81]

One of the main issues associated with queer studies is trans-gendering. Following Laura Sjoberg,[82] trans-gendering poses both a challenge and an opportunity to feminism and IR at large. Despite some tensions between feminism and trans-theorists,[83] the latter could contribute to the former in at least three ways. First, it would "encourage feminist IR to consider the difference a truly plural (rather than dichotomous) understanding of 'sex' would make for thinking about the function of gender hierarchy in global politics."[84] Second, it allows feminist to see sex and gender as 'sociobiological,' "a combination of people's knowledge, their experiences, and how people read and construct their bodies and others.'"[85] Finally, it shows how gender is relational, cut across by power relations that tend to oppress some gender expressions over others. As Laura Sjoberg concludes, "while it is important to be inclusive of sex and gender diversity, it is equally important not to lose sight of the power relations between and among sexes and genders."[86]

Laura Sjoberg argues that trans-theorising can also contribute to the discipline writ large through the problematisation of concepts such as hyper/invisibility, transition and liminality, crossing and disidentification.[87] It will ultimately enable the discipline to ask better questions and offer better answers in terms of studying difference seriously.[88] The influence and visibility of queer work in IR is already unavoidable, and its presence is a constant in all the major international IR conferences, including the ISA convention. According to Cynthia Weber, that was more or less inevitable once "a new generation of scholars doing cutting edge queer, international, and queer transnational/global/international work . . . claim[ed] IR as among their disciplinary homes."[89] Overall, queer studies are currently a fast growing area in IR. The same could be said of the slightly more established postcolonial studies.

Looking beyond the West

Postcolonial studies were born out of different academic subjects – history, anthropology, cultural studies and literature. The works of some of its biggest authors, Edward Said, Frantz Fanon, Ranajit Guha, Gayatry Spivak and Homi Bhabha, are interdisciplinary in nature, cutting across what they perceive to be Western-centric forms of knowledge organisation.

Frantz Fanon, the Martiniquan psychiatrist (1925–1961) who was a leading intellectual (and activist) in the post-Second World War anti-colonial movement, along the likes of Amilcar Cabral and Mahatma Gandhi, also became a reference in terms of postcolonial studies. Colonialism is, for Fanon, the structural denial of diversity, of humanity.[90] His final work, *The Wretched of the Earth* (1961), is a polemical call for arms to those under colonial rule, for there is no other possibility of liberation from colonial rule other than through violence, as that is embedded in the relationship between the coloniser and the colonised: "decolonization is the encounter between two congenitally antagonistic forces."[91] For Fanon, the world is fundamentally divided along racial lines,[92] in which the "dividing line, the border, is represented by the barracks and the police stations."[93] In that regard, "challenging the colonial world is not a rational confrontation of viewpoints. It is not a discourse on the universal, but the impassioned claim by the colonized that their world is fundamentally different."[94] Violence is important not only to remove the colonial Power but to free the native from the inferiority complex imposed on them by the colonising Power.

Not only should the colonies remove the colonial Powers from their lands, they should seek compensation for what they did, akin to what was demanded of the Germans at the end of the Second World War. All of that could be achieved once the European 'masses' acknowledged their responsibility, an idea seconded by Jean-Paul Sartre in the Preface to the book: "Let's take a good look at ourselves, if we have the courage, and let's see what has become of us."[95] Fanon's apology of violence was defended by some[96] and criticised by many.[97] Its influence extended way beyond academia, inspiring movements as diverse as the Black Panthers, the anti-apartheid movement in South Africa, and even the IRA.[98]

There obviously is a strong Marxist element that cuts across Fanon's work – "capitalism . . . objectively colludes with the forces of violence that erupt in colonial territories"[99] –but that needs to be stretched in order to accommodate the fact that the former is a foreigner and not merely part of a bourgeois elite. Stretching Marxism was certainly part of the early postcolonial literature, also visible in another important work, *Orientalism*.

Edward Said's *Orientalism* (1978) was no less polemical and influential, another critical point in the development of postcolonial studies. Said establishes a relation between politics, knowledge and race, in a work that builds on both poststructuralism (Foucault) and Marxist studies (Gramsci). There is, in his view, a relation of power and dominance of the West over the East that is materialised in the meanings attributed to those terms: Occident (good, superior) over Orient (bad, inferior). The production and maintenance of this relation is very much at the basis of the West's domination. In that regard, colonialism is more than just oppression and violence; it is about shaping and transforming the 'other' according to a specific world view. These are to be silent subjects that will be represented by 'us.' Many criticise Said. Homi Bhabha argues that Said "fails to investigate the process in which the colonial subject is historically constructed, making Orientalist discourse appear monolithic, undifferentiated and uncontested."[100] This is an argument similar to those of postcolonial feminists when referring to the universalising experiences of being a woman that many feminists portray in their studies.

Said's influence in IR has arguably been more reduced than in other disciplines, as recognised by Sheila Nair in the Introduction to the *Millennium* Forum *Edward W. Said and International Relations*.[101] One could ask whether that lack of influence is to an extent related to the lack of attention the discipline paid to postcolonial studies through much of its existence. Most IR manuals have until recently neglected postcolonialism as a theoretical approach deserving of an exclusive chapter. Although many factors may contribute to include or exclude a specific theory or approach, the reality is some of the most important textbooks in the discipline do not as yet have a chapter dedicated to postcolonialism – which is the case with *Theories of International Relations*[102] – or took some time to do so: *Globalization of World Politics* only dedicated a chapter to postcolonialism in its fourth edition (2010). It probably is also rather elucidating that one of the most sophisticated volumes taking stock of the evolution of IR after the end of the Cold War, *International Theory: Positivism and Beyond*,[103] did not dedicate an individual chapter to postcolonialism.

Unhiding invisibilities and inverting (historical) narratives

Postcolonialism is a very recent, but growing voice in contemporary IR. Very much like feminism, postcolonialism does not offer a unified theory of IR.[104] It builds on pre-existing approaches offering its 'partial perspective'[105] of the world. In epistemological terms postcolonialism offers a "partial perspective" embedded within "situated knowledges."[106] It engages directly with the power dynamics that the discipline of IR and the world it represents reproduce; a Eurocentric[107] world built on centuries of colonial domination.[108]

From this perspective, it was not so much anarchy as colonisation being the ordering mechanism of the international system. The majority of the world lived under conditions of imposed sovereignty, not as functionally equal 'units' of the system, to use Kenneth Waltz's language. In that regard, the norms of the English School's international society have been experienced quite differently depending on whether you were in London or Nairobi. As Branwen Gruffydd explains in the Introduction to *Decolonizing International Relations*, whereas IR as a discipline has focused on the expansion of the international society as "the spread of European forms of state, sovereignty, democracy, law, and rights to non-European areas and peoples," to the rest of the world that expansion has also meant "authoritarianism, theft, racism, and, in significant cases, massacre and genocide."[109] What for some was the natural flow of inter-state relations, for others was nothing but oppression. But colonialism was not only oppressive but also transformative. Picking on a point already raised by Frantz Fanon, colonialism and imperialism shaped the subjugated societies according to their interests, but they were also often shaped by their interaction with those colonies, in interactive, hybrid[110] processes. This transformative power of colonialism continued after the independence of these countries. After decolonisation, oppression was transformed into integration: to be 'integrated' into international society was to accept a whole set of Western-centric rules and norms. As argued by Geeta Chowdhry and Sheila Nair, "the postcolonial does not signify the end of colonialism, but rather that it accurately reflects both the continuity and persistence of colonizing practices, as well as the critical limits and possibilities it has engendered in the present historical moment."[111] Colonial independence does not correspond to the formal emancipatory event to which the term is associated. Not only does the colonial Power often keep strong political and economic ties with the ex-colony, but those oppressed by decades of colonial rule are defined by that relation. Even if the colonial Power is formally outside, it is inside the social tissue of these societies and an integral part of the constitution of these subjects in the Global South.

From that recognition results the attempt to set the record straight in terms of how history is told, the possibility of enabling actors in both the Global North and Global South to come to terms with the past, but also, arguably more importantly, the possibility of rejecting the imposition of specific Western-centric versions of the truth and offering alternative narratives of the world,[112] including those of the subaltern.[113] How one writes and re-writes IR and its history becomes a space of struggle and resistance.[114] For instance, the Cold War when viewed from the Global South was a very different, and far from cold, historical process.[115] Viewing the international from such a perspective is, in Vivienne Jabri's view, to first, "gain access to the international and on terms equal to that of the European" and, second, "to draw upon the political-juridical structure of the international as a guarantor of freedom from resurgent colonial domination and subjugation."[116]

Finally, postcolonialism problematises and confronts IR as a discipline that results, to a large extent, from and is dominated by, Eurocentric practices and Western institutions.[117] Progressively, the discipline has been incorporating these critiques,[118] opening itself to different voices and trying to be "more global and more decentred."[119] In the voice of postcolonial authors, the discipline needs to be progressively decolonised, that is, it needs to be understood "how Eurocentrism has informed the basic categories and vocabularies of social and political inquiry,"[120] and it needs to acknowledge (and act accordingly that) it has so far failed to "study the weak and the strong together, as jointly responsible for making history, hamstrings IR and security studies' ability to make sense of world politics generally and North-South relations in particular."[121]

Both regarding the discipline and the 'real' world, postcolonialism also identifies and explores a topic that is very uncomfortable to the discipline: racism. "By problematizing global social relations, postcolonial authors draw attention to the racist assumptions underlying much Western social scientific scholarship in the portrayal of the Third World."[122] Although the topic is still relatively untouched in the discipline, there have been some efforts towards giving it more relevance. For instance, the 2016 Millennium Conference 'Racialized Realities in World Politics' and the ensuing Special issue have certainly helped in what is a fast-growing topic in the discipline.

Critiques and future paths

Postcolonial studies have been, very much since its early stages, mired in controversy, which is hardly surprising given its critical and often disruptive *raison d'etre*. Some of the most common critiques echo what is said about other post-positivist approaches, such as critical theory or poststructuralism in its lack of scientific rigour and method. More poignant and relevant critiques have to do with the embedded Eurocentrism of postcolonialism and the often essentialising view of it.

Despite having Eurocentrism as part of its constellation of key concepts, postcolonialism is often accused of being a product of that same Eurocentrism. Indeed, many of its most famous authors were educated and work or worked in Western institutions (with all the privileges associated with it), were inspired by Western authors and use or used Western systems of thought.[123] This leads to two problems. First, that these authors might be as distant from the views and ideas of those in the Global South as those from the Global North. Second, that they may end up reproducing the same ordering principles – not least in academia – they themselves criticise. A Harvard or Cambridge scholar will certainly have more and better opportunities to be heard than a scholar in a university in Mozambique or Peru.

Postcolonial approaches also often engage in essentialising dynamics, in which the world is divided along clear dichotomies (North-South for instance) that reify and simplify often much more nuanced and complex issues. This type of approach tends towards what John M. Hobson labels "Eurofetishism," in which Western imperialism is reified: "a fetish serves, albeit unwittingly, to eternalize Western domination of the non-Western world."[124] As postcolonial studies grow in stature and diversity, both these issues will probably dissipate in the future.

A factor that may certainly bear an important weight in diversifying postcolonialism and IR is how in the 'real' world we seem to be moving towards a post-Western world.[125] As wealth and prestige are redistributed across the globe, and previous colonies become global actors (such as India or Brazil), the views from these countries and from their universities will become increasingly central to the discipline and to international politics at large. Fundamentally, postcolonial studies will play a central role in aiding academics and policy-makers to navigate in this increasingly decentralised multipolar world.

Notes

1 His 'Social Forces, States, and World Orders: Beyond IR Theory,' published in 1981, would, six years later, be at the basis of his famous book *Production, Power and World Order* (New York: Columbia University Press, 1987).

2 Andrew Linklater, *Men and Citizens in the Theory of International Relations* (Basingstoke: Palgrave, 1982).

3 For Robert Cox's observations on being a Marxist, see 'Reflections and Transitions,' in Robert W. Cox (ed.) with Michael G. Schechter, *The Political Economy of a Plural World. Critical Reflections on Power, Morals and Civilization* (Oxford: Routledge, 2002).

4 According to Robert Cox "I read and thought a lot about Gramsci at the time and people started to call me a neo-Gramscian. I wonder, 'what was the neo for?'" in Brincat, S., Lima, L. and Nunes, J. '*For* Someone and *For* Some Purpose,' in Brincat et al. (eds), *Critical Theory in International Relations and Security Studies. Interviews and Reflections* (Oxford: Routledge, 2012), p. 18.

5 Brincat, S., Lima, L. and Nunes, J. 'Introduction,' in Brincat et al. (eds), *Critical Theory in International Relations and Security Studies. Interviews and Reflections* (Oxford: Routledge, 2012), p. 5.

6 Mark Hoffman 'Critical Theory and the Inter-Paradigm Debate,' *Millennium: Journal of International Studies*, Vol. 16, No. 3, p. 234.

7 Horkheimer, Max (ed.), 'Traditional or Critical Theory,' in *Critical Theory: Selected Essays* (New York: Seabury, 1972 [1932]), pp. 188–243.

8   Hoffman, 'Critical Theory,' 1987.

9   Richard Wyn Jones, *Security, Strategy, And Critical Theory* (Boulder, CO: Lynne Rienner Publishers, 1999), p. 9.

10 *Ibid.*, p. 3.

11 Richard Wyn Jones, 'Introduction: Locating Critical International Relations,' in Richard Wyn Jones (ed.), *Critical Theory and World Politics* (Boulder, CO: Lynne Rienner Publishers, 2001), p. 6.

12 Shapcott, Richard, 'Critical Theory,' in Christian Reus-Smit and Duncan Snidal (eds), *The Oxford Handbook of International Relations* (Oxford: Oxford University Press, 2010), p. 328.

13 Robert W. Cox, 'Social Forces,' p. 128.

14 *Ibid.*

15 *Ibid.*, p. 129.

16 *Ibid.*, p. 130.

17 Andrew Linklater, 'The Question of the Next Stage in International Relations Theory: A Critical-Theoretical Point of View,' *Millennium: Journal of International Studies*, Vol. 21, No. 1, 1992, p. 86.

18 See Chapter 11 for a discussion on the positivist merits of Waltz's theory.

19 Andrew Linklater, 'The Question of the Next Stage in International Relations Theory: A Critical-Theoretical Point of View,' pp. 86–87.

20 For an overview of Cox's critics, see Michael G. Schechter, 'Critiques of Coxian Theory: Background to a Conversation,' in Robert W. Cox (ed.) with Michael G. Schechter, *The Political Economy of a Plural World. Critical Reflections on Power, Morals and Civilization* (Oxford: Routledge, 2002).

21 See in particular, Roger D. Spegele, 'Is Robust Globalism a Mistake?' *Review of International Studies*, Vol. 23, 1997, p. 224.

22 Michael G. Schechter, p. 18.

23 Brincat et al., '*For* Someone and *For* Some Purpose,' p. 20.

24 Andrew Linklater, *The Transformation of Political Community*, p. 20.

25 *Ibid.*, p. 148.

26 Brincat et al., '*For* Someone and *For* Some Purpose,' p. 27.

27 Linklater, *The Transformation of Political Community*, p. 116.

28 *Ibid.*, p. 220.

29 Robert W. Cox with Michael G. Schechter, *The Political Economy of a Plural World. Critical Reflections on Power, Morals and Civilization* (Oxford: Routledge), p. xx.

30 Cox with Schechter, p. xxi.

31 *Ibid.*

32 Following Stephanie Lawson, standpoint feminism "is based on the primary claim that all knowledge is socially situated and that the knowledge we acquire as females or males is conditioned by our gender," Stephanie Lawson, *Theories of International Relations: Contending Approaches to World Politics* (Cambridge: Polity, 2015), p. 184.

33 'Facts and Figures: Leadership and Political Participation,' *UN Women*, Available at: www.unwomen.org/en/what-we-do/leadership-and-political-participation/facts-and-figures.

34 J. Ann Tickner, 'Feminist Responses to International Security Studies,' *Peace Review*, Vol. 16, No. 1, 2004, p. 44.

35 Elizabeth G. Matthews and Rhonda L. Callaway, 'Where Have All the Theories Gone? Teaching Theory in Introductory Courses in International Relations,' *International Studies Perspective*, Vol. 16, No. 1, 2015, pp. 190–209.

36 Lucian M. Ashworth, 'Feminism, War and the Prospects for Peace,' *International Feminist Journal of Politics*, Vol. 13, No. 1, 2011, p. 26.

37 *Ibid.*

38 J. Ann Tickner, 'Feminist Responses,' p. 44.

39 Lene Hansen, *Security as Practice. Discourse Analysis and the Bosnian War* (Oxford: Routledge, 2006).

40 J. Ann Tickner, 'Feminist Responses,' p. 45.

41 Laura Sjoberg and J. Ann Tickner, 'Introduction,' in J. Ann Tickner and Laura Sjoberg (eds), *Feminism and International Relations. Conversations About the Past, Present and Future* (Oxford: Routledge, 2011), p. 5.

42 Sjoberg and Tickner, p. 6.

43 J. Ann Tickner and Laura Sjoberg, 'Feminism,' in Tim Dunne et al. (eds), *International Relations Theories. Discipline and Diversity* (Oxford: Oxford University Press, 2016), fourth edition, p. 186.

44 Bill Aschcroft, Gareth Griffiths and Helen Tiffin, *Post-Colonial Studies. The Key Concepts* (Oxford: Routledge, 2000), p. 94.

45 Katrina Lee-Koo 'Feminist International Relations in Australia,' *Australian Journal of Politics and History*, Vol. 55, No. 3, 2009, p. 419.

46 Cynthia Enloe, 'Carmen Miranda Returns,' in Ken Booth and Toni Erskine (eds), *International Relations Theory Today* (Cambridge: Polity, 2016), second editon, pp. 154–155.

47 Others were to follow in the 1990s, including J. Ann Tickner, *Gender in International Relations* (New York: Sage, 1992); and Jindy Pettman, *Worlding Women* (St Leonards, NSW: Allen & Unwin, 1996).

48 Stephanie Lawson, *Theories of International Relations: Contending Approaches to World Politics* (Cambridge: Polity, 2015), p. 182.

49 Cynthia Enloe, *Bananas, Beaches and Bases. Making Feminist Sense of International Politics* (Berkeley, CA: University of California Press, 2000), second edition, p. xvii.

50 *Ibid.*, pp. 1–2.

51 *Ibid.*, p. 3.

52 *Ibid.*, p. 197.

53 *Ibid.*, p. 200.

54 *Ibid.*, p. 201.

55 J. Ann Tickner *Gender in International Relations. Feminist Perspectives on Achieving Global Security* (New York: Columbia University Press, 1992), chapter 1.

56 Tickner, *Gender in IR*, chapter 5.

57 Laura Sjoberg and J. Ann Tickner, 'Introduction,' in *Feminism and International Relations*.

58 Fred Halliday, 'Hidden From International Relations: Women and the International Arena,' *Millennium: Journal of International Studies*, Vol. 17, No. 3, 1988, p. 419.

59 Sarah Brown, 'Feminism, International Theory, and International Relations of Gender Inequality,' *Millennium: Journal of International Studies*, Vol. 17, No. 3, 1988, p. 461.

60 *Ibid.*, p. 464.

61 *Ibid.*, p. 473.

62 Philip Windsor, 'Women and International Relations: What's the Problem?' *Millennium: Journal of International Studies*, Vol. 17, No. 3, 1988, p. 458.

63 J. Ann Tickner, *A Feminist Voyage through International Relations* (Oxford: Oxford University Press, 2014), p. 5.

64 *Ibid.*, 17.

65 *Ibid.*

66 *Ibid.*

67 Fred Halliday, 'Gender and IR: Progress, Backlash, and Prospect,' *Millennium: Journal of International Studies*, Vol. 27, No. 4, 1998, p. 833.

68 *Ibid.*, pp. 840–842.

69 *Ibid.*, pp. 836–838.

70 Marysia Zalewski, 'Where Is Woman in International Relations? "To Return as a Woman and Be Heard",' *Millennium: Journal of International Studies*, Vol. 27, No. 4, 1998, p. 848.

71 *Ibid.*, p. 864.

72 Kimberly Hutchings, '1988 and 1998: Contrast and Continuity in Feminist International Relations,' *Millennium: Journal of International Studies*, Vol. 37, No. 1, 2008, pp. 97–105.

73 Gayatri Chakravorty Spivak, 'Gender and International Studies,' *Millennium: Journal of International Studies*, Vol. 27, No. 4, 1998, pp. 809–831.

74 Hutchings, K., Zalewski, M., Tickner, A., Sylvester, C., Light, M., Jabri, V. and Halliday, F. 2008, 'Roundtable Discussion: Reflections on the Past, Prospects for the Future in Gender and International Relations,' *Millennium: Journal of International Studies*, Vol. 37, No. 1, 2008, pp. 153–179.

75 *Ibid.*, p. 159.

76 *Ibid.*, p. 161.

77 *Ibid.*, p. 168.

78 Cynthia Enloe, 'Carmen Miranda Returns,' p. 155.

79 Cynthia Weber, 'Why Is There No Queer International Theory,' *European Journal of International Relations*, Vol. 21, No. 1, 2015, p. 28.

80 Cynthia Weber, *Queer International Relations: Sovereignty, Sexuality and the Will to Knowledge* (Oxford: Oxford University Press, 2016).

81 For a symposium discussing queer IR, please see https://thedisorderofthings.com/2016/11/21/queer-international-relations-a-symposium/.

82 Laura Sjoberg, 'Toward Trans-gendering International Relations?' *International Political Sociology*, Vol. 6, 2012, pp. 337–354.

83 *Ibid.*, p. 340.

84 *Ibid.*, p. 341.

85 *Ibid.*, p. 342.

86 *Ibid.*

87 *Ibid.*, p. 343.

88 *Ibid.*, p. 351.

89 Cynthia Weber, '"What Is Told Is Always in the Telling": Reflections on Faking It in 21st Century IR/Global Politics,' *Millennium: Journal of International Studies*, Vol. 45, No. 1, 2016, p. 124.

90 Himadeep Muppidi, 'Frantz Fanon,' in Jenny Edkins and Nick Vaughan-Williams (eds), *Critical Theorists and International Relations* (Oxford: Routledge, 2009), p, 152.

91 Frantz Fanon, *The Wretched of the Earth* (New York: Grove Press, 2004 [1963]), p. 2.

92 *Ibid.*, p. 5.

93 *Ibid.*, p. 3.

94 *Ibid.*, p. 6.

95 Jean-Paul Sartre, 'Preface,' in Fanon, *The Wretched of the Earth*, p. lvii.

96 Jean-Paul Sartre, 'Preface,' pp. xliii–lxii.

97 Homi K. Bhabha, 'Foreword: Framing Fanon,' in F. Fanon (ed.), *The Wretched of the Earth*, pp. xxviii–xxix. Also see Hannah Arendt, *On Violence* (London: Harvest Book, 1970).

98 Homi K. Bhabha, 'Foreword: Framing Fanon,' in F. Fanon (ed.), *The Wretched of the Earth*, pp. xxviii–xxix

99 Fanon, *op. cit.*, p. 27.

100 Catarina Kinnvall, 'Gayatri Chakravorty Spivak,' in Jenny Edkins and Nick Vaughan-Williams (eds), *Critical Theorists and International Relations* (Oxford: Routledge, 2009), p. 322.

101 Sheila Nair, 'FORUM: Edward W. Said and International Relations,' *Millennium: Journal of International Studies*, Vol. 36, No. 1, 2007, p. 80.

102 Scott Burchill et al., *Theories of International Relations* (London: Palgrave, 2013), fifth edition.

103 Ken Booth, Marysia Zalewski and Steve Smith (eds), *International Theory: Positivism and Beyond* (Cambridge: Cambridge University Press, 1996).

104 Charlotte Epstein, 'The Postcolonial Perspective: An Introduction,' *International Theory*, Vol. 6, No. 2, 2014, pp. 294–311.

105 *Ibid.*, 295.

106 *Ibid.*, 295.

107 Eurocentrism can be defined as a "set of practices – scientific, cultural, political – which overtly (mostly in the era of colonial imperialism) or tacitly (mostly in the postcolonial era) seek to establish and maintain the primacy of post-Enlightenment European political and epistemic culture at the expense of alternative political systems and epistemologies," Rosa Vasilaki, 'Provincialising IR? Deadlocks and Prospects in Post-Western IR Theory,' *Millennium: Journal of International Studies*, Vol. 41, No. 1, 2012, p. 4.

108 See Dipesh Chakrabarty, *Provincializing Europe: Postcolonial Thought and Historical Difference* (Princeton, NJ: Princeton University Press, 2000).

109 Branwen Gruffydd Jones, 'Introduction,' in Branwen Gruffydd Jones (ed.), *Decolonizing International Relations* (Boulder, CO: Rowman & Littlefield, 2006), p. 4.

110 Hybridity can be understood as "the creation of new transcultural forms [e.g. creole language] within the contact zone produced by colonization." See Bill Aschcroft et al., *op cit.*, p. 108.

111 Geeta Chowdhry and Sheila Nair, 'Introduction: Power in a Postcolonial World – Race, Gender, and Class in International Relations,' in Geeta Chowdhry and Sheila Nair (eds), *Power, Postcolonialism and International Relations. Reading Race, Gender and Class* (Oxford: Routledge, 2004), p. 11.

112 *Ibid.*, p. 26.

113 A subaltern is someone "cut off from lines of social mobility." Gayatri Chakravorty Spivak, 'Gender and International Studies,' *Millennium: Journal of International Studies*, Vol. 27, No. 4, 1998, p. 817.

114 Chowdhry and Nair, p. 28.
115 Shampa Bisawas, 'Postcolonialism,' in Tim Dunne, Milja Kurki and Steve Smith (eds), *International Relations Theory. Discipline and Diversity* (Oxford: Oxford University Press, 2016), fourth edition, p. 227.
116 Vivienne Jabri, *The Postcolonial Subject. Claiming Politics/Governing Others in Late Modernity* (Oxford: Routledge, 2013), p. 11.
117 Tarak Barkawi and Mark Laffey show in their excellent article, 'The Postcolonial Moment in Security Studies,' how both IR and security studies are Eurocentric in nature. Tarak Barkawi and Mark Laffey, 'The Postcolonial Moment in Security Studies,' *Review of International Studies*, Vol. 32, 2006, pp. 329–352.
118 Rosa Vasilaki, 'Provincialising IR? Deadlocks and Prospects in Post-Western IR Theory,' *Millennium: Journal of International Studies*, Vol. 41, No. 1, 2012, p. 4.
119 Charlotte Epstein, 'The Postcolonial Perspective: An Introduction,' *International Theory*, Vol. 6, No. 2, 2014, p. 331.
120 Tarak Barkawi, 'Decolonising War,' *European Journal of International Security*, Vol. 1, No. 2, 2016, p. 200.
121 *Ibid.*, p. 333.
122 Catarina Kinnvall, 'Gayatri Chakravorty Spivak,' in Jenny Edkins and Nick Vaughan-Williams (eds), *Critical Theorists and International Relations* (Oxford: Routledge, 2009), p. 323.
123 Lawson, p. 215.
124 John M. Hobson, 'The "R-Word" and "E-Word" Definitional Controversies: A Dialogue with My Five Interlocutors,' *Postcolonial Studies*, Vol. 19, No. 2, 2016, p. 215.
125 Oliver Stuenkel, *Post-Western World* (Cambridge: Polity, 2016).

15 Barricades and bridges

Putting the 'I' into IR[1]

In plotting the evolution of IR as an emerging discipline, we are engaging in an endeavour which is not merely an intellectual history but also an analysis of sociological and political trends. Where we have come from explains more than a little of what we are. Moreover, memory is a guide for the future, since we can draw upon its lessons, not only from our past failures but also from our past successes. In plotting this evolution, a number of way stages can be identified. However, most great events, which may be signified by a particular act or period, are in fact part of a larger process. There is room for agency in bringing about particular acts, but there is also a need for a cognisant awareness of the structure of the greater process within which the agent acts. Our purpose is first to take some 'snap-shots' of the structure in evolution and then to look at agency in the form of institution building before drawing some lessons for IR as it goes global.

An encounter with the 'Other': building a barricade

For all the debates, theoretical innovations and disciplinary expansion, IR as theory and as practice have always been defined within the parameters of two binomials: the inevitability of reality versus the possibility of a better future, on the one hand, and the recurrence of history versus its constant evolution, on the other. As we had the opportunity to see throughout this volume, these two binomials have been, and will continue to be, contested by multiple theories in multiple debates. The question is where those debates will be taking place and whose voices will be heard.

Our starting point is a moment in which there were three entities, the Caliphate, the Byzantine Empire and the Far West, in Europe. The three interacted, to a mutual benefit, until January 2, 1492 when Granada fell to the Christians, thus ending 700 years of Muslim governance, culture, science and philosophy in Western Europe. At the same time, the conquest of the Americas by the Iberians and others got underway. The Muslims and the indigenous American civilisations were quickly characterised and treated as the 'Other' by the conquerors. The origins of modern IR, as we know it, are therefore, in essence, colonial. The institutions reflect this. Europe is seen as the centre of the civilised world, and other conceptions are denigrated or ignored. IR grew out of a framework of the suppression of the 'Other.'

IR emerged to analyse a world in which notions of sovereignty increasingly took root. Sovereignty involved the idea of sameness or a similar standing and of equality, and it became the basis of the Westphalian system. Muslims were beyond this system and not allowed to take part in it. An important exception was the Ottoman Empire, which interacted on a regular basis with the European system. Indeed, it was, in effect, a frequent part of it. The idea of being the same was not applied to the new world of the Americas, nor to the old world of the Muslims as their home in Europe switched from Iberia to the Balkans. In this sense we can say that IR grew out of a stratified European world. The 'world' was Europe and the rest was the 'Other.' IR as a discipline therefore developed within a system where the primacy was with the European sovereign state. Europeans asserted their supremacy, the superiority of their civilisation, their right to exercise their manifest destiny, to bear the white man's burden, to engage in a *mission civilisatrice* and to pillage the world as the process of globalisation took root from the 1500s onwards. While relations between European states were hierarchical, because of their differing capacities, this stratification was nothing when compared with that between the European-centric world and the 'Other.'

Three great traditions: conceptual barricades

As Europe began to conceptualise the study of IR, it did so in a framework which reflected three great traditions of political thought concerning intergroup relations. These go back beyond the Westphalian system to the ancient European world, and indeed, they go beyond Europe to other parts of the world, such as China and India, through thinkers such as Sun Tsu and Emperor Ashoka. Martin Wight summed up these three traditions as that of the realist, the rationalist and the revolutionary.[2] Michael Banks suggested a similar division, which he called realists, world society approaches and structuralists.[3]

In the nineteenth century all three of these traditions were evident as IR was emerging as a social science. A realist framework could be seen through the operation of the balance of power and its institutionalisation in the Concert of Europe. It was an approach that was state-centric, which saw power politics as the main medium of influence and exhibited an overriding concern with the security dilemma. At the same time, it was also possible to identify a more rationalist, progressive and pluralist approach in the development of international public unions, the early attempts at arms control through the Hague Peace Conferences, the growth of arbitration and international courts, the humanitarian development of human rights and the involvement of civil society in such questions as the establishment of the International Committee of the Red Cross, the abolition of the slave trade and then, eventually, of slavery itself. The revolutionary or structural approach in the nineteenth century manifested itself in the analysis of Marx and others about the growth, evolution and ultimate downfall of capitalism, which was associated, in their eyes, with imperialism. Lenin wrote a pamphlet entitled 'Imperialism: the Highest Form of Capitalism'[4] during the Great War, which was his contribution to a debate involving others, such as Hobson and Schumpeter, about the relationship between capitalism and imperialism. This was not the only concern of structuralist analysis, since geopolitics, which had its early roots in Sweden, became a major structural approach. It could be seen in the writings of Mahan and Mackinder,[5] and later in the academic writings of Haushofer and others in Munich, in its twisted use as a 'scientific' base for racist expansion by Hitlerite Germany.

The First World War was a catastrophe for the Eurocentric world. It was a European civil war, world-wide in its scope and effects. 'Pride comes before a fall,' as the saying goes, and the Europeans were undoubtedly arrogant to an almost unbelievable extent in their utter conviction of their racial superiority, and that of their religion, of their forms of political, social and economic organisation, and of their force of arms. The fall was equally great, as those who had thought of themselves as bringing civilisation to the world, destroyed their own civilisation in the Fields of Flanders, in the Dolomites, in the Levant and Near East, and on the Great Steppes of Central and Eastern Europe. This catastrophe could not but give food for thought, and the question arose of how to prevent another such collapse of civilisation. It was in this atmosphere that the modern academic discipline of IR was founded.

The agenda was clear: there were two fundamental questions, namely, what are the causes of war, and what are the bases of a stable, long-term peace? Of the three traditions to which we have just made reference, two were, in fact, out of the running, in the sense that the balance of power system of power politics had failed in 1914, and the consequences of this failure were evident to all. On the other hand, structuralist approaches were, in their economic form at least, taken up by a revolutionary state, namely, the USSR, which sought to eliminate the bourgeoisie and bourgeois states elsewhere in the world, but especially in Western Europe. The potential victims were not amused. This left the tradition of rational, progressive thought, of large-scale social engineering as the 'winner' by default. Under the aegis of many groups in civil society, through such forms as the League of Nations Union, a grand attempt was made to create a new world order which would bring out the natural harmony of interests between peoples who could have no interest in the conduct of wars which were essentially dynastic. States which were democratic and nations which became states were deemed likely to be of the liberal internationalist way of thinking. They could settle their differences peacefully if there were created, at the same time, an organisation of a universal nature. It could promote not only functional integration but also establish a regime of international peace and security. This organisation was the League of Nations.

Founding an academic discipline: tentative bridges

IR grew out of the experience of the nineteenth century and reflected a long tradition of thought. The first Chair of International Relations was established after the First World War at the University of Wales in Aberystwyth, a small seaside town on the Welsh coast, and this was followed quite quickly by Chairs at LSE and at Oxford. At the same time, what later became the Royal Institute of International Affairs (Chatham House), was also founded. All of them were concerned with what was deemed to be the scientific study of the causes of war, and the conditions for permanent peace. Similar institutions followed quickly in the United States. The tradition in the UK grew out of a concern with international history, whereas that in the United States was much more influenced by international law and the recently established political science. Both in the United States and in the UK the State was not given the salience that was evident in continental countries. Indeed, the reference was usually to the government rather than to the State. There was no strong notion of *l'État régalien* with a republican tradition, such as predominates in France and in many other continental countries. From the beginning, IR was essentially Anglo-American, but not exclusively so. The Graduate Institute of International Studies in Geneva, established in 1927, was a case in point. As the League of Nations developed in areas beyond that of collective security, it established groups, such as the Institute for Intellectual Cooperation, which in turn organised many academic conferences in the 1920s and 1930s. These attracted academics in the newly established field of IR and also from international law and international history.

This collegiality involved scholars from many of the independent states of the world, which at that time were essentially European, North American, the British Dominions and Latin American, with a few additions. It was broken by the rise of the Nazis in Germany, and more generally of Fascism and Social Darwinism in much of continental Europe. At the same time it brought an emigration from Europe, and more especially from Germany, of leading IR scholars, who brought a continental input of a more philosophical sort to the essentially empirical or historical analysis which then pertained in the UK and the United States. The scholars included Georg Schwarzenberger in the UK and Hans Morgenthau, Ernst Haas, Arnold Wolfers and Karl Deutsch in the United States. They quickly made their contribution along with the existing leaders of the field, who included E.H. Carr, Sir Charles Webster, Sir Alfred Zimmern and David Mitrany in the UK, and Quincy Wright, William and Annette Fox, Norman Palmer, Pitman Potter and George Kennan in the United States. Thus, while on the continent there was little development in terms of professorial positions, departments and the like, nevertheless, the continental voice was heard in the Anglo-American domain, even though it had a German accent.

This phase of the continentalisation of IR in the United States is now over. Global IR is perhaps the worse for it, since there are disturbing elements of hegemony and insularity leading to an ever greater parochialism in some aspects of academic life in the United States. There is now little or no European influence on US scholarship and research, which may be because Europe has nothing to say. But it could also be because the United States is increasingly inward looking, despite the nature of the field, and in particular because many US scholars are not able to read that which is written in other languages. Translation often loses the subtleties of thought of the original.

As IR became more heavily concentrated in the United States during the second half of the twentieth century, at least in terms of quantity, then the study reflected the world as seen by a super Power and its clones. The famous article by Stanley Hoffmann,[6] who had received much of his training in France, but who was, nevertheless, a leading figure in IR in the United States, suggested that IR was an American Social Science. However, there were challenges to such approaches in the United States, for example by Karl Deutsch[7] and James Rosenau[8] in the 1960s, and also in the writings of John Burton[9] and David Mitrany[10] in the UK, which circulated quite widely in North America. These writers began to regard the question of units of analysis, whether states or systems of transactions, and levels of analysis, with pluralist views of world society, as being of greater significance than was usually attributed to them in the United States. Other new voices began to be heard, for example, in foreign policy analysis, where Indian scholars such as A.P. Rana developed notions of non-alignment,[11] while structural theories of a centre-periphery nature emanated from Latin America.[12] The original 'English' school flourished in the UK, with Martin Wight, Herbert Butterfield, C.A.W. Manning and later, Hedley Bull, Adam Watson, Richard Little and Barry Buzan.[13] Moreover, historical sociology was not neglected in the writings of Michael Mann.[14] However, strangely, a key US enterprise was the development of integration theory, particularly when applied to the empirical case of the EU. The Europeans paid scant attention conceptually to what was happening on their own doorstep, at least initially.[15]

There is no doubt that, in terms of quantity and quality, the United States produced an enormous amount of excellent work. In most of the main areas, or sub-fields, of IR, the European contribution was considerable and independent of that of the United States. Indeed, it could be said that there was a greater variety of high quality work in Europe than in the United States, but while the Europeans were very aware of what was happening in North America, the reverse was not true, to the detriment of both.

Coming together: the beginning of convergence

In various parts of Europe during the 1950s and 1960s there gradually emerged centres where IR studies were to some degree institutionalised in the form of departments or research institutes. Examples of this can be found in the UK, France, the Netherlands and in the Scandinavian countries. These centres clearly made a contribution of great importance to the subject world-wide in the fields of international political economy, conflict studies, strategic studies, international history, international law, and the conceptualised study of geographical regions, particularly in the developing world. For example, the phrase *tiers-monde* is an indicator that developing world studies began in the framework of French social science. At the same time, there was the original English School, which was formed by a number of scholars with an historical and philosophical background, and who shared, for the most part, a Christian ideology. They put international political theory back on to the agenda. Likewise, political geography was a subject that was strong in France.

Nevertheless, IR, as an academic subject, was spread around Europe in penny packets, sometimes in the humanities, sometimes in social science or in law, and at other times attached to departments of political science, economics, political economy or history depending on national traditions and conceptions. There were few departments or Chairs, and very few research institutes, although there were some academic think-tanks, such as Chatham House and its equivalents in countries such as Belgium, the Netherlands, the Scandinavian countries and Germany, not forgetting the Academy of Science Institutes in the Soviet sphere. There were very few professional associations. However, two began to give a degree of coherence to work in the field on both sides of the Atlantic. The first occurred in the United States with the setting up of the International Studies Association (ISA) in the 1960s, which was initially based on the West coast, and then spread throughout North America, and indeed, beyond, so that it is now a North American organisation with an international membership. A little later, in 1974, the British International Studies Association (BISA) was founded in the UK. It grew out of something called the Bailey Conference, which in its turn was a hangover from meetings organised under the League of Nations' auspices between national groups in the inter-war period. To give an indication of the growth in size in the UK, a Bailey Conference in 1966 had, from memory, twenty-seven participants, and that represented *grosso modo* the academic field of IR. It was small and concentrated in very few centres such as London, Aberystwyth and, to a lesser degree, in places such as Aberdeen. However, in the decade that followed there was an expansion of posts so that it made sense to create BISA, and this was done by the leading Professorial figures in the UK at that time, such as Alistair Buchan, Susan Strange, Philip Reynolds, David Wightman, Jack Spence and a few others. The *rite de passage* for graduate studies in IR still remained to go to the United States, although some graduate students from the Commonwealth and the Continent came to the UK. But this was all to change, and a European dimension was in the offing.

Creating a European dimension

The stimulus for building beyond national associations towards creating a European dimension for the study of IR, was a joint conference organised by BISA and ISA in London in 1989. At that time ISA was in a phase of what can only be called imperialistic expansion. It had aspirations to become not the national association in the United States or regionally in North America, but to create a global hegemonic organisation under US leadership, finance and mentoring. It saw, or so it seemed to people in BISA, that the proposed London conference would be an opportunity for ISA to establish itself in Europe, and for Europe to be a regional body of the ISA in a traditional centre-periphery structure. The planning for the conference on the BISA side was undertaken by a committee led by the Chairpersons or Vice-Chairpersons of BISA, who in the period 1986–1992 were Jack Spence, Barry Buzan and A.J.R. Groom. They expressed the view that if Europe was to organise it should be done by Europeans, and not done for Europeans by a US association.

It soon became evident that there was a market for some form of European dimension for the study of IR. Informal meetings were held at BISA Conferences and also at ECPR

Joint Sessions, which led eventually in 1989 to a Workshop on International Relations in Europe in the Paris Joint Sessions of ECPR. Many of the participants in that Workshop then formed an informal committee to take the matter further. They were a group of individuals who had imagination, commitment and the willingness to work hard. They were not put off by predictions of failure, and they were careful not to turn anybody away, whether because of their nationality, their approach or whatever. Indeed, the aspiration was clearly to be pan-European and it was a good moment in the sense that establishing ties with the Central and East European countries began to be easier due to the end of the Cold War.

There were a number of building blocks that the Committee used. One was to ensure that there was a strong French participation, because that would be a gate to participation by scholars in Mediterranean countries, such as Spain and Italy. At the other end of Europe was the Scandinavian group, which already had ties among themselves, and there were particular strengths in the Netherlands, Germany and Russia. This process then culminated in the First Pan-European International Relations Conference, which was organised at the University of Heidelberg. Something approaching 500 scholars from all parts of Europe attended, as did a sprinkling of leaders in the field from North America. Indeed, by now the leadership and attitude of ISA towards Europe had changed radically from being that of incorporating the periphery to one of a welcome consensual and cooperative collaboration. So what was to be the next step?

It was evident that there was a clear demand, and that some form of association needed to be created. Three options were considered. The first was to accept the notion of leadership from the ISA and to become a regional body in ISA. This was rejected on the basis that if Europeans were to be organised they must organise themselves, and not lean unduly on the ISA, valuable though its support and experience turned out to be. The second option was to be an independent body, but this raised financial questions, especially the establishment of a secretariat, which also raised the issue of membership. Given that the aim was to be pan-European, it was extremely difficult in those days for any individuals or institutions from East and Central Europe to pay dues in hard currency. A solution was found in the framework of the European Consortium for Political Research, which had been set up in 1970 on the same basis as the IR organisation, namely to create a European dimension so that Europeans did not have to go to North America to talk to each other. ECPR was therefore able to provide a legal framework, in the sense that it is a charity registered in England, under English law, and it had sub-groupings which were known as Standing Groups of which the IR Committee became one. In other words, the ECPR provided a broad framework within which a largely autonomous International Relations Association on a European scale found a home. More recently, the Standing Group has become a fully fledged European International Studies Association (EISA).

The Standing Group Committee had ambitions to go beyond that of simply holding a pan-European Conference every three years. The idea was quickly expressed that Europe needed a European journal, and negotiations were started with publishers to investigate the possibilities. Two publishers appeared interested, and eventually the Standing Group chose the contract offered by Sage as the most advantageous for the European dimension. The Standing Group Committee chose Walter Carlsnaes as the first Editor, and he made ample use of his connections in Scandinavia, in the UK, in various other parts of Europe, as well as in North America He set out his philosophy for the new journal, called the *European Journal of International Relations*, in the first issue, which was in March 1995. The *European Journal of International Relations* was – and still is – a great success in both its content and its contribution to IR as it goes global.

Going global

IR is in the process of going global, not through a process of cloning but by aspiring to the genuine opening of mind, spirit and research to the Other and to the agenda of the Other. In East Asia, Japan has had an independent voice in the field since the 1920s, although it was essentially a discussion in international political theory. India and China are now developing professional associations, and Brazil has a very vibrant critical mass in the field of IR. Just as the Pan-European Conferences and the recently created EISA brought the notion of a European IR community into embryonic being, then such a global community may also be in its embryonic stage, visible in the increasing participation of academics from outside Europe and North America in the annual ISA Convention, and also by the proliferation of other conferences and organisations across the world, including the World International Studies Committee (WISC). No national association, no regional association can act in a fully global manner from its own base. It must create a new base, and one that is acceptable to all, in short a global base.

Technology, freedom and plurality

The construction of this global base is enriching IR as a discipline and arguably making it, for the first time ever, truly plural. Many obstacles within the academic practice remain, starting with the Western-centrism of academic journals and their problematic gatekeeping. As highlighted by Arlene Tickner, for all the openness in recent decades, top journals still are dominated by US-based scholars and US-dominant theoretical and methodological approaches.[16] Changing these dynamics will take time and certainly investment in alternative ways of presenting peer-reviewed research. Technology can, in that regard, be both a blessing and a curse. A blessing, in that it seems to facilitate the use of open access, particularly through university repositories. A curse, as it increasingly attaches the value of academic work to metrics and social media dissemination, which is often independent of the real quality of the text and benefits those that are technologically well informed or have institutional support to do so.

Another, very significant problem has to do with the ideological basis of this academic encounter. For all its flaws, IR developed as a discipline primarily in liberal democratic settings. Its opening up to the world means negotiating its place in a context of very different political realities (including within the Western world). Guaranteeing a genuine plurality might thus demand the adoption of firm stances by organisations such as the ISA or WISC. Those stances could be perceived as political, but they should ultimately speak to the values and principles of academic freedom. Only then can IR be truly global.

Notes

1 Parts of this chapter were published in Frederik Bynander and Stefano Guzzini (eds), *Rethinking Foreign Policy* (Oxford: Routledge, 2013), a *Festschrift* in honour of Professor Walter Carlsnaes.
2 Wight, Martin, *International Theory: The Three Traditions*, Gabriele Wight and Brian Porter (eds) (Leicester: Leicester University Press, 1991).
3 Banks, Michael, 'The Inter-Paradigm Debate,' in Margot Light and A.J.R. Groom (eds), *International Relations: A Handbook of Current Theory* (London: Frances Pinter, 1985), pp. 7–26.
4 Vladimir I. Lenin, 'Imperialism: The Highest Stage of Capitalism,' *Collected Works*, Vol. 22 (London: Lawrence and Wishart, 1964).
5 Alfred Thayer Mahan, *The Influence of Sea Power upon History 1660–1783* (London: Methuen, 1965); Halford J. Mackinder, *Democratic Ideals and Reality* (London: Constable, 1919).

6 Stanley Hoffmann, 'An American Social Science: International Relations,' *Daedalus*, Vol. 106, No. 3, 1977, pp. 41–60.
7 Karl Deutsch, *The Nerves of Government* (New York: Free Press, 1964).
8 James Rosenau, *Linkage Politics* (New York: Free Press, 1969).
9 John W. Burton, *World Society* (Cambridge: Cambridge University Press, 1972).
10 David Mitrany, *A Working Peace System* (Chicago, IL: Quadrangle Press, 1966).
11 A.P. Rana, *The Imperative of Non-Alignment* (New Delhi: Macmillan, 1976).
12 The starting point was the UNECLA in Santiago under the leadership of Raul Prebisch. See Raul Prebisch, *The Economic Development of Latin America and Its Principal Problems* (New York: United Nations, 1950).
13 Herbert Butterfield and Martin Wight (eds), *Diplomatic Investigations* (London: Allen & Unwin, 1966).
14 Michael Mann, *The Sources of Social Power* (Cambridge: Cambridge University Press, 1986).
15 Ernst Haas, *Beyond the Nation-State* (Stanford, CA: Stanford University Press, 1964).
16 Arlene Tickner, 'Core, Periphery and (Neo)Imperialist International Relations,' *European Journal of International Relations*, Vol. 19, No. 3, 2013, pp. 627–646. Also see Arlene B. Tickner and Ole Wæver (eds), *International Relations Scholarship around the World* (Oxford: Routledge, 2009).

Index

Note: page numbers in italic type refer to figures.

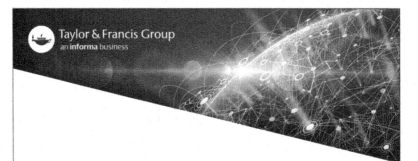